COLD WAR MODERN

COLD WAR MODERN

Edited by David Crowley
and Jane Pavitt

DESIGN 1945–1970

V&A Publishing

First published by V&A Publishing, 2008
V&A Publishing
Victoria and Albert Museum
South Kensington
London SW7 2RL

Distributed in North America
by Harry N. Abrams, Inc., New York

Paperback edition ISBN 978-1-851-77570-5

10 9 8 7 6 5 4 3 2 1
2012 2011 2010 2009 2008

Hardback edition ISBN 978-1-851-77543-9
Library of Congress Control Number
200069286800

10 9 8 7 6 5 4 3 2 1
2012 2011 2010 2009 2008

A catalogue record for this book is available
from the British Library.

Publication and typefaces designed by:
A2/SW/HK

New V&A photography by Christine Smith,
Ken Jackson and Paul Robins, V&A Photography
Studio

Printed in Singapore

Note on Transliteration

The transliteration of Russian words in this book
is based upon the system used by the US Library
of Congress. Common English renderings of certain
proper names or titles in common usage override
the transliteration rules (for example, Lissitzky,
not Lissitskii).

Frontispiece: Karel Šourek (designer) and Tibor Honti
(photographer), *Hail to the Red Army, Protectors
of the New World.* Poster, Czechoslovakia, 1945.
Private collection

V&A Publishing
Victoria and Albert Museum
South Kensington
London SW7 2RL
www.vam.ac.uk

Contents

List of Contributors

Greg Castillo is an historian and Senior Lecturer at the University of Sydney. His research on Cold War architecture and urbanism has been supported by fellowships from the Getty Research Institute and the Canadian Centre for Architecture. *Cold War on the Home Front: The Soft Power of Midcentury Design*, his book currently in press, will be published in 2009.

Anne Collins Goodyear is Assistant Curator of Prints and Drawings at the National Portrait Gallery, Smithsonian Institution, Washington, DC. Recent publications include 'The Portrait, the Photograph, and the Index', in *Photography Theory* (edited by James Elkins, 2007), and 'From Technophilia to Technophobia: The Impact of the Vietnam War on the Reception of "Art and Techno-logy"', *Leonardo*, vol.41, no.2 (2008). She is co-curator, with James W. McManus, of the forthcoming exhibition 'Inventing Marcel Duchamp: The Dynamics of Por-traiture' at the National Portrait Gallery, London (2009), and is an author and co-editor of the accompanying catalogue.

David Crowley is the consultant curator of 'Cold War Modern'. He is an historian working at the Royal College of Art, London. His specialist interest is in the cultural history of Central Europe in the nineteenth and twentieth centuries. He was an academic consultant to the V&A exhibition 'Modernism: Designing a New World 1914–1939' (2006) and a contributing author to its accompanying catalogue. Recent publications include *Socialist Spaces: Sites of Everyday Life in the Eastern Bloc* (co-edited with Susan E. Reid, 2002), *Warsaw* (2003) and *Posters of the Cold War* (2008).

Barry Curtis is Emeritus Professor of Visual Culture at Middlesex University, a Fellow of the London Consortium and a visiting lecturer at the Royal College of Art. His book *Dark Places: Haunting in Film* will be published in 2008, when essays on 'Dinosaur Design' and a contribution to the event/publication *If Looks Could Kill* will also appear. He is working on a book on *Imaginary Architecture* for Reaktion, for which he co-edits the 'Locations' series.

John Harwood is Assistant Professor of Art at Oberlin College, Ohio, where he teaches modern architectural history and theory. His recent publications include essays in *Grey Room*, *PIN-UP* and *do.co.mo.mo*, and he is at work on a book entitled *The Redesign of Design: Computer, Architecture, Corporation*.

Caroline Maniaque, an architectural historian at the Ecole Supérieure d'architecture, Lille, is interested in the history of alternative culture in the twentieth century. Recent works include *Le Corbusier et les maisons Jaoul* (2005); an essay in *Ant Farm 1968–78* (2004); 'The American Travels of European Architects: 1960–1975', *Space, Travel, Architecture* (forthcoming); and *Cultures savantes et alternatives: les architectes français et les Etats-Unis* (forthcoming).

Katarzyna Murawska-Muthesius teaches art history at Birkbeck College, University of London, Faculty of Lifelong Learning. In 2000 she edited a collection of essays, *Borders in Art: Revisiting Kunstgeographie*, and she is the author of *National Museum in Warsaw: Guide* (2001). Her publications on the visual culture of the Cold War include essays on Socialist Realism, public sculpture, caricature, maps and film in recent issues of *Third Text*, *Artmargins* and *Centropa*, and in the Royal Academy of Arts exhibition catalogue *Paris: Capital of the Arts 1900–1968* (2002).

Paola Nicolin is an art critic and historian teaching at Bocconi University, Milan. Currently at work on a study of exhibition theory, she is art editor at *Abitare*, and publishes reviews and essays in *Artpress*, *Untitled* and *Corriere della Sera*. The author of *Palais de Tokyo. Sito di Creazione contem-poranea* (2006), she completed her Ph.D. in 2007 with a dissertation on the 14th Milan Triennale.

Jane Pavitt is the curator of 'Cold War Modern' and the University of Brighton Principal Research Fellow, based in the Research Department of the Victoria and Albert Museum. Her research interests include design history post-1945 and contemporary design and museological issues. She was co-curator (with Gareth Williams) of the V&A exhibition 'Brand.New' in 2000 and editor of its accompanying book. Other exhibitions that she has curated include 'The Shape of Colour: Red' (V&A/Glasgow 1999 Festival of Architecture and Design) and 'Brilliant' (V&A 2004). She is co-curator (with Glenn Adamson) of the V&A's forthcoming show, 'Postmodernism' (2011).

Susan Emily Reid is Reader in Russian Visual Arts, University of Sheffield. She has published widely on Soviet art and design history, focusing on the 1950s–60s. Publi-cations include: 'Cold War in the Kitchen', *Slavic Review* (2002); 'The Khrushchev Kitchen', *Journal of Contemporary History* (2005); 'Khrushchev Modern', *Cahiers du Monde russe* (2006); and two volumes edited with David Crowley, *Style and Socialism: Modernity and Material Culture in Post-War Eastern Europe* (2000), and *Socialist Spaces: Sites of Everyday Life in the Eastern Bloc* (2002).

Jana Scholze is the assistant curator of 'Cold War Modern' and was previously the assistant curator of 'Modernism: Designing a New World 1914–1939' (V&A 2006). Her research interests include museum theories and the design history of the twentieth century. She has curated a number of exhibitions in Germany. Recent publications include: *Medium Ausstellung. Lektüren musealer Gestaltungen* (2004) and an essay in *Museumsanalysen* edited by Joachim Baur and Gottfried Korff (2008).

Jane A. Sharp is Associate Professor in the Department of Art History and Research Curator of the Dodge Collection at the Zimmerli Art Museum at Rutgers University, New Jersey, USA. She is author of *Russian Modernism Between East and West: Natal'ia Goncharova and the Moscow Avant-Garde, 1905–1914* (2006) and numerous articles on Russian and Soviet art of the twentieth century.

Sarah Wilson is Reader in the History of Art in the Modern Department at the Courtauld Institute of Art. She was invited Professor at Paris-Sorbonne IV from 2002–4. Her work on Socialist Realism extends from contri-butions to *Paris-Paris* (1981) and *Face à l'Histoire* (1996) with the Centre Georges

Pompidou, Paris, to the neo-marxists involved in *Art and Theory: The Secret History* (in preparation for Yale University Press) and a current project for the Franco-Russian celebrations in 2010. She was principal curator of the exhibition 'Paris, Capital of the Arts, 1900–1968' (Royal Academy of Arts, London, and Guggenheim Museum, Bilbao, 2002) and the recent Pierre Klossowski retrospective (London, Cologne, Paris, 2006–7).

Acknowledgements

The planning and staging of the exhibition 'Cold War Modern: Design 1945–1970' and the preparation of its accompanying publication could not have been undertaken without the generous collaboration of many colleagues, both from within the V&A and outside, over a sustained period of time. The lenders to this exhibition have assisted not only in the selection and preparation of objects, but have given generously of their time and expertise to make this possible. Although space precludes the naming of all who have contributed, we extend our grateful thanks to those who have participated in the making of this project.

Chief amongst these are our close colleagues at the V&A, who have formed a vital part of the core project team, and have made a sometimes arduous process into a delightful adventure. Jana Scholze, the Assistant Curator to the exhibition, has worked with dedication, scholarly determination and continual good humour since its early days. Maria Mileeva, also Assistant Curator, has not only helped to bring this project to fruition, but also provided huge expertise and commitment to the research and negotiation of Russian loans. Charlotte King, Exhibition Organizer, has managed the exhibition project in a calm and dedicated manner, under the leadership of Linda Lloyd Jones, Head of Exhibitions, with Rebecca Lim, Ruth Cribb and Sarah Sonner from the Exhibitions Department. Without them the project could not have been realized. Alongside them, several skilled research assistants have given us the support we have needed in key areas, namely Verity Clarkson, Lorna Dryden, Katie Feo, Inessa Kouteinikova,

Catherine Rossi and Nadine Stares. Volunteers, always an essential part of the life of a museum project, have offered unstinting support, particularly John Hoenig and Chiara Micallef.

Two institutions have provided us with their generous and collegiate support. The Faculty of Arts and Architecture at the University of Brighton has funded Jane Pavitt in her role as Research Fellow at the V&A since 1997. In its institutional partnership with the V&A, the University has therefore facilitated the research and development of this key project. We are particularly grateful to the support and expertise of Professor Jonathan Woodham at Brighton. The Royal College of Art, where David Crowley is Senior Tutor in the Department of Humanities, has also provided institutional support and funding for David's period of extended research leave, which was also supported by the Arts and Humanities Research Council with a grant in 2006.

Two key research events were fundamental to the development of the project. The first, a scholarly workshop held in November 2004, brought together academics to advise on the initial shaping of our ideas. A second, two-day international symposium, entitled 'The Cold War Expo' organized at the V&A by the University of Brighton in January 2007, provided the opportunity for the presentation and debate of this key area of research. We are immensely grateful to the participants of both events, many of whom have provided us with their continued and generous support. We would also like to recognize the considerable support and advice given to us by the contributors in this book. Leading academics in their fields, they have not only shared their ideas in the forms of the essays which appear here: they have also in many cases led us to exhibits which feature in the exhibition.

Whilst we gratefully acknowledge the contribution of all our lenders, we would also especially like to thank the following individuals for their unstinting and expert help: Sir Kenneth Adam; Sir Christopher Frayling; Jack Masey; Shoji Sadao; Kristen Harrigen and William Ahern; Stacy L. Fortner, IBM Archives; Barry Bergdoll and Christian Larsen, Museum of Modern Art, New York; Bonnie Rychlak and Larry Giacoletti, Noguchi

Museum; Olga Korshunova, Irina Sedova and David Sarkisyan, Schusev State Museum of Architecture, Moscow; Elisabetta Barisoni, Clarenza Catullo and Gabriella Belli, MART (Museum of Modern and Contemporary Art, Rovereto, Trento); Lolita Jablonskienė, National Gallery of Art, Vilnius; Laima Kreivytė, Vilnius Capital of Culture 2009; Helena Koenigsmarková and colleagues from the Museum of Decorative Arts, Prague; Jola Gola, Muzeum Akademii Sztuk Pięknych, Warsaw; Anna Frąckiewicz, Anna Manicka and Katarzyna Nowakowska-Sito of National Museum, Warsaw; Snježana Pintarić, Museum of Contemporary Arts, Zagreb; Noëlle Chabert, Musée Zadkine, Paris; Phillipe Jousse, Jousse Entreprise, Paris; Rosalind Pepall, Museum of Fine Arts Montreal; Howard Schubert, Canadian Centre for Architecture, Montreal; François Dallegret; Jean Louis Cohen; Tim Benton; Paolo Scrivano; Paul Betts; Alla Rosenfeld; Karen Kettering, Hillwood Museum, Washington; Maria Morzuch, Muzeum Sztuki in Łódź; Vit Havranek; Boris Groys; Ľudovít Kupkovič; Viera Mecková; Alex Mlynarčik; Krystyna Łuczak-Surówka; Andrzej Szczerski; Naum Kleiman, Museum of Cinema, Moscow; Birgit Beumers; Kai Lobjakas, Museum of Applied Art and Design, Tallinn; Andres Kurg; Soraya Smithson; Jeremy Aynsley; Joe Kerr; Vojtěch Lahoda; Piotr Piotrowski; Małgorzata Wróblewska Markiewicz, Muzeum Włókiennictwa in Łódź; Andrei Erofeev and Ludmila Marz, Tretyakov Gallery, Moscow; Yuri Avvakumov; Francisco Infante-Arana; Gianpiero Frassinelli; Roberta Cerini Baj; Václav and Jakub Cigler; Jiří Jiroutek; Zdeněk Lukacs, Prague Castle; Ann Bennett and Meg Simmonds, Eon Productions; Ladislav Pflimpfl and Renata Clark, Czech Centre, London; Anna Tryc-Bromley, Polish Cultural Centre, London; Johannes Wimmer, Austrian Cultural Forum, London; Rainer and Patricia Zietz; Sarah Mahurter, Kubrick Archive, University of the Arts, London; Flora Turner, Croatian Embassy; Frances Guy, Pallant House, Chichester; Roger Tolson, Imperial War Museum; Andrew Nahum, Science Museum, London; Frances Morris and Victoria Walsh, Tate, London; Mark Adams, Vitsoe; Dieter Rams; Christof Groessl; Tommaso Tofanetti, Triennale di Milano; Helmut Geisert and the Henselmann family; Marjan Boot,

Stedelijk Museum, Amsterdam; Paul Clark; Nikolai Delvendahl; Florian Hufnagl, Petra Hölscher, Josef Straßer, Die Neue Sammlung, Munich; Winfried Nerdinger; Hans-Peter Reichmann, Deutsches Film-museum, Frankfurt am Main; Marcela Quijano, HfG Archiv, Ulm; Gereon Severnich, Martin Gropius-Bau, Berlin; Isabelle Godineau and Delphine Studer, Fondation Le Corbusier, Paris; Marie-Ange Brayer, FRAC, Orléans; Siegfried Hermann; Hans Hollein; Timo Huber; Martina Kandeler Fritsch, MAK, Vienna; Günter Zamp-Kelp; Peter and Felix Ghyczy; Gijs Bakker; Diana Wind, Ludo Van Halen and Christel Kordes, Stedelijk Museum Schiedam; Madelief Hohe, Gemeentemuseum Den Haag; Yvonne Joris, Stedelijk Museum, s'Hertogenbosch; Jeffrey Head, Stanford University; Rika Devos and Mil de Kooning, Ghent University; Irena Murray, RIBA, London; Richard Barbrook; Eric Schuldenfrei; Eames Demetrios; Pat Kirkham, Bard Graduate Center, New York; Sarah Lichtman; Alexander Payne, Philips Depury; Jean-Claude Ameline, Centre Georges Pompidou, Paris; Robert Little, Royal Ontario Museum, Toronto; Andrew Bolton, Metropolitan Museum of Art, New York; Cathleen Lewis, National Museum of Air and Space, Washington, DC; Justinian Jampol, The Wende Museum, California; Henry Meyric Hughes and Irene Wiedmann, Council of Europe; Conway Lloyd Morgan; Lars Müller; Markéta Uhlířová; Alison Clarke; Jonathan Zimmerman; the late Ettore Sottsass Jnr.

V&A colleagues, past and present, have offered us support and expertise often beyond the bounds of their professional roles in the museum. We are particularly grateful to members of the Research Department, who have not only shared their knowledge and similar experiences in the preparation of such projects, but have also made the congenial atmosphere in which we have worked. We would especially like to thank: Glenn Adamson, Christopher Breward, Alex Klar, Ulrich Lehmann, Carolyn Sargentson, Ghislaine Wood (Research Department); Claire Wilcox, Christopher Wilk, Gareth Williams (Furniture, Textiles and Fashion Department); Abraham Thomas (Word and Image Department); Jennifer Opie, Eric Turner (Sculpture, Metalwork, Ceramics and Glass Department); Ken Jackson, Christine Smith (Photographic Studio); Nigel Bamforth,

Dana Melchar (Conservation Department); Richard Ashbridge, Matthew Clarke, Robert Lambeth (Technical Services); Jo Banham, Laura Elliot (Learning Services); Laura Hingly, Jane Lawson, Nicole Newman (Development Department), Mark Hook (Webteam); Michael Casartelli and Laura Saffill (Contracts and Purchasing); Nadine Fleischer, Annabel Judd and Jane Scherbaum (Design). Alex Bratt, Olivia Colling, Debra Isaac, Jane Rosier, Tora Soderlind, Damien Whitmore, Eleanor Appleby (Public Affairs) who, with Ben Weaver, developed the exhibition's press and marketing campaigns.

Universal Design Studio, together with graphic designers Bibliothèque, not only delivered an exceptional exhibition design, but also brought their own considerable enthusiasm and knowledge to the subject. We are especially grateful to Brian Studak, Jonathan Clarke, Juri Nishi from Universal and Mason Wells, Jonathan Jeffrey and Sarah Kirby-Ginns from Bibliothèque for their continual good humour and creative vision. The exhibition design and installation were managed, with admirable dexterity, by Mike Cook of Cultural Innovations.

The publication of this book has been a major undertaking for our colleagues in V&A Publications. We are especially grateful to Mary Butler, who commissioned the book, and Mark Eastment, who saw it to completion. Monica Woods, together with Asha Savjani, managed the project. Johanna Stephenson not only did an admirable job as copy editor, but also assumed responsibility for the whole book at the most difficult and final stages of delivery, for which we are immensely grateful. Henrik Kubel and Scott Williams at A2/SW/HK have produced a skilful and sympathetic book design.

Our grateful thanks go to Emma-Louise Basset for the translation of Paola Nicolin's essay and to Rachel Fuller, who translated the whole text of the poem 'Het Uitzicht van de Duif', an excerpt of which is included on p.107.

Finally, we would like to thank our families, who have shown immense patience and support throughout the last four years. This book is dedicated to Lesley, Edie, Noah and Lily, and to Tim, Milo and Iris, with our love.

David Crowley and Jane Pavitt

Richard Buckminster Fuller, dome for covering part of New York City. Photomontage, 1962. The estate of R. Buckminster Fuller, Santa Barbara

1.1
Russian cosmonaut Aleksei
Leonov sitting in Walter
Pichler's Galaxy 1 chair
at the exhibition of the first
space conference in
Vienna, 1968

1 / Introduction

David Crowley and Jane Pavitt

Cold War battlegrounds

In 1958 British pop artist Richard Hamilton embarked on a new work, entitled *$he* (Tate, London), a portrait of the 'heroine' of the consumer society, the housewife, standing before one of the chief symbols of her age, the refrigerator (1.2). *$he* combines newsprint advertising, a lenticular image of a winking eye and the seductive curves of streamlined products and Hollywood pin-ups.[1] Hamilton's artwork is a composite picture of an American lifestyle then beginning to make its presence felt in Britain. As Christopher Booker put it,

> Deep Freeze had arrived and TV Instant Dinners and Fish Fingers and Fabulous Pink Camay.

And with so many bright new packages on the shelves, so many new gadgets to be bought, so much new magic in the dreary air of industrial Britain, there was a feeling of modernity and adventure that would never be won so easily again.[2]

Hamilton's image of the consumer society captures its novelty. Yet this vision is accompanied by some dark shadows. The rounded pink curves of the refrigerator appear fleshy, and to be leaking blood. At the bottom of the picture, a strange domestic appliance – part-toaster, part-vacuum cleaner – has fired off a projectile, the path of which is tracked, like a missile on a screen. Hamilton's kitchen seems to represent a perplexing combat zone.

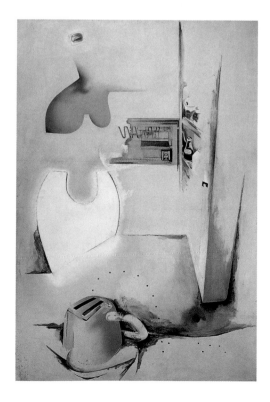

1.2
Richard Hamilton, $he. Oil, cellulose paint and collage on wood, 1958–61. Tate, London

The vision of the kitchen-as-battleground seemed less strange when, a year later, the world's two superpowers confronted each other over the issue of domestic goods.[3] At the American National Exhibition, staged in Moscow in 1959, American vice-president Richard Nixon and Soviet premier Nikita Khrushchev vied with each other with competing claims of high living standards, whilst standing next to an American kitchen on display (5.27). At a time when Khrushchev called for 'peaceful co-existence', leaders from the most powerful nations in the world stood eye to eye and argued over the productive capacities of their political and economic systems. In an attempt to produce the destabilizing effects of envy in the Soviet Union, the United States Information Agency (USIA) organized the Moscow spectacle, turning the glossy products of capitalism into weapons. In one of many sharp exchanges, Nixon challenged Khrushchev: 'Would it not be better to compete in the relative merits of washing machines than in the strength of rockets? Is this the kind of competition you want?'[4]

This was not the first time that displays of material affluence had been used to generate consumer desire in the Cold War.[5] It had been a key American strategy in the propaganda wars fought throughout Western Europe in the 1950s. In the early part of that decade, exhibitions of modern design organized in West Germany by the USIA and the New York Museum of Modern Art presented the designs of Eero Saarinen and Charles and Ray Eames as symbols of democracy and liberalism.[6] In this way, they were used to outdo the promises of the socialist regime installed by the Soviet Union in East Germany in 1949.

The 1959 exhibition in Moscow was different, however. This time, American affluence was being paraded at the heart of the Soviet empire, not in an allied nation. Khrushchev's response to the display of material affluence was characteristically robust: 'We too have such things', he bragged. He exaggerated of course, but his words were still important. As the exhibition took place, the command economies of the Soviet Union and the other states in the Eastern Bloc were already changing course. After the austerity of the Stalin years, Eastern European citizens were being encouraged to imagine a future

1.3
Interior of USSR Pavilion,
Expo '58, Brussels, 1958

1.4
Fashion show at the US
Pavilion, Expo '58, Brussels,
1958

in which modern industry would satisfy all their material needs. This new course was described – sometimes pejoratively – as 'Refrigerator Socialism'.[7]

As Hamilton's $he suggests and the 'Kitchen Debate' at the American National Exhibition made clear, consumer goods occupied a key place here, and the home was one of its many battlegrounds.[8] From the sports field to outer space, the cinema to the art gallery, many settings became arenas for Cold War competition. In this regard, the Cold War was by no means a conventional conflict: it was a coercive one in which two ideological systems asked those who lived under their rule to internalize its divisive logic (though of course many chose not to). The Cold War formed an all-encompassing horizon of experience and expectation. In that sense, it was perhaps more pervasive than the conditions of 'total war' that had occupied much of the world between 1939 and 1945.

Not only signs of military strength and power, but also glittering products, high-tech electronics, skyscrapers and their images were deployed by each side to demonstrate its superior command of modernity. By planting a flag on the Moon, by constructing the world's tallest building or quite simply by ensuring the supply of shining white refrigerators for ordinary homes, the superpowers sought to demonstrate the pre-eminence of their science, their industry, their organization and their design. These images and objects were often produced for consumption by their own citizens; but the international growth of television broadcasting and the continued importance of events like the international Expos ensured that they were seen throughout the world. In Brussels, Expo '58, the first World's Fair of the post-war period, set itself the task of demonstrating the renewal of society and of the individual after the trauma of conflict.[9] Yet the two superpowers seized the opportunity to engage in Cold War crossfire: the Soviet Union put the Sputnik, the first satellite sent into orbit in 1957, at the centre of its pavilion to demonstrate Soviet technological superiority (1.3); as well as projecting scientific achievement and high culture, the US Pavilion displayed the comfortable benefits of the 'American way of Life' (1.4).

What was at stake in such confrontations was nothing less than the future of mankind

(or so both systems proposed). This notion of futurism was built into the Soviet project, based on the tendentious ideology of Marxist-Leninism: Communism was to be man's ultimate destiny. Equally, and especially in the 1950s, champions of American ideals proclaimed an alternative vision of the future based on affluence and leisure within the framework of the consumer society. Daniel Bell, writing in 1960, famously announced 'the end of ideology' (in the sense of ideological partisanship) as democratic politics and capitalism triumphed throughout the West.[10] This, he argued, was a reflex of progress.

If consumerism and Communism represented two visions of future utopia, then the Cold War also generated the most terrifying visions of modernity in ruins. The Cold War nuclear arms race forced mankind to reflect upon the possibility of its future destruction. Furthermore, the effects of industrialization, consumerism and war conducted with chemical weapons in Vietnam led others to prophesy 'ecocide', the death of the planet by pollution and over-industrialization.[11]

Nothing could be more polarized than the visions of 'dreamworlds and catastrophe' which structured Cold War modernity.[12] But as this book reveals, utopia and distopia were not only concurrent: they could even be present in the same object. Buckminster

Fuller's overarching 'Dome Over Manhattan' (see pp.8–9) presented not only the utopian possibility of a climate-controlled eco-city, but also, when the visionary engineer asserted its potential usefulness as a shelter from radioactive fallout, the threat of nuclear war. The computer – the electronic brain of future society, with the potential to free man from the drudgery of labour – was also imagined in film and literature as hard-wired to destroy humanity once its intelligence exceeded that of its creator.[13] Concrete, the ubiquitous building material of the age, could be articulated as the 'rough poetry' of New Brutalist architecture, the prefabricated slabs used in Eastern Bloc panel housing, the protective casing of a nuclear reactor or even, as Wolf Vostell's 1972 artwork *Concreting (Potsdamer Platz)* suggests, the entombed city (1.5).[14] The duality of utopia and disaster could, it seems, be found in the most ordinary of things.

Design was not a marginal aspect of the Cold War but central – both materially and rhetorically – to the competition over the future. Taking a wide view of its subject, this book explores its many faces from the end of the Second World War to the early 1970s – a period in which modernism was, arguably, at its last peak.[15] The longer chapters, written by the curators of the accompanying exhibition, reflect on the defining faces of Cold War modernity, including the reconstruction of Europe's cities; the effect of nuclear anxieties on art and design; the revival of modernism in Eastern Europe after Stalin; the dialogue between design and high technology; the image of revolution in the late 1960s; and the changing landscapes of visionary architecture. The shorter essays, by leading scholars in their fields, explore the significance of key groups, events and artefacts of Cold War art and design.

Art and cinema also feature in this book, not in their conventional framework (for instance, in terms of the Cold War battle between abstraction and socialist realism much explored by art historians[16]) but in terms of the powerful commentaries offered by artists and film-makers on the material world. Even when conscripted into Cold War battles, artists and other image-makers frequently spoke with dissenting voices. At the Venice Biennale in 1964, for example, Robert Rauschenberg was chosen as featured artist

1.6
Robert Rauschenberg, *Kite*.
Oil and colour serigraphed
on canvas, 1963. Museum of
Modern and Contemporary
Art, Rovereto/Trento

1.7
**Zdzisław Głowacki and
Aleksander Kromer [design]**,
tapestry on the themes
of the reconstruction of
Warsaw, American dockers
destroying armaments
and the war in Korea,
woven by students in Maria
Kańska-Piotrowska's atelier
at the State High School
of Fine Art in Łódź, Poland,
1950. Central Museum
of Textiles, Łódź

in the American Pavilion: his pop canvases, with their assemblages of the signs of American hegemony, such as military vehicles, soldiers, flags and the American Eagle, as shown in *Kite* (MART, 1963; 1.6), made him seem an appropriate choice. But for all that his works employ the symbols of national identity, they are also taut with ambiguity and they can be read as critical commentaries on American military and cultural imperialism.[17]

This book focuses on modernism in design; that is, real and imagined objects that were believed by their creators and champions to be both reflections and agents of social, moral and technical progress. In concentrating on visions and projections, we inevitably deal with the ideals (and often the nightmares) of the post-war generations rather than the material reality of their everyday lives. Faith in progress was a central characteristic of the pre-war Modern Movement, a theme that was explored in a previous V&A exhibition and book, entitled *Modernism: Designing a New World 1914–1939* (2006). However, after 1945 the question of how to be modern was given an unprecedented sense of urgency by the pace of world events. The future presented prospects of unspeakable horror and hitherto unimaginable achievement. By 1949, both of the world's superpowers had acquired the capacity to annihilate one another with nuclear weapons; twenty years later, man had walked on the Moon.

A world divided

The Cold War was shaped by the intense rivalry between the USA and the Soviet Union, the two superpowers that emerged from the ruins of the Second World War.[18] In fact, the demarcation lines in Europe were drawn at summits between Roosevelt, Churchill and Stalin in 1943–5. Within months, the wartime alliance was breaking down, with Moscow accusing Washington – now armed with nuclear weapons and increased wealth and power – of having imperial ambitions on the world.[19] At the same time, Western statesmen were keen critics of the Soviet occupation of Eastern Europe and the suppression of democratic political parties there. Winston Churchill, speaking in the USA in March 1946, described life in Eastern Europe in the shadow of an 'Iron Curtain'.[20] This metaphor

1.8
Reg Butler, photomontage
of maquette for the
*Monument to the Unknown
Political Prisoner* on the
proposed site, Humboldt
Hain, Wedding, West
Berlin, 1957. Estate of
Reg Butler, Berkhamsted

describing the partition of the world was compelling, providing above all a powerful image of the incarceration of the East.

In the decades that followed, much of the world was divided along Cold War lines (with a few nations like Tito's Yugoslavia asserting their non-aligned status). Military pacts and economic alliances contributed greatly to the consolidation of two 'blocs'. The declaration of the People's Republic of China in 1949, a new ally of the Soviet Union until the early 1960s, added considerably to the sense of the march of Communism on the world. Much American money and effort was spent trying to stop its spread around the world in the years that followed. The superpowers never engaged each other in direct hostilities, but the Cold War did produce many victims, particularly in the developing world where East confronted West through its proxies. The Korean War (1950–53) (1.7), the Vietnam War (at its height in 1965–75), Latin American politics and post-colonial wars in Africa were all catalysed by Cold War antipathies and often sponsored with dollars and roubles.[21]

Berlin was a continual hot spot.[22] The division of the German capital by the Allies at the end of the Second World War meant that East faced West in a very literal sense. The Kremlin attempted to force the Western powers to withdraw from the city in 1948 by cutting off road and train access, and therefore the supply of food and fuel to the city. The Allied Forces mounted an enormous airlift of supplies to the city until Stalin backed down in the summer of 1949.[23] Just over ten years later tensions peaked again: in August 1961, with East Germany haemorrhaging people, communist leader Walter Ulbricht ordered the building of an 'anti-fascist protection barrier'. The Berlin Wall became the Cold War's most notorious symbol of division, with more than a hundred people killed trying to cross it before it was dismantled in 1989.[24]

Berlin also captures a second important aspect of the Cold War: that the division of the world into two separate camps was not, or not always, as absolute as Churchill's 'Iron Curtain' metaphor suggests. Until the Wall was built, the borders in the city were open to allow movement between zones. Even after 1961, the close proximity of the two systems meant that television signals breached the divide. Whilst the German case was pronounced, it was not unique. During periods of Cold War rapprochement, considerable numbers of images, people and things made border crossings (as the 'Kitchen debate' in Moscow illustrates).

In seeking new perspectives on Cold War modernity, it is often most interesting to view them from places such as Berlin, Prague, Warsaw or Milan (rather than Washington or Moscow, the conventional hubs of Cold War power). Berlin, for example, was selected as the site of the winning entry for the 1953 International Competition for a *Monument to the Unknown Political Prisoner* (1.8, 1.9; see also p.58). Planned for a site on the Humboldt Hain, the abstract monument (never built), well over 100 ft tall, was intended to deflect the stare of its socialist counterpart in the East, the Soviet *Victory Monument* at Treptow.[25]

The voyeuristic gaze of the Cold War, with each side obsessively watching the other, was also to be found in the skies: radar scanned the movement of planes and missiles and unblinking satellites surveyed the planet below, whilst the intelligence services of both sides engaged in espionage. Each side found

its own image in the other. Stanley Kubrick used an eccentric neologism to describe this exchange of gazes, when he gave the central character of his 1963 film exploring nuclear confrontation the name 'Dr Strangelove'. This was a powerful metaphor for the impassioned embrace in which the superpowers held each other during the Cold War years.

Modernism redux

The devastation wrought by six years of total war was viewed by many architects and designers in 1945 as both an enormous challenge and a great opportunity. For those associated with the pre-war avant-garde, here was a real chance to build truly modern cities and towns with high-rise housing and functional zoning, separating residential, industrial and recreational areas. The reconstruction of Rotterdam, the early stages of rebuilding Warsaw and the planning of cities like New Belgrade all represent the materialization of pre-war ideas.[26] At the same time, the rationalization and modernization of industry, accelerated by the conditions of war, would allow for the mass-production of practical goods to serve the needs of all mankind. In the designs advanced by such evangelizing bodies as the Congrès Internationaux d'Architecture Moderne (CIAM, the International Congress of Modern Architecture) and the Deutscher Werkbund, a long-established alliance of modernist designers and industrialists in Germany, the objects and buildings of this new era would be purposeful and, in their abstract, utilitarian forms, forward-looking.[27]

For those on the Left, the creation of new European socialist states in Eastern Europe based on the Soviet model was initially a cause for optimism. It seemed that the progressive urban projects envisaged in the inter-war years could now be built in the service of socialism. Mart Stam, a founder member of CIAM who had spent the war in his native Holland, made the decision to offer his services to the authorities in the Soviet zone of Germany, where he had hopes of reviving a Bauhaus-style school.[28] Attempting this first in Dresden and then in Berlin, his modernist pedagogy soon fell foul of the Zhdanovshchina, the cultural politics of the Kremlin exported throughout the Eastern Bloc, which labelled such progressive tendencies as 'deviant' and 'bourgeois'. Stam's approach

1.9
Reg Butler, final maquette for the *Monument to the Unknown Political Prisoner*. Forged and painted steel, bronze and plaster, 1955–6. Tate, London

1.12
Peter Ghyczy, Garden Egg
Chair. Lacquered, moulded
polyurethane with synthetic
textile upholstery over
polyurethane foam padding,
1968. Manufactured
by VEB Synthesewerk
Schwarzheide, East
Germany, 1972–4/5.
V&A: W.8-2007

1.13
**Jonathan De Pas, Donato
d'Urbino, Paolo Lomazzi
and Carla Scolari**, Blow
Chair. PVC film seam-
welded by radio frequency,
1967. Manufactured
by Zanotta S.P.A.
V&A: Circ.100:1-1970

impact on consumer goods in a myriad of ways. Glass fibre reinforced plastics had been developed in the United States by Monsanto, a company specializing in chemical products. It produced thin hubs to protect the radar equipment on American military aircraft. By 1944 the company was experimenting with entire fuselages fashioned from the material. Even before the end of war, Monsanto looked for peacetime applications: 'For the post-war world, there are promises of plastic houses, of plastic private airplanes, of thousands of other articles that will heighten the comfort of everyday life', *Newsweek* had announced in 1943.[38] Great effort was invested in imagining applications for the material, resulting in the 1953 Chevrolet Corvette made with a Monsanto fibreglass body and designed by Harley Earl, chief car stylist of the era. The Monsanto House of the Future, exhibited at Disneyland, California, from 1957, was one of a number of plastic houses fabricated on both sides of the Cold War divide in the 1950s.[39]

The plastic chair, like the plastic house, was the regular focus of design and material innovation in the East and West. In the USA Charles and Ray Eames had been the first to exploit the aesthetic effects of fibreglass, leaving glass rope fibres clearly visible through the polished sheen of the moulded furniture that they designed for Herman Miller (1.14). In communist Poland, Roman Modzelewski experimented with fibreglass armchairs, seeking to encourage interest for his designs amongst architects in the West (1.15).[40] In the 1960s, the use of polyurethane led to many innovations in furniture design, such as Peter Ghyczy's Garden Egg Chair, a lacquered and moulded polyurethane shell for Reuters Plastics (West Germany, 1968; 1.12).[41] Also in the 1960s, advances in plastics allowed designers to challenge ideas of rigidity and permanence in furniture, with mass-produced, inflatable and potentially disposable furniture such as the Blow Chair by De Pas, d'Urbino, Lomazzi and Scolari of 1969 (1.13).

The history of plastics after the Second World War conforms to a general idea in the history of technology, that the 'needs' of war accelerate developments which are then, often slowly, found peacetime applications.[42] The arch of wartime invention and peacetime application had a different profile during the Cold War. The competition between the superpowers saw sustained investment in military and technical research over an exceptionally long period, even to the extent that American politicians protested the grip that the 'military-industrial complex' had on their nation.[43] Not only governments, but corporations were at the heart of Cold War machinations, desperate to protect their assets

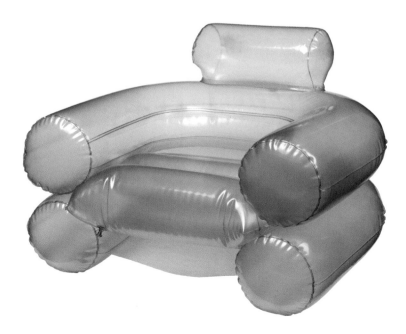

1.14
Charles and Ray Eames, armchair. Grey moulded shell with rope-edge, seng swivel mechanism and dowel legs, 1950. Manufactured by Zenith Plastics for Herman Miller. V&A: W.15-2007

1.15
Roman Modzelewski, armchair. Fibreglass, 1959–60 (patented 1961). National Museum, Warsaw

and contracts.[44] The Soviet Union, which seemed almost chronically unable to innovate – often creating ersatz copies of Western goods – and failing to meet the most basic needs of its citizens, supplied the most startling achievements in the field of space technology, from the launch of the Sputnik in 1957 to Yuri Gagarin's triumphant journey into orbit in 1961.[45] Viewed from the perspective of ordinary citizens of the Soviet Union, the 'benefits' of the triumphs of the Soviet space programme were, however, largely ideological (even if drawing genuine feelings of pride) and not material.[46]

Visionaries or technocrats?

Architects and designers played a crucial role in the Cold War competition to demonstrate superior modernity. If corporations, scientists, engineers, the military and others created the material world over and through which this conflict was fought, designers gave it form. The roles played by architects and designers (whether obliged, given or assumed) were the subject of much controversy during the period. Should the designer be a technocrat, preparing expert designs in the service of State or corporation, or visionary, independently pursuing a search for alternate ways of living?

For a generation of designers, characterized in this volume as the 'last utopians', assuming the role of visionary was a means by which to seize back modernism from its narrow commercial and instrumental uses. Ant Farm in the USA, Superstudio and Archizoom in Italy and the Utopie group in France are the best-known champions of radical design in these years: in their company we consider the work of Eastern European visionaries including NER (Novye elementy rasseleniia/New Element of the Urban Environment) in the Soviet Union, VAL (Voies et Aspectes du Lendemain/Ways and Aspects of Tomorrow) and a generation of glass artists in Czechoslovakia. Václav Cigler, for example, whose establishment of an experimental school of glass design at the Academy of Arts in Bratislava (Vysoké škole výtvarných umění) in 1965 allowed him to produce extraordinary works of creativity, evading the narrow utilitarianism of official design culture. Through his chosen medium of glass, Cigler explored the relationship between body, object and environment. His highly engineered glass lenses, sometimes cut with oblique edges and volumes produced unexpected distortions of the surroundings in which they were placed (1.16). Cigler also imagined massive mirrors – an early form of land art – functioning as great transmitters or shields which could bounce laser beams or electronic pulses from around and above the world.[47]

In Eastern Europe the dichotomy of technocrat and visionary has to be understood within the context of a near-monopoly over futurism held by the communist state. Organized and managed in central architectural offices and bureaucratic design institutes, architects and designers were given the task of realizing this vision. Glossy products were, for instance, designed and manufactured in small runs, often as prototypes of prospective designs that would one day find their way into the lives of ordinary citizens of socialist societies. Reproduced on television or in the pages of magazines, or exhibited at home and abroad, they represented a promise that the regimes often failed to meet. In featuring their output, this publication arguably risks reproducing Soviet dissimulation. But it is nevertheless important to stress that what some of the original and imaginative products and buildings produced during the Thaw period following Stalin's death represent are sincere hopes in the possibility of a modernized and reformed socialism. In the cosmic work of the Dvizhenie (Movement) Group in Moscow, for instance, we confront perhaps the last Soviet avant-garde group to have sincere faith in the possibility

1.16
Václav Cigler, glass object
with concave surfaces.
Optical cut glass, 1968–70.
Museum of Decorative
Arts, Prague

of Communism, the final breath of an avant-garde body that had been born in 1917 and died around 1970. Little such enthusiasm survived the stagnancy and self-interest which characterized the Brezhnev era, particularly after the Soviet-led forces crushed the Prague Spring.

In the 1960s an important vein of critique emerged, largely but not exclusively in the West (as Cigler's case shows), which focused on the twin props of Cold War modernity: consumerism and militarism. A generation that had grown up in conditions of relatively affluence and security, without memories of the war, made critical judgments of the Cold War order once they came of age. Opposition to the war in Vietnam and the ecological devastation caused by industrialization was sometimes coupled with a romantic and often naïve enthusiasm for 'primitive' or pre-modern lifestyles. Counter-cultural communes adopted teepees and yurts, particularly but not exclusively in the deserts of California and New Mexico, as signs of opposition to modernity.

These themes were combined in the late 1960s in a series of artworks by Italian artist, Mario Merz, in which he adopted the form of the igloo. One of these, *Objet cache toi* (*Object, Hide Yourself*, private collection, 1969; 1.17), bears an injunction that originally appeared as graffiti on the walls of the Sorbonne University in Paris during the student protests of May 1968.[48] Perhaps Merz invites the viewer – objectified by power – to hide in his shelter. Alternatively, the work expresses a demand for the disappearance of commodity culture in favour of a world without possessions. This collective dream was the subject of much critical reflection at the time by architectural groups such as Superstudio in Italy, as discussed in the final chapter of this book.

Alongside other radical counter-cultural groups of the late 1960s, Superstudio represented the last wave of utopianism in architecture and design in the twentieth century. Floating structures that favoured a new mobility, geodesic domes for communal existence or electronic networks connecting the entire planet suggested the possibility that mankind might not only be freed from the irrational attachment to places and possessions, but that he could find entirely new ways of living on the planet. Within such schemes, however, one can also trace the outline of doubts about the effects of modernity and the shadows of irony. In this way the last utopian schemes not only cast back to the radical avant-garde of the 1910s and 1920s, but also look forward to what would emerge as Postmodernism in architecture and design in the course of the 1970s.

Whilst the Cold War enmities continued until Eastern European societies threw off communist rule in 1989 and, ultimately, the Soviet Union imploded in 1991, the conditions of Cold War modernity were much changed in the 1970s. Economic recession and the oil crisis of 1973 ended the long post-war boom in the West which had fostered the growth of mass consumerism in the 1950s and provided the counter-culture at the end of the 1960s with the freedom to 'drop out'. The shocks now registered in the world's economy have been described as the beginning of a new 'age of crisis'.[49] At much the same time the legitimacy of the regimes which formed the Eastern Bloc was contested by new generations of dissidents and undermined by a pervasive and intractable lack of faith in the communist project. Design too took on new and different faces in the 1970s, to the extent that some commentators could announce with ringing confidence the death of modern architecture.[50] On both sides of the East–West divide there was a sharp rise of interest amongst architects and designers in what were described as postmodernist concerns such as the role of ornament and the function of design as language, as well as the specificities of place and history.[51] Coupled with a growing critique of functionalist aesthetics and the alienating effects of urban planning, these shifts cast considerable doubt over many of Modernism's central convictions.[52] In this regard the early 1970s marked a significant shift in the history of design, if not necessarily in the politics of the Cold War.

If design and politics had been in sync with each other during the 1950s and 1960s, the efforts of counter-cultural architects and designers of the late 1960s did much to break that relationship. One such disruptive work is *Klima 1* (*Climate 1*; 1971) by Viennese architectural group Haus-Rucker-Co, a design for an exhibition scheme that involved covering Mies van der Rohe's Haus Lange

1.17
Mario Merz, *Objet cache toi*. Metallic net, tubular metallic structure, tarred cloths, clay blocks, neon (1969), 2001. Private collection

(1929) in Krefeld with a massive inflatable (1.18). The image is a visual diagnosis of Cold War modernity with powerful resonance for the present: an icon of architectural modernism sits under a great dome. Functioning as a life-support system, described in a handwritten caption as a 'climatic island', the robust architecture of the Modern Movement now apparently needs protection. Or perhaps it is the possibility of utopia that is under threat. In front of the house, a second, far more contemporary face of modernity co-exists under this protective skin: members of a nuclear family, dressed in bright leisurewear, enjoy the benefits of affluence. One dream has perhaps been replaced by another. What is less clear is the nature of the threat facing them. High in the sky is a burning sphere: captioned 'artificial sun', it is an alienating image of what is conventionally a symbol of life. This scene of anxious domesticity is also framed by ruins producing a disturbingly

vertiginous effect: the viewer is left uncertain whether they represent the future or the past.

We live in a world still shaped – materially, environmentally and imaginatively – by Cold War modernity. The threat of nuclear warfare may seem somewhat more distant today, but the legacies of aggressive industrialization in the 1950s and 1960s are all too evident in our global environment. Moreover, many of the key questions of Cold War modernity – such as how to exploit new technology for the benefit of humanity without producing inhuman effects, or how to imagine modern lives outside conditions set by the marketplace – remain present today. And if we are to manage our future, we need to understand our Cold War past.

1.18
Haus-Rucker-Co (Klaus Pinter), *Cover, Klima 1 (Climate 1)*, in connection with the exhibition project 'Haus Lange, Covered', Krefeld. Mixed media, 1971. Archive Klaus Pinter, Paris

From Monuments to Fast Cars: Aspects of Cold War Art, 1946–1957

Sarah Wilson

1.19
Ossip Zadkine, model for monument *La Ville Détruite* (*The Destroyed City*). Bronze, 1947. Musée Zadkine, Paris

The city of Paris was not only 'capital of the nineteenth century', as Walter Benjamin famously declared, but the nerve centre of intellectual life and political ferment in Europe until well after 1945. It absorbed waves of immigrants from Eastern Europe and Russia before 1914, after the Russian Revolution and at the end of the First World War. Anti-Nazi Jewish intellectuals from Germany and beyond found refuge in Paris in the later 1930s. The bravery of the French Communist Party in resisting the Nazi Occupation gave them tremendous political and moral authority in 1945. It is no surprise, therefore, to learn that Stalin chose Paris as an important centre for both Comintern operations before 1939 and Cominform operations after 1947. Cultural strategies were crucial to their success.[1]

In the arts, the so-called 'School of Paris' reflected the ethnic diversity and exhilarating internationalism of these waves of immigration in the 1930s; after 1945, though many of the heroic pre-war figures had emigrated or perished, the story continued. The style wars played out in the European art world during the 1930s had complex origins; hence polarizations of figuration versus abstraction in the Cold War period seen as relating to pro- or anti-communist positions are often far too simple. The case of Ossip Zadkine and Naum Gabo in Rotterdam – Russian exiles and contemporaries – is a case in point. And while the fabric of bombed cities contrasted with the beauty of Paris, whose heritage from the medieval to the nineteenth-century was essentially preserved, the growing pace of reconstruction and modernization meant that memories as well as monuments could become inappropriate or simply disappear. The case studies discussed here – covered at the time by an international press, both communist and anti-communist – relate, therefore, to a far wider picture.

Ossip Zadkine's *Monument to the Destroyed City* (1951–3), which dominates the port of Rotterdam, is a major public monument expressing the fate of Europe in 1945 (1.19). Returning from America to France – his spiritual and artistic homeland since 1909 – the artist was greeted by the sight of the port of Le Havre razed to the ground. Yet artistic life, which had continued under duress during the war years, started flourishing again, a symbol both of rebirth and continuity. Zadkine's *First sketch for a monument to a destroyed town*, conceived as a small terracotta in 1946, was included in the exhibition 'La Sculpture française de Rodin à nos jours' held in Prague from May to June 1947, and then in Berlin in July.[2] Zadkine travelled to see friends in Holland in the same year: his vision of Rotterdam, saturation-bombed in May 1940, was of 'an enormous and mournful plane stretching ahead of me: not one house left … sinister and depressing'. While his terracotta returned from Berlin in fragments, the idea of a tribute grew. A new sculpture exhibited in Brussels and Amsterdam in 1948 led to a major commission, and in May 1949 the maquette was exhibited as *Project for the destroyed town of Rotterdam* in Paris; the Paris retrospective travelled to Rotterdam during the winter of 1949-50. The towering 20ft-high public monument was dedicated in the Leuvehaven in May 1953, 'a statue which would commemorate, for the inhabitants of this great city-port and for all their future descendants, the impardonable injustices of war'.[3] Zadkine recalls these words by G. van der Wal, director of the Jewish-owned department store De Bijenkorf, who first had the idea of a commemorative monumental sculpture for the city. English Marxist critic John Berger called it 'the best modern war monument in Europe':

> You walk around the plain granite block on which the figure, cast in dark bronze, simultaneously stands, dies and advances.… The hands and the head cry out against the sky from which the man-aimed bombs fall. I say man-aimed because this makes the anguish sharper and fiercer than that of an Old Testament prophet crying out against the wrath of his God, and this extra anguish partly explains, I think, the violence of the distortions in modern tragic works like this. The torso of the man is ripped open and his heart destroyed.… The man represents a city, and this sculpture is of bronze and so the wound, which is in fact a hole right through the body, is seen in terms of the twisted metal of the burnt-out shell of

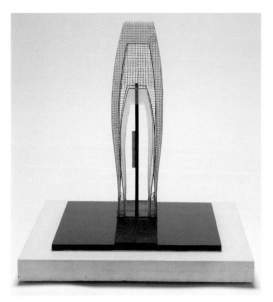

1.20
Naum Gabo, model for
*Monument to the Unknown
Political Prisoner*. Plastic
and wire mesh, 1952.
Tate, London

1.21
Double-page spread from
J.W. de Boer (text) and
Cas Oorthuys (photographs),
*Rotterdam, dynamische
stad*, 1959, showing Naum
Gabo, *Bijenkorf Construction*
and Ossip Zadkine, *The
Destroyed City*.
V&A/NAL: 19.R.82

a building. The legs give at the knees.
The whole figure is about to fall.

Yet the monument exemplifies a dialectic.
Berger continues: 'This is also a figure
of aspiration and advance. The figure has
no back – and so cannot retreat.... And so
the curses also become a rallying cry.'[4]

Ironically, the Bijenkorf department
store, which had stood throughout the
bombing, did not survive the reconstruction
of the city: a new, modernist building designed
by Marcel Breuer with Dutch architect
A. Elzas replaced the old, and for reasons
connected with new city vistas, the same
Van der Wal would commission the Russian
sculptor Naum Gabo's *Bijenkorf Construction*
to be placed against the building. This was the
first and only constructivist public monument:
eight storeys high and free-standing, it was
fabricated from pre-stressed concrete, steel
ribs, bronze wire and marble. Based on a
similar design submitted to the 'Monument
to the Unknown Political Prisoner' competition in London in 1953, Gabo's work eschewed
the multiple resonances of Reg Butler's
winning entry at that time: crucifixion,
aerial, Orwellian watchtower (1.20).[5]

Similarly, his Rotterdam sculpture had
no obvious commemorative function. Entirely
abstract, thrusting upward, its curvature,
membranous and sinewy qualities added
connotations of vitalism to an otherwise
purely technological vision. Approved in 1955,

the monument was dedicated in May 1957.
Gabo declared: 'I have tried to express the
indomitable spirit of the people of Rotterdam
and the miracle of a modern city rising from
the rubble.' Critics, from Herbert Read and
John Berger at the time to the present day,
have discussed Gabo's sculpture work in terms
of the success or failure of this late constructivist project, whose style originated in post-
Russian Revolutionary ideals.[6]

From a Cold War perspective, however,
the dialectic between Zadkine's anguished
figure and Gabo's forward-looking vision
epitomizes debates between figurative and
abstract, memory versus amnesia, the past
versus the future. The two images were
juxtaposed (the Zadkine a dramatic night-
time silhouette) by Cas Oorthuys in *Rotterdam, dynamische stad* (1959), a large-scale
book of black-and-white images celebrating
the rebuilt city. The velvety black photographs
of children, workers and sailors in the docks
underline the European tradition of humanist
photography that co-existed with debates
around realism in the fine arts. Oorthuys
shows not only new modernist banks and the
concert hall, but the continuing development
of 'new town' public sculptures, from busty
nudes by Renoir to Nordic bear cubs at play,
the latter a gift to the city in its reconstructive
phase (1.21). These secondary works modify
the idea of a simple confrontation between
Zadkine and Gabo: the two major commissions
were not only geographically distant from
each other, but separated by time – the period
spanned, from 1946 to 1957, is one of major
change in European cities on both sides
of the Iron Curtain.

Both artists, contemporaries, were
Russian-Jewish emigrés. Gabo's commitment
to abstraction may, perhaps, link him to other
Russian-Jewish artists.[7] Zadkine, while not
mentioning his Jewish roots in his memoirs,
was supremely aware of the Holocaust;
his wife, the artist Valentine Prax, suffered
great humiliation proving her Aryan descent.
Yet in terms of both monumental scale and
its outstretched arms, *Monument to the
Destroyed City* may be compared, poignantly,
to Zadkine's *Christ*, sculpted from the trunk
of a huge elm tree in the village of Arques in
1940.[8] Artists from Chagall to the communist
Boris Taslitzky created Christ figures
during this period of Jewish persecution

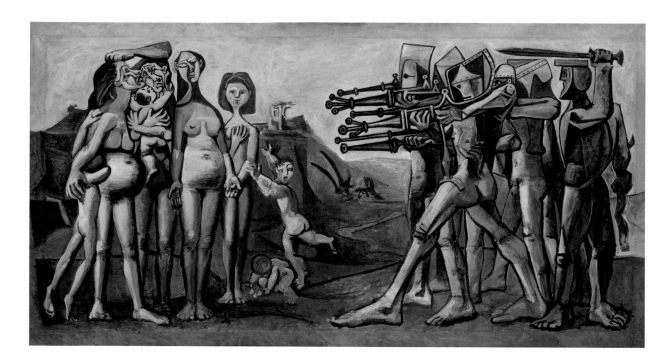

1.22
Pablo Picasso, *Massacre in Korea*. Oil on plywood, 1951. Musée Picasso, Paris

and increasing terror, while the eschatological and indeed religious dimensions of post-war sculptures, from works by Alberto Giacometti to Germaine Richier, have too often been subsumed in discussions of post-war existentialist humanism and what Herbert Read memorably called the 'geometry of fear'.[9] Berger's recollections of Job, the 'Old Testament Prophet', in his discussion of Zadkine's piece and the significance of 'man-aimed bombs' in a world without God, set the Rotterdam monument within theological debates of the time.[10]

The artistic configurations of pre-1939 Europe and their relationship to artistic diasporas from Russia and the East must be understood as a backdrop to the post-1945 Cold War 'battle of the styles'. The first twentieth-century emigrations to Paris by intellectuals before the First World War and Russian Revolution accompanied pogroms and economic migrants from the East. Some, like Kandinsky and Chagall, returned with revolutionary zeal, but as bureaucratization and ultimately Stalinism replaced revolutionary and artistic structures, many artists who had gone back to Russia returned to Europe. Gabo trained in Munich, spent the First World War in Scandinavia, worked in Moscow, 1920s Berlin, 1930s Paris, wartime Britain and, from 1946, the United States. His

abstraction may be linked to similar trends ranging from the De Stijl group from Holland to the biomorphic abstraction of Hans Arp. All varieties mingled in the 'Abstraction-Création' Salon in Paris, where Gabo exhibited from 1932 until 1935. Here, an international abstract language contained its own memories of revolutionary, theosophical or utopian-socialist origins.

In contrast, Zadkine was an exemplary sculptor of the School of Paris and, like so many of his contemporaries, never relinquished figurative, post-cubist forms. As politically 'engaged' realisms, both social realist and fascist, began to supplant the 1920s 'return to order' in the arts in Europe, Communism as a political creed linked to forms of workers' organization, and Socialist Realism as an artistic style, were promoted from the USSR after 1932, coinciding with the impact of the Depression. The crude Soviet idea of 'reflection theory', grounded in Georgi Plekhanov's turn-of-the-century writing on 'bourgeois' literature, was inadequate to address what in 1930s Paris was already a conflict between various forms of abstraction (geometric and expressionistic), realism ('bourgeois' or socially engaged), and surrealism, under whose aegis the poet Louis Aragon moved towards Communism and the painter Salvador Dalí cultivated

increasingly pro-Franco right-wing sympathies during the decade.

A revival of Plekhanov was not sufficient to cope with the style wars between late modernism and its opponents, and particularly an emblematic figure such as Picasso. The German emigré Max Raphael's *Marx, Proudhon, Picasso*, published in Paris in 1933, attempted the impossible: to create a Marxist theory of art that could embrace stylistic pluralism. And Picasso, after *Guernica* in 1937 and having joined the French Communist Party in 1944, continued to pose a problem. Significantly, in 1965 John Berger would dedicate his Marxian analysis *The Success and Failure of Picasso* to Max Raphael, whose theories still seemed relevant; and by 1966 the French sociologist Pierre Bourdieu had likewise searched out *Marx, Proudhon, Picasso* in an attempt to challenge Marxist aesthetics on their own territory.[11] The 1960s saw a continuation of the Cold War communist arts policy in France, in which Picasso was deeply implicated, and from which Zadkine kept a significant distance.[12]

Paris, then, chosen after Weimar Germany's collapse as the centre for the Soviet Comintern's Western operations, was from the 1930s pre-eminently inappropriate for Soviet directives in the fine arts.[13] In the Soviet Union, the site for revolutionary art shifted from the city to the sports ground and ultimately to the battlefield. The military epics and panoramas produced for the New York World's Fair and the All-Union Exhibition in Moscow in 1939 marked a climax.[14] Stalin subsequently dissolved the Comintern to facilitate his role as major agent in the drawing-board division of Europe at Yalta; later, in response to the Truman Doctrine and Marshall Plan, he set up the Cominform in 1947 as a new organ of coordination for satellite communist countries: Paris, with the strongest Western communist party, became yet again the focus of Cominform operations, including those in the cultural domain.

Andrei Zhdanov, responsible for the formulation of Soviet Socialist Realism in 1934, became the USSR's cultural spokesperson at the first Cominform conference in 1947. His 'two camp' theory, one 'imperialist and anti-democratic', the other 'anti-imperialist and democratic', quickly extended to the arts.[15] Surprisingly, however, the term 'Socialist Realism' does not occur in the minutes of these Cominform sessions.[16] The priority was the creation of the Peace Movement, with its multi-language publications, art exhibitions, poster campaigns, processions and protests such as the Stockholm Appeal in March 1950 against the atomic bomb and nuclear proliferation (of its over 273 million signatures, the entire Eastern Bloc's vote was co-opted).[17]

Despite their anachronism, national realist traditions were employed to legitimate painting and were promoted in communist periodicals such as *Arts de France* and *Realismo* in Italy. This strategy of promotion was employed to mask Soviet directives on the use of realism. In France, Louis Aragon became the effective cultural spokesman for the Communist Party; painters looked back in time to sources in David, to Courbet and to Daumier; Picasso was seen as representing a tradition extending from Poussin's *Massacre of the Innocents* (1632–4) to the present.[18] A two-tier policy allowed a 'modernist' communist art to flourish: Picasso, Fernand Léger, even Matisse were shown in the elegant Maison de la Pensée Française off the Champs Elysées; worker-based exhibitions were held elsewhere. The grand tradition of history painting continued: Boris Taslitzky's *Death of Danielle Casanova* (1950–51),

deployed the tropes of Christian martyrdom to evoke extermination at Auschwitz, in homage not only to Danielle (wife of Party cultural spokesman Laurent) and her extensive cult, but also to his own deported Jewish mother. Evidently anti-German, this painting was exhibited as part of the Communist Party's ultimately successful propaganda war against the European Defence Community:[19] large-scale works were often used as scenic backdrops for the collection of signatures of protest.[20]

Picasso's *Guernica* and *Massacre in Korea* (1951; 1.22) in reproduction became catalysts for discussion on both sides of the Iron Curtain; the artist became the most famous communist in the world after Stalin and Mao Tse-tung. Two months after he joined the Party, before the end of the war and the Yalta Conference, he was under FBI surveillance. Senator George Dondero's charge that 'so-called modern art contains all the "isms" of depravity, decadence and destruction', naming Picasso as 'one of the leaders of the art of "isms"', was reproduced from the *Chicago Daily Sun-Times* (17 August 1949) in the FBI dossier 'Subject Pablo Picasso. File no. 100-337396'.[21] For the more enlightened cadres of the CIA and the Museum of Modern Art, New York, Western European modernism was a bastion of liberty, of avant-gardism, of art as an autonomous practice to be funded and promoted against realism, the art of the communists.[22] In this manichean light one should compare the peace conference exhibitions of 1948 and 1950, held under the Cominform aegis, with the Venice Biennale shows of the same years.

Ruined Wrocław was chosen as the venue of the first International Peace Congress.[23] The mobilization of Cold War intellectuals meant that transportable and reproducible artworks were required, plus film and souvenirs. These served as powerful forms of representation and cultural legitimation, and as ritual objects in an era where congresses, youth festivals, processions, debates and cell meetings replaced – or competed with – the spiritual and emotional functions of Church and pilgrimage. In Wrocław Picasso exhibited his Vallauris ceramic plates; Fernand Léger, Paul Eluard, Aimé Césaire, Ilya Ehrenburg and Renato Guttuso from Italy also went to the Peace

Congress. However, the second World Peace Congress, banned by the Labour government in Britain and forced to move from Sheffield to Warsaw at the end of 1950, reflected changes since 1948, with the closing of the celebrated collection of abstract art in Łódź and the imposition of a Socialist Realism rooted in Polish nineteenth-century sources.

In Warsaw Picasso received the Lenin Peace Prize, not for his painting but for his dove poster, produced for the Salle Pleyel Paris–Prague Conference of November 1949. In the show 'Artists for the Defence of Peace', Wojciech Fangor's *Peace inviting dockers of imperialist countries to throw their murderous armaments into the sea* demonstrated how French Socialist Realism was used as an authoritative model for Eastern Bloc painting: the anti-colonialist subject matter had been specified by Maurice Thorez at the Twelfth Party Congress at Genevilliers in April, 1950.[24] Chinese revolutionary themes were also present in the Warsaw show, and by 1949 Maoist socialist realist works of art were reproduced in the communist periodical *Arts de France*. Portraits of Ho-Chi Minh joined the Stalinist themes of the exhibition 'De Marx à Staline' held in Paris in early 1953, a long-forgotten apotheosis of the 'cult of personality'.[25]

At the post-war Venice Biennales, left-wing artists such as Guttuso exhibited huge history paintings, communist in theme, expressionist and Picasso-like in style. He exhibited *Occupation of the Sicilian Lands* (1949) in 1950, recalling peasant demonstrations in 1946–7 (1.23); in 1952, *Battle at the Ponte Ammiraglio* showed bodies clashing in shirts of brilliant red. The British movement of communist painters and fellow travellers adopted Guttuso as their mentor and inspiration.[26] American counter-strategies, increasingly sophisticated, emphasized liberality and 'cultural freedom' by exhibiting the left-wing realist Ben Shahn in conjunction with Willem de Kooning at the next Venice Biennale, in 1954.[27] Literature and film were of course additional arenas of confrontation.[28]

Picasso's peace dove was so internationally successful that a CIA-funded peace campaign was set up as a riposte. Appropriating a slogan from its communist rivals for its name, the 'Paix et Liberté' organization waged a pro-American propaganda campaign. The

1.24
Anonymous, *Jo-Jo-la colombe (Jo-Jo the Dove)*, anti-communist propaganda poster issued by Paix et Liberté, France. Ink on paper, colour lithograph, 1952. V&A, E.629-2004

visibility of their posters, their memorable catchphrases and their use of humour and caricature were aimed at hearts, minds and tongues. Most celebrated were the exploding tank-dove, *La colombe qui fait boum!* (1950), and *Jo-Jo-la colombe* (1952; 1.24), Stalin the 'peace dove'. Simultaneously, posters with accurate maps of Soviet labour camps exposed the systematic denial of broad swathes of the Left in France, caught up in what they saw as an American propaganda war.[29] Ephemeral yet intrusive, the posters became part of a cityscape which during the 1950s became increasingly covered with the signs of capitalist prosperity: the advertising billboards that the Nouveau Réaliste *affichistes* would later rip to shreds and exhibit as symbols of France's continuing schizophrenia during the Algerian war.

While there were innumerable commissions for monuments of Stalin in the USSR or cities in the East, Western European communist parties lacked the political legitimacy to invest public space with permanent sculptures.[30] Yet the masterpiece of Western European Cold War history painting, André Fougeron's *Atlantic Civilisation* of 1953 (Tate, London), is predicated precisely upon this absence – or rather upon the redundancy of the monument altogether (1.25).

1952 was the year in which Paris chose to celebrate two thousand years of its existence; it was decreed 'Victor Hugo Year' by the French Communist Party, which in January held a debate about the proposed replacement of the grandiose monument to the poet by Barrias, removed by the Nazis from the city's Place Victor Hugo.[31] Anticipating the Congress of Cultural Freedom's 'Masterpieces of the Twentieth Century' celebration, an enormous American car, 'lit up by projectors like Notre-Dame de Paris', was placed on the very spot where Hugo had reigned from his Guernsey rock encircled by muses.[32] The symbol of French culture sacrificed to the Nazis became the invisible presence behind the magnificent blue Ford Consul MK1, which, larger than life, was to dominate Fougeron's *Atlantic Civilisation* of the following year. Above, replacing Hugo himself, like an empty throne, is the electric chair used to execute Julius and Ethel Rosenberg, who were believed by the communists to have been framed as spies by the CIA.

Louis Aragon's response is a Cold War classic: a hymn of hatred whose dazzling rhetoric becomes a paean to American capitalism:

A Ford car, the civilisation of Detroit, man on the conveyor belt, from Mac Gee [sic] to the electric chair, with Einstein and Charlie Chaplin under suspicion, the civilisation which can only persist under the appalling shadow of Hiroshima, of atomic menace surrounded with a belt of napalm. A Ford automobile in the Place Victor Hugo, here's the very symbol of the men who set up Eisenhower in Marly and their war installations in fifty-five departments of France – for the war which will continue in the Brittany arena transformed into a Korea, here's the symbol in broad daylight of this subjection to the dollar, docilely applauded ... Here's the lacquered God, the bull's eye of foreign industry, the Atlantic Totem which chases away the glories of France for the profit of Marshall's stocks and shares, the varnished and chromium-plated statue of its imports, and, more arrogant than the Nazi iconoclast, the Yankee substitutes a machine for the poet ... for poetry the Coca-Cola of commercial deals, American advertising for *La Légende des Siècles*, the mass-produced car for the Genius, the Ford automobile for Victor Hugo![33]

A re-armed German sniper stands upright in the American car as though in a tank. In *Atlantic Civilisation* politics have gone global: domestic expenditure (on housing and pensioners) is contrasted with armaments procurement and France's military engagement in Korea. Military recruitment posters decorate modernist apartment blocks for NATO personnel; children of the poor, canon-fodder for imperialist war, contrast with the American 'occupier' reading his girlie magazine. Despite closely following Aragon's speech and new Soviet directives requiring more satire in painting, the work is prophetic. It anticipates – a year before France's military defeat at Dien Bien Phu in Indo-China – the equations made in the very title of Kristin Ross's analysis: *Fast Cars, Clean Bodies, Decolonization and the Reordering of French Culture*.[34] It spells the future: the inevitability of France's NATO alliance, the triumph of the pro-American arguments of Raymond Aron in *Le Figaro* and of James Burnham's *The Managerial Revolution*, which Aron had had translated as early as 1947.[35]

The title *Atlantic Civilisation* recalls arguments contrasting American democracy with the French Revolutionary political heritage going back to Alexis de Tocqueville.[36] In 1950, Fougeron had based the striking miners of his painting *National Defence* on Jacques-Louis David's *Oath of the Horatii*. (Was the use of a revolutionary metaphor now increasingly compromised by an association with terror?) As for the painting's spatial contruction (denounced by Aragon as 'old photomontage procedures'), while Mexican muralism had changed Fougeron's perspective devices, the overall impact is of a kaleidoscopic and American modernity. Spaces are multiple, time is static or accelerates forward. And Stalin was dead. In this period of uncertainty and ensuing power struggles, Aragon's condemnation of Fougeron (and hence the socialist realist programme as a whole) and Fougeron's forced 'self-criticism' in Stalinist mode, have been eclipsed by later vindications of this work.[37] For in its satire and inadvertent humour, the painting

Modernism between Peace and Freedom

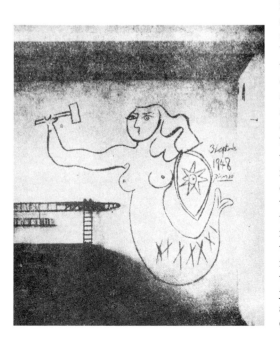

Despite its unique scale and its 'avant-gardist' appeal, the Congress was roundly discredited in the mainstream Western media of the time. It is remembered today as little more than a second-rate rally against 'Anglo-American warmongering', and as an arena for the dissemination of the Stalinist vilification of modernism as the product of Western imperialism. Recorded as the defining moment of the Cold War, which left even the most loyal fellow travellers disillusioned with Soviet Communism, the Congress has been notoriously reduced to a two-dimensional clash between the Russian author Alexander Fadeyev and the British socialist historian A.J.P. Taylor. When Fadeyev famously compared Jean-Paul Sartre and T.S. Eliot to 'hyenas and jackals' using typewriters and fountain pens, Taylor denounced the event as incitement to hatred, and called for the defence of 'freedom behind the Iron Curtain'.[6]

I wish to argue that the Congress remains one of the most significant and least studied events of the cultural Cold War. Although striving to abolish the East–West binaries, the Congress helped to strengthen them; moreover, it has been continuously assessed through their homogenizing lens. The Wrocław Congress is waiting to be examined not only as the seminal event of the World Peace Movement, but also as a vital moment in the debates on the politicization of science, as well as a step towards the post-1945 revolt against the notion of the superiority of the West and, finally, as a demonstration of the importance of communist ideas for anti-colonialist struggles. By focusing on the arts at the Congress, we can see that Picasso's statement, redeeming the belief of the historical avant-garde in art committed to revolution both aesthetic and social, was fully in accord with the world-building activity he witnessed in Wrocław. The Congress might have contributed to the articulation of the peace-versus-freedom opposition, but at that time the rhetoric of peace and the communist plan for a wholesale conversion of Polish society were undistinguishable from the avant-garde ideal. Indeed, the setting of the Congress in war-ravaged capital of Silesia (which had just become Polish territory), its timing in the shadow of the Berlin blockade, its stupendous exhibition and surreal parade of the world's celebrities among the ruins – all was conceived as a grand-scale enactment of the avant-garde utopia, equating the political with the aesthetic in the drive to construct a new world on the ashes of the old one.

Orchestrated on the eve of the expansion of the blunt anti-formalist dogma, the Wrocław Congress has been perceived as merely an overture to it. And yet the stockpile of 'formalist' ideas developed in Wrocław during that summer of 1948 survived the Stalinist campaign against 'formalism', keeping the undercurrent of modernism alive in Polish design into the early 1950s. Similarly, Picasso's art, interventionist and 'formalist' at the same time, was to play a seminal role in the process of stretching the boundaries of 'anti-formalism' to the extent of eventually abolishing the socialist realist hegemony of the Communist Bloc.[7]

Organized by the Polish and French communist parties as a non-governmental call for peace outside the structure of UNESCO, the Congress was a very French event from the start, with the French language dominating the speeches and French exhibitions in the *couloirs*. Despite allegations that the Congress was a Cominform plot, the idea originated in the mind of the Polish publisher Jerzy Borejsza, a Francophile, as well connected with the French Communist Party as he was with Moscow, and his ambition was to turn the Congress into a *bombe atomique de la paix*. What must have gained him the approval of the Zhdanov Politburo was the location of the Congress in Wrocław.[8] As argued by Davies and Moorhouse in 2003, this city at the crossroads of *Zwischeneuropa* had been for centuries a microcosm of the Central European past.[9] In the post-Yalta reality Wrocław became uniquely suited for the display of both the traumas of the past and the dialectical triumphs of the present, exposing the foreign guests to tangible evidence of the recent Nazi atrocities as well as to Poland's historical claims to the western territories and, significantly, to the virility of Communism, thus legitimizing the new geography of Europe.

Following the tradition of the inter-war anti-fascist congresses 'which sought to rally personalities', invitations were sent to the world's top scientists and artists, and during those few days of August of 1948 Wrocław

was transformed into a veritable microcosm not just of Central Europe, but of the whole intellectual world, colonial countries included, rallying against war and imperialism. As the British communist and film-maker Ivor Montagu recalled, 'At no conference before or since have I seen so exalted and so assorted a galaxy of celebrities, in so appropriate a setting'.[10] Picasso was a star guest. He overcome his fear of air travel, gave a speech in defence of his friend Pablo Neruda and was invited on a two-week-long tour, during which he was shown around the ruined cities, visited Auschwitz and the Warsaw Ghetto, as well as the housing settlements being constructed by the new Poland. His gift of a set of his own ceramics to the National Museum in Warsaw, his mural of a Siren with a hammer sketched spontaneously on the freshly plastered wall

of a worker's flat (1.29) and his manifest interest in Polish folk art were all presented as his blessing of the country's new cultural politics. Picasso's *Sketch of a New Poland*, as a communist, anti-American and folklorized image, won him a major state award presented by the Polish President Bolesław Bierut.[11]

Apart from Picasso, the immensely long list of luminaries attending the Congress included Julian Huxley, the renowned British biologist and the president of UNESCO; the Nobel laureate Irène Joliot-Curie, who with her husband Frédéric was in the forefront of the campaign against the military use of science; Fernand Légér and Paul Eluard; and the poet from Martinique and a forerunner of the Négritude movement, Aimé Césaire. Le Corbusier cancelled at the last moment.[12] Albert Einstein, George Bernard Shaw and

Stephen Spender (who later became a contributor to the Congress for Cultural Freedom) sent notes of support. Among those who declined the invitation were Graham Greene; the American journalist who coined the term 'Cold War', Walter Lippmann; and Louis Aragon, who refused to lend his name to an event not organized by the Soviet Union. Jean-Paul Sartre, André Malraux and Albert Camus, deemed 'formalists', were not invited.[13] The Soviet delegation, led by Ilya Ehrenburg, included the novelist Mikhail Sholokhov, the avant-garde film-maker Vsevolod Pudovkin and, surprisingly, the composer Dmitrii Shostakovich, who a few months before had been denounced as formalist and forced to repent.[14] Among the foremost Marxist intellectuals from outside the Soviet Union were the Hungarian philosopher Georg Lukács,

1.30

Feliks Topolski, drawing
of the Russian delegation
at the World Congress
of Intellectuals in Defence
of Peace in Wrocław,
1948, from his *Confessions
of a Congress Delegate*
(London 1949).
V&A/NAL: Box I G 28 G

1.31

Feliks Topolski, drawing
of the ruins of Wrocław
during the World Congress
of Intellectuals in Defence
of Peace in Wrocław,
1948, from his *Confessions
of a Congress Delegate*
(London, 1949).
V&A/NAL: Box I G 28 G

the German communist author Anna Seghers, and Jorge Amado, the Brazilian writer in exile in Paris. From Britain they were joined by a particularly strong representation of 'red scientists', led by the crystallographer J.D. Bernal, the future president of the World Peace Movement who, after his return to London, engaged in a polemical campaign against a 'deliberate omission or misrepresentation of the Wrocław Congress' in the mainstream British press.[15] The British delegation, with 43 members, was one of the largest and the most diverse in its political outlook. It included a number of fellow travellers, such as the editor of *The New Statesman and Nation* Kingsley Martin, whose article 'Hyenas and Other Reptiles' sealed the negative reception of the Congress, and the aforementioned 'troublemaker' A.J.P Taylor. A sharp riposte to Taylor's lecture about freedom and 'bad manners' in politics was given by Peter Blackman, a poet from the West Indies, who pointed out the persistent lack of such concerns in British colonial relations. On the last day of the Congress the 'Red Dean' of Canterbury, Hewlett Johnson, famous for preaching Christianity and Communism as if they were one and the same, delivered an oration in the huge space of the Jahrhunderthalle.[16]

A unique, 'film-like' record of the event was published in book form by Feliks Topolski, a painter and draughtsman of Polish origin. Entitled *Confessions of a Congress Delegate* and written in a lively metaphorical prose, the book describes the turmoil caused by the two opposing resolutions of the Congress, the official 'communist' one and the counter-resolution prepared by the British. Topolski signed both of them, unable to maintain the neutrality of a detached observer when caught 'between two lines of fire'.[17] His ferocious drawing of a collection of bespectacled heads, wrinkled and pensive, bending low over their notes, disengaged from their companions, isolated by headphones and buried in their own thoughts, conveys a gloomy vision of the Congress (1.30). His haunting images of Wrocław provide a striking context to the portraits of the celebrities, showing empty streets where peace banners in foreign languages float pathetically over the ruins, unnoticed by the occasional pedestrians, and where ghosts of old German Kraftwagens and horse-drawn carts compete with a new tramway carriage (1.31). Topolski's pessimistic record of the Congress's 'meaningless universe' reminds the reader of Sartre and Camus, and appears closer to its denigration by Taylor or Huxley

than to its alternative evaluations published under the auspices of Bernal or *Les temps modernes*.[18]

A totally different vision of the Wrocław Congress is preserved in the sketchbook of Max Frisch mentioned above. Here the Congress is presented as a journey of self-recognition on the part of the 'Western intellectual'; an event unfolding in time and space; a spectacle composed of official speeches and scandals and of informal dialogues in *couloirs*, such as that between Picasso and his Soviet critics; of gala dinners and evening drinks in a hotel bar; and of chance encounters and lonely tours around Silesian countryside and war-ravaged Poland. On his arrival in Warsaw, 'a silhouette of insane destruction, worse than anything I have so far seen', Frisch visits the building sites and the Old City, and wanders off to the Warsaw Ghetto, the history of which he had been researching for a new play. He recovers over an 'excellent coffee' in an improvised café among the ruins. Before his departure Frisch goes to a meeting with some fellow architects, among whom are the future West-Berlin's planner, Hans Scharoun, Jiří Kroha of Czechoslovakia, Luigi Cosenza of Italy and Berthold Lubetkin representing Britain, all of them invited by Helena Syrkus, who held the vice-chairmanship of the Congrès International d'Architecture Moderne (CIAM) at the time. Frisch devotes a long paragraph to the reconstruction of Warsaw, clearly enthralled by the 'unique chance of building a city of our century', thanks to the abolition of private ownership of land.[19]

> ... The city will not be built by a state department but will bear the hallmarks of many individual architects.... Their architectural outlook, by no means alien to ours, is modern ... they show much imagination, in most cases a human scale of values, much feeling for cubic rhythms.... And so each of them ... has something of that healthy self-confidence of the early pioneers.[20]

Frisch's diary testifies to the widespread excitement generated by the reconstruction, felt even by visitors, for whom Poland presented an unmissable opportunity to build a new and better world. And there were no doubts at the time that this would be a radically and truly modern world. In Wrocław, Picasso's ceramic plates and contemporary French paintings were put on display in the Polytechnic where the Congress was held. A real star, however, was the 'Exhibition of the Lands Regained', opened a month earlier on the outskirts of the city and dominated by a giant steel needle. It was here that the 'feeling for Cubic rhythms' and 'healthy self-confidence of the early pioneers' were most articulated. No matter how critical Western dispatches on the Congress itself may have been, the exhibition was universally praised for its intelligence, originality, artistry and aesthetic quality, as well as for the speed and efficiency with which it was built. Kingsley Martin, writing in the *The New Statesman and Nation*, went as far as to suggest that 'Gerald Barry, seeking hints for the British Exhibition of 1951, should pay a visit'.[21]

Located on 150 acres of the German Ausstellungsgelände of 1913, the 'Exhibition of the Regained Lands' was a stunningly modern proclamation of the belief in social and economic utopias made possible by the communist system. It was devised as a 'book', and its main objective was to justify the post-Yalta division of Europe. One hundred new pavilions and numerous installations were set up with astonishing speed, having consumed huge funds earmarked for this event by the Polish government. This vast undertaking was said to have employed three thousand artists, including architects, engineers, graphic designers, photographers, painters, sculptors and craftspeople, and synchronizing in one impressive project a wide range of media, from architecture, design and fine art to film, music and performance. Three wooden arches, designed by the architect Marek Leykam, ran diagonally across the square in front of Max Berg's Jahrhunderthalle of 1913, while the soaring needle in the middle, designed by the engineer Stanisław Hempel, over 100m high and wonderfully slim, dominated the whole site. Other remarkable installations, such as the black Coal Rotunda with coal-clad walls, a tower built of shiny buckets and an abstract composition of a Duchamp-like fountain composed of car radiators, were blurring the boundaries not only between architecture and sculpture, but also, in a truly avant-garde manner, between art and life (1.32). Wrocław itself was also turned into a huge installation, in which ruins formed part of the whole assemblage, and gigantic plans of reconstruction set among them promised to transform the old Festung Breslau into a thriving new Polish city. As was readily pointed out by triumphant modernist critics, the exhibition testified to the transformative potential of modernism and, remarkably, to its ability to communicate with the public. The artistic director of the exhibition, the architect and designer Jerzy Hryniewiecki claimed enthusiastically:

> We are entering the world of artistic concepts which transgresses the framework of traditional thinking. We are entering 'applied Surrealism', we are getting close to abstract art. We live again by the awakened dynamism of Futurism, we are surrounded by the visual movements which have been inaccessible so far. 'Elitist' art is ultimately finding its own method of appealing to the masses. That which is an illegible and difficult form at the salons of art – starts speaking the language of propaganda and advertisements at exhibitions and fairs.[22]

As the Polish art critic Bożena Kowalska argued in the 1970s, the exhibition became an experimental field for artistic adventures, anticipating 'pop-art, ready-mades, environment and even *arte povera*'.[23] It also proved instrumental to the future development of Polish design, and in particular to exhibition design as a specific discipline which, virtually unaffected by Stalinist constraints, was practised by the same designers, especially in displays staged abroad.[24] Many of the young designers employed in Wrocław, such as the poster artist Henryk Tomaszewski, the Zamecznik brothers, the architects Hryniewiecki and Leykam, as well as cartoonists Jan Lenica and Eryk Lipiński, would continue to play significant roles in Polish art world, both under and after Stalin. A new periodical, *Projekt*, launched by Hryniewiecki in 1956, was to become a conscious revival of the ideas generated in Wrocław in 1948 (1.33).

However, these events were still in the future, so let us return to the summer of 1948. Despite the death Zhdanov a few days after the end of the Wrocław Congress, the meaning of anti-formalism was drastically reduced to a pro-socialist realist offensive, changing the art world of Poland considerably. Just as in the Soviet Union in the early 1930s, the most spectacular acts of the avant-garde went hand-in-hand with its sudden demise. Socialist Realism, which was emerging here and there at Wrocław exhibition grounds, received a supporting hand during the Congress. Among the artists invited to participate were the leading Soviet painter Alexander Gerasimov, who in just over a year's time would oversee the first socialist realist exhibition in Warsaw, and the French communist sculptor Emmanuel Aricoste, who would become instrumental in promoting French Socialist Realism behind the Iron Curtain. The Italian painter Renato Guttuso, a member of the Central Committee of the Italian Communist Party, at the time considered to be one of the leading Italian artists, was elected as one of the Congress's four presidents, declaring his choice of 'dynamic realism' as the only creative idiom answering contemporary needs.[25] In hindsight, even the exhibition of seventeen 'Contemporary French Painters' shown during the Congress could have been interpreted as heralding Socialist Realism. It featured

1.32
The tower of zinc buckets
and the fountain at the
'Exhibition of the Regained
Lands', Wrocław, 1948.
National Museum, Warsaw

1.33
Cover of *Projekt* (vol.1, no.2,
1956), featuring the design
of a Warsaw sports stadium
by Jerzy Hryniewiecki and
a plate by Pablo Picasso.
V&A/NAL: PP 61 G

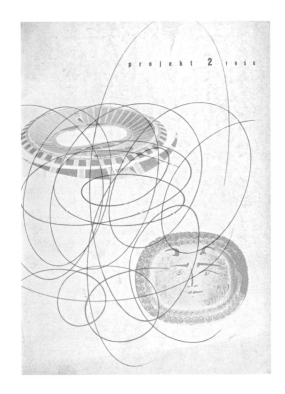

Modernism between Peace and Freedom

Picasso's *Seated Woman in a Hat* (1939),[26] two of his drawings and his set of ceramic plates; but, apart from several still lifes and a nude, the largest work was Boris Taslitzky's *Delegation* (1947; Courneuve Town Hall) representing a group of steelworkers on strike. Jean Marcenac's introduction to the catalogue ended with a declaration of the political function of art, while striving to find an excuse for Picasso's formal experiments:

> The era in which painting was a test of skill is over. Today, it is the test of conscience. Painting is not satisfied by illusory truths, but wants to transgress and go beyond them, to reach reality; make-up is no longer considered art.... Picasso's woman and Boris Taslitzky's workers speak the same language, and express what they essentially are. The woman is what she has been made by the world; the workers are the ones who want to remake this world.[27]

By the time the French exhibition arrived at the National Museum in Warsaw in late November 1948, official art policies in Poland were undergoing a radical shift, and only a few lukewarm reviews of the show were published. As argued by Bernatowicz, Picasso the potter was now universally praised, while Picasso the formalist was shunted into the back seat.[28] After the official declaration of Socialist Realism as the only acceptable artistic idiom of the socialist era at the General Meeting of the Union of the Polish Artists in Katowice in June 1949, it was now the violent realism of Guttuso and the heroic allegories of his French counterpart André Fougeron, as well as the monumental compositions of the Mexican muralists, which would dominate the official discourse of art in Poland for the next few years.[29]

And yet, as early as April 1952 Picasso was to return once more to the front pages of both professional journals and the media. His *Massacre in Korea*, 1951 (Musée Picasso, Paris), abhorred in New York as 'modernism for propaganda purposes', was held to be sufficiently anti-American to be shipped to the exhibition of Progressive Artists in Warsaw, even despite its formalist outlook. Re-legitimized by official discourse, Picasso's art was to play a significant role in diversifying anti-formalist formations, in stretching the boundaries of realism and dismantling socialist realist orthodoxy.[30]

Even after that watershed moment, *Massacre of Korea* repeatedly returned, deployed and redeployed in the tug-of-war between peace and freedom and in the constant battle of values in the Polish art world. A huge reproduction of the painting was included by Jerzy Hryniewiecki in a gigantic anti-war installation, strongly reminiscent of the Wrocław exhibition, during the International Festival of Youth in Warsaw in July 1955. Picasso was seen once again as the patron of modernist glamour, and *Massacre in Korea* represented both peace and formalist freedoms.[31] A year later, however, when a copy of the work was displayed on a main thoroughfare in the Polish capital by Warsaw Academy of Art students in protest against the Soviet intervention in Budapest in October 1956 (1.34), it entered yet another battle for re-signification, inviting the viewer to read it primarily as an anti-war protest. However, it turned now into the accusation of the Soviet 'peace makers'.[32] Paradoxically, this brought the painting back to its anti-formalist, essentially political function, testifying yet again to the ambiguity of modernism which, just as Picasso had implied, was capable of accommodating formalism and anti-formalism within the same frame. It was the viewer who activated one or the other.

2.1
Dmitrii Chechulin (architect) and I. Tigranov (structural engineer), administrative building in Zariad'e, the eighth high-rise tower-block planned for Moscow (unbuilt). Watercolour and ink on paper, 1947–9. Schusev State Museum of Architecture (MUAR), Moscow

2 / Europe Reconstructed, Europe Divided

David Crowley

Cold War challenges

In 1949 the Congrès Internationaux d'Architecture Moderne (CIAM) gathered in the historic city of Bergamo in Italy (2.2). This occasional meeting of minds had been the major intellectual clearing house for new ideas about modern architecture and planning in the inter-war period. Its members had confidently announced to the world the minimal dwelling in 1929 and the credo of the 'functional city' with its high, widely spaced apartment blocks and green belts separating zones outlined in the Athens Charter (1933/42). But four years after one war had ended and with a new one seemingly on the verge of breaking out, the mood of the CIAM was less bullish. Gone were the utopian pronouncements of the pre-war years. Nevertheless, reconstruction of Europe's war-torn cities was a common concern and a great opportunity for the Congress to demonstrate its indisputable relevancy. Reconstruction should, perhaps, have been a unifying theme. But the event was disturbed by dispute, a symptom of a Cold War freeze in the relations between former allies. One-time constructivist, Polish architect Helena Syrkus took the stage to signal her unequivocal support for the new order that was being imposed East of Berlin.[1] Before an audience made up of such architectural luminaries as Josep Luis Sert, Ernesto Nathan Rogers, Le Corbusier and Max Bill, some of whom had once been her close allies and colleagues, she argued that the kind of technological invention and abstract volumes of Le Corbusier's luxurious villas or *Existenzminimum* social housing in the late 1920s, when CIAM had first met, were redundant in the advanced conditions of Soviet socialism:

The formalism of CIAM was positive in the early days – it was a revolt. It made use of analytical methods, which were also socialist methods ... but its importance has grown less and less.... Construction is but a skeleton. It has great interest for the anatomist, but for the rest it only becomes beautiful when it is covered with fine muscles and a lovely skin. We had nothing else to offer when CIAM began, and so we made a fetish of the skeleton. The countries of the East have come to the conclusion that we should have a greater respect for the past.[2]

Soviet modernity, she argued, outstripped that of the capitalist West and no longer had, therefore, any need for the transitional experiments of the Modern Movement. (In this way, Syrkus revealed a talent for the twisting analytical method of dialectical materialism.) The architect needed, she further argued, to suppress his or her ego: the needs of 'the people' should dictate his or her line of action. Abstruse theory or abstract conceptions of space should be foregone in order to serve the tastes of the working classes.

Syrkus spoke at the height of the *zhdanovshchina* when Soviet ideologues, led by Cominform boss Andrei Zhdanov, went on the attack against the West. He divided the world into 'the imperialist and anti-democratic camp, on the one hand, and the anti-imperialist and democratic camp, on the other'.[3] Furthermore, the announcement of the Marshall Aid scheme for Europe in June 1947 (and its rejection by Eastern European states under pressure from the Kremlin) triggered a paranoid response in the East, with one newspaper celebrating 'those countries and people that refuse to trade their national independence, preferring to ... build up ... their own industries rather than ... [accept] American handouts'.[4] A 'vast ideological disinfection campaign' against American culture was launched throughout the Eastern Bloc in its earliest days, focused largely on Hollywood films and jazz music. A new coded vocabulary entered into political discourse in which 'cosmopolitan' was a synonym for American and 'democratic' signalled countries under communist rule aligned to Moscow.

2.2
Max Huber, poster promoting
the Congrès International
d'Architecture Moderne
meeting in Bergamo, Italy,
1949. M.A.X. Museo,
Chiasso

2.3
Helena and Szymon Syrkus,
Koło East housing estate
under construction,
Warsaw, 1947–51 (Source:
B. Bierut, *Sześcioletni plan
odbudowy Warszawy*,
Warsaw 1949)

All communists loyal to Moscow were now under an injunction to attack the 'forces of reaction'.[5] In the East German *Handbuch für Architekten (Guide for Architects)* of 1954, the reader was to be left in no uncertainty about where the menace of modern architecture was coming from:

> As in other capitalist countries, building is predominately formalist and subordinated to the cosmopolitan ideology of American imperialism. This is why buildings look alike whatever their location, whether they are in West Germany, Italy, France, or America. The housing, banks, administration buildings, hotels, and stores in the form of shapeless boxes are an expression of the profit hunger of monopoly capitalism under American dominance. The obliteration of all national character continues relentlessly. This is evident as well in the destruction of valuable historical complexes. Thus architecture is replaced by mere construction.[6]

Syrkus's speech was also, as she freely admitted, a 'self-critique'. In this way, she gave her audience a public demonstration of the Soviet ritual of *samokritika*, a public confession of the 'errors' in one's earlier thinking or actions. There were, as in all such confessions, traces of involuntary surrealism in her actions. As she spoke, social housing schemes in precisely the modernist idiom that she had designed with her husband, Szymon Syrkus, were being erected in Warsaw. Pre-dating the imposition of Stalinist aesthetics on the city (announced in the *Five Year Plan for the Reconstruction of the Warsaw*), the Koło East estate (designed 1947–8 and constructed 1949–51), spare social housing-blocks built from prefabricated panels and composed in the manner of pre-war *Siedlungen*, had slipped through the ideological net that she was herself now casting (2.3).

2.4
Lev Kerbel' (sculptor),
Vladimir Zigal (sculptor) and
Nikolai Sergievski (architect),
Soviet cenotaph in the
Tiergarten, West Berlin,
1945–6

Syrkus was not alone on the path taken by former modernist architects towards Stalinism. In East Germany, one of the most forceful figures driving Socialist Realism was Kurt Liebknecht, once an employee in the studio of Mies van der Rohe, the last director of the Bauhaus. Following a period of forced exile in the Soviet Union, Liebknecht became the most prominent spokesman for Stalin's new order and vigorous Cold War critic of the Modern Movement.[7] In Hungary the new city of Stálinváros was designed by former Bauhäusler Tibor Weiner to serve the Dunai Vasmű (Danube Steelworks). Infected with the 'war psychosis' which gave priority to military-industrial needs over all other social priorities, the steel town was built at break-neck speed. Weiner, in Stálinváros's early phases, explored a number of core modernist preoccupations such as industrialized housing construction. But this national project required more spectacular architectural propaganda than efficient schemes for laying cinder-blocks. In fact, in 1952 Weiner came under ideological attack for not bringing enough 'socialist enthusiasm' to his designs. His Communist Party headquarters in the steel town, a modest box framed with columns and a classical pediment, did not express the 'power of the Party' with sufficient force.[8]

It is difficult to say whether ambition, opportunism, fear or genuine commitment to the Soviet programme motivated these abrupt changes of orientation (and historians are only now exploring the careers of some figures who were largely dismissed as hacks after the Stalin years[9]). It was clear that the sovietiza-tion of architecture and city planning in the emergent Eastern Bloc required unambiguous statements of loyalty from the most prominent architects, particularly those who had been most closely connected with the old faith of modernism. Syrkus's speech made this plain. The response of her CIAM colleagues, gathered from around the world, was

unsympathetic. Soviet cities – with their long, formal avenues with monumental sculpture and buildings dressed with classical columns and lintels – hardly looked like the future.[10]

The disagreement at Bergamo was not whether architects should have wide ambi-tions and effects (as CIAM delegate Ernesto Nathan Rogers put it, from 'the spoon to the city') or even whether the State should be the chief client for whom architects would work.[11] For most European architects these were the given conditions of reconstruction. What was being contested in Bergamo was, at heart, a debate about the form that buildings and cities should take. In this regard, monuments formed a particularly fierce front in Cold War disputes about the future face of the city. The prospect of casting history aside – a theme of much inter-war rhetoric – was somewhat harder to countenance when so much had been destroyed. Which buildings and monuments should be rebuilt or restored to assume pre-war appearance or what should be forsaken in the name of progress occupied many minds in the first post-war decade.[12] Parallel debates attended to the question of new memorial art. That the trauma of the Second World War and

its victims required some kind of memorializa-tion was largely accepted: what was far more controversial was the question of what formal languages public memorials were to take. This was perhaps most pronounced in the different sectors of Germany, where it formed one face of a pained debate about the effects of abstract and realist art in the wake of Nazism, known as the *Realismusstreit*.[13] As the Cold War unfolded, abstract art was increasingly associated with a 'Western' orientation whilst realism appeared to be tainted with 'Eastern' associations.

Evidence of the latter was plentiful. Germany – and the nations liberated from Nazi rule by the Red Army – had little choice but to accept the innumerable monuments expressing their gratitude for the efforts of Soviet forces in defeating Nazism. Berlin, for instance, acquired three massive memorial complexes, including the Tiergarten complex (1945–6) in the very centre of the city (2.4).[14] (Built before the decisive drawing-up of zones in the city in 1948, it was located in the Western sector.) This Soviet memorial – with its lonely Red Army soldier on a tiered plinth, colonnade and Soviet tank – was a standard

2.5
Eduard Ludwig, *Monument
to the Victims of the
Berlin Airlift*, Tempelhof,
West Berlin, 1951

'kit of parts' widely configured elsewhere. Largely indifferent to the existing architectural settings, such memorials served as the backdrop for political and military ceremonies marking the imposition of Soviet order on Eastern and Central European societies.[15] Collectively, they acted as belligerent territorial markers mapping out the extent of what was euphemistically called 'the Soviet sphere of influence'.

Perhaps not surprisingly, Cold War Berlin was the site of one of the first abstract public monuments erected in post-war Europe. In 1951 former Bauhäusler Eduard Ludwig's concrete *Monument to the Victims of the Berlin Airlift* was erected at Tempelhof airport in the Western sector (2.5). Its three-pronged form, organized as a tall, curving wall, represented the three air-corridors that had supplied food and other essential items for life during the Soviet blockade of the city in 1948 and 1949. Ludwig's design was surprisingly monumental, its unrelieved concrete form towering above the visitors who paid homage to the American and British airmen who had lost their lives serving the city. It also struck the strongest possible contrast with the three Soviet memorials already erected in the city.

In the confrontation with 'totalitarianism', a term that grew in currency in the West during the 1940s, monumentality itself was seen as a threat to democracy.[16] Gregor Paulsson, a liberal promoter of Swedish modernism, joined a debate on the pages of the *Architectural Review* in September 1948, to make his views plain:

> The totalitarian society has always taken monumentality into its service to strengthen its power over people, the democratic society in conformity with its nature is anti-monumental ... Intimacy not monumentality should be the emotional goal, even in cities, as far as this is possible.[17]

Other contributors to the debate identified monumentality with dictatorship, with the editorial criticizing Soviet Russia for an attachment to 'pseudo-monumentality', a double offence which not only produced false emotional effects in the city but also buildings which in Sigfried Giedion's words lacked the 'strong artistic vision that leads to new results'.[18] Paulsson did not specify what an intimate monument might be, though at the time he spoke a number of architects were designing buildings that can be understood in his terms (see p.56 below).

By 1950 it seems that views of the ideal city were divided on clear Cold War lines. Ideology and events should not, however, be confused. The years of the *zhdanovshchina* (1947–54) throw up many unexpected buildings and schemes that cannot be neatly squared with the excited political rhetoric of the day. The first of these ideological inversions was the strange phenomenon of 'American' skyscraper aesthetics in Moscow.

Monuments to victory

Although the principles of Socialist Realism had been declared in the 1930s, Soviet architecture was not unchanged by war.[19] In fact, a 'new' building type, the *vysotnye zdaniia* (tall building) was introduced in the 1940s as an expression of the triumphalism of the late Stalin period. The Soviet Union had saved the world from Fascism: now its capital was to become the hub of a new Empire that would draw admiring visitors from across the globe. A set of eight buildings, ostensibly initiated to commemorate Moscow's eighth centenary, was announced by a Council

of Ministers' proclamation in 1947 (2.1). They were to be 'in terms of size, technology and architecture, a new form of construction, seen for the first time in our country'.[20] In fact, these additions to the Moscow skyline had already been proposed by Boris Iofan – a favourite of the Stalin regime – before the Soviet Union went to war with Nazi Germany. He had argued that its undulating terrain was naturally suited to such eye-catching monuments. They were also related to the Palace of Soviets competition (1930–33). Iofan's winning design had been an icon of Stalinist mania: a stepped skyscraper capped with a figure of Lenin that was to tower 400m above the ground. Building work had begun on what was to be a national parliament in the 1930s, but the project stalled in 1941 and the unfinished steel framework of the Palace was dismantled to provide war materials.[21]

By contrast, seven of the eight buildings planned to crown Moscow were eventually constructed and continue to dominate the Russian capital today. Six new post-war towers were erected in strategic sites in the centre of the city: the Leningradskaia and Ukraina hotels; three massive housing schemes on Kotelnicheskaia Quay, Krasnye Vorota and Vosstania Square; and the Ministry of Foreign Affairs on Smolenskaia Place.

They rose above the wide radial and ring roads which threaded the city together, a fact emphasized in most of the monumental presentation drawings produced in the late 1940s: all feature sweeping profiles of ZIL cars, the vehicle of choice for the Party elite.

A seventh building, a 'Palace of Science', was built in the south-west of the city centre, high up on what were then called the Lenin Hills. Moscow State University was connected to the core by a sight line to the Kremlin towers, the centre of Soviet power. In this regard it followed a key pattern in Soviet city aesthetics: centres of power like the Party headquarters and public monuments were not only to be highly visible, they were to be connected to one another as if fixed on a grid that would distribute ideological 'electricity'. Architects like Lev Rudnev – author of Moscow University – approached the design of buildings like sculptors, determining their visual appearance and positioning in the cityscape before attending to the arrangement of rooms and other 'internal' matters. This represented not only an indifference to private space characteristic of Soviet architecture, but also the priority given to the ideological impact of buildings. The Soviet metropolis in the Stalin era was conceived as a set of vivacious images, ignoring the experiential and sensory qualities of the city. The eye can travel in an instant along a vista; the body takes considerably longer. Henri Lefebvre, describing the general appeal of architectural images to authority, has called this phenomenon, 'the reign of the façade'.[22] These glittering images reflected back on their authors. Ultimately they were public monuments to the 'genius of world history', Stalin himself, disquieting cathedrals in the cult of personality (2.6).

Despite differences in the stone and terracotta facings in which these structures were clad, their varying ornaments and profiles, these tiered towers represented a distinct and new building type within the context of Soviet architecture. But what was even more obvious was that Moscow's new towers owed much to the American skyscraper of the early twentieth century, typified by structures like the Woolworth Building in Manhattan by Cass Gilbert (1911–13).[23] A 25-storey tower capped with a sculptural spire emerging from a massive main block,

2.6
N. Petrov, *Glory to the Great Stalin, the Architect of Communism*. Poster, USSR, 1952. Private collection

2.7
Opening of the Palace of Culture and Science in Warsaw, 22 July 1955 (Source: Jan Jacoby and Zygmunt Wdowiński, *Pałac, Kultury i Nauki im. Józefa Stalina*, Warsaw 1955)

the Woolworth Building is a steel frame dressed in Gothic terracotta mouldings, traceried marbled and bronze trimmings and glass. A self-proclaimed 'cathedral of commerce', it was an unmistakable symbol of Western capitalism. The uncanny return of this building type to the heart of the Soviet Empire was a kind of perverse historical echo which Soviet architectural critics worked hard to explain.[24] Moscow-trained architectural theorist Edward Goldzamt

explained to Polish readers that it was not the arrangement of space or the building technology that made these buildings Soviet; it was their legibility and order.

The American skyscraper reflects the chaos and internal contradictions of the capitalist economy. Piled up near one another in a state of disorder, they grow without clear function. This can only be supplied by thinking carefully about composition of the city and its streets. The tall buildings set in Moscow's extensive squares has created a genuine system which responds to the needs and the structure of the city. It has created the affecting unity of its silhouette and image.[25]

According to this Soviet-minded commentator, the market also determined the austere form of the modernist slab block.[26] This was an emerging building type that invited comparison with the opulent materials and rich decoration of the Soviet *vysotnye zdaniia*. The towering slab dressed with a glass and aluminum curtain wall was an architectural 'degeneration' rather than – as its champions in the West claimed – the expression of modernity. 'The economic power which drives the New York skyscraper upwards', wrote Goldzamt, 'also determines its degenerated slab form. Stretched like a sky-high matchbox on extended foundations, it is awkward in construction and in use'.[27] The chaotic and ugly Western city was, on the basis of Stalin-era criticism, the pivot of modern alienation: it was shaped by the selfish interests of capital and the technological fetishism of the architectural profession.

In Stalin's shadow

Plans were made to export the new order of Soviet skyscrapers throughout the rest of the Union and the People's Republics. Few Stalinist skyscrapers, however, were realized: Prague's International Hotel, which opened its doors to guests in 1951, was reduced in scale. Designed by František Jeřábek with Russian architectural advisors, it was for this reason almost more kitsch than its Moscow forebears.[28] By contrast, Warsaw's Palace of Culture and Science was a direct implant from Moscow (2.7). A vast building at the heart of

the city on plac Defilad (Parade Square), this building was a gift to the city from the people of the Soviet Union, in recognition, as the press loudly trumpeted, of Warsaw's heroism and sacrifice during the fight against Nazism. It was designed as a cultural centre with sports facilities, museums, cinemas and theatres, a massive enlargement of the workers' clubs and houses of culture that were built in the Soviet Union from the 1920s. Beyond its practical uses, the building had a symbolic function in its scale and as the prime site of public parades (for which a tribune was built in front of its main, eastern elevation). Indeed, the authority of this building lay in its visibility, and Polish advocates of Soviet architecture championed the reciprocity of sight that it afforded all inhabitants of Warsaw. So self-consciously belonging to Moscow, it was as if Warsaw's Palace of Culture and Science could offer a glimpse of the heart of empire 'just' over the horizon. To demonstrate the claim that the building adhered to the socialist realist maxim that ensured 'correct' design, 'Socialist in content and national in form', Rudnev, its architect, and his Soviet colleagues went on a widely reported tour of historic buildings in the region. He adopted the historicist ornament characteristic of the Renaissance architecture of the central Polish towns of Sandomierz, Cracow and Toruń to form decorative crenellations on Warsaw's new Palace.

Despite the 'Polishness' of its architectural garb, the Palace of Culture and Science was an aggressive imposition on the urban and architectural traditions of the city. It has now been generally recognized that even the Polish communists did not want this 'gift' to the city conferred by Stalin himself.[29] As if to offset the violence done to Warsaw by the imposition of this Soviet skyscraper, a campaign stressing dizzying innovation was launched to proselytize diffident Poles. The Palace of Culture and Science was almost invariably described as 'the most beautiful and most original building of socialist Warsaw'.[30] The building became a kind of didactic symbol of Communism's imminence. The metaphor of architectural construction was interlaced with one of social construction. A Trojan Horse, it was designed by Russian architects and constructed by Russian labour using imported materials. The 4,000 Russian

workers building the Palace were encamped on the edge of the city in barracks. These brigades of young enthusiasts enjoyed, according to contemporary reports in the popular press, sport and gymnastics, amateur theatre, ballet led by instructors from the Bolshoi Theatre and the Red Army after their daily toil. The workers' camp was presented as a premonition of the future: 'The visit of our Soviet friends', reported a journalist in Stolica, 'strengthened our conviction that Soviet peoples should not only work hard, but should also spend free time from work in a cultured way'.[31] Furthermore, work on the building continued day and night using automated technology, a fact frequently repeated to emphasize the 'advanced' nature of Soviet civilization.

Exporting the style

The Palace of Culture and Science in Warsaw is a rare exception to the general pattern of the Sovietization of architecture in the Eastern Bloc during the reconstruction years.[32] Very few buildings were designed by Soviet architects or constructed with Soviet labour (excepting the first wave of liberation memorials in the region). Far more effort was invested in nationalizing the building industry and compelling architects to conform to the official creed. The process by which this was achieved was remarkably uniform in all the countries that formed the Eastern Bloc. Experts trained in Moscow returned home to occupy prominent positions in the government and professional hierarchies and, conversely, architects – often combining young communist enthusiasts and established figures – were sent on tours of the Soviet Union as guests of the Main Council of the Union of Soviet Architects.[33] The route was a uniform one: it focused on Moscow, where they learned how the new monumental tall buildings, beautiful squares and avenues were 'harmonized into an architectural unity', and 'beautiful, historic and heroic' Leningrad, where they were 'inspired' for their return home and the task of building socialism. For those who did not have the benefit of a ticket east, a series of conferences were called throughout the region in 1949–51 in which the official creed of Socialist Realism was broadcast to the profession. If architects were uncertain about how to interpret the new creed, dozens

of articles in the architectural press were reproduced from Architectura SSSR. In Czechoslovakia, the most loyal of Moscow's satellites, a new Czech journal entitled Sovětská architektura was published in 1951 with the sole purpose of trumpeting Soviet designs. Architectural competitions, widely reported in the press, not only drew attention to the muscular vision of socialism: they also served a disciplinary function, providing the ideologues with the means to reward orthodoxy and publicly criticize difference.

To meet the ideological requirement of 'national form', a limited repertoire of historic precedents was licensed in each country: in Poland, for instance, a 1910 neoclassical tenement on plac Małachowski in Warsaw designed by Jan Heurich was selected to supply the genetic code from which all new buildings in the city undergoing reconstruction would be generated.[34] In a very literal manner, the five- and six-storey elevations of apartment buildings dressed with classical cornices, lintels and miniature porticos – the preferred taste of the haute bourgeoisie in 1900 – were adapted for ostensibly similar new buildings for the workers in capital's model district, Marszałkowska Dzielnica Mieszkaniowa (Marszałkowska Housing District), in the 1950s.[35] Czech architects were given different models to follow. In Marxist historiography, fourteenth- and fifteenth-century Bohemia carried strong historical resonance as an age when the Hussites, an alliance of peasants and merchants, fought off the Germans and supporters of the Pope. Hussite decorative motifs – richly decorated gables, ornamental parapets and sgraffito embellishments – were adopted as the appropriate language of Czech architecture. In East Germany, Karl Friedrich Schinkel's nineteenth-century neoclassicism was prescribed as the model for the future. Here East German ideologues had the difficult task of distinguishing 'politically correct' neoclassicism from the disfigured aesthetics of the Nazi regime. As Greg Castillo has noted, there was a paradox at the heart of East German socialist realist schemes that celebrated 'Prussian neoclassicism whilst denigrating its social and political context'.[36] Ultimately, however, the sophistry of the new cadre of Party ideologues counted for

Horst E. Schulze, publicity photograph of Stalinallee from the roof garden of the 'Children's House' on Straussberger Platz, Berlin, 1956

less than the unassailable fact that the State now managed architectural practice and building construction. Large central planning and design offices were organized to serve the only client, the State, which also controlled the supply of building materials and plots. With few exceptions architects had one choice: design or resign.

'The most beautiful street in Europe'

The most important Soviet thoroughfare in Central Europe was Stalinallee, the new ornament of East German capital (2.8). Berlin had effectively split in two after the Soviet Blockade and the Western airlift of 1948–9, when Stalin had tried to force the Allied Forces to withdraw from the city deep behind the East-West border. The Western Sectors were increasingly orientated to the West German state, whilst the Soviet Sector – turned into the capital of East Germany – looked eastward. In the course of the 1950s two separate urban infrastructures took shape (power networks, communication lines, and so on). East and West Berlin began slowly to turn their backs on each other, with architects, planners and politicians tacitly accepting the divisions that operated there.[37] The East German authorities, for instance, shifted the centre of the city away from its historical focal point, the Brandenburg Gate on Unter den Linden, towards Friedrichshain district further east. The centrepiece of this heavily ruined area was the Frankfurter Allee, which was renamed Stalinallee in the Soviet leader's honour as a birthday gift in 1949. It was presented with loud propaganda as a national project to which ordinary citizens should commit their money or labour, and national combines should give materials.

Stalinallee was an effective barometer of the changing political-aesthetical climate in East Berlin during the 1950s. The earliest buildings on the boulevard, built in 1949–50, were designed by Ludmilla Herzenstein, a close associate of Hans Scharoun, and Richard Paulick. In their utilitarian form and square proportions they represented a return to the low-key modernism that had flourished in Weimar Germany. The western end of the avenue, constructed in the early 1960s after the Stalinist aesthetics fell out of favour, was equally plain with the housing blocks organized at right-angles to the main axis. But it

2.9
Hermann Henselmann,
drawing of façade of
building on Marchlewski-
strasse, the precursor
of Stalinallee, East
Berlin, c.1952. Berlinische
Galerie, Landesmuseum
für Moderne Kunst,
Fotografie und Architektur,
Berlin

was the vision of the city represented by the building between these modernist bookmarks that attracted both garlands of praise and jeers of ridicule from the considerable numbers who came to visit the street (before the Wall was built in 1961 the city was 'open' and Berliners could travel between the zones). The apartments as well as the ordinary shops which occupied the ground floors were dressed with classical details and clad with stone and ceramic tiles, amplifying their luxurious impression in a city where many buildings still stood as semi-ruins.

This wide avenue was designed to broadcast the new priorities of the East German regime to its own citizens and to the rest of the world. High-quality housing for the workers not only represented the social priorities of the regime, it also formed a critique of the suburbanizing effects of city planning in the West. The official declaration of the 'Sixteen Principles for the Restructuring of Cities' (1950) had demanded that residential districts should be urban: 'pastoral' life in the suburbs represented the past.[38] Cities required centres – the 'political midpoint of the life of the populace' – for political demonstrations, parades and other 'popular celebrations'. The boulevard was widened to 80m and the individual blocks extended over 200m in length. Different architectural collectives led by six of the leading architects working

for the regime – under the overall leadership of Hermann Henselmann – designed the long seven- to ten-storey residential housing blocks (2.9). By articulating the façade with different arrangements of balconies and projecting bays, and decorating their buildings with classical devices, the architects were expected to produce variety within the symbolic unity of the scheme.

Eventually 5,500 apartments were provided, largely to prominent figures in the arts, members of the nomenclatura and favoured workers. At 12m deep, the blocks were strangely narrow, adding to their 'Potemkin village' effect. The flats inside were based on very small, *Existenzminimum* proportions and provided only one or two rooms plus a kitchen. Meeting the collective emphasis of the 'Sixteen Principles' and functioning as a showcase for Soviet-style socialism, Stalinallee was supplied with communal facilities like laundries and childcare centres. Here was 'proof' of the benefits of collective life under the protection of the State over the private and individualistic values encouraged by the market. Stalinallee was a model avenue, which would over the course of time assume national proportions. All East German cities would come to share its 'joyful' appearance (this smooth rhetoric was disrupted when workers on Stalinallee in July 1953 rioted over pay and conditions[39]).

2.10
Max Bill, poster for 'USA
Builds', an exhibition at
the Kunstgewerbemuseum,
Zurich, 1945.
V&A: E.217-1982

kunstgewerbe museum zürich

USA baut

9. september – 7. oktober 1945

Here was a city in perfect order, a chilling vision that sought to spare the comrade-citizens of East Germany the anxieties of modernity. At the same time, its monumental proportions and limited repertoire of forms extinguished the excitement and unpredict-ability that characterize modern urban life.

The new world in the old

To talk about the Sovietization of architectural design and city planning in Eastern Europe during the Stalin years is not an exaggeration: the same cannot be said of the Americaniza tion of European architecture, despite the loud protests of Zhdanov's sharp-shooters. This is not to say that American materials and ideas had no impact on the reconstruction of Western Europe or that the Cold War warriors in Washington saw no uses for architecture in their battles with Communism. As Greg Castillo demonstrates below (p.66), Marshall Fund administrators in West Germany (as well as in Italy and France) were keen to exploit housing exhibitions as a way of promoting 'the American way of life', an ideological concept predicated on envy. In 'living exhibitions' that toured West Germany in the 1950s, domestic appliances were used to forge connections between individualism, reconstruction and consumerism. This was but one face of America in Europe. Reconstruc-tion was a complex affair in which the American influence was met by modernist architects in Western Europe with enthusi-asm and resistance.[40]

A notable feature of the first post-war decade was the movement of people and ideas across the Atlantic. Architects, as well as planners, engineers and other technocrats, were taken on extensive study tours to North America in the late 1940s and early 1950s.[41] European architects could see American building technology at first hand and meet its liberal champions, including writers like Lewis Mumford and émigrés from Nazi Germany including Mies van der Rohe and Walter Gropius, both former directors of the Bauhaus. The French Ministry of Reconstruc-tion organized a delegation of French archi-tects to travel to Chicago and the new towns that had been built under the aegis of the Tennessee Valley Authority in the 1930s, a massive Depression relief scheme. The response of one delegate was to discover

Soviet-style state planning in the American economy.[42] This was not, perhaps, the inten-tion of his hosts.

This transatlantic process was not simply a matter of American *noblesse oblige* or Cold War propaganda: the French Ministry of Reconstruction set up an office in Washington in 1945 from which it investigated new construction materials and prefabrication structures in the USA.[43] Moreover, not all Europeans were happy consumers of *Ameri-kanismus*. In the Netherlands, the Contact Group for Increased Productivity sent Dutch delegations to the United States. The second tour in the spring of 1953 was made up of architects and urbanists who made pilgrim-ages to meet the same heroes of the Modern Movement as their German counterparts. One delegate, architect Leo De Jonge, was not consumed with passion for the New World: 'I was not pro-American. And I thought that a lot of the trip was pure propaganda ... our presence was to supposed to sell the American people on the idea that so much money was going to Europe ...'.[44]

At the same time, touring exhibitions focusing on the construction techniques employed by American buildings, as well exhibitions celebrating the achievement of modern architects in America, came to Europe (2.10). Frank Lloyd Wright, for instance, was the subject of a major retrospective exhibition entitled 'Frank Lloyd Wright: Sixty Years of Living Architecture', which opened in Florence in 1951 before travelling to Zurich, Paris, Munich and Rotterdam. The sponsor of this event was the United States Informa-tion Agency, the chief organization promoting American culture abroad in the Cold War.[45]

The Museum of Modern Art (MoMA) in New York was an enthusiastic conscript in this war of images. In its famous 1932 exhibition, MoMA had already done an effective job of decontaminating what Henry-Russell Hitchcock and Philip Johnson called 'the International Style' from its Marxist associations by emphasizing its formal qualities over its social aims. This had been an important part of modernism's translation into the social and political setting of America in the 1930s. In the 1940s and 1950s, MoMA's defenders of modernism worked hard, in the face of loud resistance, to demonstrate its democratic bona fides by exhibiting it as the choice of an informed and, ultimately, free individual. 'Modern design', wrote Edgar Kaufmann, Director of the Industrial Design Department, in 1950, 'is intended to implement the lives of free individuals'.[46] Demonstrating its democratic credentials in postwar Europe was part of the same logic.

In 1948 the International Style returned back to Germany in an important publication, *In USA erbaut 1932–1944*.[47] It supplied not only information about the development of modern architecture in the period since MoMA's 1932 exhibition but, crucially, new American achievements in the field. New models were presented to the German public, including the curtain wall systems which had been used by Mies van der Rohe in the United States from the late 1940s onwards (and were to be popularized by Gordon Bunshaft for Skidmore, Owings & Merrill, architects of the iconic Lever Building [1952] in New York). Mies' sparkling innovations and the undeniable originality of Frank Lloyd Wright's output had the benefit of demonstrating the high intellectual ambition of America, a rebuttal of the Soviet image of the US as a land in thrall of Coca-Cola and pornography.

Despite this transatlantic traffic in ideas and technologies, few significant new building schemes in Europe can be described as 'American' in a meaningful sense in the 1940s and early 1950s. As Paolo Scrivano notes of the situation in Italy, the intense building programme to address the extensive homelessness after 1945 – largely funded by the USA – recycled existing vernacular building types.[48] The exigencies of reconstruction made traditional techniques and building types an immediate solution to immediate problems. It was only in the late 1950s, when US businesses sought to capitalize on the economic recovery, that a more visible Americanization of the European cityscape occurred, with corporate headquarters and air-conditioned hotels.[49] In 1957 Conrad Hilton wrote in his autobiography that each of his international hotels was a 'laboratory' where the peoples of the world could 'inspect America and its ways at their leisure'. Hilton considered his international hotels, particularly those in 'hot' Cold War settings, as 'bulwarks against the communist threat'.[50] For instance, the Berlin Hilton, designed by LA firm Pereira and Luckman and located in the old Tiergarten, with its chequerboard façade in vibrant blue and white *Mittelmosaik*, was highly conspicuous in a city still full of ruins.

In the early reconstruction period, American images were refracted by the mixed attitudes to the New World in the minds of Western European architects. The chief task during the reconstruction years was, unquestionably, to provide housing for the millions of homeless and displaced people in Europe. This priority was then followed by other social needs such as schools, hospitals and roads. In this respect, the impression of American suburbs – sprawling landscapes of brick and timber houses under low-pitched roofs – offered little attraction to architects who had been stimulated by the idea of the integrated city of functional zones propounded by CIAM. In fact, Le Corbusier, who visited America in the 1930s and then again in 1946 when he was invited to be the French delegate in the United Nations Commission, described the suburbs as 'the Great American Waste'.[51]

By contrast, manufacturing industry offered more arresting images of American modernity. 'What power, what plenitude', was French architect Marcel Lods' laconic response to his first visit to the USA in 1946.[52] He was drawn to the organizational power

of industry and saw in it the potential to realize his long-held twin goals of the industrial prefabrication of building elements and mechanization of housing construction. They could, he believed, provide a solution to the twin problems of homelessness and labour shortages in post-war France.

Lods' enthusiasms were shared by Sigfried Giedion's *Mechanisation Takes Command* (1948), a book that charted the deep penetration of anonymous industrial organization into the rhythms of everyday life in the USA. CIAM's first secretary-general, Giedion had spent much of the Second World War deep in the archives of companies like Westinghouse Corporation and General Electric to produce his contribution to what he called 'anonymous history'. This technocratic sentiment was transferred, later, into widespread enthusiasm for glass curtain walls, air conditioning and elevators.[53] Eventually, of course, many European architects, planners and politicians came to imagine the future cityscape in these 'American' terms. West Berlin, for instance, acquired its Europa Centre (1962–5), a 22-storey office block dressed with a glass curtain wall and an adjacent shopping centre designed by Karl Heinz Pepper, the architects Helmut Hentrich and Hubert Petschnigg. This slab employed the full set of International Style signifiers which, in the words of Alexander Sedlmaier, had by the early 1960s 'come to signify faith in economic growth and technological progress'.[54]

Communauté

Perhaps the most influential and controversial architectural image to emerge during the reconstruction period was the Unité d'Habitation designed by Le Corbusier for the city of Marseilles in the late 1940s. The scheme resulted from an invitation to the architect from the first Minister of Reconstruction, M. Raoul Dautry, and survived numerous changes in the Ministry largely because of Le Corbusier's dogged pursuit of the project to completion.[55] Marseilles was selected as the site for what the architect imagined would be a prototype building because it had been very heavily bombed during the Second World War by both the Allies and the Germans, leaving 50,000 people homeless at the end of the conflict. Dautry approached Le Corbusier

as the famous author of ambitious vertical garden schemes before the war.

The result of the commission was a far richer architectural form than the vertical slabs that characterized his pre-war urban visions. The Unité is a long 17-storey frame containing 337 cell-like apartments for 1,600 inhabitants (2.11). Recessed behind concrete balconies and *brises soleils* (projecting embrasures to provide relief from the sun), they occupy the entire width of the block, each arranged over two floors. A central access corridor runs through the core of the building on alternate floors, providing interior 'streets'. The Unité also contains many different kinds of communal facilities: the roof garden was provided with a gymnasium, two solariums, a paddling pool, a children's nursery and garden, an open-air theatre and a 300-m running track; an internal street – *rue commerçante* – was to provide a shopping arcade on the seventh and eighth floors.[56] The design also accorded a great deal of variety in the arrangement and sizes of the apartments in the unit to accommodate different sizes of household.

The Unité was to be a 'social condenser', bringing the community together into close spatial and social relations. This was an idea with deep historical foundations that have been traced back to Fourier's Phalanstère at the beginning of the nineteenth century.[57] It is important to note that Le Corbusier's scheme was also influenced by Soviet precedents (that he had seen during his three visits to Moscow in the late 1920s and early 1930s, a transforming and somewhat bruising experience).[58] The *dom kommuna* (the collective house) had been a major preoccupation of the Soviet avant-garde in the 1920s, realized in the form of the Narkomfin Apartment Building (1928–30) in Moscow, designed by Moisei Ginzburg.[59] The Soviet architect's concern had been to produce new socialized domestic spaces that would destroy the closed, private world of the bourgeoisie. In the Narkomfin house he developed a spatial arrangement – similar to that employed at Marseilles – based on four double-floor apartments which created hallways every third floor. These 'street decks' would, he claimed, provide free social communication between the inhabitants of the block. And like the Unité, Ginzburg's design specified a cafeteria, gymnasium,

library and day nursery. In reviving this Soviet vision, at that time cast into oblivion by Stalinist aesthetics, Le Corbusier produced the most complete architectural image of community in the reconstruction period.

The Unité was envisaged as one unit in a considerably larger housing scheme. Le Corbusier claimed that all the homeless in France, some four million people at the end of the Second World War, could be accommodated in Unités providing the dense urban experience that would save the country from suburban sprawl and maintain a 'proper' relation between man and nature.[60] Protecting their occupants from the venality and barbarism of a world that had yet to throw off its wartime mentality, the Unités d'Habitation would also serve as mechanisms for the just distribution of resources nationally. Writing of black marketeers in France in 1948, he said: 'the speculation of these sharks could be ended in one strike if the distribution of food were undertaken by co-operatives and incorporated in the Unités d'Habitation.'[61] Here was a complete world, providing the community services needed for modern life as well as privacy in the family home. Expensive and controversial, Le Corbusier's vision never came to pass. Only three such Unités were built in France (and one more, as I will describe, in Berlin).

The sculptural aspect of the building – which drew much attention – was achieved in part by the treatment of the concrete from which it was made, abandoning the pre-war fascination with machine-perfection. Its surfaces revealed the imprint of the timber formwork used in the process of building as well as the 'messy soup of suspended dusts, grits and slumpy aggregate' in the concrete. This was famously described as *béton brut*.[62] The building's striking appearance was also achieved through its massive thick, tapering columns and abstract roofscape with surreal protrusions and ramparts. Through the building Le Corbusier expressed his cosmological ideas about man's relation with nature. For instance, it was conceived as a massive astronomical instrument onto which the sun would projects its rays. Protected within the Unité, 'humanity' would be put back 'into proper harmony with "the dance" of the cosmos'.[63] The building and its interiors were governed by a system of proportions which

2.14
Max Bill, entry in
the 'Competition for
a Monument to the
Unknown Political
Prisoner'. Photomontage,
1952. max, binia + jakob
bill foundation, Zurich

subscribed to the Sartrean precept that 'existence precedes essence'.

Abstract monuments

It is perhaps no surprise that Max Bill in the Bergamo debate should settle on Corbusier's Unité as the most appropriate model for 'public art' in the uncertain years of the early Cold War. Bill was, in fact, close to Le Corbusier, having spent time in Paris in 1938 editing one of three volumes cataloguing his output published before the War.[77] And the Modulor was very close to Bill's own conception of art. 'I am of the opinion', he famously asserted, 'that it is possible to develop an art largely on the basis of mathematical thinking'.[78] Science and art were, he admitted, different things, but the laws provided by the former could lead to 'new formal idioms expressive of the technical sensibilities of our age'. While the Unité was still a building site in Marseilles, it was easy for Bill to overlook the primitive qualities sought by its architect. At that time Bill, a Swiss citizen and former Bauhaus student (1927-9), was gaining prominence in discussions about the role and purpose of modern art and design. His credentials as a major exponent of Concrete Art, that is, an abstract aesthetic that asserted the 'pure' expressive

value of colour, space, light and movement, as well as having a record unblemished by any associations with Nazism, lent his views particular authority. His now famous 1936 essay on Concrete Art acquired new significance in 1949 when it was reprinted in the catalogue of 'Züricher Konkrete Kunst', an exhibition that toured Germany. To claim, again, that 'Concrete Art ... is the expression of the human spirit, destined for the human spirit, and should possess that clarity and that perfection that one expects from the work of the human spirit' was a powerful assertion of man's power to act rationally after the irrationality of Nazism.[79]

In his entry to the 'Competition for a Monument to the Unknown Political Prisoner', Bill rejected monumentality both in his design and, explicitly, in the statement he supplied to accompany his scheme (2.14).[80] This 1953 competition has been well recorded as the clearest evidence of CIA conscription of modern art, through the agency of the Institute of Contemporary Art under Sir Herbert Read in London. Ostensibly claiming a universal theme – a tribute to 'those individuals who had dared to offer their liberty or lives for the cause of human freedom' – and earmarked for a West Berlin setting, the competition had clear anti-communist overtones.[81] This seems to have been widely understood by the 3,500 participants, the majority of whom appear to have offered abstract or semi-abstract schemes. Bill proposed an architectural scheme in which the visitor could pass through three granite and marble hollow cubes to a central core containing a stainless steel triangular column. This device was to symbolize the 'unconditional and independent attitude of a responsible human being' (perhaps the prisoner of conscience), while the cubes were to make a sharp contrast between the sombre exterior and bright interior (thereby suggesting the political environment of a 'dictatorship'). Set in a green park with small paths, the visitor was free to enter or leave the sculptural environment. Action was presented by Bill, in his words, as 'free choice'. In his conception of the public monument, monumentality was understood in Corbusian terms as the 'measure of man'.[82] In this case, the 'monument ... speaks to each human being as an individual. Its proportions should therefore be in proper relationship to human proportions'. Bill was

2.15
Postage stamp
commemorating 'Interbau',
the international
architecture exhibition in
the Hansa district of West
Berlin, 1957. Private
collection

explicit in his rejection of the gigantic public work of art that is 'not grand but bombastic ... nowadays the small in size once again gains in strength'.

Mathematics, abstraction and humanist values all sought to strike universal chords that could rise above the East-West ideological battles of the 1950s. 'We have good reason to be sceptical about any "political art"', wrote Bill in 1949, 'regardless [of] whether it emanates from the right or left; especially when, under the cloak of antagonism to the prevailing order, its aim is to bring about a new, but in all essentials, almost identical structure of society because this is not art at all but simply propaganda'.[83] But the aspiration of escaping politics was a delusion. Abstract works exploring organic abstraction or formal reduction, eschewing allegory or symbolism, were still given ideological functions by the discourses into which they were inserted; in the ways in which they were titled; or by the locations they were given. A sculpture initially entitled *Large Spherical Form* by Karl Hartung, a key figure in the revival of abstract art in Germany, offered the most inscrutable form, a hollowed sphere (although it should be noted that it is fabricated from concrete, an intensely symbolic material in the reconstruction years). After appearing in the 'Constructa' building exhibition held in Hanover in 1951, Hartung's sculpture was the subject of public discussion about its meaning and future use. Godehard Janzing has shown that contemporaries drew a connection between its hollowed form and the nation's supposed incompleteness.[84] This

interpretation provided the pretext for the addition in 1959 of a dedication to the East German Uprising of 17 June 1953, which had turned Stalinallee into a battle ground. (This date had been given unmistakable public significance by being declared a public holiday in the Federal Republic of Germany as early as 1954.) In such circumstances, partisanship – whether desired or not – was inevitable.

Back to Berlin

The conscription of the Modern Movement to Cold War ends was evident at Interbau, the West Berlin response to Stalinallee. During the summer of 1957, 1.4 million people, including many East Berliners, visited the Internationale Bauausstellung in the Hansa district of the city (2.15).[85] The area had been in ruins since a devastating night of Allied bombing in November 1943, and its dusty wilderness was known to Berliners as 'Sahara'. There were elements of restoration about the Interbau scheme: the Kaiser Friedrich Memorial Church designed by Ludwig Lemmer, with a striking 60m-high openwork bell tower was, for instance, built on the site of a church. The idea of turning urban development into a living exhibition also had a celebrated pre-war history.[86] Interbau carried strong trace memories of the 1927 Weissenhofsiedlung organized by the Deutscher Werkbund in Stuttgart and the Bauausstellung in Berlin in 1931. Like a number of major projects, including the German Pavilion at the Brussels Expo in 1958 (3.24), Interbau represented the strong desire of the West German authorities to claim an honourable heritage in Weimar

modernism.[87] But this new district was also a confident statement about the future urban development of the city – based on modern construction techniques and materials as well as family apartments and car ownership – and, ultimately, on the superior claims of capitalist democracy over Soviet-style socialism.

Measured against the impoverished state of the West German economy, considerable funds were invested into the Interbau project, reflecting – like Stalinallee – its primary significance as an exercise in ideology. Prosperity, as Greg Castillo shows in his discussion of Marshall Aid exhibitions in the city (p.66), was a Cold War tool. After securing the support of the Bundestag, the competition to redesign the district was launched in June 1953. German architects Willy Kreuer and Gerhard Jobst were selected to design the site plan. Their overall conception of the district as a green and 'natural' site, on the edge of the Tiergarten, was published in 1953 and an international commission appointed to select and oversee the designs for construction. In its green setting, Interbau represented a picturesque updating of the Weimar planning concept of the *Zeilenbau* based on the parallel arrangement of apartment blocks. It was also an answer to the rhetoric of collectivism that reigned in the East. Jobst made this point plain when he wrote 'the free man does not want to live in an army camp, not buildings in rows, like workers' barracks'. Arranged organically and eschewing axiality, the buildings were to convey the impression of 'people turning to one another in conversation'.[88]

Despite Kreuer and Jobst's aim of creating a communion of buildings, the city authorities sought to emphasize the differences between architectural visions within the broad stylistic and intellectual priorities of International Style Modernism. This, they believed, would appeal to the premier league of modernist architects and, as Francesca Rogier argues, allay common prejudices against collective living.[89] The policy was not entirely successful: Walter Gropius, former director of the Bauhaus and now practising and teaching in the USA, was disturbed by the emphasis on individualism, objecting privately to the 'coordination' as being 'more like a patternbook of architects than an organic integration'.[90] As he wrote in 1956:

> The two opposites – individual variety, and a common denominator expressed by creating form symbols of human fellowship – need to be reconciled to each other. The degree of success in shaping and fusing these opposites indicates the depth of culture reached and is the very yardstick for judging the architectural achievements of a period.[91]

In its rush to distance itself from the regimented architecture of East Berlin, Interbau risked mannerism.

Gropius was one of glittering cast of architects who designed housing for the Hansa district (2.16). The fact that he had been forced to flee Nazi Germany added to his post-war credentials. Others included Arne Jacobsen from Denmark, Alvar Aalto from Finland and Le Corbusier, who designed a *Unité d'habitation* (though not on the Hansa district site).[92] Bakema and Van den Broek too contributed the design of a high-rise apartment which – like the Lijnbaan – combined complex arrangement of geometric forms, particularly in its façade, and careful attention to the social effects of space. Each double-height storey provided its inhabitants with common spaces for social exchange (2.17). In its range of contributors, Interbau, as its promoters stressed, was to be testimony to the transforming power of international collaboration and a desire to see a democratic West Germany prevail.

One building, the Kongresshalle situated close to the Tiergarten, was an American import (as was an Amerika Haus exhibition, entitled 'Amerika Baut', curated by Peter Blake, editor of *Architectural Forum* for the United States Information Agency, which contained a scale model of the curtain wall of the Union Carbide Building designed by Gordon Bunshaft and the façade of the Mies van Der Rohe's Seagram building, both then under construction in New York[93]). The Kongresshalle was a gift of the US Benjamin Franklin Foundation established by Eleanor Dulles, commissioner at the American State Department and sister of CIA head Allen Dulles and Secretary of State John Foster Dulles. Franklin's words were inscribed in stone in the entrance: 'God grant that not only the love of liberty, but a thorough knowledge of the rights of man may pervade all the nations of the earth so that a philosopher may set his foot anywhere on its surface and say "this is my country".' The function of the Kongresshalle was as a cultural centre, with a theatre auditorium and restaurant as well as numerous smaller rooms for seminars and meetings (2.18). In this respect it was a challenge to the palaces of culture that were appearing across the Soviet-controlled sector of Germany, as well as

a retort to the Soviet claims that the USA was a cultural desert. Its functions were to stimulate lofty exchange, as testified by the state-of-the-art simultaneous translation facilities and radio equipment that were later installed into this putative UN of the suburbs of Berlin. The opening of the building in September 1957 was followed by a series of high-profile events, including a conference chaired by Raymond Aron, a key figure in the CIA-financed Kongress für Kulturelle Freiheit.[94] The same week saw performances by Martha Graham and seven one-act plays selected by Thornton Wilder reflecting on social problems in America.[95]

Designed by Hugh A. Stubbins, Gropius's former assistant at the Harvard School of Design, the Kongresshalle was as ambitious in architectural terms as its programme was in cultural ones. It is dominated by an arching twin-roof structure, sometimes described as an 'oyster shell', supported on both sides by steel posts. Under this dramatically engineered form, the building itself was organized into three stepped levels containing a large theatre auditorium, as well as a two-storey restaurant overlooking the river Spree. A large bronze known as 'Big Butterfly' was sited before the entrance of the building in the middle of a large pond. The primary function of the building was symbolic, an assertion made when leading German engineer Frei Otto mounted sharp criticism of its organicism, suggesting that it masked structural deficiencies: 'The unresolved question remains. Does each part of the building serve the organism as a whole?'[96] (Otto proved

prophetic when the structure collapsed in May 1980 and had to be rebuilt.)

Interbau's organizers wanted to draw international comparisons with Stalinallee (and, by this limited standard, the living exhibition was a ringing success: every report compared the two districts). Capitalism and real democracy were positioned against socialism and what was by then widely being called totalitarianism. The apparently informal arrangement of buildings in the leafy cityscape, as well as the variety and utility of the architectural forms found there, were to demonstrate the 'natural' qualities of modern architecture. But, like Stalinallee, this was an ideological effect: the cost involved in building Interbau's housing required heavy subsidies and, moreover, it offered its inhabitants the security of social housing but not the opportunities of private ownership. In other words, it was demonstration of the social benefits of State investment into housing (a thesis that was hardly controversial in Europe in the 1950s). Furthermore, its ideological effects were already circumscribed by the time the exhibition opened to the world. The architects working in the Soviet Bloc had been given a new set of priorities and blueprints by their masters, which ruled historicism and monumentalism out of court.

In 1954, after Stalin's death, Nikita Khrushchev – then first Secretary of the Communist Party of Soviet Union – launched an attack on Socialist Realism at the Moscow Conference for the Building Industry (a statement that was widely published in the architectural press in the Eastern Bloc in early

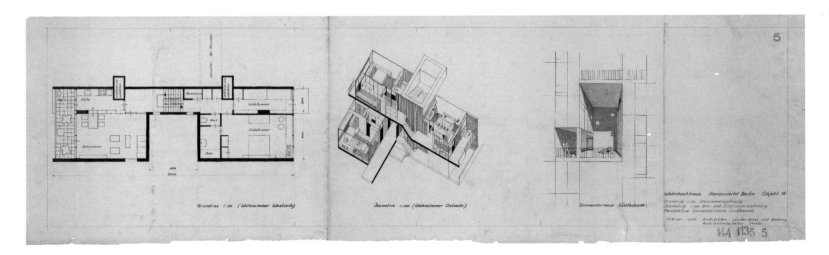

1955). Architects were charged with building efficiently by designing standardized and industrialized building elements and eschewing their interests in superfluous decoration (2.19).[97] Modernism, after five years in detention, was rehabilitated. In the course of the mid-1950s a new architectural vocabulary of utilitarian, even industrial forms fashioned from glass, concrete and steel was licensed. Many of the most vocal advocates of Stalinist aesthetics – including the figure of Syrkus, with whom we started this essay – were quick to recant.[98]

Although few buildings in the East ever achieved the experimental spirit or expressive vigour of, say, Gropius or Bakema's contributions to Interbau, the differences between Eastern Bloc and Western architecture and town planning were never to be as wide again. East Berlin, for instance, acquired a new 'modern' face in the Alexanderplatz district at the end of Stalinallee. Buildings like the 'Teachers' House' (1959–62), designed by one of the Stalinallee architects, Henselmann, represented the new image of Socialism, one that apparently differed little from the American models that had been under prohibition a few years earlier. A slab lifted off the ground with narrow columns and dressed with a glass curtain wall, *Haus des Lehrers* (Teachers' House) 'needed' a massive mosaic frieze by Walter Womacka narrating the achievements of socialist society to demonstrate its political bona fides (2.20). Like the Soviet skyscrapers in Moscow and Warsaw, this building was a sublimation of what had become the latest architectural symbol of American capitalism. This was less an ideological inversion than a recognition that American technologies were more advanced than those in the East. Khrushchev was candid on this matter, encouraging his technicians, designers and planners to learn from the West in order to overtake it. By the time of Interbau in 1957, the competition to be modern – which characterized the Cold War – was, as we explore in Chapter 5, shifting ground.

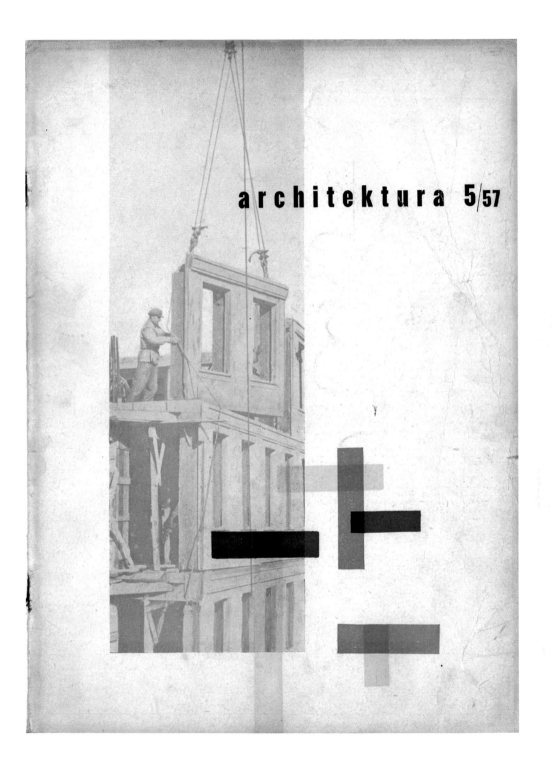

2.19
Wojciech Zamecznik, cover of *Architektura* (May 1957) depicting the use of prefabricated panels on a construction site, Poland

architektura 5/57

2.20
Walter Womacka, mosaic
frieze *Our Life*, 1964,
on the Teachers' House
by architect Hermann
Henselmann, East Berlin,
1962–4 (photographed
in 2008)

Marshall Plan Modernism in Divided Germany

Greg Castillo

2.21
Publicity photograph for the 1951 Marshall Plan exhibition, 'Industry and Craft Create New Home Furnishings in the USA', Stuttgart

2.22
'We're Building a Better Life', view of the exhibition, West Berlin, 1952

As strange as it may sound, the cultural Cold War forged weapons from modern home furnishings. Divided Berlin was the pre-eminent 'home front' of a propaganda battle involving domestic consumer goods. Until the infamous Wall went up in 1961, East and West Berlin met at a relatively permeable border crossing. East Berliners might spend an afternoon in the West taking in a Hollywood matinée; West Berliners headed East for cheap goods at favourable exchange rates.[1] Inspired by the ways in which consumers exploited the city's oddness for their own ends, propagandists transformed divided Berlin into a matched set of ideological showcases. Khrushchev acknowledged the city's 'battle between socialism and capitalism' in 1956: 'There, the borders are simply open ... [and] the comparison is made: which order creates better material conditions, that in West Germany or East Germany?'[2].

The US Marshall Plan for Western Europe's economic and political reconstruction linked consumer affluence to economic stability and an enfranchised democratic citizenry. As expressed by Marshall Plan director Paul G. Hoffmann, 'Today's contest between freedom and despotism is a contest between the American assembly line and the Communist Party line'.[3] US State Department officials deployed one of their most potent propaganda instruments in Berlin: the well-provisioned model home. With much of West Germany's housing stock devastated by wartime bombardment, the post-war home became an icon of social and economic reform and its promise of 'prosperity for all' (Wohlstand für alle), the motto of West German Finance Minister Ludwig Erhard.

Modernist product design also played a strategic role in the Marshall Plan blueprint. Continental elites typically regarded America as the purveyor of 'a primitive, vulgar, trashy

Massenkultur... whose importation into Europe had to be resisted', in the words of historian Volker Berghahn.[4] Perceptions of a degraded American 'non-culture' undermined the legitimacy of its mass-consumer society, which US advisors hoped to recreate in Western Europe. To counter such prejudices, the US State Department contracted Edgar Kaufmann Jr, curator of the industrial design department at New York's Museum of Modern Art (MoMA), to organize a travelling exhibition displaying 'American design and craftsmanship as adapted to American home living'.[5] For the 1951 Marshall Plan exhibition 'Industry and Craft Create New Home Furnishings in the USA' (Industrie

und Handwerk schaffen neues Hausgerät in USA), Kaufmann assembled 500 examples of 'progressive American design' characterized by 'simple lines and functional forms' (2.21). The selection of objects recycled the contents of the 'Good Design' exhibitions that Kaufmann produced annually for MoMA and the Chicago Merchandise Mart. His advocacy of household modernism was impassioned and politically charged. Kaufmann declared it indispensable to post-war democracy, proclaiming: '*Modern design is intended to implement the lives of free individuals*' (emphasis in original).[6] A West German critic, Heinrich König, correctly observed that the products displayed at the Marshall Plan's 'New Home Furnishings' show were not 'representational' in style.[7] Rather than merely representing 'the American Way of Life', modernist household objects were its physical embodiments, according to Kaufmann.

The most spectacular American household exhibition staged in Cold War Germany, and the one that most clearly demonstrated the ideological utility of modernist design, was 'We're Building a Better Life' (*Wir bauen ein besseres Leben*), which debuted at West Berlin's 1952 German Industrial Trade Fair before heading to subsequent venues in Stuttgart, Hanover, Paris and Milan. It featured a house within a house – an 'ideal dwelling' built within the George-Marshall-Haus trade pavilion. Just as at a nineteenth-century ethnographic spectacle, where exotic natives were displayed for public edification, the model home served as the backdrop for a 'man-wife-child family team actually going through [the] physical actions of living in [the] dwelling, making proper use of [the] objects in it', according to a US State Department planning document. The show would stress 'arguments for a high-production, high-wage, low-unit-cost, low-profit-margin, high consumption system ... Emphasis to be placed upon [the] fortunate outcome of American economic philosophy when combined with European skills and resources'.[8] All of the 6,000 products placed on display were to be contemporary in style and manufactured in a Marshall Plan member nation. A modernist domestic environment based on New World ideals, but assembled from continental products, would convey the benefits of the American-style economic system presented

by the US for Western European emulation.

During its three week run, the 'Better Life' dream home drew over half a million visitors, over 40 per cent of them from the East. Its detached, single-family suburban residence was realized down to kitchen gadgets and garden tools, but built without a roof. A billboard beside the home's front door announced:

> The objects in this house are industrial products from many countries in the Atlantic community. Thanks to technology, rising productivity, economic cooperation and free enterprise, these objects are available to our western civilization.[9]

This stage-set for the domestic life of 'an average skilled worker and his family' was manned by a model family, in the literal sense. Two couples and eight pairs of children, all professional actors, worked alternating shifts,

going about the household tasks and leisure rituals of a consumer wonderland. A narrator, dressed in white and perched in an elevated crow's-nest (2.22), described the model family's interaction with the luxurious environment. Visitors became voyeurs, staring through windows or crowding overhead catwalks for a bird's-eye view as they observed the power of modern household objects to define new post-war subjects (2.23).

As displayed at 'A Better Life', modernist household design provided aesthetic redemption for bourgeois domesticity. It also advanced cultural cosmopolitanism, a notion reviled by Third Reich ideologues, through transnational patterns of consumption. As a primer in 'the modern approach to interior decoration', 'Better Life' publicity releases proclaimed, the exhibition demonstrated how 'rationally designed products from different countries in the Atlantic community can be combined harmoniously'.[10] 'The show says

2.23
'We're Building a Better Life', living room with furnishings from Germany, Italy and the USA.
V&A/NAL: PP.42.U

that just as these items from the various countries combine to form a homogenous whole, so the nations themselves can combine to form a homogenous community.'[11] That underlying message was accurately reprised in the West German daily *Der Tag*:

> The new style, realism plus simplicity, finds its strongest expression in the US Marshall-Haus.... There are different versions of one style and one way of life typical for a 'western bourgeois' household. Nothing is foreign to us, whether it comes from Berlin or Los Angeles, from Stockholm, Sicily or New York.[12]

To counter the notion that the 'Better Life' vision was a crass exercise in cultural Americanization, US information officers carefully explained the installation's international emphasis. 'To some visitors, this home of a future "average consumer" would appear perhaps to be "American," but that is incorrect', a West German journal glossed from Marshall Plan press releases. 'John Smith or Hans Schmidt would be perfectly capable of affording such a house when certain conditions were met: we must make the Atlantic community of nations a reality,

eliminate tariff barriers, and raise productivity, thereby allowing us to lower prices and raise wages.'[13] Indeed, for 1950s Europe, the goods on display were anything but affordable for a typical family. A US State Department report acknowledged that 'many of the items in the house (refrigerator, automatic dishwasher, television set, etc.) are still beyond the average German budget'. Parked around the home were a bicycle, a kayak, a motorcycle, a motor scooter and a Volkswagen (chosen for its 'direct appeal to local pride'). 'No average worker could possibly own all these forms of transportation', the memo noted.[14] At 'A Better Life', the term 'International-style' described both a modernist aesthetic and a prescription for global production and consumption.

The model home's calculated mix of products from various Marshall Plan member nations ended at the kitchen door. America's rapid advances in domestic mass technology made the kitchen the only room in the dream house in which nearly every piece of equipment was imported from the US (2.24). It was also the room that made the strongest impression upon visitors and the local press. An actress portraying a housewife effused: 'This house is so perfect that I am afraid we will not want to move out.... What will happen if I fall in love with the kitchen too?'[15] Germans were mesmerized by the 'completely automatic, mechanized wonder kitchen ... somehow reminiscent of the control panel of an airplane', as a journalist gushed.[16] 'For women and all men interested in mechanics, it is a white paradise....'.[17] This appliance-laden paradise was home to a new Eve, conservative in appearance but radical in her economic behaviour. Beneath the actress-*Hausfrau*'s traditional apron, pinned-up braids and *Kaffee-Klatsch* charm lurked a new postwar persona charged with a new household task: negotiating a Fordist revolution in mass consumption. It was a chore that also entailed cleaning up a messy past. Hitler's 'total war' had infused advanced technology with an aggressive, sinister masculinity. Feminization would help render a post-war machine age *gemütlich*. The restrictive gender role of the idealized *Hausfrau* may have been limiting, but also liberating, as Erica Carter has argued, in that it endowed a privileged status, 'housewife as consumer-citizen', establishing the stay-at-home mom as a 'bearer of the values

2.24
The traditional German
Hausfrau is modernized
with American kitchen
technology, as demonstrated
to a crowd of German
observers at the 1952
'We're Building a Better
Life' exhibition

2.25
'We're Building a Better Life', West Berlin, 1952. The model home's 'model family' enacting leisure activities within their modern domestic setting as exhibition visitors peer through a window behind the dining-room table

2.26
'We're Building a Better Life', Stuttgart, 1952. The exhibition's culminating display, as staged for the second opening in Stuttgart

Marshall Plan Modernism in Divided Germany

of a specific form of post-war modernity, one dominated by scientific and technological rationality'.[18] With her unbridled optimism and faith in an incipient 'better life', the idealized housewife was the true 'new man' of West Germany's first post-war decade.[19] Excluded from this visionary ideal and its domestic economy, however, was an historically unprecedented number of female heads of household. Of West Germany's 15 million households, nearly one-third were headed by widows or divorced women. The 'typical' household portrayed at 'We're Building a Better Life' was a speculative social fiction reflecting the ongoing 'political reconstruction of the family' taking place in both the US and West Germany.[20]

A circuit of the 'Better Life' show ended at a display introduced by a panel showing a male labourer and the headline: 'This man is a worker and at the same time a consumer' (2.26). For East Germans it was an obvious reference to the lack of material rewards for labourers under Stalinist socialism; for male visitors it provided a cue to the presence of an exhibition discourse of broader interest than they might expect, given the era's standard gendering of household consumption as female. In this final display area, furnishings seen earlier in the model house could be examined at close range. Attached to every item was a tag indicating country of origin, retail price, and the number of hours of labour – as measured by a skilled worker's wage – needed to purchase the object. This seemingly guileless calculation of purchasing power entailed a fundamental repudiation of Marxist ideology, which used the concept of labour value to define capitalist production and distribution as exploitation. Profit, according to Marx, was the unpaid labour value that industrialists appropriated from workers when manufactured goods were sold at retail price. 'We're Building a Better Life' arrogated Marx's concept of labour value and used it to express the amount of work needed to *purchase* an item rather than to *produce* it. This shift in emphasis radically redefined labour value to quantify capitalist reward systems, rather than to measure exploitation. The ideological subtext was not missed by the East German authorities. They saw Marshall Plan advocacy of barrier-free trade as an assault upon national sovereignty and vilified

modernist design as a plot to 'disassociate the people from their native land, from their language and their culture, so that they adopt the "American lifestyle" and join in the slavery of the American imperialists'.[21] While alarmist, the assessment was not baseless. The 'Better Life' exhibition revealed that the US State Department was indeed grooming modernism as the stylistic lingua franca of transnational consumer capitalism and its idealized American 'good life'.

The Treaty of Rome, ratified by Belgium, France, Italy, Luxemburg, the Netherlands and West Germany in 1958, laid the foundation for today's European Union. Its calls for a tariff-free Common Market echoed the blueprint for economic integration promoted by Marshall Plan advisors. In retrospect, their notion of mobilizing international modernism as the Esperanto of continental consumer culture seems both visionary and flawed, as European consumers soon revealed. Enfranchising workers through escalating purchasing power – as measured in household goods – was a Marshall Plan strategy that worked. As Michael Wildt has argued, 'West Germans became democrats through consumption: they did not fight for democracy, but struggled for prosperity'.[22] However, the idea that transnational consumption demanded aesthetically standardized goods was profoundly misguided. As West Germany's Miracle Economy gained momentum through the 1950s, it did so without the benefit of a unifying product style. Modernism, as it turned out, was just one of many viable design strategies for consumer seduction, a reality that provoked dismay among the aesthetic's proponents. 'It is a sad fact', an English industrial design journal reported, 'that some of the worst examples of British goods find a ready market across the North Sea and the Channel, because for so many Continentals the pseudo-Jacobian, Byzantine and Gothic horrors of ... lodging houses in Bayswater are forever England'.[23] There was no need to purge Tudor roses or Florentine filigree from tableware to assure its viability in an international marketplace: least of all in Germany, where Nazi cultural isolation had left in its wake a taste for the exotic – a predilection nowhere more apparent than in the post-war kitchen. West German home-making magazines of the 1950s promoted a gastronomic cosmopolitanism,

much of it deliriously ersatz, with concoctions like 'Cabbage à la Strausborg', 'Fish Milanese', 'Portuguese spinach rolls' and 'Steak à la Hawaii'.[24] As the unfolding process of globalization demonstrated, one of the things consumers enjoy consuming most is cultural difference: a maxim as true today as it was during the Cold War.

3.1
Berlin Blockade 1948–9.
Berliners watching the
landing of a transport plane
at Tempelhof Airport, Berlin
(Western Sector), 1948

Design and the Democratic Ideal

Jane Pavitt

After 1945, as Europe counted the cost of six years of war, voices began to be heard from some of the most wounded parts of the continent calling for a kind of reconstruction that would be devoted not only to physical rebuilding, but to a comprehensive social and spiritual rehabilitation. The German graphic designer Otl Aicher wrote: 'We now have to deal with the most beautiful task; however, it requires our full responsibility: the new beginning.'[1]

The 'beautiful task' he referred to was no less than the social, political and moral re-education of Germany in order to eradicate any vestiges of militarism, nationalism and prejudice, and to create instead a democratic and progressive society.

In Italy also, the desperate need for reconstruction was seen as the opportunity to build a better world where the signs of the nation's rehabilitation would be visible in buildings, homes and everyday goods. As Ernesto Rogers, architect and editor of the magazine *Domus*, stated in 1946: 'It is a question of forming a taste, a technique, a morality, all terms of the same function. It is a question of building a society.'[2]

3.2
Eduardo Paolozzi, page from a scrapbook featuring cut-outs from American magazines. Collage, *c.*1947–52. V&A: AAD.1985.3

3.3
Alexander Zhitomirsky, *'Pentagon' eating up among others 'School' and 'Hospital'.* Photomontage, n.d. Private collection

3.4
Selman Selmanagic (in cooperation with Herbert Hirche and Liv Falkenberg), Type 602 Seminar Chair. Beechwood, laminated wood, 'Skai' cover, 1947. V&A: W.7–2007

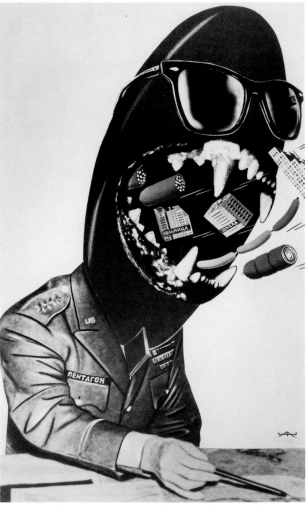

The first stage of reconstruction, of course, was the immediate alleviation of suffering and the provision of shelter and sanitation, tasks which preoccupied the grim years of 1945–7. At the 8th Milan Triennale in 1947 – the first time the influential design fair had been staged since the war – the theme of the exhibition was workers' housing, and featured emergency shelters for the homeless, with basic furnishings designed for cheap, mass manufacture. For many designers schooled in the modernist principles of rationalism and 'fitness to purpose', the rebuilding of Europe was an ideal opportunity to bring these principles to benefit society.

But another, equally compelling argument made in the late 1940s for the role of design in the reshaping of Europe lay in consumerism. The economic recovery that could be spurred by the reconstruction of industry would, in turn, generate increased demand for consumer goods. In this, the USA offered a bright vision of material abundance to assuage the privations of Europe (3.2). Advertising, Hollywood and other forms of popular entertainment provided a seductive view of idealized American lifestyles. In the context of growing tensions of the Cold War, this prospect of Americanization generated considerable disquiet in intellectual and political circles in Europe where its potent signifiers, such as Coca-Cola and the juke-box, became the subjects of anti-American protest.[3] The French left-wing critic Henri Lefebvre defined Americanization as 'that ideological commodity imported in the name of technical progress, "consumer society" and the mass media'.[4] Communist condemnations of 'decadent' America depicted it as bawdy and louche, grasping and selfish, spending its wealth on militaristic and imperialistic gestures, rather than on social provision (3.3). Nevertheless, a vital image of the USA's potential role as rescuer of Europe was created during the Berlin Blockade of 1948, after Soviet authorities closed access to the Western sectors of the city following disagreement over Western currency reforms. US planes, together with British ones, parachuted a steady stream of emergency rations over 'enemy' lines (3.1).

In the few short years after the war, these divergent arguments for the role of designed goods in the service of democracy emerged.

Put simply, one view privileged social needs, the other, individual wants. The first, informed by the pre-war theories of the Modern Movement, was progressive, reformist, devoted to the 'values of economy, honesty and good form'.[5] Ernesto Rogers, with his 1946 call to arms (quoted above) and his elision of taste, morality and social responsibility, was an advocate of this position. So too was Aicher, one of the founders of the Ulm Institute of Design (Hochschule für Gestaltung) which became a bastion of high-minded German modernism in the 1950s (alongside the Deutscher Werkbund, an alliance of manufacturers and designers promoting design reform, founded in 1907 and revived in 1947[6]). They were not the only ones who cast their discourse in moral terms. Nor was this rhetoric confined in the 1940s to the Western sectors of Germany. At the Deutschen Werkstätten in Hellerau, East Germany, a revival of Bauhaus practices was attempted before the bitter debates about 'formalism' called a halt to them. These attacks were led by Kurt Liebknecht, head of the East German architectural association (DBA), who denounced the so-called formalism (or 'form without ornament')

of Bauhaus-style modernism as both 'foreign' and 'hostile' to the people.[7] These attacks were endorsed by Walter Ulbricht, who became the General Secretary of the SED (Sozialistische Einheitspartei Deutschlands, the Socialist Unity Party of Germany) in 1950.[8] The 'Seminar Chair' designed by Selman Selmanagic and a Werkstätten team for the SED Parteihochschule, the Unified Socialist Party of Germany's training academy in Berlin, is an example of the simple and efficient furniture later deemed unacceptable by the communist state (3.4). The spartan interiors and furnishings of the Parteihochschule were singled out for political criticism, as an example of inappropriate style.[9]

A second view of the potential post-war role of design was cast in terms of freedom of consumer choice and the marketplace, and the means to self-expression through the acquisition of goods.[10] American models of modern domesticity promoted in 1950s West Germany 'conflated democratic freedom with rising private consumption'.[11] Consumer culture offered a seductive image of 'democracy' at a time of privation in Europe. When framed in terms of 'freedoms', 'choices' and

'self-expression', it also had the added benefit of suggesting a positive alternative to the imagined conditions of a communist state.[12]

The question was which was a better expression of the democratic ideal. This chapter focuses on key instances of modern design reform and promotion in the period from the interregnum of 1945–7 (the end of the Second World War to the 'start' of the Cold War) to the so-called 'economic miracle' years in Western Europe (or *'Wirtschaftswunder'* in Germany) beginning in the late 1950s. During some of the iciest years of the Cold War, and with the memory of fascist dictatorship still so raw, the need to align practices of both design and consumption with democracy took on a great urgency. For the United States, committed to curbing the spread of Communism, the greatest weapon in its arsenal in this respect was the Marshall Plan.

The Marshall Plan

On 5 June 1947 US Secretary of State George C. Marshall outlined his proposed programme of economic assistance to Europe in a speech at Harvard University. Shocked by his firsthand experience of European devastation and, following a failed attempt to devise an Allied solution to the problems in Germany (at a Moscow meeting in April that year), Marshall advanced a scheme for a long-term programme of US investment in Europe. The purpose of the European Recovery Programme (better known as the Marshall Plan) 'should be the revival of a working economy in the world so as to permit the emergence of political and social conditions in which free institutions can exist'.[13] The key to its success, as Marshall saw it, was that Europeans would themselves take responsibility for its implementation (3.5).

The Marshall Plan was to be the bedrock of *Pax Americana*.[14] It was an extraordinarily far-reaching and innovative scheme. Between 1947 and 1952, support for European reconstruction under the scheme cost the US in the region of thirteen billion dollars.[15] It replaced the short-term programmes of emergency aid which had already seen huge financial investment by the USA in the ravaged parts of Europe, largely directed towards the immediate alleviation of suffering.

Under this scheme, nations once in thrall to Fascism (Germany, Italy) were to be the subject of a concerted US campaign of modernization.[16] Germany was the target of a comprehensive programme of re-education and democratization, through every facet of political, economic and cultural life. A comparable story of US investment and recovery describes events in Japan, which was under US occupation from 1945–52. During this period the US government sanctioned a programme of training and technology transfer, which in turn helped to shape the Japanese consumer boom of the 1950s and 1960s. One example of this was the transistor, developed by Bell Laboratories in the USA, but made commercially successful in radios and televisions by the founders of the Sony Corporation in the mid-1950s (3.6).[17] By the late 1950s, modern living in Japan had become equated with the ownership of what

3.6
Sony Corporation, 8 301 W,
portable television. Metal,
grey lacquered, partially
chromed, 1959. Manu-
factured by Sony Corpo-
ration, Tokyo. Die Neue
Sammlung, Munich

Simon Partner has called 'certain talismanic possessions, notably electrical goods such as television, washing machine and refrigerator'.[18]

The Marshall Plan was not simply a programme of aid: it required the recipient nations to structure and implement their own reconstruction plans, based on the development of a competitive economy and with the aim of raising standards of living. It offered goods which could be traded, the profits used to buy more imports and invest in infrastructure (so-called 'counterpart funds'). The Plan was promoted through a comprehensive propaganda programme of films, exhibitions and events, many of which were aimed at embedding it in specific local and national contexts, to inculcate a sense of shared ownership in different parts of Europe. The film *Me and Mr Marshall* (c.1949), for example, introduced the effects of the Plan in Western Germany through the character of a young coal miner from the Ruhr.[19]

The Plan followed in the wake of President Truman's speech to Congress in March 1947 (the 'Truman Doctrine'), which had announced aid to Greece and Turkey as a means of 'containing' the spread of communist influence to vulnerable nations.[20] In some respects the Marshall Plan was part of this US policy of 'containment'. By securing the future of market economies in Western Europe, the US was effectively building a bulwark against Communism.[21]

The Plan was initially offered to all European governments, with Franco's fascist dictatorship of Spain the only major exception.[22] Both Britain and France took a leading role in negotiating the terms of the Plan to maximize its benefits but minimize dependency upon and the influence of the USA. Resistance to the US dollar was strong in many parts of Europe, as was the hope that European reconstruction plans did not necessarily have to follow a US model of free-market capitalism. The Plan was rather at odds with the majority view of European governments after 1945, which were exploring policies of welfarism based on protected markets and nationalized industries to foster full employment.[23]

Political instability in Europe was one of the USA's greatest fears, not only for ideological reasons but also because of the damage it would inflict upon both European economic recovery and the potential loss of markets for US goods. However, left-wing interests had to be appeased, particularly in France where communist influence was strong. France, therefore, insisted the USSR be involved in the planning stages. Soviet Foreign Minister Molotov travelled to Paris to meet with French President Bidault and British Prime Minister Bevin in June 1947, but, unable to either stop the plans or win any significant concessions, Molotov returned to Moscow having rejected any chance of Soviet involvement in a Paris conference arranged for July 1947.

States within the Soviet 'sphere of influence', such as Czechoslovakia, Poland and Hungary, were a different matter, and they initially responded positively to the scheme. Representatives of all European nations had been invited to the July conference. Moscow, after some vacillation, set a firm line and ordered Eastern European states not to participate. After stormy discussions between the Czechoslovak government and the Kremlin, the Czechoslovaks eventually complied. Moscow then acted to harden the divisions between East and West Europe, accelerating the Stalinization of the Eastern Bloc.

By the spring of 1948 the money from the Marshall Plan had started to flow into Europe. Britain and France, of course, were major recipients. US expertise in industry and business was exported to Europe via the thousands of managers and skilled workers – including engineers, technicians and architects – who were sent on 'productivity missions' to observe and learn from US industry.[24] Within a short time, forms of Americanized modernization impacted upon key industries, particularly the automotive industry.[25] The idea of the perfectly synchronized automobile production line had been fetishized by a generation of modernists following the First World War. By the 1950s, US car manufacturers had set in place a practice of frequent model changes and designed-in obsolescence. The private car, with the material wealth it implied and the mobility it promised, became a ubiquitous symbol of modern life consumed primarily through film and advertising.[26] The luxurious styling of the new European cars, such as the Italian Cisitalia 202 GT (designed by Pininfarina in 1947 though manufactured in small quantities) and the French Citroën DS (in production between 1955 and 1975), may have paid homage to American streamlining but, more importantly, they served as symbols of national pride despite the fact that these models were not affordable by most when they were launched.

In fact, in the immediate post-war years the production of bicycles, motor-scooters and cheap but under-powered models of micro-cars flourished in Europe as an affordable alternative that could be quickly manufactured in large quantities (3.7). These models were initially aimed at providing utilitarian mobility for factory workers (the Vespa scooter; 3.8), farmers (the Citroen 2CV) and even disabled war veterans (the Messerschmidt micro-car of 1955; 3.9). Their popularity also led to some of these vehicles becoming youthful symbols of cool by the late 1950s. In Italy, the scooter was just one of a number of products which were transformed from object of utility to cultural sign of fashionability.

3.8
Corradino D'Ascanio, Vespa
125CC, motorscooter.
Manufactured by Piaggio
& Co., 1951. Die Neue
Sammlung, Munich

3.9
Fritz Fend, Messerschmitt
Kabinenroller KR 200.
Designed in 1955. Manu-
factured by Fahrzeug-
und Maschinenbau
GmbH, Regensburg, 1959.
Die Neue Sammlung,
Munich

The case of Italy

Like Germany, Italy faced the daunting task
of rebuilding a defeated nation. Industry
seems crippled, housing stocks and the
transportation infrastructure were shattered,
unemployment was rife and inflation ram-
pant. Massive internal economic immigration
of workers from south to the industrial north
in the immediate aftermath of war added
to the urgent housing crisis.[27]

Crucial to the revival of Italy after 1945
was the American view that the country
would form a front line in the fight against
Communism in Europe. With a powerful
communist party of its own (the Partitio
Comunista Italiano or PCI), elected to power
in the parliamentary elections of 1946, Italy
had to be brought swiftly into the US sphere
of influence. The first wave of investment
came through the relief funds established
immediately after the Allied victory, with
housing and industry the first targets.[28]
Concern about the poor state of housing in
Italy was amplified by public discussions
of the cave dwellings known as 'I Sassi'
in Matera, Southern Italy. Hovels without
sanitation, these peasant homes were
described across the political divide as 'the
shame of Italy'.[29] The caves were made the
subject of a Marshall Plan film, showing how
the Italian government, with Marshall funds,
built a new community for the inhabitants.[30]

The task for social reconstruction was
clear, but the years 1945–7 were characterized
by debate amongst architects and planners
rather than a great deal of building, although
some construction had taken place with
funding from UNRRA (the United Nations
Relief and Rehabilitation Administration).
A US-funded handbook on building standards
and materials of 1946 entitled *Manuale
dell'architetto* (*Architects' Handbook*) had
been made freely available.[31] Emergency
relief was also reflected in home furnishings,
and explored in exhibitions of the late 1940s,
where (on the whole) prototypical objects
produced by artisanal methods were exhibited
as blueprints for industry, for example the
RIMA (Riunione Italiana per le Mostre di
Arredamento) popular furnishings exhibition
of 1946, held in Milan. Designers worked with
the limited means at their disposal, attempting
to emulate the mass production methods and
materials available to US designers (which

they knew through magazines).[32] Marco Zanuso, for example, collaborated with the manufacturer Arflex to produce, in 1951, the 'Lady' armchair, made with elastic banding and foam rubber, the latter having been developed by the industrial rubber company Pirelli.[33]

These social and technological concerns had given a seriousness of purpose to the revived 8th Milan Triennale in 1947. Devoted to the theme of mass housing, it featured the experimental housing quarter QT8, then in the process of being built in the San Siro district of Milan. The commissioner of the 8th Triennale and coordinator of QT8 was communist architect Piero Bottoni, a leading member of the inter-war rationalist architectural movement and of the Congrès Internationaux d'Architecture Moderne (CIAM).[34] QT8 was intended as a testing-ground for industrialized building methods, furniture and interiors, to house 13,000 residents, and was to have involved a wide range of international architects; however, the project was beset with problems and criticisms, and was built on a more limited scale. Successive additions to the site were showcased at the Triennales of the 1950s.[35] Ernesto Rogers commented afterwards that Bottoni's 'self-imposed task' of initiating a social programme for architecture had been more difficult to achieve than if he had followed the 'brighter roads of decorative arts outside of any architectural framework and any social preoccupation'.[36]

Indeed, by the time of the next Triennale both Italy and its design industry had entered a new phase of transformation. In the Italian elections of April 1948 the Christian Democrat Party (Democrazio Cristiana) won a decisive victory against the incumbent Communist Party. Despite the financial support of Moscow (which continued through to the 1970s), the PCI was no match for the centre-right politics gaining ground with the support of highly visible US aid. After the elections a new economic framework was devised to implement housing plans, in the form of the INA-Casa housing legislation. INA-Casa, so called because the Italian National Insurance Institute (Istituto nazionale delle assicurazioni or INA), charged with its implementation, was a subsidized building programme created in 1949. INA was responsible for a host of building projects across Italy, one of the first

3.10
Gio Ponti, 'La Cornuta' coffee-making machine. Manufactured by La Pavoni, 1947/8

of which was Ludovico Quaroni's neo-realist Tibertino Quarter in Rome (1949).

The 9th and 10th Triennali of 1951 and 1954 respectively demonstrated the journey down the 'brighter roads of decorative arts', albeit still with a strong architectural context. With spectacular displays of interior and industrial design, presented with greater flamboyance and less social urgency than the first revived event, the Triennale began to attract greater international, and particularly US, attention. Significant steps towards a clearly identifiable 'Italian style' had been taken. A central figure in this direction was architect and design polymath Gio Ponti, who had founded *Domus* and resumed its editorship in 1947 (replacing Ernesto Rogers). Ponti bridged the divide between decorative arts and industrial design, as demonstrated by his showy masterpiece for the Italian company La Pavoni, a coffee machine of 1947/8 (3.10).

With Marshall Plan funding and a plentiful supply of inexpensive labour (due in part to internal migration), northern Italian manufacturers from the late 1940s were able to revive their factories, employing economical and efficient methods of mass-production to produce standardized products, as in the Italian automobile industry.[37] Artisan industries such as ceramics and basketry, based on traditional methods of craftsmanship, were also revived by Marshall funds and were regarded as an important aspect of modern Italian style destined for export.[38] The furniture industry straddled artisanal and large-scale production, but some companies, such

as Cassina, Arflex and plastics company Kartell, were quick to embrace the possibilities of new materials and production methods to produce strikingly contemporary forms.

The revival of Italian industry marked a new phase in the role of the designer, and the rise to prominence of the consultant designer to industry. Figures like Gio Ponti were able to work across a broad range of disciplines, from luxury goods to corporate architecture. Designers had worked in consultative roles to Italian manufacturers before the war, but by the 1950s certain companies had established far-reaching corporate design policies. Chief amongst these was the manufacturer of typewriters and business equipment, Olivetti. Olivetti's distinctive design programme was largely the work of architect Marcello Nizzoli, who had worked with the company in a consultative capacity since 1938, and designed the highly successful Lexikon 80 (1948) and Lettera 22 (1950) typewriters. This programme won the admiration of US corporations, such as IBM, in the 1950s. Olivetti also employed artists and graphic designers to produce advertising materials (3.11), and subsequently industrial designers such as Ettore Sottsass Jr and Michele De Lucchi had long-running associations with the company.

Olivetti was run by Adriano Olivetti who took over from his father in 1932, since when he had rationalized production methods whilst developing an alternative vision of corporate responsibility based on a kind of benevolent paternalism. Olivetti's programme

3.11
Giovanni Pintori, poster for
Olivetti Lexikon typewriter.
Colour offset, 1953.
V&A: Circ.634-1965

of corporate welfarism (providing, for example, housing, community and educational facilities for workers[39]) was a long way from the business model being offered up by the USA. Instead, Olivetti stands as testimony to the ways in which Italian industries adapted US models of business organization to their own ends, creating a distinctive form of modern corporation which cannot be said to be comprehensively 'Americanized'.

'An Italian Shopping Trip'

Design developments in Italy were widely publicized in the USA as evidence of the successes of the Marshall Plan. In 1950 a touring exhibition entitled 'Italy at Work' opened at the Brooklyn Museum of Art. In its press release, the show was described as revealing 'the Resurgence of [a] Nation Freed of Dictatorship and Aided by [the] Marshall Plan'.[40] It showcased artisanal works from across Italy including ceramics, glass, basketry, furniture and interior design. It contained a number of room sets, designed by luminaries such as Ponti and Carlo Mollino.[41] There were also examples of industrial design, including an Olivetti Lexikon 80 typewriter and a Lambretta scooter. 'Italy at Work' eventually toured to 11 institutions across the USA, funded by the Compagnia Nazionale Artigiana (CNA), a company financed by the Italian Ministry of Foreign Trade which was, in turn, supported by American funds.[42] The selection committee included leading industrial designer Walter Dorwin Teague, who wrote an account of the research visit to Italy for *Interiors* magazine under the title 'An Italian Shopping Trip', in which he stressed the mutual benefits of such a model of cultural and economic exchange between two nations.[43]

Italian goods made a rapid and sustained impact on US consumers in the wake of the Marshall Plan. US department stores made a feature of special Italian promotions in the early 1950s, including an extravagant event at Macy's, New York, which included a Venetian gondola installed in the centre of the store.[44] In terms of industrial design, the company Olivetti had been effectively canonized by the Museum of Modern Art in 1952 in an exhibition which showed not only Olivetti's elegant streamlined products, but also graphics, architecture and shop interiors, with a description of the company's paternalist, humanitarian ethos. Olivetti made a decisive impression on New York again in 1954 with the opening of its Fifth Avenue store designed by the company BBPR (a partnership which included Ernesto Rogers[45]). The store itself was a showpiece of Italian design and craftsmanship and featured marble stands for products rising from the floor like stalagmites, Murano glass light-shades, a wall relief by Constantino Nivola and the typewriters and calculators displayed as if pieces of sculpture, some of them turning on a giant display wheel (3.12). Other similarly unconventional store designs were to follow. What is also remarkable about these stores is that they positioned a manufacturer of office products alongside high fashion stores, imparting an image of elegance and fashionability to industrial design in general, and Italian goods in particular.[46]

The fragile state of Italy in 1945–7 was gradually replaced, during the 1950s, by a democratic and consumerist society. This was not without its critics, despite the optimism and gloss of the boom years.[47] By the late 1960s this discontent was becoming more frequently and publicly articulated, as Robert Lumley has shown[48] and Paola Nicolin attests below (p.228). Contemporary design, so closely aligned to this version of consumerist democracy, was to attract the criticisms of a new generation of radical designers protesting against the alienating effects of capitalism, arguing once more for a newly politicized role for design instead of 'a uniformity of design (which) mirrored the uniformity of consumer society'.[49]

Design ambassadors

As the 'carpet bombing' of the Soviet Union with consumer goods imagined by David Riesman in his parodic 1951 essay 'The Nylon Wars' suggested, the idea of material abundance distributed as *largesse* was a key part of the USA's post-war image.[50] At the point when Europe foundered, the USA promoted itself as a highly seductive model of a modern consumer society.[51] But the processes of Americanization in Europe in the post-war period were manifold and complex. They ranged across many areas of influence, from systems of factory production and business methods to pop music and film. They varied

3.12
BBPR Studio, Olivetti Corporation Showroom at 584 Fifth Avenue, New York, 1954

in degrees of effectiveness – US corporate, cultural and institutional forms were not absorbed into Europe smoothly or in a wholesale manner, but rather by a process of selection and adaptation, peppered with instances of outright rejection. US streamlined design (in particular the work of Raymond Loewy) was often singled out for critical attention, as wasteful, tasteless and irresponsible.[52] Loewy's own location of design in a democratic context was forthright. In a speech to Harvard Business School in 1950, he asserted that 'no-one has yet been able to make [democracy's] high spiritual values of freedom, liberty and self respect a packaged item to be sold to the rest of the world'. Consumer goods, however, could substitute for this: 'The citizens of Lower Slobovia may not give a hoot for freedom of speech but how they fall for a gleaming Frigidaire, a stream-lined bus or a coffee percolator.'[53]

A contrasting form of high modernist design, such as the work of Charles and

Ray Eames, Eero Saarinen, Harry Bertoia and George Nelson, manufactured by Knoll International and Herman Miller, was used to counter a view of US consumer products as vulgar and lacking aesthetic maturity. As Greg Castillo argues (p.66), modern design was frequently assigned an ambassadorial role in Europe. Exhibitions were vital tools in the drive to raise the cultural profile and change expectations of the USA in Europe.[54] The ambitious touring exhibition '50 Years of American Art' organized in 1955 by the Museum of Modern Art, New York, and sent to Paris, Zurich, Barcelona, Frankfurt, London, The Hague, Vienna and Belgrade, featured industrial design and architecture alongside the main displays of American art and photography. MoMA's selection of objects was in line with the basic tenets of its 'Good Design' programme, established in 1949 by curator Edgar J. Kaufmann, an ambitious attempt to unite art with commerce, through the selection and exhibition of 'approved' products in tandem with the wholesale company The Merchandise Mart of Chicago.[55] Despite MoMA's careful selection of stylish products alongside modernist buildings which proclaimed the relocation of the European Modern Movement to the USA, thoughts of another America – that of brash consumerism and militarism – were never far away. One French reviewer in the communist weekly paper *Lettres Françaises* commented scornfully:

> an extensive section has been given over to saucepans, lemon-squeezers, can openers, and plastic chairs ... only a Cadillac, a jet plane, and an H-bomb are lacking but will undoubtedly be included another time.[56]

Despite such expressions of scorn, the USA did offer an industrious model of design renewal. Peacetime uses had been found for inventive materials, many of them the product of accelerated development during the war years (such as nylon and polythene). The stimulus of the wartime economy produced, in turn, countless examples of technology transfer which impacted upon the design and production of housing, furniture and household goods. The use of moulded plywood and glass-reinforced plastic (GRP or fibreglass)

by the aircraft industry, for example, was enthusiastically adopted by innovators in furniture design. Charles and Ray Eames had developed a moulded plywood leg splint for the US Navy in 1942, allowing them to further their own experiments in plywood furniture and gain access to privileged technical information (3.13).[57] A furniture competition of 1948, organized by the Museum of Modern Art in New York and entitled 'The International Competition for Low-Cost Furniture', showed prototypes which utilized experimental materials and novel methods of production, such as Davis Pratt's chair based on a vehicle inner tube (3.15). After the competition, the Eames were awarded a grant (in Charles's name) to develop their seat-shell made from metal sprayed with neoprene (3.14), produced in collaboration with research engineers from the University of California at Los Angeles. By the time the finished products were exhibited in 1950, they had changed the material to fibreglass to make a single shell armchair (see 1.14), which immediately went into production with Herman Miller and Zenith Plastics (which had used fibreglass in the manufacture of radar domes during the war).[58] The chair, together with its upholstered close cousin, Eero Saarinen's evocatively named 'Womb Chair' (3.16), produced by Knoll from 1946 onwards), became stalwarts of US touring exhibitions of the 1950s. They were also immediately taken up by the European design press, spawning a wealth of imitations. At the same time, the Eames were also achieving European recognition for their prototype mass-manufacturable home, designed for the Case Study House Programme in California in 1949 (3.17).[59] As Beatrix Colomina has observed, the house appeared to be 'one of the Eameses plywood cabinets blown up in scale ... a lightweight, demountable, infinitely rearrangable storage system' (3.18).[60] An easily assembled flexible structure (erected in a day), made from ' off the shelf' products, the house must have appealed to those facing the task of reconstruction with limited resources.[61]

In numerous exhibitions at home in the USA and abroad, 'progressive' US designs were displayed alongside exhibits with strong European associations (sometimes because they were the output of émigrés like Mies van der Rohe who crossed the Atlantic before

3.13
Ray and Charles Eames, leg splint. Moulded plywood, designed 1941-2. Manufactured by Plyformed Wood Company, Los Angeles 1942-3; Evans Products Company 1943-5. V&A: W.49-1983

3.14
Charles Eames and University of California Team (group design), full-scale model of Rocking Armchair RAR. Neoprene-coated aluminium shell, metal rods and wood runners, 1948. The Museum of Modern Art, New York

3.15
Chair designed by
Davis J. Pratt, from Edgar
Kaufmann, *Prize designs
for modern furniture
from the International
Competition for Low-Cost
Furniture Design*, exhibition
catalogue, New York, 1950.
V&A/NAL: 47.K. Box 1

3.16
Eero Saarinen, Womb
Chair. Upholstered
latex foam on fibreglass-
reinforced plastic shell
and chrome-plated steel
rod base, 1946. The Museum
of Modern Art, New York

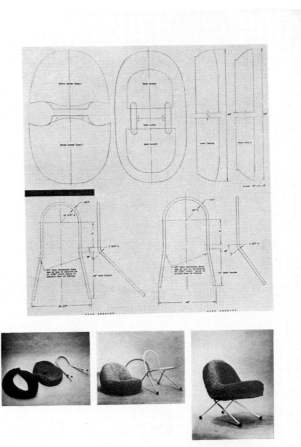

Co-winner of Second Prize, Seating Units

Chair Designed by **Davis J. Pratt**, Chicago

One of the most important problems in furniture design is that of a really soft, comfortable chair. Few modern designers until now have chosen to try their hand at it. Davis Pratt went to one of the forms of cushioning most available in modern life—an inflated tube, particularly because the technical problems had in large part been solved by the automobile tire industry. After some experimentation, Mr. Pratt determined that maximum comfort could be secured by containing an inflated ring within a fairly heavy envelope which distributed resilience over a large surface. He later determined that by separating the ring into two parts, one for the seat and the other for the back, comfort could be considerably increased. These procedures have allowed him to avoid the unnecessary uniform resilience provided in air mattresses, for example, as well as the somewhat personal touch which anyone will remember who has sat within an inflated inner tube on some summer picnic.

The rubber-tipped metal legs devised by Mr. Pratt may be folded nearly flat for convenient shipping, which is also aided by the other collapsible features of the chair. The retail price has been estimated at $30.

24 **Seating: Pratt**

Seating: Pratt 25

Design and the Democratic Ideal

3.17
Ray and Charles Eames,
Eames House, Case Study
House No.8, completed 1949

3.18
Ray and Charles Eames,
storage unit. Zinc-plated
steel, birch-faced plywood,
plastic-coated plywood
and lacquered fibreboard
(masonite), designed 1949–
50. Manufactured by
Herman Miller Furniture Co.
V&A: W.5:3-1991/ W.5:4-
1991/ W.5:5-1991

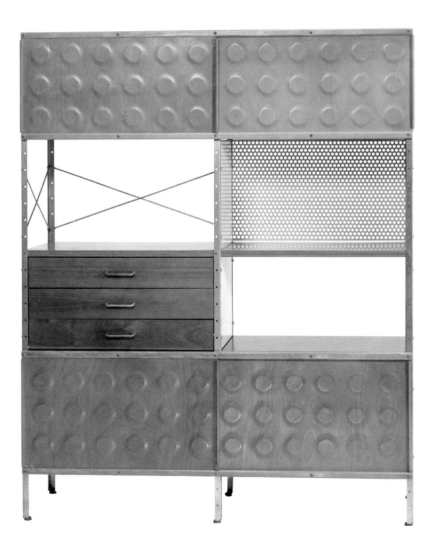

the Second World War), serving to shape an idea of 'internationalist' modernism flowering under Western democratic alliance. In other words, modern design constituted a North Atlantic community.[62] In Germany this was especially true. The diligence with which MoMA and the United States Information Agency, a body established by the Department of State to promote US culture abroad, had integrated progressive American design into a European conception of international modernism paid dividends. Aside from the high prominence given to the products of companies such as Knoll International and Herman Miller in European journals of architecture and design, they were also exhibited by European design organizations such as the Deutscher Werkbund.[63]

For the reconstituted Werkbund, the German appeal of an internationalist perspective on design was obvious. Positioning itself as a key vehicle in the economic, cultural and spiritual re-education of the nation, the design association realized the need to distance Germany from statements of national character or identity (as a means of separation from Nazi rhetoric). When the Brussels Expo was announced, the Werkbund, together with the German Design Council (Rat für Formgebung), was awarded the task of organizing the German Pavilion. The organizing team strove to present an image of inward-looking and modest Germany to suppress recent memories of her belligerence and to demonstrate her commitment to spiritual renewal. A transparent structure fashioned from plate glass and thin metal frame (in the manner of Mies Van der Rohe), designed by Egon Eiermann and Sep Ruf, was used to suggest the openness of the new state and society (3.24).[64] The pavilion's contents (directed by Hans Schwippert, Werkbund president 1947– 63), was devoted to the theme of 'Living and Working in Germany' and presented an image of wholesome, dignified and productive lifestyles, lived modestly. It was to be an evocation of a renewed humanism, where objects served not as the glossy signs of a prosperous consumer culture, but as the humble artefacts of use and 'honest living'.[65] The press release for the Pavilion marked it as the culmination of ten years' work, 'giving birth to a new conception of life' based on 'wholesome principles' and 'spiritual

3.19
Aerial view of the building
of the Hochschule für
Gestaltung Ulm, 1955

enjoyment'.[66] But this version of German design culture was far from the mainstream of the *Wirtschaftswunder*, and did little to stem the tide of brash and genuinely popular consumer goods in the country. From the mid-1950s, the concept of 'good form' was to come increasingly under attack as a delusional vision which failed to recognize or challenge the powerful exigencies of the marketplace.[67]

The Beautiful Task: The Hochschule für Gestaltung

Probably the most considered meeting of design with democratic ideals after the war was found in the construction of a progressive design school, the Hochschule für Gestaltung (HfG), on a hilltop above the devastated city of Ulm in southern Germany, which lay in the US Occupation Zone.[68] Opened in 1953, the school, a cluster of low-lying functionalist buildings furnished with simple, spare furniture and frequently referred to as a 'cloister' or 'sanatorium',[69] was widely regarded as both a bastion of high-minded aestheticism, and a beacon of hope for the revival of the Modern Movement (3.19).

As plans for the school developed, they found favour with the US priorities for West Germany of re-education (later termed 'reorientation') and democratization, particularly via the support of John McCloy, the American High Commissioner for Germany.[70] Whilst the spiritual and philosophical basis of the school may seem at odds with a pragmatic, market-oriented view, nevertheless the school went on to forge close links with major German businesses. Commercialism was ameliorated by Ulm's focus on the tenets of modernist functionalism, which had long been situated within a moral discourse. During its short history, which ended with its closure in 1968 (following financial crisis and a turbulent internal debate about its teaching methods and independent status), the HfG came to represent (quite literally) the high ground of West German Modernism, through its role in the generation of coolly minimalist industrially produced goods (3.20) and identity schemes for leading corporations, such as Lufthansa and Braun.

The school was the inspiration of Inge Scholl, who had been a founder member of an anti-Nazi resistance group called The White Rose (Die Weiße Rose) during the war. Together with her siblings Hans and Sophie Scholl and a close circle of friends she had advocated passive resistance as a means to overcome National Socialism and restore social democracy to Germany.[71] In 1943 three members of the group, including her brother and sister, were arrested by the Gestapo and executed.[72]

After the war Scholl and Aicher (who were later to marry) sought a means to memorialize her siblings in a manner that would pay tribute to their democratic ideals. They chose an educational path, with plans to found a publicly funded community college (*Volkshochschule*) in Ulm. This scheme was inaugurated with a programme of events focused on the city's rebuilding programme and bolstered by a series of philosophical, literary and historical talks by a glittering list of speakers. Only months after the arrival of US troops, the first of the famous Thursday evening lectures began (in August 1945), organized by the Aicher-Scholl community of supporters known as the *Ulmer Kreis* (Ulm Circle), and publicized with posters designed by Aicher. In the years 1945–50, talks on town planning, home crafts and jazz were juxtaposed with lectures on Marxism and Existentialism (3.21).

3.20
Max Bill and Ernst Moeckl,
kitchen clock with timer.
Metal, glass, ceramic and
plastic, 1956–7. Manufac-
tured by Gebrüder Junghans
AG, Schramberg, Germany.
V&A: M.224-2007

3.21
Otl Aicher, lecture posters
for the Volkshochschule.
Lithographs on paper,
1947–50. Ulmer Museum,
HFG Archiv

But their ambition for a more permanent college was stalled by City Council concerns that their programme was too politically radical. Instead, Scholl and Aicher laid plans for an independent institution where they could pursue a vision of an integrated curriculum combining artistic, philosophical, political and contemporary cultural instruction (such as their pioneering interest in media studies). Their pedagogical vision was based on the firm belief that such all-round education was the key to a humanist sensibility.

The school was also to have an internationalist outlook, and in order to achieve this, Scholl and Aicher approached the Swiss artist and designer Max Bill to be its first Director. Bill's presidency of the Swiss Werkbund, and well-known proselytizing on behalf

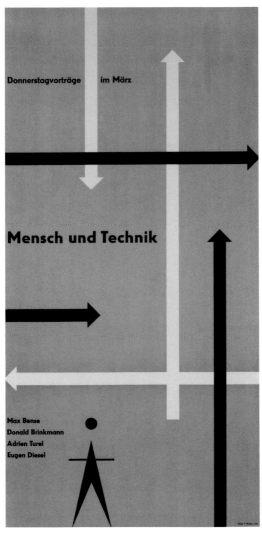

3.22
**Dieter Rams and Hans
Gugelot**, Phonosuper,
SK55 (a later version of the
1956 SK4 model). Metal,
wood and acrylic plastic,
manufactured by Braun
AG, Taunus, West Germany,
1963. V&A: W.51-1978

of functionalist design (through his touring exhibition 'Gute Form', or 'Good Form'), were amongst his credentials for the job.[73] A former Bauhäusler who had expressed the wish to see the Bauhaus ethos revived, Bill agreed to Aicher's and Scholl's request with the proviso that the school should become more firmly directed towards design.

Bill was not the only new partner with vested interests. Although the conventional histories of the HfG have tended to assert that its origins lay in the ideals of high-minded individuals, recent scholarship has shown that the school was also the product of a highly complex and contested Cold War climate.[74] As was necessary under the terms of the Allied Occupation Zones, the school curriculum was submitted for approval to the US High Commission in 1950. High Commissioner McCloy was instrumental in directing plans for the school, not only through the provision

of funding, but also through the imposition of US educational advisors.[75] In his view, the encouragement of a German-run educational programme with democratic ideals was of great potential benefit to the American objectives of de-Nazification, plus the HfG had the added advantage of being focused on design, which suggested that it would play a key role in serving the material interests of a stable Germany committed to peace and democracy. As Paul Betts has shown, the Ulm ethos was cast in terms of a 'spiritual Marshall Plan' for a democratic West Germany.[76]

Scholl and Aicher had to tread a careful path in order to establish the school's legitimacy, adhering to their ambitions for a politically informed programme whilst fighting off suspicions that their aims were positioned too far towards the political left. Castillo has shown how Bill stressed the

school's political neutrality in his negotiations with McCloy and the extent to which the founder of the Bauhaus, Walter Gropius (now domiciled in the USA) was instrumental in both endorsing the school, initially aligning its ideals with those of the Bauhaus.[77] Although Gropius's alignment of the Bauhaus with the Ulm school was not to last,[78] at the time it may have been instrumental in securing support for the HfG. Bill's appointment also mollified concerns about the political orientation of the school, as between 1951–3 he shifted it towards being an institute of design. Bill wrote to McCloy in 1952 describing his ideal graduate:

> The designer who emerges from the Ulm school will influence society in two ways: first, as a responsible citizen, and secondly, as a designer of products which are better and cheaper than any others, thus contributing to raising the living standards of society in general, and creating a culture of our techno-logical age.[79]

Once satisfied, the US High Commission granted the school the funding of one million Deutsche Marks in 1953.[80]

The first generation of Ulm tutors, selected by Aicher and Bill, defined the initial programme. The painter Josef Albers was an early appointment, followed by British graphic designer Anthony Froshaug and the Argentinian painter and designer Tomás Maldonado. This strong graphic focus helped to shape the school's attitudes to mass communication, where design was seen as a means to cleanse the visual incoherence of modern life with simple typographic solutions. It also paved the way for a pro-gramme of identity design which united product, graphics and other communication methods such as advertising.

Alongside Bill's established industrial design skills, Hans Gugelot was appointed to run the product design programmes. The school immediately benefited from a commission from the company Braun, which approached the school in late 1954 with a proposal that the school take charge of the company's integrated design policy. Gugelot and Aicher headed the commission which incorporated the design and redesign of

Braun's electrical products, as well as exhibi-tion design and corporate identity. This programme of design was managed effective-ly, with a smooth transition from Ulm as the external design consultancy to an internal Braun design team headed by Dieter Rams. Rams, a young architect, worked alongside Gugelot to develop Braun's first iconic product, the SK4 radiogram, colloquially known as 'Snow White's Coffin' (*Schneewittchensarg* in German) due to its transparent plastic lid and box-like form (3.22). Rams subsequently took over the role as chief designer for Braun, employing an Ulm ethos of functionalist design for the duration of his long career with the company (3.23).

Ironically, it was Ulm's commercial success in this field of corporate identity and industrial design that seems most at odds with the lofty ideals of its founders. Certainly, as Paul Betts has argued, the Braun design programme reflected its concern to move German products away from cosy domesticity towards the status of technical equipment based on use-value rather than on style or taste – in the words of Herbert Lindinger, to 'reduce the design object to the irreducible'.[81] The objects were intended to be the antithesis of cheap consumerism, to appeal to an informed, wealthy clientele (achieving international recognition through their frequent mention in design and architecture publications, and exhibitions).

The Ulm vision of functionalist design as the embodiment of the democratic ideal was not without its detractors. Bill's announcement of the school's programme and intentions in 1953 inflamed those who objected to his effective annexation of the Bauhaus legacy. The Danish artist and former COBRA member Asger Jorn counter-attacked with the announcement of the founding of the 'International Movement for an Imaginist Bauhaus'. A lively exchange between Bill and Jorn took place.[82] In Jorn's view, the strictly rational and functionalist HfG programme was based on a narrow reading of Bauhaus principles. Instead, Jorn would form 'a united organization capable of promoting an integral revolutionary cultural attitude' in homage to early Bauhaus ideals. Artists 'must get hold of industrial means and subject them to their own nonutilitarian ends, embracing experimentation and play'.[83]

Although Jorn's Imaginist Bauhaus was conceived largely as a provocation (rather than as an actual institution), he found an outlet for his plans in the artistic centre of Alba, Italy, where the studio of his friend, artist Giuseppe Pinot-Gallizio, attracted a host of experimental artists from 1954 onwards. Ceramics, the traditional artisanal production of the town, was the main material exploited in these acts of free, experimental play. In September 1956, Jorn hosted the Alba Congress of Free Artists, in the name of the Imaginist Bauhaus and the leftist organization the Lettriste International. The Congress was an international gathering of avant-garde artists with openly political intentions. Many delegates were former members of COBRA (the acronym for a group of experi-mental artists, coined in 1948 in Copenhagan, Brussels and Amsterdam), from eight countries, East and West (although Czech delegates were prevented from entering Italy). The delegates saw the Congress as a vital moment in a turbulent political year, meshing their acts of artistic experimentation with 'real' revolutionary events:

> The Alba Congress will probably one day be seen as a key moment, one of the difficult stages in the struggle for a new sensibility and a new culture, a struggle which is itself part of the general revolu-tionary resurgence characterising the year 1956, visible in the upsurge of the masses in the USSR, Poland and Hungary...[84]

At Alba, Jorn called for a 'new Institute of Artistic Experiment and Theory' which would claim back the political territory of the early modernist avant-garde and reject the prag-matic moves taken by Bill. To be avant-garde, Jorn claimed, a movement 'must be isolated, without direct support from the established order, and given over to an apparently impos-sible and useless struggle'. It also needed to be of direct relevance to the 'forces in whose names it struggles – in our case, human society and artistic progress'.[85]

The Alba congress demonstrated how the 'rational' path of a modern design philosophy based on the elision of function-alism with democracy was increasingly under attack, a position that was to gain critical ground in the later 1960s. Furthermore, the position at Ulm itself had begun to shift, after Bill's 1957 resignation following disagreements over his style of leadership. Tomás Maldonado, who took over the running of the school in partnership with Aicher and Scholl, shifted the pedagogical focus of the school from functionalism to the discussion of semiotics and systems thinking.[86] This shift was based on the view that the Ulm approach was in danger of becoming another form of elitist style choice in a prosperous economy. In the place of 'good form' (with its suggestion that the designer was some sort of ascetic individual) he proposed that the designer take his or her place in a culture of specialists, which would include technologists, as well as experts in the market, consumer behaviour and communications. This would foster what Maldonado termed a culture of 'scientific operationalism', which would provide the means by which a critical function for design could be developed within a highly complex economy. Maldonado's repositioning of the school's ethos was based on the concern that the *Wirtschaftswunder* was a symptom of a perverse condition in which democratic freedom was confused with consumer 'rights'. Only by a systematic analysis of this 'consumer manipulation' could design be liberated from its uncritical role as the supplier of unnecessary wants rather than needs.[87] He left Ulm in 1967, months before its closure, to an academic post in Italy. His close colleague Gui Bonsiepe, co-author of many statements on their shared design-as-science vision, moved to Chile, aided by Maldonado's contacts in Latin America. Fittingly, Bonsiepe was to become involved in the enactment of a vision of scientific operationalism – a project for the cybernetic rationalisation of the socialist economy (see pp.187–8).

The collapse of the school scattered its members far afield. The reasons for its demise due to financial and institutional difficulties are complex and have been described elsewhere.[88] Students and staff were split over the degree to which Ulm could square its moral conscience with corporate contracts. Some protested that the school take a more extreme stance against what they termed 'Kommerzterror'.[89] Infected with the radical student culture of the late 1960s, and aware the authorities wished to make the school

a department of Stuttgart University (thus removing its independence), as a final act the students erected a makeshift sign renaming the school 'Karl-Marx College' and waved placards declaring '50 years of repression: weimar, dessau, berlin, ulm' (all in typical lower-case ulm type), seeking to associate the closure of the school with that of the Bauhaus by the Nazis in Berlin in 1933.[90] The school was officially closed on 31 December 1968.

The quest to imbue designed products with the 'democratic ideal' was thus a persistent theme of the 1950s. It united, at least in mission if not in method or objective, the rather disparate interests of design reformers, social modernizers and state programmes devoted to economic recovery. For the proselytizers of Modernism, this purpose was given greater urgency by the conditions of the Cold War.[91] But for all the studied neutrality of Ulm-designed products, or the easygoing modernity of Italian goods in the 1950s, design was never far removed from its political context. And how could radios, chairs, typewriters and scooters be inherently democratic? Could the clean lines and unadulterated forms of such goods embody ethical principles, regardless of how they were used? Not only was the elision of design ideals with moral or political constructs a factor in Cold War politics, but it was also the fault-line along which the persistent tensions within modernism were found. This line of argument, which equated 'good design' with moral consciousness, increasingly came under attack in the 1960s, from a position within modernist discourse which called for a new radicalization of the modernist project which would question the limitations of consumer capitalism and, by implication, design.

3.23
Dieter Rams, T 1000 radio world receiver. Coloured aluminium, manufactured by Braun AG, Taunus, West Germany, 1963. V&A: W.12-2007

Cold War Front Lines: The Architecture of Defence

Caroline Maniaque

3.25
Double-page spread
contrasting the 'Atomic
City' of Oak Ridge and the
city of Hiroshima in ruins.
The Architectural Forum,
October 1945, USA.
V&A/NAL: PP. 4.J

It is a commonplace to say that the Cold War's effects were primarily indirect rather than inscribed in the built environment. Unlike the anxieties of Existentialism or the bluff and bluster of international trade fairs, the material reality of defence against nuclear annihilation has rarely occupied centre stage. Only now, as historians begin to work on the period and sites come up for consideration as heritage monuments, is the physical landscape of the military Cold War becoming apparent. Tom Vanderbilt's book *Survival City: Adventures among the Ruins of Atomic America*, published in 2002, has led the charge.[1] The very terminology he uses to describe the monuments of the Cold War – white and black spaces – is a good indication of their special character. The black spaces are the secret underground bunkers and test sites hidden from public view, whereas the white spaces are visible and even visitable, though they too might be 'hidden in plain sight'. Of these two orders of space, Vanderbilt writes, 'the existence of one not only presupposes the other, but they inevitably seep into each other, corrupting both in the process'.[2] In the 'visible' world of progress and unstoppable capitalism, the reaction to potential annihilation through nuclear weaponry was sometimes one of denial. Vanderbilt argues, citing Lewis Mumford, that the International Style office block with its fragile glass surfaces was a defiant statement ignoring the threat of nuclear blast and can in this way be seen as one kind of response to the Cold War.[3]

In other words, the real subject of Cold War architecture is not just its visible forms but also the psychological effect of the invisible, of the anxiety of annihilation in the midst of plenty. The closest most ordinary Americans came to this was what Vanderbilt calls 'the domestication of Doomsday',

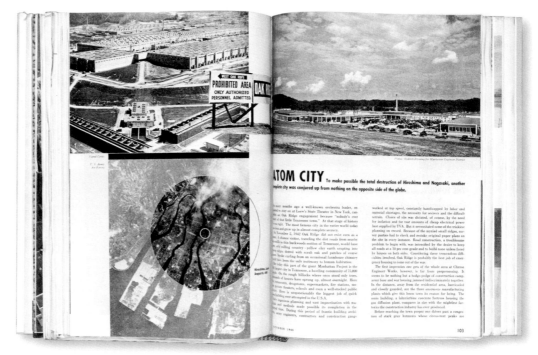

the construction of underground shelters.[4] At the other extreme were those Cold War megastructures that most influenced the popular imagination of the James Bond films and Stanley Kubrick's *Doctor Strangelove: Or how I learned to Stop Worrying and Love the Bomb* (1964), both designed by Kenneth Adam. The sources of inspiration for such visions included Oak Ridge, Tennessee, built in 1942, the 'atomic city' that helped bring Skidmore, Owings & Merrill to prominence as one of the country's most efficient architectural firms; 'Cheyenne mountain', the hardened, self-contained core of the North American Aerospace Defense Command (NORAD) Centre, designed to operate for nearly a month after a nuclear blast; and NASA's 'Vehicular Assembly Building', designed by Max O. Urbahn, which for a time possessed the largest interior volume in the world'.[5]

The history of these structures pre-dates the outbreak of the Cold War. Oak Ridge, Tennessee, for instance, was an entire town built between 1942 and 1945 to service America's programme to produce the atomic bomb, known as the Manhattan Project.[6] The town was kept largely secret until the war ended. Only then could *The Architectural Forum* (3.25) announce:

To make possible the total destruction of Hiroshima and Nagasaki, another complete city was conjured up from nothing on the opposite side of the globe. Today this part of the giant Manhattan Project is the fifth largest city in Tennessee, a bustling community of 75 000 people. On the rough hillocks where once stood only trees, thousands of houses have sprung up, almost overnight.

3.26
One of 31 Distant Early Warning radomes designed and supplied by R. Buckminster Fuller's Geodesics Inc., Cambridge, MA, in 1955-6. The radomes, weighing less than a pound per square foot, survived winds exceeding 150 miles per hour. This efficient use of material permitted excellent radar performance

Here are restaurants, drugstores, supermarkets, fire stations, motion picture theatres, schools and even a well-stocked public library. Here is unquestionably the biggest job of quick town building ever attempted in the U.S.A.[7]

The fact that this report, published just weeks after the end of the Second World War, contrasts an image of the huge plants in Oak Ridge and an image of the city of Hiroshima after its destruction on 6 August 1945, offers a revealing insight into the ambiguous 'pride' of the architectural community in the prosecution of the war.

Within Vanderbilt's category of the 'black spaces' of Cold War architecture hidden from the public, we should include the new structures that set out to resolve the practical problems of operating military-derived technology in uninhabitable space. But, as this short discussion of the distant and alien structures of the Distant Early Warning (DEW) Line shows, they too seeped into public consciousness in the course of the 1950s and 1960s. The specialist technology of rapid construction, prefabricated or pneumatic domes that formed part of an electronic network in the mid-1950s, was transferred later into commercial and peacetime use in international exhibitions and satellite intercommunication networks.

The DEW Line

Defensive walls have always served to reassure those within as much as to deter those without. This was certainly the case with North America's attempts to construct a defence system to provide a shield from the threat of its Soviet neighbour. The DEW Line was an integrated chain of more than 50 electronic listening posts deployed along the 69th Parallel, 200 miles north of the Arctic Circle. Radar and communication stations stretched 3,000 miles from Cape Lisburne in Alaska to Cape Dyer on Baffin Island (3.26). Far out in the frozen North and consisting of fragile half-hidden structures, its reassuring role might appear paradoxical. And yet its very secrecy and invisibility, part of an interconnected electronic network, gave it precisely the required aura of technological supremacy necessary to withstand what were dubbed the 'Russian bears' (Soviet bombers).

The DEW Line, the purpose of which was to give early warning of incoming Soviet bombers, was one of the most significant initiatives of the Cold War. It marked the edge of an electronic grid controlled by the new SAGE (Semi-Automatic Ground Environment) Computer System and was ultimately centred on the Colorado Command hub of NORAD (3.27). Initial research at a Massachusetts Institute of Technology (MIT) summer study group chaired by Jerrold R. Zacharias in 1952 had demonstrated the inadequacy of the existing early warning system.[8] The construction of the DEW Line was made possible by a 1954 bilateral agreement between the Canadian and American governments, and an alliance between the US Department of Defense and the Bell 'system' Companies. The Western Electric Corporation, Bell's manufacturing arm, was in charge of supervising the construction of the system, a task that was completed in just three years by some 25,000 people. The DEW Line included 63 stations, the construction of which was hampered by, among other things, the cold, the never-ending darkness of the Arctic winter, and the extreme wind. Ten people were required to operate each of the manned outposts, once completed; in addition, some automated stations could be left to operate for months at a time, as explained in the booklet written at the end of the 1950s, to commemorate the titanic achievement.[9]

The communication and radar detection equipment available at the time was known to be unsuited to the weather and atmospheric conditions encountered in the Arctic. Thus the most prominent visual elements of the DEW Line stations were the covers that housed the radar and protected them from the winds and snow. These were the radomes, large geodesic domes designed by American architect-engineer Buckminster Fuller, made of fibreglass and plastic to avoid interfering with the radar transmissions. Buckminster Fuller's experiments with fibreglass were typical of his enthusiasm for new materials. Technical developments during the Second World War had made fibreglass practical, and it was already well on its way to taking the place of wood in the construction of boats. Radomes for the Army and the Air Force provided an important market for Fuller's geodesics. Often sited at high altitude and in inaccessible

regions, the standard structure that Buckminster Fuller proposed was a 17-m diameter, 75 per cent non-metallic sphere made from diamond-shaped fibreglass components, which could be delivered by helicopter in kit form to the most difficult locations and erected in 14 hours. First employed in 1956, these structures were decommissioned after 1990 but were not entirely dismantled. Some of them have since become heritage sites.[10]

The Cold War uses of the radome were not limited to DEW Line outposts. As several scholars have shown, the dome became a much-employed tool and prominent symbol of Cold War corporate and military America:

> In the 1950s the Air Force and Marine Corps took geodesic domes to the front lines of the Cold War, using them in radar pickets and integrating them into beachhead invasion plans. The department of Commerce used them as pavilions for American exhibits at international trade fairs. To fair organizers, if not the millions of Afghans, Poles, Japanese and others, geodesic domes became 'tangible symbols of progress'

3.27
Diagram showing the network of surveillance and missile systems connected by SAGE (Semi-Automatic Ground Environment) computer system, late 1950s, USA. Computer History Museum, Mountain View, CA

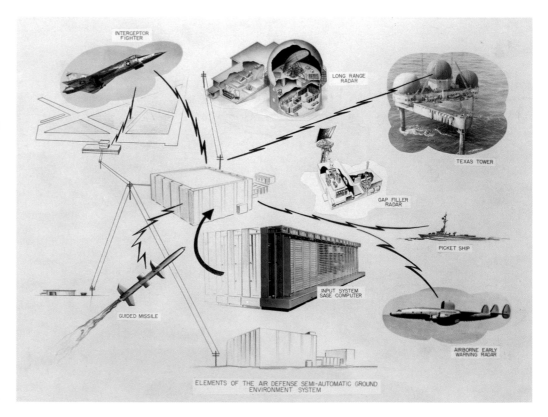

ELEMENTS OF THE AIR DEFENSE SEMI-AUTOMATIC GROUND ENVIRONMENT SYSTEM dramatizing 'American ingenuity, vision and technological dynamism.'[11]

After the construction in 1953 of the Ford Motor Co. dome at Dearborn, Michigan, a massive structure that covered the Corporation's headquarters, interest spread to large and open multifunctional structures like the demountable 30-m and 60-m exhibition domes with their suspended synthetic fabric envelopes that were used by the United States Information Services overseas. The advantage of these domes was the ease with which they could be transported and erected. They could be put up and taken down by unskilled local labour in few days. Like the radomes, these exhibition domes too were produced by Fuller's wholly owned companies Geodesics Inc. and Synergics Inc.[12]

Commentators have often pointed to the diverse and even contradictory applications of Buckminster Fuller's ideas in the Cold War. Architectural historian Felicity Scott argues that his 'Revolution by Design' was predicated on imminent threat of nuclear war and that he exploited this anxiety in promoting his geodesic domes.[13] Yet they were also the structure of choice for hippies and artists dropping out of conventional culture. A variation constructed in a field near Trinidad, Colorado, with its brightly coloured panels hacked out of automobile wrecks with axes, was, for instance, the centre point of Drop City (see pp.261–2 below). This coincidence is perhaps less contradictory than it might at first appear. The use of Fuller's domes in American trade fairs across the globe made them symbols of liberating technical progress, a key element of US propaganda in the Cold War period. This ideology was not so distant from the view that technology could be harnessed to create utopian spaces for personal liberation – the vision that shaped Drop City. The peculiar mixture of do-it-yourself improvisation and recycling of scrap materials with up-to-date structural systems and advanced electronics (hi-fi sound systems, television and film) was typical of the hedonistic survivalism of the counter-culture of the second half of the 1960s, and bears comparison with the DEW outposts.[14] Similarly, both the DEW Line and, in a very different way, the counter-cultural movement, with its global outreach through the *Whole Earth Catalog*,[15]

conformed to aspects of Marshall McLuhan's 'global village', a phrase coined by the Canadian writer to describe the world that had been 'shrunk' by modern advances in communications. The DEW Line, with its electronic surveillance across the Arctic, was indeed a feature of the global village.

Pneumatics

Instrumental to the shrinking of the planet was the first direct transatlantic television broadcast between North America and Europe. On 11 July 1962 the site of Pleumeur-Bodou (near Lannion, France) received the first transatlantic transmission of a television signal from a twin station in Andover, Maine, USA, via the TELSTAR satellite. This achievement relied on two large radomes at both locations. The immense 60-m high sphere, set up in Pleumeur-Bodou to protect the horn antenna broadcasting American television live for the first time to Europe, still stands out today against the Brittany skyline. Here we pass from the geodesic dome to another technology with roots in the military industrial complex: the pneumatic dome.

In the 1940s the US military needed lightweight, expendable structures to protect its remote missile sites in hostile climates. In 1946, Walter W. Bird and the engineers at the Aeronautic Laboratories at Cornell carried out this research. An aeronautical engineer who had graduated from MIT, Walter Bird was a pioneer in the design of lightweight structures and advanced the development of air-supported structures and tensioned membranes.[16] New airtight materials such as nylon, rayon, PVC-coated polyester, Dacron and fibreglass were developed, financed by the army and the aeronautic industry, which also invested in the development of lightweight, foldable structures and the miniaturization of electronic components. Early pneumatic radomes served alongside Buckminster Fuller's geodesic structures on the DEW Line in the severe climate of the Arctic.

Riding on the success of the first radomes that he designed for the US military, Bird made the transition from military engineering to the leisure industry. In 1955 he set up Birdair Structures Incorporated, producing and selling inflatable structures with which to cover tennis courts, swimming pools and exhibition

sites. In 1957 his work made the front cover of *Life* magazine (3.28), with a photo of teenagers bathing in a swimming pool covered by a semi-cylindrical membrane envelope: the craze for air-supported structures was born. Other fabric, tent and parachute manufacturers began producing inflatable buildings, for the most part simple semi-cylinders or hemispheres. Like Buckminster Fuller's geodesics, pneumatic structures were adopted for a wide range of uses, from the practical roof of Boston Arts Centre Theatre, designed by Carl Koch and engineer Paul Weidlinger at the end of the 1950s, to the nonconformist experiments of the Ant Farm Group ten years later. Considerable experiment was also made with the design of pneumatic shelters capable of supporting life on the dusty surface of the Moon. Working for NASA, Goodyear Aerospace designed capsule-like inflatable buildings with double skins to provide a pressurised internal environment capable of supporting life and an external membrane forming a second space in which the large amounts of water needed for the oxygen supply, food and waste disposal could be stored. The Stay Time Extension Module (STEM) was to support two astronauts for eight days on the surface of the Moon (3.29).[17]

Pneumatic structures had the advantage of creating dramatic shapes with spectacular visual forms, an effect that was not lost on the American authorities and the architects and designers they employed to promote their interests. Pneumatic structures were drawn into the propaganda war. By the late 1950s, for instance, the secrets of the Cold War were coming out into the open: 'Thus, by 1957, the place of nuclear energy in American life, an issue that for almost a decade had been confined to the secret councils of the federal government, had become the subject of a significant public debate'.[18] 'Atoms for Peace', a travelling exhibition, was one such official attempt to influence public opinion around the world. According to historians Richard Hewlett and Jack M. Holl, 'The search for redeeming values, as much as the desire to demonstrate the superiority of the American system over Soviet communism, explained the fervour with which the Atomic Energy Commission and its scientists and engineers pursued the shining dreams of Atoms for Peace'.[19] The curves and counter-curves of

3.28
A Birdair inflatable
structure on the cover
of *Life* magazine,
11 November 1957

the United States Atomic Energy Commission
(USAEC) travelling pavilion that housed
the display, designed in 1960 by architect
Victor Lundy and engineers Severud and
Bird, stretched for 90m. It contained a theatre
with a capacity of 300 seats, a technical
laboratory, and considerable exhibition space.
The exhibits included a model of an experimental atomic reactor housed within
a transparent pneumatic dome, a 'bubble
within a bubble'.[20] Erected in three days and
then folded away ready to be transported
to the next site, this travelling pavilion was an
important tool in the North American information strategy targeting the country's Latin
American neighbours.

In 1986 Bird reflected on the challenge
involved in designing one of the most demanding inflatable structures of the age, Pleumeur
Bodou Radome, in these words:

> The early BLT (Bell Telephone Laborato-
> ries) Telstar satellites were not fixed in
> orbit and needed to be tracked, requiring
> antennas with precise tracking capa-
> bility. BLT had developed a large horn
> antenna but needed protection from the
> weather. Proposals were solicited. Birdair
> proposed a two hundred and ten foot
> diameter air supported radome standing
> one hundred and sixty-five feet high.
> Nothing had ever been built this large
> and no material had ever been developed
> that would meet the strength and service
> requirements.[21]

Both this temporary shelter – installed to
house the construction site for the antenna –
and the final radome measured 64m in
diameter. The permanent radome, installed
in the summer of 1962, is made of Hypalon
coated Dacron and weighs over 30 tons.
Although a remarkable technical achievement, it is important to note that the radome
at Pleumeur-Bodou also produced important
Cold War media effects. The unexpected
and fascinating sight of this bright white
geometric shape in the Brittany landscape
was a monument to the technological edge
and media strength of the United States at
that time. A chain of antennas covered with
brilliant white air-supported shells – like
literal examples of Vanderbilt's 'white spaces'
– relayed electronic information from the

3.29
Stay Time Extension
Module, an experimental
lunar inflatable produced
by Goodyear Aerospace
for NASA in the late 1960s
(Source: Roger N. Dent,
*Principles of Pneumatic
Architecture*, London 1971)

USA via Pleumeur-Bodou to Raisting in Bavaria. Moreover, the transmission of television programmes designed to unite the 'free' capitalist world in simultaneity was a challenge that also involved industrial and technological competition between companies.[22] In the passage from Cold War survival to peaceful global colonization, American technology not only played a role of cultural ambassador: the wonder and beauty of these structures disguised their real function, of transmitting American cultural values and economic supremacy.

Looking back

Soon after its completion the DEW Line, which was conceived to detect and deter bombers, lost most of its significance with the arrival of Soviet Intercontinental Ballistic Missiles and submarine-launched missiles. Although some of the stations were decommissioned, the chain as a whole remained in place until the mid-1990s. Some stations still exist and are being considered as heritage sites.[23] The websites of these communities are a vivid illustration of Cold War culture, bringing

together the technical expertise of American engineers with the survival skills of the Inuit people who serviced the stations.[24] Classified as a historical landmark in 2000, the radome at Pleumeur-Bodou is the home of the National Museum of Telecommunications, curated by France Telecom since 1991, and it still protects the cornet antennas as an eloquent example of transatlantic co-operation.

4.1
Herbert Matter, *Atomic
Head*. Photomontage, 1946.
Matter Archive, Stanford
University Libraries,
Stanford, CA

4 / The Bomb in the Brain

Jane Pavitt

In 1946, the cover of the American journal *Arts and Architecture* carried an image of a photo collage by Herbert Matter – a head in profile, which contained the image of a mushroom cloud rising to fill the brain cavity (4.1). The 'bomb in the brain' was a potent representation of the overpowering presence of nuclear anxiety initiated by the USA's atomic bombing of the Japanese cities of Hiroshima and Nagasaki in August 1945.

By 1949, the knowledge that the Soviet Union possessed the same nuclear capabilities as the USA raised Western anxieties to fever pitch, which only abated slightly following the death of Stalin in 1953.[1] Despite much talk of the 'peaceful uses' of atomic power after 1953, tensions rose again in the early

1960s, when the world was brought to the brink of nuclear confrontation during the Cuban Missile Crisis. This was a period of history lived in the shadow of the bomb.

4.2
Kenneth Adam, storyboard for the Bomb Release sequence in *Dr Strangelove Or: How I Learned To Stop Worrying and Love The Bomb*, directed by Stanley Kubrick, 1964. Ink and wash on paper, 1962. Sir Kenneth Adam, London

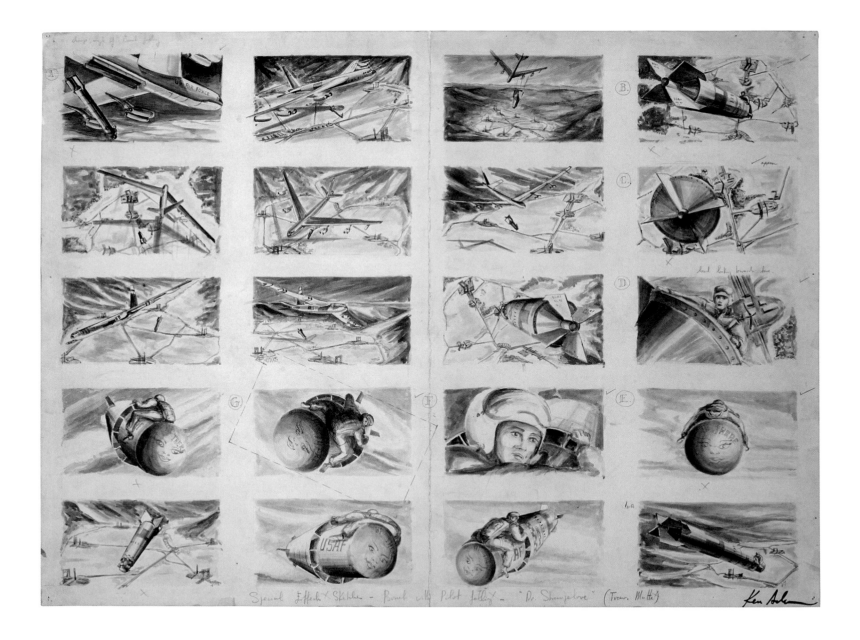

Yet in the West this anxiety was absorbed into everyday life as the dark consequence to the breezy and optimistic vision of a future world empowered by technology, and made pleasurable and efficient by the influx of new consumer goods. No such parallel could be found in the Eastern Bloc (although during the Khrushchev years the complete harnessing of thermonuclear reactions for peaceful uses was sometimes claimed as a prerequisite for the transition to full Communism).[2] In the US, magazines such as *Life* would match articles on the newest gadgetry for streamlined kitchens with descriptions of how to provision one's domestic fallout shelter. Civil defence was even given commodity forms in capitalist America.

Atomic science, marked by pioneering nuclear physicist Robert Oppenheimer's portentous and perhaps apocryphal quotation from Hindu scripture as he recalled witnessing the first atomic explosion on July 16th 1945 – 'Now I have become Death, the destroyer of worlds'[3] – was nevertheless promoted through widespread campaigns as a means of achieving peace and international co-operation. Indeed, this idea was

advanced by President Eisenhower in his December 1953 speech to the United Nations, which called for the formation of an International Atomic Energy Agency, to include the USSR, to develop 'peaceful' uses for atomic energy, in medicine, industrial research and as a cheaper source of power:

> It is not enough to take this weapon out of the hands of the soldiers. It must be put into the hands of those who will know how to strip its military casing and adapt it to the arts of peace.[4]

Although many of Eisenhower's proposals for international collaboration (particularly with the USSR, which rejected the proposal) did not come to fruition, his speech did set in train a propaganda campaign to 'rehabilitate' the image of atomic science, known as Atoms for Peace.[5] An abstract symbol of scientific progress, the atom had already been absorbed into a popular and jaunty visual design vocabulary in the early 1950s, appearing in print, on textiles, in animation and furniture, and even in giant architectural form, as in André Waterkeyn's Atomium Building, centrepiece of the Brussels Expo in 1958 (4.3).[6]

The Atoms for Peace campaign was to become both an ideological offensive against the USSR, which had refused to support it, as well as a means of distracting public attention away from the military implications of atomic science towards such benefits as cheaper energy. The International Atomic Energy Agency, following approval from the United Nations, was to oversee the verification, safety and security of nuclear power, and to develop the potential for technology transfer. Atoms for Peace continued through the 1950s and 1960s, its core mission hampered by the political climate, but nevertheless continuing to promote a 'benign' image of the atom by means of conferences, travelling exhibitions and visual media.

The Atoms for Peace message was also adopted with enthusiasm by some of the commercial partners of the US defence industry. In 1955, the US company General Dynamics had been invited to take part in the International Conference on the Peaceful Uses of Atomic Energy in Geneva. The company, which owned a portfolio of interests including electronics, astronautics, jet engines and

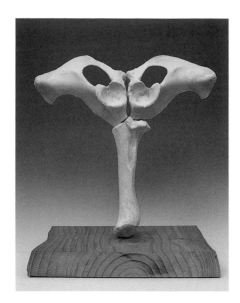

EMERGENCY
POWER STATION

TRANS-HIGHWAY BELT

QUONSET HUT HOSPITALS

MOTOR
POOL

HOSPITALS

FUEL
STORAGE

CAMPSITES

SHOPPING
CENTERS

RAIL TERMINAL

WAREHOUSES

6-TRACK RAIL BELT

BY-PASS POWER LINE

LIFE BELTS AROUND CITIES WOULD PROVIDE

The Wiener civil defense plan is calculated to meet two urgent needs in the after-bomb crisis. It would tend to check panic among the survivors of a city that has been A-bombed by giving them a definite place to head for, an escape route that could be reached by moving in any direction away from the city. It would also enable vital transportation services to continue functioning, taking food and supplies to the bombed city and bringing casualties out. The emergency transportation system suggested by Wiener would be tied in with existing rail and road facilities; thus no city would be completely cut off from outside aid.

The drawing above shows a mythical U.S. city equipped with the three major elements in Wiener's proposed escape route and communications network: 1) additional roads, radiating like the spokes of a wheel from the center of the metropolitan area, to serve as exits for the people, 2) an express highway that encircles the city about 10 miles from the edge of the built-up area to intersect every road that leads out of the city, 3) a railroad belt line five

← MAP OF MYTHICAL CITY (TOP) BEFORE THE PLAN

A PLACE FOR BOMBED-OUT REFUGEES TO GO

miles beyond the express highway to provide a direct auxiliary link between existing rail routes (pp. 80, 81).

Between the city and the express highway that rings it, zoning regulations will prohibit almost all construction. This area will be kept as clear as possible to serve as a safety zone, permitting an unhindered exit from the city. But along the highway life belt will be built the hospitals, supply warehouses, truck depots and power stations necessary to cope with the emergency. Nearby land will be reserved as parks

and made ready for large tent cities which could quickly be erected to shelter the refugees. Supermarkets, suburban homes and small businesses would be permitted to grow up near the life belt to supplement the emergency rations and housing set up for a fleeing population.

In any circumstance the Wiener plan would be useful. In war it would bolster the nation's civilian defenses. In peace it would expand and accelerate the current trend of many city dwellers toward the suburbs and help relieve the traffic congestion which plagues most U.S. cities.

SAME CITY WITH PROPOSED OUTER BELTS →

CONTINUED ON NEXT PAGE

The Bomb in the Brain

as Tristan Sauvage) recollected that, at one event, the Chair of Physics at Milan University, Professor Polviani, 'at a certain point fled in horror, dismayed by the "scientific" theories of the painters'.[16] The Nuclearists' fascination with the beauty and horror of atomic science led them also to propose a link between primordial nature, ancient myth and the conquest of outer space, as expressed in their 1959 manifesto, *Interplanetary Art*:

> Our imagination lands on the volcanic and calcinated pock-marked surfaces of the different planets before they may be reached by the stinking, noisy, metal carcasses, all horns and spheres, that the technicians and scientists have conceived.[17]

Those 'pock-marked surfaces' immediately recall the paintings of the Nuclearists' contemporaries Yves Klein and Lucio Fontana. Even before the inception of Arte Nucleare, Fontana had exhibited works that drew critical attention as the first examples of 'atomic' art as early as 1949;[18] throughout the 1950s and 1960s his work occupied a 'cosmic' terrain, as evident in this 1963 painting *Concetto Spatiale (La Fine di Dio)* (*Spatial Concept, The End of God*; 4.10). Cosmology, in both the philosophical and scientific senses a concern for the origins of the universe, was a preoccupation of many artists through the period.

If cosmology was Fontana's terrain, then other artists saw the post-nuclear landscape in terms of ruins. Artists including Jean Dubuffet, Asger Jorn and Constant Nieuwenhuys (known as Constant) continued to paint devastated landscapes well into the 1950s: in this they mapped not only the recent experience of war but also the persistence of anxieties in the present. Filtered through the ideas of Existentialism, such raw landscapes can be read as terrains of anxiety, about purposeless existence and the ever-present threat of annihilation. The Dutch artist Constant, for instance, captured this ruined vision in his celebrated painting *Scorched Earth* (*Verschroeide Aarde*, 1951; 4.11), a scene of twisted metal, bent wheels and outstretched limbs. Reusing these motifs to illustrate the words of Dutch poet Jan Elburg, *Het uitzicht van de duif* (*The Dove's*

View; 4.12), both artist and poet connect the raw experience of the Second World War with a condition of perpetual anxiety:

> Since time immemorial, the eyes prefer
>   to see down than blood, that down
>   grows on Picasso's doves:
> there the splinters stab like knives,
> there the incendiary bombs burst into
>   flames,
> that's what those who spit at us make
>   fun of,
> there the past blows the trumpet
> of the dead oppressors.

Dispersal and fallout

Of course, Europeans could equate their fear of potential nuclear destruction with the very real experience of being bombed during the Second World War. Unless they had served in the Forces, however, most Americans could only have experienced this vicariously, through media images. Even before the end of the war, American military strategists and urban planners had begun to gather evidence of the effects of heavy bombing on both

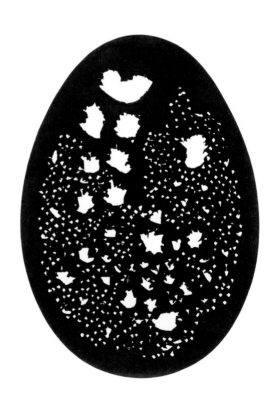

HET UITZICHT VAN DE DUIF

JAN ELBURG en CONSTANT

Koud als de vis, als het kijken van kruipende dieren,
als onderkoeld zonlicht onder ijs;
planten zijn stom en de dieren zwijgen.
Ik heb mijn eigen ontredderd leven
om te weten hoe het met anderen is
in dit opgepompt en geverfd paradijs.

Wat de arbeiders met de rug van hun kinderen
en met het vel van hun handen betalen,
betaal ik mee: een losgeld van onrecht
met de gehavende taal van mijn blinde
ontevredenheid, maar altijd betaal ik te weinig:
slechts met de tijdelijke tik van mijn hart;
niet met de koekoeksklok van mijn bloed.

Met het beschadigd protest om een vrijheid
van veilig te zijn tegen zonbrand en regen
en honger en hoon van de windbuilen,
betaal ik mee aan een nooit te voldoene
hypotheek die de voorouders voor is gelogen
met de prenten van helden en stadhouders,
met de rekensommen van a naar b
en de doodgewone hooghollandse taalles.

Uitsluitend aan de gedachten als kamerplanten,
bestoft in het avondlicht, gaan steden dood;
uitsluitend aan de terrassen met krakante vrouwen,
uitsluitend aan de wanhoop thuis en de gregoriaanse
schooldeun achter de geeuwende ramen
slijten fabrieken en handelshuizen.
Uitsluitend aan haat sluit het hart zich, de wenk
van de handen met lettertekens als rook;
uitsluitend aan leugens sterft het woord,
aan leuzen en lessen het goed vertrouwen
van wind en water en oevervogels.

Wij, die de wereld bekijken met een vers
op de tong als een fluittoon van hoon,
wij dragen in wangen opgeborgen
een koperen doodshoofd dat boos is:
door hamers van binnenuit nors gebeukt;
in het zoeklicht van buiten verstard tot een grijns:
de lach van het cynische incasseren.

Zo kunnen de straten en kamers ons opleveren.
Wij zijn, want de straat kan ons opleveren,
met een voet en een voet en een hand
en een handtastelijk duidelijk gelijk,
grof en verongelijkt, omdat wij zijn de wij zijn:
met handen en voeten en monden ontkomen
aan deze onmenselijke mentaliteit:
lipstick te zijn van de klassenstaat.

Maar de ogen gezouten door zweet en tranen,
maar het tergende ruien van de kalenders:
dat doen de dagen hem, wat doen de dagen?
Wat doen wij? Wij schuren de muren dun
met schampere krassen van kinderkrijt,
met een mes en een vijl van gewone wensen,
om eenmaal bewust de lamlendigheid
van het bukken, omkeren en bezwijken
aan de veiligheid van het onrecht en leed
van het arbeiderskind en de ongelijke
bevoorrechting ver om ons dood te weten.
Voorwaarts, en niet vergeten.

Wie biedt? Wat baat mij de stapelplaats
janmaats en machinegeweren? Wie biedt meer,
biedt mij een plaats zonder praatjes
van maan, mooie mogol of moloch of mammon,
een gewone plek zon, zonder gouden verleden?
Magnaat, magistraat, advocaat van de duivel,
wie biedt? En ik vraag geen afbraak.

Zij hebben octrooi op instortende huizen
en kleerscheuren, alleenvertoningsrecht
van mijn regen, op de rechte weg
de tol, om mijn geld te geven, te heffen,
het vruchtgebruik van gewassen:
koolzaad en graan en de zoete peen.

Ik moet: zoet zijn, soldaten betalen,
betaalde moed, onvergoed bloed en pijn
eisen en goedkeuren, leugens bewijzen
en leuren met jabroers en harlekijnen,
bonen van broodroof eten.

Ik moest beter weten, Marx niet lezen,
kieskeurig wezen, niet de kant kiezen
van de blauwkielen onder het kolengruis,
uit het achterhuis, de armzalige achter-
en arbeidersbuurten, neen, fijn u alure
zijn en mij spijzen met het overschone,
ten hemel wijzen en God vertonen
(dat is: op een werf van bederf werken).
En de H-bommen doen de deur dicht.
Wie biedt een simpel uitzicht,
zonder aalmoezen angst, zonder pleinen van angst?

Dit is de keuze: onheuse leuzen,
delicaat gepraat van vingertoppen
op een toetsenbord met alfabet der kaballa,
of staan en weer vallen in het wisselvallig
gevecht om brood en recht en een nieuwe wereld,
met de veeltalig-veeltalige menigten:
kinderen, huismoeders, hardknuistige kerels:
een eenstemmig veemgericht van vrede.

Kameraden, wie een eerlijk besluit
in een lied uit en bij zijn klasse staan gaat,
zal door hofmeiers, honden en verstokte kohorten
gezocht en gejaagd worden, gehaat worden
als veepest. Maar het zal lang laat worden
eer hij van zijn vermaningen aflaat.

Van oudsher zien de ogen liever dons dan bloed
dat dons groeit op de duiven van Picasso:
daar steken de scherven als messen naar,
daar steken de fosforbommen de brand in,
daar steken die naar ons spugen de draak mee,
daar steekt het verleden de loftrompetten
van dode verdrukkers.

Vleselijk is onze vrede, gewone begeerte
naar een veilige wieg met een kleine stem,
een vriendelijk woord en een snee kruimig brood:
daar knaagt de dood aan, daar slaat een gele haan
de vlam van zijn vleugels aan,
daar komt men aan met een hand als brand.

Persoonlijk willen wij een vaderland,
door de koeien betreden en gegeten,
met karen en zonnige wegen, zelfs in de regen:
dat egt men met prikkeldraad,
daar legt men vulkanen aan,
daar vecht zich een waanzin van wagenraderen
door dat zware broodgraan, dat laaien zal.

Werkelijk zijn wij met velen,
een werkelijkheid met blote handen:
daar zet men de tanden in,
daar duwt men geweren in van gewin,
daar neemt men de koperen centen uit,
daar wil men de lijnen in lezen,
hoe het zal wezen.

Het is bewezen dat hun rijk heeft uitgeluid:
wij zijn tot moed gedoemd, grauw van vertrouwen,
dat wij varen zullen, dit land bebouwen,
als vrijen in de fabrieken staan.
Daar helpt geen lievemoederen aan,
geen god in een heilig huis aan,
geen wichelroede, geen maan,
geen muizenval die op niets slaat,
geen huilen, geen politiestaat:
de toekomst ligt in de vuisten
van het proletariaat.

4.12
Constant A. Nieuwenhuys and Jan Elburg, *The Dove's View*. Woodcut and letterpress on paper, edition no.100/125, 1952. Poem by Elburg, woodcuts by Constant. Stedelijk Museum, Schiedam

the physical environment and the collective psyche, as a means of learning lessons for post-war social planning. In 1944 the US Strategic Bombing Survey was initiated in order to calculate the effects of airborne warfare against Nazi Germany, and soon to investigate the physical, social and psychological impact of the bombing of Hiroshima and Nagasaki. As Peter Galison has observed, the experts enlisted by the Survey soon began to project their findings on to the possible scenario of similar attacks on American cities.[19] One of the proposals put forward to minimize the cost to human and economic life in the event of such a scenario was that of dispersal planning – the de-centring of conurbations to provide small-scale, uncongested suburban communities. This formed part of the civil defence culture which encouraged the drive to build domestic and communal fallout shelters, to teach children the habits of 'duck and cover' in the event of nuclear blast, and to instil vigilance, if not paranoia, in the American people in the face of possible nuclear threat.

The argument for dispersal followed these lines: a congested, large-scale city was vulnerable to attack not only because of the concentration of industry, resources and people, but also because it would render the community unable to respond with retaliatory action in the chaos that followed. Smaller communities, banded by empty green space (which could act as a firebreak), were not only seen as more efficient, but disturbingly, were also more expendable. Once of the first proponents of this theory, planner Tracy Augur (who had contributed to the planning of the 'secret' Manhattan Project city at Oak Ridge, Tennessee) proposed in 1948 a circular cluster of 20 urban units, 2 by 3 miles in area, separated from each other by open country.[20] Another advocate of dispersal was Ralph E. Lapp, the atomic scientist who had been one of the first to disseminate information on the effects of radiation in the mid-1950s.[21] His influential book *Must We Hide?* (1949) proposed a number of different urban plans, including the so-called 'Donut City', a model of dispersal that imagined communities removed from the centre to a perimeter ring.[22] In a version of the dispersed city illustrated in *Life* magazine in 1950, cybernetics theorist

Norbert Wiener proposed a civil defence plan for the atomic age that separated the suburbs from the urban centre with a green belt, identified as 'lifebelts' in the event of atomic bombings (4.9).[23] These imagined cities were based on patterns that chillingly echoed the concentric rings of diagrams so frequently published in the period to measure the effects of a nuclear bomb on property and people.

An uncanny echo of this is seen in Richard Buckminster Fuller's iconic scheme to install a 'Dome over Manhattan' of 1962. He proposed changing the skyline of New York by installing a massive structure spanning the city from the Hudson to the East River. One mile high at its centre, this hemisphere was to be three times taller than the Empire State Building: 'The dome's skins, consisting of wire-reinforced, one-way-vision, shatterproof glass, mist-plated with aluminium, will have the exterior appearance of a mirrored dome.' At a distance, the structural elements would become almost invisible, little more than a 'glistening translucent form'.[24] The warm air inside the dome would provide lift, so the structure would not require a foundation: it could be tethered to the ground.

Fuller's logic was, at least initially, environmental. Life inside the dome would be a happy arcadia of outdoor restaurants and street art. The warm air that would gently lift the structure off the ground would also deliver a hospitable habit and a new sensibility. It was to be a high-tech antidote to the volatile, polluted atmosphere of the industrialized city. Writing in 1965, Fuller also hinted a darker dividend: 'the dome would provide a prime shielding against atomic radiation fall-out, reducing the radiation effects of neighbouring regions' atomic explosions to below lethal or critical impairment magnitude.' He even imagined that domes of pre-stressed and post-stressed steel and concrete could be made so strong that they could be covered with earth and become man-made, air-conditioned mountains. Although never described as such, these were surely nuclear bomb shelters on a gargantuan scale.

Although many forms of dispersal planning were not applied in actuality, some forms did leave their mark on the landscape of America. Dispersal was to have been made

possible by the network of inter-state highways derived from a model of the 1930s, but pushed through by General Eisenhower who had observed in wonder the efficiency of the German Autobahn system during the Second World War.[25] The National System of Inter-state and Defence Highways, announced by Eisenhower in 1956, was designed to facilitate the efficient movement of military and civilian personnel in the event of nuclear attack.

Within a short period following the end of the war the imagined consequences of airborne attack shifted from an idea of carpet-bombing based on wartime experience, to one that contemplated a new spectre: fallout, the radioactive dust from a nuclear explosion. Fear of fallout resulted in the widespread discussion of fallout shelters, and also in more imaginative forms – namely science fiction films where alien infestations or the spread of deadly viruses were ways of evoking the threat of radiation. This popular genre included *Them!* directed by Gordon Douglas (1954), in which giant radioactive ants emerge from the New Mexico desert following a-bomb tests, and *The Incredible Shrinking Man* directed by Jack Arnold (1957), about a man contaminated by a radioactive cloud. A sense of creeping dread was captured by those aware of the distances over which harmful fallout might spread. Public anxieties about the effects of weapons testing the early 1950s were raised when radioactive rain fell over Chicago in 1955 and, a few years later, when Strontium-90 began to be detected in foodstuffs such as wheat. Fears were hardly allayed by such popular studies as Ralph E. Lapp's *Radiation: What it is and How it Effects You*, published in 1957, or Stephen Spencer's two-part article in the *Saturday Evening Post* two years later entitled 'Fallout: The Silent Killer'.[26] In Nevil Shute's evocative novel *On the Beach* of 1957 (set in 1963), a world war conducted with atomic weapons has decimated the Western Hemisphere, leaving a community of survivors in Australia to await the inevitable drift of deadly radiation. Although scientifically implausible that radiation drift could be so deadly over such a large area, Shute's novel and the film adaptation of 1959 stated the bleakest terms that global nuclear confrontation would mean the end of the human race.

Whilst the cinema became the place to enjoy the frisson of fearful pleasure induced by sci-fi fantasy and horror, the popular press in the USA was full of practical advice on protecting oneself and family in the event of attack. Following the shock wave that had pulsed around the world after the news that the Soviets had successfully tested a nuclear weapon on August 29, 1949, the Truman Administration embarked on a programme of civil defence that included the building of fallout shelters. Planning for shelters and bomb-proof homes became a popular topic for discussion in the press, reaching a state of near ubiquity in the pages of *Life*, *Time* and magazines aimed at women and the home. The 1950s was the age of American home ownership, with near-obsessive pride in the family home as the ideological centre of American values, and the shelter was its dark flip side.[27] Public information publications such as *How to Survive an Atom Bomb* (1950) and *The Family Fallout Shelter* (1959) took a practical, hands-on approach to constructing and equipping the shelter in a manner that made these tasks seem like commonplace advice about house maintenance. As Sarah A. Lichtman has observed, the advice on fallout shelter construction was pitched to appeal to the D.I.Y. enthusiast, who could even engage the whole family in the provisioning and decorating of the shelter.[28] And, if purpose-built structures were rare,[29] then the common household cellar or basement room could be easily converted from rumpus room or den to family shelter. These publications had little if nothing to say about life after the initial bombing. Of course, the most horrific consequences of nuclear war would only begin with the bombing itself (assuming that survival was possible). The threat of radiation fallout to the survivors was just as deadly. As Kenneth D. Rose has argued, the building and equipping of shelters and other such advice was viewed by some as a part of a kind of morale-building exercise, to counter the inevitable sense of futility. In actuality, the shelter-question generated much discussion, but little action, on the part of most American people.[30]

The years 1961 to 1963 saw the discussion of fallout shelters reach its most obsessive level. Tensions rose between the USSR and the Kennedy administration, first over the defence of Berlin, as Kennedy promised retaliatory action, nuclear if necessary, should Khrushchev pursue his threat of closing Western access to Berlin. On 15 September 1961 *Life* magazine published a special issue on 'How to Survive Fallout', featuring cutaway illustrations of domestic shelters (4.13). Another issue a year later (12 January 1962) featured community shelters. By October of that year, panic reached feverish levels in the US as the Cuban Missile Crisis brought the world to the brink of nuclear confrontation. Only the Limited Nuclear Test Ban Treaty of 1963 appeared to stave off any immediate threat.

The underground shelter, whether a permanent dwelling or a temporary refuge, was the main form of Cold War 'defence' to be recast in upbeat and popular form, as Beatrix Colomina has argued.[31] Several architects and developers saw the opportunity for the commercial development of a modern shelter-home that would appeal to this nervous nation. The Hungarian émigré-architect Paul Lázsló, who had established a successful design and architecture office in California, developed a model of a domestic shelter aimed at his wealthy private clients. He also attempted to sell his concept of a nuclear city, Atomville USA, to the US Military. Lázsló's concept featured an underground community centre built around a well-appointed bomb shelter, which would function as an ordinary leisure facility, complete with swimming pool and roofed with a sweeping concrete curve (which also served as landing strip for helicopter or space vehicle; 4.14). In the event of a bomb strike, the facility would instantly seal itself from outside contamination. Although no military commission transpired, Lázsló published his ideas and executed one shelter for a private client, John Hertz, in Woodland Hills, California, in 1955 (4.15).[32]

Unsurprisingly, the shelter-home was also a feature of the 1964–5 New York World's Fair[33] (alongside the more familiar display of the positive benefits of atomic science[34]). Like Lázsló, the property developer Jay Swayze had recognized the opportunity for developing shelter-homes for the more opulent end of the market. Swayze, with the backing of General Electric, presented an exhibition on the Underground Home at the Fair. The ranch-style suburban home featured climate, atmosphere and sound control, high security and a facility to 'dial up' any time of day or night by artificial lighting. The panoramic

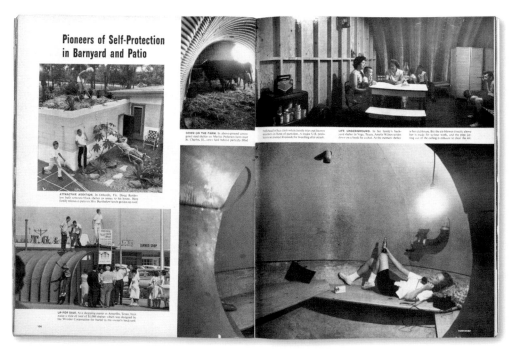

4.13
'Pioneers of Self
Protection in Barnyard
and Patio', from *Life*
magazine, 15 September
1961

4.14
Paul László, *Launch Pad
with Helicopter*, Atomville
USA (project). Photostatic
on paper, 1950. Architecture
& Design Collection,
University Art Museum,
University of California,
Santa Barbara

4.15
Paul László, *Longitudinal
section, John A. Hertz
Residence Fallout Shelter,
Woodland Hills, California*.
Ink and graphite on board,
1955. Architecture & Design
Collection, University Art
Museum, University of
California, Santa Barbara

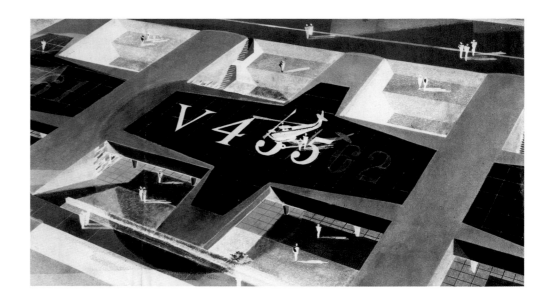

4.16
Frederick Kiesler, Endless
House. Ink and ink wash
on paper, 1951. The Museum
of Modern Art, New York

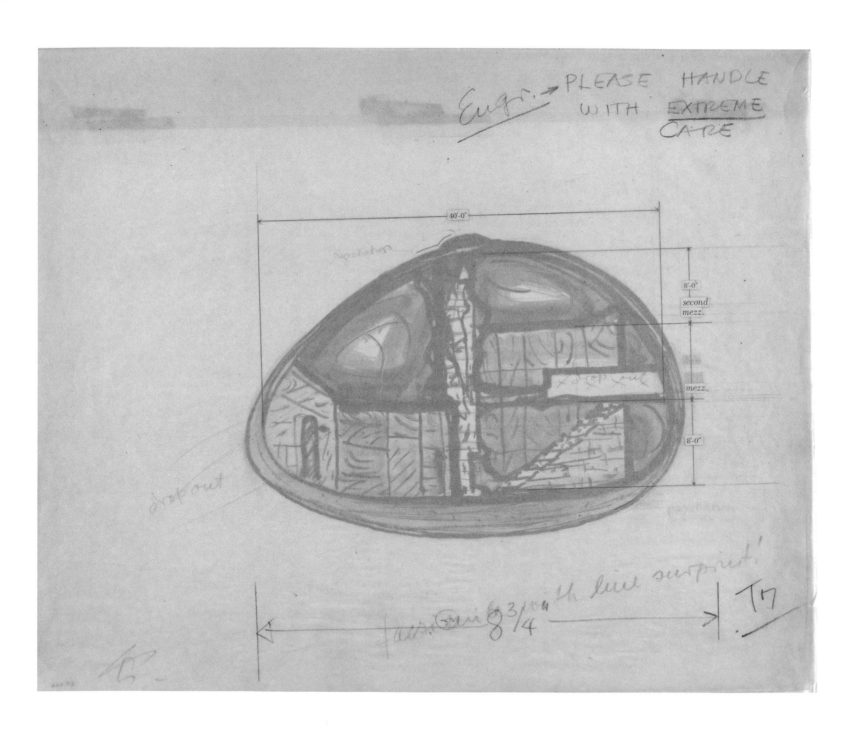

windows looked out on to breathtaking views – which could be chosen from a selection of slides including the Golden Gate Bridge or the New York skyline. Swayze's vision of underground life is euphemistically described in the accompanying brochure as 'carefree',[35] yet he drew his plans at the height of the Cuban Crisis in 1962. As he stated later, the crisis precipitated his plans for structures which 'utilised the earth as protection against radioactive fallout'.[36]

But the possibility of underground homes and communities offering real protection in the event of conflict, or of providing a desirable post-nuclear environment in which to live, was recognized by some as untenable by the early 1960s. Veteran planner Lewis Mumford offered a warning in 1961:

> [Those] in the underground city ... are the prey of compulsive fears and corrupt fantasies ... and the more they devote themselves to adapting their urban environment to this possibility, the more surely they will bring on unrestricted collective genocide ... the underground city threatens in consequence to become the ultimate burial crypt of our incinerated civilization.[37]

An alternative approach to the fear of nuclear proliferation came through protest. Rather than accept the inevitability of conflict and prepare for it, others took action to question the principles of Mutually Assured Destruction (MAD). MAD seemed an appropriate acronym to describe the defence strategy that assumes that the massive nuclear capacity possessed by both the USSR and USA would act as deterrent against either side attacking. It was the basis of the US policy of 'massive retaliation', threatened by Kennedy on several occasions in the early 1960s to counter Khrushchev's own threats over Berlin and Cuba. MAD was also the basis for numerous film and fiction scenarios where a rogue element, whether a malfunctioning computer or maverick general, could start a nuclear war. To counter the consequences of MAD, American anti-nuclear protestors formed the National Committee for a Sane Nuclear Policy (SANE) in 1958, the same year that the Campaign for Nuclear Disarmament was founded in Britain.[38] Anti-nuclear protest took

the visual form of the disturbing posters by F.H.K. Henrion and Hans Erni, and the visceral, horrific depiction of the aftermath of a nuclear strike in British film-maker Peter Watkins's BBC production *The War Game* of 1964–5, as discussed by Barry Curtis (p.122 below).

Sheltering forms

As Lewis Mumford had observed in 1961, the underground dwelling may have been predicated on a plan for survival, but ultimately could also imply burial. These contradictions invaded the designs of a generation of architects occupied with *Existenzfragen*, or questions of existence, in the 1950s. The image of the crypt, cave or bunker was often evoked in architectural schemes after the Second World War, albeit often as a kind of unconscious symbol. In their influential book *Phantastische Architektur*, first published in German in 1960, Ulrich Conrads and Hans G. Sperlich use the category of the 'Sheltering Cave' as one of their conventions of fantasy architecture.[39] In the nuclear age, the sheltering cave looked less like fantasy and more like a necessity. Inspired in some part perhaps by the ruined landscape of Europe and the brooding remnants of defensive military architecture, some architects adopted the use of brutalist materials like rough, unfinished concrete. Euclidean geometry was rejected in favour of curved, womb-like forms. Frederick Kiesler's project for his Endless House (1950–60; 4.16) explored the possibilities of a freeform, biomorphic dwelling, where spaces would flow one into another like chambers of the body. Kiesler's thinking was indebted to Surrealism and psychoanalysis, and to his personal theories of Correalism, which he saw as the investigation of the shared lifeforce between objects, people and spaces.[40] Indeed, Sigmund Freud had made clear the psychoanalytical connection between the womb, shelter and grave in his essay on *The Uncanny* in 1919:

> To some people the idea of being buried alive by mistake is the most uncanny thing of all. And yet psychoanalysis has taught us that this terrifying fantasy is only a transformation of another fantasy which had originally nothing terrifying about it at all, but was qualified by a

certain lasciviousness – the fantasy, I mean, of inter-uterine existence.[41]

The growth of a vocabulary of organic and sheltering forms in architecture and furniture was in part a development from the preponderance of biomorphic imagery in art in the 1930s and 1940s,[42] and also a consequence of experimentation with materials and new constructional and moulding techniques. These allowed architects to design large spans and curved structures inspired by nature, as well as chairs that moulded to and embraced the body, as exemplified by the work of Eero Saarinen. Saarinen's 1948 Womb Chair (3.16), as the name implies, was designed for Florence Knoll to 'curl up in'. Made from foam moulded over a fibreglass form, the chair suggests a cocoon in which the body could hide.

The idea of the cave had also taken a special significance after 1940, when the palaeolithic caves of Lascaux, with their wealth of paintings, were discovered in the Dordogne region of France.[43] Although prehistoric cave-paintings had been a source of inspiration to modern artists throughout the twentieth century (such as those at Altamira in Northern Spain), the discovery of the caves at Lascaux appeared to strike a chord within contemporary French culture. As Douglas Smith has argued, Lascaux 'comes to represent the suspended and precarious nature of human existence in the post-war years'.[44] Writings inspired by Lascaux, such as Georges Bataille's *La Peinture préhistorique: Lascaux, ou la naissance de l'art* (1955), dealt with questions of human origins – in Bataille's case the paintings indicated the ludic, creative side of human nature. For Bataille, Lascaux demonstrates 'the world of art in which communication between individual minds begins'.[45] This fascination with origins also came at a time when the ultimate destruction of humanity seemed imminent. The drawings of Lascaux and Altamira were the source for innumerable primitive references in the period, such as the celebrated *Zoomorphic Stones*, by Stanislav Libenský and Jaroslava Brychtová, a series of mould-melded glass stones with internally modelled images based upon the cave paintings, shown in the Grand Prix-winning Czechoslovak Pavilion at the Brussels Expo of 1958 (4.17).

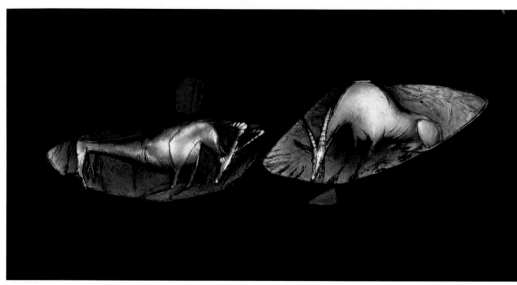

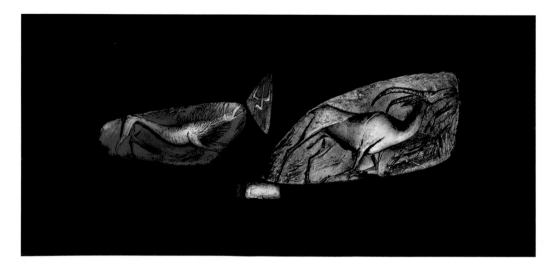

In its various architectural and philosophical forms, the cave, then, came to stand for both the cradle of humanity (the womb) and its tomb.[46] This is evident in Isamu Noguchi's landmark project (unbuilt) for a memorial to commemorate the Hiroshima dead of 1952 (4.18). Noguchi's memorial was his response to an invitation from architect Kenzo Tange and the Mayor of Hiroshima to commemorate the victims of the 1945 bombing. He was already designing bridge railings for Tange's Peace Park, which was to be the site of the memorial. The memorial needed to accommodate an underground chamber that would serve as a repository for the 200,000 names of the Hiroshima Dead. Noguchi proposed a giant granite parabolic arch straddling the chamber, its legs descending underground. The form of the granite arch was to symbolize peace, and was based on the shape of the mounded roofs of prehistoric *haniwa* houses (*haniwa* were ancient clay representations of possessions made to adorn the tombs of the wealthy). For Noguchi, the memorial was a cave, a womb, a place to commemorate the dead but also to symbolize rebirth: '[a] cave beneath the earth (to which we all return), it was to be the place of solace to the bereaved – suggestive still further of the womb of generations who would in time replace the dead'.[47] The form of the arch could also be said to suggest the shadow of a mushroom cloud.

The spiritual dimension of the womb/crypt structure is further expressed in Le Corbusier's Chapel of Notre Dame du Haut at Ronchamp in North-Eastern France (1950–55). Its interior spaces are cave-like, its outer walls buttressed and solid so that it appears as a defensive structure with few visible religious iconographic references. Given the context of the commission (the former church on the site had been destroyed by artillery fire in 1944) and Le Corbusier's own rejection of organized religion, it is unsurprising that he viewed the chapel at Ronchamp as a 'pacifist sanctuary, as well as a symbol of the peace and "silence" which he increasingly saw as the ultimate expression of human happiness'.[48] The building is intimately connected to its situation on top of a hill. Its sharply curved walls support the heavy bulk of the roof, which is steeply inclined to act as a water collector; the three towers (like the conning towers of submarines) indicate the three chapels on site.

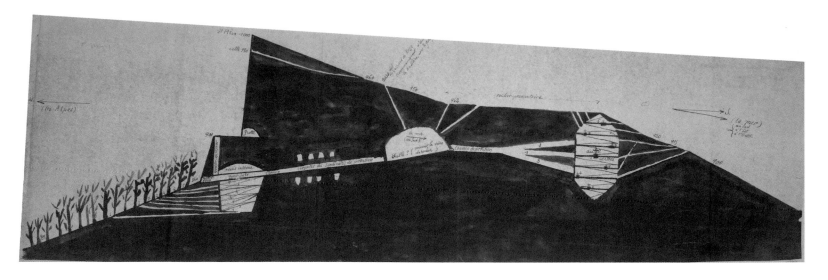

4.17
Stanislav Libenský and Jaroslava Brychtová, *Zoomorphic Stones*, eight glass objects in three-part concrete mount, made by Železnobrodské sklo Glassworks, 1957–8. Steinberg Foundation, Vaduz

4.18
Isamu Noguchi, photomontage of model for *Memorial to the Dead of Hiroshima*, 1952. The Isamu Noguchi Foundation and Museum/ARS, New York

4.19
Le Corbusier and Edouard Trouin, *Basilique La Sainte-Baume*, 1948. Heliotype, 1948. Fondation Le Corbusier, Paris

Le Corbusier created two other religious buildings, the monastery of La Tourette (1953–9), and the church of Saint-Pierre, Firminy (designed in 1960/1 but construction did not begin until the 1970s), both of which employed the same language of rough concrete and massed form. In addition to several other sketches for churches, he also embarked on plans for a magnificent underground cathedral in the mountains at La Sainte-Baume in 1947 (4.19).[49] This structure was to be carved out of the rock and only accessible by a bridge across a ravine (where hotels, a museum and a pilgrimage centre would be situated). Although the project never got off (or under) the ground, the funnelling of light and air into the underground chambers found their echo in the designs for Ronchamp, reinforcing the idea that the chapel is, in a sense, a cave or crypt.

Cave of the future

In 1956 British architects Alison and Peter Smithson, together with Eduardo Paolozzi and Nigel Henderson, created an installation for the Whitechapel 'This Is Tomorrow' exhibition entitled *Patio and Pavilion* (4.20).[50] This was a roughly built, square wooden shack with a corrugated plastic roof on which were arranged 'found' objects, including bicycle wheels, an old pistol, and a toy aircraft. A fence made from aluminium-faced plywood ran around the site; the floor of the 'patio' was sand with objects arranged in it as if from an archaeological dig; the pavilion was furnished with a rickety bench, more

found and made objects and a photo collage by Henderson. In the accompanying catalogue the creators described *Patio and Pavilion* as representing 'the fundamental necessities of the human habitat in a series of symbols':

> The first necessity is for a piece of the world: the patio. The second necessity is for an enclosed space: the pavilion. These two spaces are furnished with symbols for all human needs.

The installation was reminiscent of a bomb-site; even in 1956 the bombed-out landscapes of London were still very visible.[51] The objects in the pavilion also spoke of a recent militarized world – the old revolver, the aerial photographs used by Henderson to create his collage (*Head of a Man*, 1956, now in the Tate's collections), which in likelihood recalled his active service as a pilot during the Second World War.[52]

Patio and Pavilion demonstrated its creators' fascination with the materiality and authenticity of things, overlaid with human associations. Objects were selected for their gritty realness – 'the woodness of wood, the sandiness of sand', as Alison Smithson put it later[53] – as a means of conveying a concern with the qualities and experience of everyday life. This kind of authenticity, coming from a heightened awareness of one's surroundings, situates *Patio and Pavilion* within the broader (4.21). The artists of the Independent Group were fascinated by Dubuffet, as they were with the action painting of Jackson Pollock.

4.20
**Nigel Henderson, Eduardo
Paolozzi and Alison and
Peter Smithson**, 'Patio and
Pavilion', section of the 'This
is Tomorrow' exhibition, at
the Whitechapel Art Gallery,
London, 1956

Both embodied what Reyner Banham called the 'rough poetry' of Art Brut, a tendency that the Smithsons were attempting to translate into architecture, named by Banham in 1955 as 'New Brutalism'.[54] Dubuffet's art, they felt, was primitive, raw and authentic – deliberately anti-hierarchical and haphazard, using rough materials including sand, glue and earth on the picture surface.

In common with the paintings of Dubuffet, *Patio and Pavilion* suggested a landscape that could be either from the primordial past or the post-Holocaust future. Others connected with the exhibition noted this association some time later: Richard Hamilton described the installation as 'standing for post-atomic earth', and Reyner Banham commented that 'one could not help feeling that this particular garden shed ... had been excavated after the atomic holocaust, and discovered to be part of European tradition of site planning that went back to archaic Greece and beyond'.[55] As Ben Highmore has observed, what is surprising about the press commentary surrounding 'This is Tomorrow' is the lack of discussion of the atomic threat shadowing Britain at the time of its opening. What is clear is that the

reminders of a recent and brutal past also served as a warning for the future.[56]

In a seemingly contrasting vision of the future, the Smithsons created another imaginary dwelling in 1956, this time for the *Daily Mail* Ideal Home Exhibition held four months before 'This is Tomorrow'. *The House of the Future* was an urban dwelling made to give the impression that it was fashioned entirely from plastics[57] – a prefabricated space-age unit furnished with the latest concepts in labour-saving appliances, projected into the year 1981 (4.22, 4.23). Like *Patio and Pavilion*, *The House of the Future* was another attempt by the Smithsons to reconcile architecture to everyday life, this time to the culture of advertising, mass production and industrial design. The house was to be designed and fabricated like a product, in a manner borrowed from the car styling and production methods of Detroit.[58] This was not simply mass production, but mass production with seasonal styling changes, incorporating obsolescence into the design process by anticipating (or fuelling) the desire for regular alterations to appearance and detailing. This idea of an expendable architecture was taken

up by others in the 1960s, including the British group Archigram.

Like *Patio and Pavilion*, *The House of the Future* embodied 'the fundamental necessities for the human habitat', but this time necessities were provided for in the form of hi-tech solutions to human needs for washing, cooking, sleeping, cleaning and so on. The food contained in this home had been 'bombarded with gamma-rays, an atomic byproduct' to ensure long life, suggesting perhaps the conditions of the shelter. Even the sunlight, as the original proposal suggested, was to be artificial: the house was self-contained, the rooms arranged to face onto an inner courtyard, with no external windows (except the viewing gaps through which the public could peep inside). As Beatriz Colomina has shown in a brilliant analysis of the design, the Smithsons' house was full of defences.[59] Visitors to the house were required to walk through a draft of warm air, as if being decontaminated; the steel door through which they passed was itself a kind of electronically operated air-lock, like that required for a spacecraft or for a submarine, implying the possibility of sealing the house from the

outside world. The external threat was both invisible and deeply penetrating, not unlike the nuclear threat posed by the Cold War itself. Like a spaceship, a submarine or a bunker, this was also a home without an outside: the pod-like rooms, with curved organic walls, emphasized the fluid nature of their construction material, but were also suggestive of a cave. Despite its futuristic nature, the ultimate form of *The House of the Future* was that of a womb or underground shelter, suggesting complete isolation and protection from the exterior world, within which the rituals of everyday life could be observed with obsessive detail.[60] If *Patio and Pavilion* was a 'post-atomic bombsite' then *The House of the Future* was its bunker counterpart.[61]

Of all the architectural schemes of the period, the Smithsons' *House of the Future* captured the duality of Cold War modernity with remarkable insight: like nuclear technology with its 'peaceful' and apocalyptic faces, it represented both utopia and distopia. Unlike the rough-cast, sheltering forms shaped by Kiesler and Le Corbusier's imaginations, this was a glossy and seamless world of high-tech perfection. Exhibited almost a decade before the Underground Corporation's bourgeois 'luxury' shelter at the New York World's Fair, it anticipated the bizarre commodification of anxiety on display there: what could be more disturbing than finding in these objects of desire the chilling conditions of survival after nuclear war?

Self-consciously ambiguous, *The House of the Future* seemed to represent mankind's uncertain destiny. What might it look like from the conditions of the future it anticipated? One answer was given almost two decades later in an installation by Italian architect Gaetano Pesce at the landmark 'Italy: The New Domestic Landscape' exhibition at the Museum of Modern Art, New York, in 1972. A series of proposals for future environments, each exploring domesticity through its rituals and social patterns as well as through artefacts, were exhibited by young Italian architects. The exhibition was a vigorous attempt to reinvest design with a philosophical, political and social purpose. Pesce's installation, of a subterranean housing commune, was based on the premise that this 'house of the future' from the end of the twentieth century had been discovered by

4.23
Alison and Peter Smithson, House of the Future, entrance. Ideal Home Exhibition, London, 1956

4.24
Gaetano Pesce, 'The Period of Great Contaminations': Housing Unit for Two People, project, axonometric section. Gouache, water-colour, and graphite with scoring on paper, 1971. The Museum of Modern Art, New York

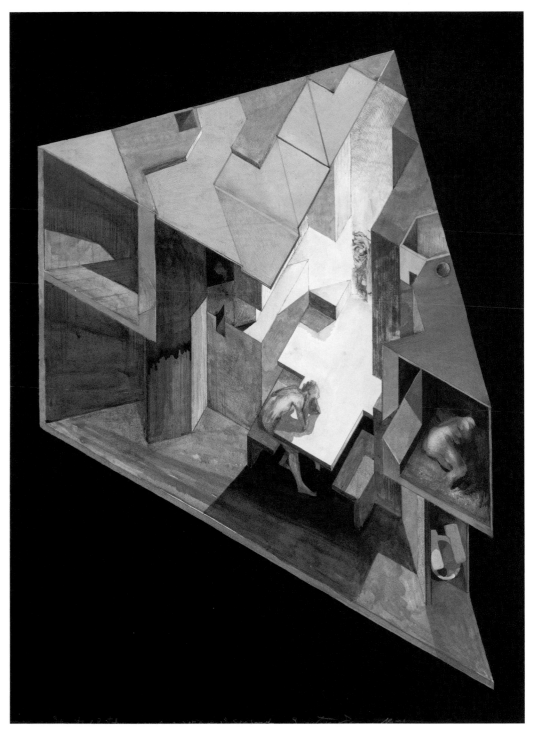

an archaeologist in the next millennium.[62] The house, part of a small underground city supposedly unearthed in the Alps, reveals evidence of a community of troglodytic dwellers, forced underground by what Pesce refers to as 'The Period of Great Contaminations' (4.24).[63] Pesce's accompanying essay, written as if it were an archaeologist's summary account of the find, decodes the architectural typology of the underground house as deriving from isolation, insecurity, a yearning for meaningful ritual, a loss of faith in technology, non-communication and minimal human contact. All that is left of this subterranean house is the stone outer shell, with only traces to show that it was once almost entirely constructed and furnished with plastic. The 'Great Contaminations' of Pesce's imagination, whether the result of nuclear explosion, ecological disaster or pestilence (or all three), had forced late-twentieth-century man into a bunker city, where the plastic house of the future had indeed become his tomb.

The Bomb in the Brain

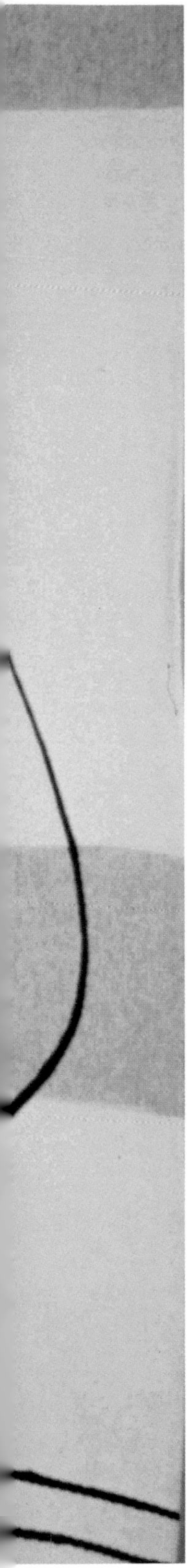

4.25
Le Corbusier, *The Hands* (*Les Mains*). Tapestry, 1951. Fondation Le Corbusier, Paris

War Games: Cold War Britain in Film and Fiction

Barry Curtis

On the second day
The radios failed; we turned the knobs;
    no answer.
On the third day a warship passed us,
    heading north,
Dead bodies piled on the deck.
On the sixth day
A plane plunged over us into the sea.
Thereafter
Nothing. The radios dumb;
And still they stand in corners of our
    kitchens,
And stand, perhaps, turned on,
    in a million rooms
All over the world. But now if they
    should speak ...
... We would not listen, we would
    not let it bring
The bad old world that swallowed
    its children quick
At one great gulp.[1]

In Britain, the gladiatorial confrontation of West and East was present in the popular imagination as remote events at frontiers and flashpoints, coinciding with a withdrawal from Empire and a sustained remoteness from Europe. In keeping with Britain's shifting national and international identity in the 1950s, the signs and scenarios of Cold War conflict were relatively subdued and repressed. Britain was imaginatively positioned somewhere in the middle of East–West competition, between aggressive austerity and assertive luxury, with fantasies of a mediating role. Anxieties of imminent conflict were omnipresent, but they were characterized by a mood of secrecy and absence. The geographer W.G. Hoskins described the landscape in the 1950s as 'England of the Nissen hut, the "pre fab" and the electric fence, of the high barbed wire around some unmentionable devilment', while overhead 'the obscene shape of the atom bomber [was] laying a trail like a filthy slug upon Constable's and Gainsborough's sky'.[2] Undisclosed locations, the spy and the traitor, were public manifestations of a momentary war perpetually deferred.

A bleak vision of a future Britain laid to waste by nuclear conflict appeared in films and comics, often depicted as a devastated landscape not too dissimilar from the Second World War bombsites that were still very much a feature of Britain in the 1950s. In the film *Seven Days to Noon* (Boulting Brothers, 1950) a scientist who shares the public school and Oxbridge backgrounds of the spies Guy Burgess and Donald Maclean and was a 'member of the British team to New Mexico in 1943' becomes convinced of the immorality of nuclear deterrence. He defects from his secluded rural laboratory and finds lodgings in London, carrying an atomic bomb in a battered Gladstone bag and threatens to detonate it unless the government agrees to disarm by noon on the following Sunday. As he waits for a decision he makes his way through an exhausted urban landscape, marked by bombsites, decayed buildings and stoical cockneys – a zone of austerity suggestive of Orwell's bleak vision of a city perpetually at war. When his threat is made public the population is evacuated in an impressively comprehensive Civil Defence operation, reminiscent of Dunkirk and D-Day for the soldiers involved. A 12-square-mile section of an ominously deserted London is explored by troops in a memorable sequence that emphasizes the surreal nature of the threat of destruction. In one particularly ominous scene the Churchillian voice of the Prime Minister, invoking Britain's lack of preparedness in 1939 and its responsibility to defend 'the Free World', is broadcast to the bomber as he mingles with members of the public among the skeletons of extinct dinosaurs in the Natural History Museum.

Rehearsals for a devastated and depopulated London pre-dated the Blitz, but they became a prominent feature of science fiction in the 1950s. First appearing in the popular *Eagle* comic in 1950, the 'chief pilot of the Interplanet Space Fleet' Dan Dare fulfils the fantasy of British ambassadorial presence as a type of a Battle of Britain pilot projected into the future to police the territorial ambitions of various alien races. In 'The Red Moon Mystery' (starting in April 1952), the London of 1999 is devastated by the effects of a mysterious wandering asteroid on the Earth's magnetic field causing earthquakes and a tidal wave in the Thames. In February 1957, Dare returns to Earth after a ten-year absence in space, to find the London of 2011 deserted and derelict after an extra-terrestrial invasion. The Mekon, Dare's alien arch-enemy, and his grim 'Treens' have taken over the Earth and are experimenting on the native population, regressing them to a Stone Age environment, where small tribes of survivors have to do battle with extinct beasts whilst other enslaved groups are set to rebuilding the pyramids.

John Wyndham's novel *The Kraken Wakes*, published in July 1953 and performed on radio shortly afterwards, continues the apocalyptic post-civilization theme of his better-known *Day of the Triffids* (1951). Mysterious creatures from space colonize the ocean depths and, although a nuclear arsenal is deployed against them, use their own inscrutable technology to melt the ice caps and reduce Britain to a landscape of fortified hilltops and localized conflicts. The narrative is remarkable for its dawning awareness of the effects of global climate change. The lone scientist who predicts the likely outcome of the cumulative disaster

is mistrusted and accused of being a spy. The novel ends with a wistful optimism that links the newly depopulated remains of Britain with the vitality of Tudor times, a suggestion that this downsizing, 'with only a fifth or an eighth of us left', might be viable as an appropriate corrective to the insane contradictions of the Cold War world and the diminished authority of Britain in the post-war era.

Wyndham demonstrates how the division of the world into two mutually suspicious armed camps obstructs the response to a global threat. The first sight of the unidentified flying objects is greeted as a hallucination and quickly becomes an official secret. The reaction of the Soviet Union is characterized as irrational and obtuse, the Americans are thoughtlessly aggressive. As Barry Commoner argued in his early formulations of the laws of ecology,[3] the wasteful technological advances of the post-war era were shrouded in secrecy and were, therefore shielded from democratic debate or monitoring. In science fictions the other side of the logic of growth and progress was countered by scenarios of entropy and regression that conformed in many ways to an emerging environmentalist awareness of the costs of pollution.[4]

H.G. Wells was an influential propagator of the notion of an Eden that could only be attained by passing through an inferno of war. This idea of Armageddon as purgation coincided with an American fascination with salvation through confrontation and violence that was played out in numerous 1950s Westerns. J.G. Ballard's *The Drowned World* (1962) describes a similar bittersweet de-evolution in which the hero/survivor greets a world systematically pruning itself whilst it moves backwards in time to fulfil what he calls a 'Triassic memory'. This theme of a salutary return to origins is cited by Kahn and Wiener in their predictive *The Year 2000* (1967),[5] where they invoke the American Walter M. Miller Jr's novel *A Canticle for Leibowitz* (1959) as a possible scenario in which all science is eliminated to prevent future holocausts.

The British Campaign for Nuclear Disarmament (CND) was formed in the aftermath of the Suez crisis and the brutal Soviet repression of the Hungarian revolt.

J.B. Priestley's novel *The Doomsday Men* (1938) had predicted the development of an atomic device in the secret desert laboratory of a mad American physicist whose fascination with the Book of Revelation leads him to plan the destruction of the Earth. It was Priestley whose article 'Britain and the Nuclear Bombs', in which he suggested that the 'spirit of Hitler' had passed into nuclear madness,[6] prepared the way for the public meeting at Conway Hall, London, on 17 February 1958 at which the CND was launched. In that year the first four-day march to the weapons research station at Aldermaston manifested a new politics of protest. The culture of the CND was created by many of the best-known emergent artists, writers, dramatists and filmmakers of the time, and was strongly identified with youth and 'anti Establishment' values, where the 'Establishment' was seen a ruling order that could be complicit, as in the case of the Cambridge spies, with subversion as well as coercion. The CND generated an iconography that configured the menace and suffering associated with nuclear war, but it also had the capacity to be what Jeff Nuttall called 'a carnival of optimism', an arena for expressive deviation.

Meanwhile, at street level, the subliminal agent who moves between East and West, resolves threats of 'nuclear blackmail' and moderates the anxiety of 'gaps' in weapons development and deployment, was the newly fascinating figure of the spy. Spies configured topical styles of existential subjectivity that were conspicuously modern and technologically enabled. James Bond, the British agent created by author Ian Fleming, who made his first appearance in print in 1952, embodied the exploratory, discriminating masculine identity that confronted and confounded charismatic evil-doers who attempted to tamper with the uneasy balance of power between East and West (4.26). The British spy is rooted in a centuries-old fascination with the manipulation of trade and empire, but after 1945, in the confrontational world of concealment, identity manipulation and accessorized masculinity, the Spy and the Playboy[7] converged in a knowledgeable manipulator of gadgets, luxury goods, travel and women. Sexual excess and deviancy were closely associated with the culture of espionage in a number of reported spy scandals, culminating in the Profumo affair and its cast of drug addicts, call girls, aristocrats, Russian spies and a Minister of Defence. The fantasy that underlay the world of Bond was the idea of Britain as an arbiter and mediator. When Bond battles to prevent the theft of the British missile in the novel *Moonraker* (1955) he is briefed by M, who conveys the Cabinet's view: 'The sooner the Moonraker could give us an independent say in world affairs, the better for us ... and quite possibly the world.'[8] M's final debriefing of Bond suggests the strong Cold War links between the lingering traces of Nazi revenge, the ever-present danger of Russian subversion and the emerging threat of 'the most deadly saboteur in the history of the world – the little man with the heavy suitcase'.[9]

Spies were loyal but not obedient, they had the unconditional backing of indulgent government agencies and were licensed to be ruthless. At one extreme spies were supernaturally powerful and charismatic, at the other, they were barely augmented civil servants. Harry Palmer, hero of *The Ipcress File*, appeared in the 1965 film of that novel as a man acutely aware of his situation, as he endures complex deceptions practised by representatives of East and West: 'What chance did I stand between the Communists on one side and the Establishment on the other, they were both outthinking me at every move'. On the film poster, Palmer/Caine pulls a gun from a crumpled trenchcoat, confronting the viewer with a stoical investigative expression. A diagonal computer tape sections off a monochrome scene representing the grim reality of the sinister partitioned East, and an unnaturally coloured image of Palmer's face suggests the psychic threat posed by new technologies of mind manipulation.

In 1969 Buckminster Fuller published a collection of his essays under the title *Utopia or Oblivion*,[10] drawing attention to a persistent paradox of the times. Everyday life was lived in an ambivalent media environment in which a future of magical empowerment was dialectically twinned with a future of potential trauma and collapse. The zombies and mutants of popular fiction were as timely as the superhero and the prosthetically enhanced citizen of tomorrow. Spiderman and The Hulk (both originally conceived in 1962) shared with Godzilla and a cast of giant insects and size- and shape-shifting humans a transformative encounter with 'radiation'. In the 1950s British writer Nigel Kneale's Professor Quatermass, in a series of televised and filmed encounters with aliens, configured a cluster of anxieties for a fascinated British public (4.27). In *The Quatermass Experiment* of 1953 an infected astronaut mutates into a monster and is eliminated on live television in Westminster Abbey. In *Quatermass and the Pit*, viewed by a third of the television audience in the winter of 1958, an alien spaceship is discovered deep underground in Knightsbridge and disinterred. Professor Quatermass's curiosity is engaged when his space exploration project is constrained by Cold War imperatives. At a time when the bomb-sites of the Blitz were being extensively

4.28
Eduardo Paolozzi, *Will man outgrow the earth?* Collage, using cover of *Time* magazine, December 1952, c.1952-3. V&A: Circ.715-1971

that focused attention on the perils of 'fallout' and the futility of assuming that 'duck and cover' responses would be adequate for survival. A 1958 Gallup Poll revealed that about 50 per cent of the British public expected less than half the population to survive a nuclear attack. F.K. Henrion's 1963 poster fuses a skull and a mushroom cloud, expressing a mood of irresistible, mythic evil (4.29). This juxtaposition was already established, as in Herbert Matter's *Atomic Head* of 1946 (illustrated on p.100). Descriptions of the first nuclear explosion at the Trinity Site, New Mexico, used apocalyptic metaphors and descriptions of the explosion as: 'a parasol', 'a gigantic mushroom' and a 'convoluted brain', already intimating a compound figuring of something protective, poisonous and internalized.

As early as 1904 Ernest Rutherford, in early experiments with the atom, suggested that the world could be vaporized as the result of a chain reaction. In 1939 The *British Journal of Discovery* was already alive to the alternative versions of the future that came to dominate public thinking in the Cold War era, suggesting that the discovery of the chain reaction in uranium could 'create a streamlined world where a pinch of salt is sufficient fuel for the Queen Mary, or shall we have a Wellsian chaos with each nation dropping bouquets of uranium bombs?'[13] The absurdity of nuclear power and the bizarre logic of deterrence inspired new forms of imaginative expression, both in the military literature concerned with 'waging peace', and the ironic response of artists and film-makers. Stanley Kubrick's *Dr Strangelove* was a 'serious' indictment that could only find expression in 'black' comic form. The idea of a 'Doomsday device' was already a staple of science fiction by 1945: a number of influential thinkers, attached to the Manhattan Project and to various 'think tanks' associated with the US military, had rehearsed the theme of 'Mutually Assured Destruction'. Herman Kahn's *On Thermonuclear War*, published in 1960, served as inspiration for Kubrick's creation of a scientist who would stop at nothing. Kahn, a RAND corporation military scientist, argued that the USA had to think 'the unthinkable' in order to face down the Soviet Union on the issue of nuclear weapons.[14] Based on military game theory and systems thinking,

reconstructed Kneale excavates a nexus of anxieties – of secret weapons, supernatural beings and the dark places of the psyche. The paradoxical linking of rocketry and burrowing into the ground that was such a feature of Civil Defence is dramatized in relation to archetypal fears of ghosts and demons.

At the 'This Is Tomorrow' exhibition, staged at the Whitechapel Gallery in 1956, artists and designers addressed the future by celebrating technology, science fiction and the new primitive forms and surfaces associated with a 'New Brutalism' in the arts with an attitudinal 'anger' that was associated by critics with 'an affirmation of life in the face of the absurd'.[11] Eduardo Paolozzi's influential collages trace connections between tribal art, prosthetics, mutations explored in Hollywood horror films and a new augmented 'nuclear' gaze made possible by aerial and micro photography, telematics, remote sensing and

'cutaway' diagrams (4.28). The mythic themes and troubled surfaces of British art testified to a perceived affinity between the complex insides of new technological devices and their potential to become disfigured archaeological remains. The new 'dead places' of the world – the Berlin Corridor, the vast concrete and earth emplacements and shelters often seen in surveillance images – were a source of anxious inspiration to artists, as shown elsewhere in this book. Richard Hamilton, considering the *Patio and Pavilion* exhibit (constructed by Paolozzi, Nigel Henderson and the Smithsons; see 4.20) at 'This Is Tomorrow', with hindsight suggests that it stood for 'post atomic earth, a dying world filled with rare fossils and touching memories'.[12]

In 1954, the 'Bravo' H-bomb test delivered five times the explosive power expected, and there were disturbing human casualties

4.29
F.H.K. Henrion, *Stop Nuclear Suicide*. Poster issued by the CND, 1963. V&A: E.3910-1983

4.30
Kenneth Adam, design for the War Room, final concept, for *Dr Strangelove Or: How I Learned To Stop Worrying and Love The Bomb*, directed by Stanley Kubrick, 1964. Felt-tip pen on card, 1962 (extended 1999). Sir Kenneth Adam, London

Kahn argued that nuclear war was both possible and winnable, but only by facing up to its calamitous consequences. The USA must be prepared to let the enemy know that it would use its weapons if necessary, whatever the cost.

In *Dr Strangelove* Ken Adam's sets contribute a link to earlier manifestations of mad and megalomaniac science, Adam admitting that he had been influenced by German Expressionism and, in particular by the film *Metropolis*. His sets for the earlier *Dr No* (1962) and for other James Bond films knowingly referenced the technological optimism that sustained fantasies of under-water cities (Buckminster Fuller patented an 'undersea island' in 1959), hollowed-out volcanoes and space stations. In *Dr Strangelove*, the baroque war-room was consistent with a real 'stealth landscape'[15] that involved hollowing out mountains for command centres, and practising 'dispersal' and concealment on a nationwide scale (4.30). Kubrick insisted that the table in the war-room should be covered in green baize (although this refinement was invisible to the monochrome photography) because he wanted the actors to feel that they were playing a game of poker for the fate of the world. Strangelove/Sellers, part of whose body is still fighting a previous war, struggles with his nuclear fallout calculator before

War Games: Cold War Britain in Film and Fiction

sketching out a hedonistic 'Playboy' underground penthouse scenario for survival.

The idea of 'survivability' was a preoccupation of Herman Kahn and other 'futurologists' whose work was constitutive of Cold War military and political theory. The ironic ending of *Dr Strangelove*, which juxtaposes a succession of nuclear blasts against a soundtrack of Vera Lynn singing 'We'll Meet Again', relates to the much-debated possibility of any post-war resumption of society. The idea of sheltering with the abundant supplies that justified free-market capitalism also suggested a mobilization of the home and domestic life in which the surrogate family space became a quasi-military 'control center'. The Berlin crisis and the erection of the Wall in 1961 saw an escalation in shelter construction. In Britain, Civil Defence pamphlets proposed more makeshift arrangements of tables, under-stairs cupboards and earth-filled bookcases.

Peter Watkins' 1965 BBC film *The War Game* used documentary techniques to explore the reality of nuclear war in a shockingly detailed and plausible scenario that it claimed as a likely event before the year 1980 (4.31). The escalation of conflict at recognizable flashpoints in Vietnam and Berlin culminates in a nuclear attack on the Soviet Union by NATO, and reprisals witnessed in one localized airburst in a small town in Kent. The shocking realism was partly effected by refusing any generic cues: there are no heroes, no authoritative institutions, no irony or black humour, just confrontations with individual witnesses and victims and a continuous relaying of disturbing information. The efficient, obedient procedures for evacuation featured in *Seven Days to Noon* are shown to be absurdly costly, emotionally unacceptable and ultimately futile. In the film, maps demonstrate that Britain has more nuclear targets than any other country in the world. After the overexposed flash of the bomb, the panic and desperate measures to cope with injuries and put out fires is accompanied by a voice-over intoning: 'This could be the way the last two minutes of peace in Britain could look'. The aftermath, for the survivors is riots, martial law, lingering trauma and death.

The BBC decided against showing the film, ostensibly on the grounds that it was too horrific for broadcast. A furious debate in the press ensued, with Watkins, having resigned his BBC job, despairing publicly at the pronouncement. Speculation was rife about government interference in the BBC's decision, although denied by both sides. However, civil servants who attended the first screening made their views clear in a report to the Cabinet Secretary, Sir Burke Trend, who recorded the opinion that:

the film has two main defects. First, it compressed into some five minutes at the beginning an exposition of how a nuclear war might begin; it omitted the whole range of Government action that would be taken to avert such a tragedy; and it did not show the American president in a very creditable role. The second main defect was that the film depicted our civil defence forces in complete disarray as a result of a nuclear explosion.[16]

The film's ironic title, *The War Game*, refers to the military, computer-enabled playing-out of scenarios of 'mutually assured destruction' and 'acceptable loss'. The possibility of taking human decision-making 'out of the loop' had led to many fictional anxieties about mad scientists, malfunctioning robots and rogue computers. Watkin's film resolutely refuses any consolations of technology, referring its audience relentlessly to the primal scenes of loss and suffering that always shadow the disturbing modernities of Cold War culture.

4.31
Still from *The War Game*, written, directed and produced by Peter Watkins, 1965

5.1
Roman Cieślewicz, poster promoting Moda Polska, a new chain of fashion shops, Poland, 1959. National Museum, Poznań

5 / Thaw Modern: Design in Eastern Europe after 1956

David Crowley

In 1950 a young Polish painter, Wojciech Fangor, produced *Postaci* (*Figures*, Muzeum Sztuki, Łódź; 5.2).[1] His socialist realist canvas is a succinct expression of the official view of consumption during the late Stalin years in Eastern Europe. Three figures stand in front of the kind of monumental crescent then being planned for the Polish capital. Two of the figures are dressed in the stereotypical uniform of the worker, their productivity symbolized in the firm grasp of a pickaxe or, perhaps, a shovel. The third figure, heavily made up and clothed in a fashionably cut dress printed with the words 'Coca-Cola' and 'Wall Street', clutches onto her purse, a sign of selfish desires. The steady gaze of labour casts an accusation at this extravagant creature who hides her intentions behind dark sunglasses. As Fangor's canvas made visible, a clear hierarchy of values was being introduced to Eastern European societies – largely unwilling allies of Stalin's Soviet Union – in the late 1940s. Production was superior to consumption and public life was to prevail over private interests. When the small pleasures associated with leisure and the everyday luxuries of the consumer society were acknowledged, it was usually in terms of deferral. Endure hardship and work hard today, was the broad message, because the nirvana of Communism will follow tomorrow.

Ten years later, official attitudes to consumerism could hardly appear more different, particularly in Moscow's satellites in Central Europe. Fashion had been reconsidered, becoming a 'legitimate' interest in the late 1950s with new fashion stores such as Moda Polska, a ready-to-wear chain in Poland (5.1), and Sybille in East Berlin being established, and catwalk shows from Paris being exported to Moscow. Glass-walled supermarkets, neon advertising and other spectacular symbols of capitalism began to be imported into the streets of Eastern Bloc cities. Forms of culture such as pop and jazz music, which had only recently been interpreted as signs of vulgar Americanism, were sponsored by the State in the form of teen movies and, later in the 1960s, pop singles and long-playing records (5.4).[2] Furthermore, Socialist Realism – the official artistic creed that determined how the artist had painted *Postaci* – had been overturned in Poland and Fangor had become a hero in the controversial field of abstract art.[3] He was also the enthusiastic designer of a poster for Georges-Henri Clouzot's 1956 film celebrating the work of Picasso, the subject of a major exhibition in Moscow in the same year (5.3).[4] Picasso's instinctive drawing style and visual wit provided a new expressive vocabulary not only for a young generation of decorative artists and designers in the Bloc, but also for consumers.[5] Brightly printed textiles with abstract patterns, expressive handmade ceramics and enamel-wares acquired the nickname *pikasy* in Poland: in ordinary homes they functioned as inexpensive markers of a popular and pent-up desire for modernity.[6] Even advertising – conventionally a function of capitalism – was to be encouraged if it could be put to socialist ends. The first International Congress of Advertising Specialists was held in Prague in December 1957 and by the early 1960s most Eastern Bloc states, including the Soviet Union, had built advertising infrastructures.[7] The new orientation to the consumer was accompanied by periodic attempts to reform the command economy in different Eastern Bloc states, usually by introducing greater flexibility and pluralism into their planning mechanisms.[8]

Little more than a decade old, the Bloc was, it seems, already being remade in the image of the consumer society. Whilst this process was uneven and some societies

'advanced' further along this path than others, the general orientation towards consumerism was clear. But how can this apparent *volte face* be explained?

Goulash socialism

The immediate explanation is that Eastern European regimes, struggling to maintain power during the turbulence of the 'Thaw' years following Stalin's death, turned to the products of modern consumerism to pacify angry societies.[9] Revelations made about the brutality and irrationality of Stalin's rule – made by Nikita Khrushchev in his famous 'Secret Speech' given to the Twentieth Congress of the Communist Party of the Soviet Union in February 1956 and then leaked to the rest of the world – were a catalyst for considerable anger in the Bloc.[10] In the months that followed, ruling parties and their allies across Eastern Europe struggled to maintain power in the face of sharp criticism from students, intellectuals and workers, many of whom had once been their enthusiastic supporters. To sustain their claims of legitimacy, communist regimes purged their ranks and promised reform. Some states relaxed censorship and tolerated, initially at least, a degree of free speech. In Poland and Hungary – countries where criticisms were vented most forcefully – events seemed to spin out of control during the course of 1956. Anti-Stalinist sentiment provoked unrest on the streets of Poland, particularly in the city of Poznań. The threat of revolt was only staved off by promises made by new leaders – installed despite the machinations of the Kremlin – to pursue a 'national path' to Communism.

In Hungary, attempts to throw off Moscow's influence, led by protestors demanding freedom of speech and the evacuation of Soviet troops from the country, escalated into mass rallies climaxing in the demolition of Stalin's monument in the city (5.5).[11] With the public engaging the Secret Police in pitched battles, the authorities panicked and installed Imre Nagy, a popular and independent-minded communist, as prime minister. The insurgents were not pacified by this gesture and, fearful of losing its grip on the country, Moscow sent in the tanks in October and again, in greater numbers, in November (following a temporary withdrawal that the fighters interpreted as a fantastic victory). The Hungarian revolution was a short-lived affair and the *rappel à l'ordre* which followed was brutal: Nagy and other leaders who had appealed for Western support against the Soviet forces were executed in 1958; 20,000 Hungarians were imprisoned and thousands more sent to Soviet labour camps; and almost 200,000 escaped across the border to Austria.[12]

After the violence in Hungary, super-markets, abstract art, hitherto unavailable consumer goods and fashionable clothes in the Eastern Bloc seem like inducements offered in exchange for political acquiescence. Khrushchev himself dubbed consumerism in Hungary 'Goulash Communism', such was the spread of relative affluence there after the trauma of the suppression of the Revolu-tion.[13] One commentator, noting the extraordi-nary rise in standards of living in the country between 1956 and 1960, concluded that consumerism was the principal means by which the State built its bridges with the people.[14]

Hungary was not, however, alone in this. The new generation of post-Stalinist leaders made extraordinary promises on future material progress. These pledges were in part motivated by a Cold War desire to outdo the West. For instance, during the famous 'Kitchen Debate' between Khrushchev and American Vice-President Richard Nixon at the American National Exhibition, a vivid

demonstration of Western affluence in Moscow in 1959 discussed by Susan E. Reid in this volume (pp.154–61), the Kremlin leader used the event to trumpet Soviet progress in the sphere of consumerism. He boldly claimed that the minor miracles of washing machines and refrigerators on display were nothing new: 'You think the Russian people will be dumbfounded to see these things', barked the Soviet premier, 'but the fact is that newly built Russian houses have all this equipment right now'.[15] And whilst Khrushchev admitted that America was more advanced in many ways, he stressed that this was only a temporary state of affairs. At the Twentieth Congress of the CPSU three years earlier, Khrushchev had announced:

> In setting ourselves the task of over-taking and surpassing the capitalist countries in per capita output, we are setting ourselves the task of overtaking and surpassing the richest capitalist countries in the matter of per capita consumption, of achieving a complete abundance in our country of every type of consumers' goods.[16]

High living standards were now set at the heart of the vision of the communist future.[17] Progress was increasingly measured in material terms (alongside other indices of achievement such as levels of higher education). Eastern Bloc planners constantly sought to establish how far socialist states were behind their Western equivalents and, crucially, when they might catch up and overtake them (in the Soviet case 1980 was the key date; the East German authorities were more ambitious, imagining in 1958 that they would overtake their neighbour within six years[18]). That the peoples living in what was invariably claimed to be the most enlight-ened social system were entitled to modern consumer goods and single-family apartments was now indisputable. The question was rather about how best to organize and distribute the goods? And what form should they take?

The approach to these questions was not consistent, either across the Bloc or even within regimes (and historians are only beginning to untangle the different profes-sional and sometimes sectarian interests

which constituted 'authority' behind the uniform face presented by the one-party state[19]). Heady promises of bounty were accompanied by prescriptions about the 'correct', rational attitudes to consumption (and the State's primary mechanism for controlling consumption – prices and wages – was managed erratically: goods which were once categorized as luxuries would suddenly be reclassed as staple goods[20]). For idealists living in the Bloc – amongst them designers and architects – consumer goods raised the spectre of a privatized society in which individuals would be more motivated by selfish interests than the collective project of building Communism. Good design was to serve the collective interests of society rather than the whims of the individual.[21] Thus modern design was given a key role in shaping cultivated, self-possessed individuals capable of resisting hollow desires. The ideal purpose of socialist advertising, for instance, was not to create objects of consumer desire, but rather to 'treat human needs as a social and developing phenomenon, and direct the interest of consumers towards those goods which best satisfy cultural needs'.[22] Far from promoting the appetite to consume, 'contem-porary style' products – fashioned from industrial materials, with light and simple constructional forms and a tasteful asceticism – were to mould the taste and even the behaviour of their users. The former editor of the leading design magazine in the Soviet Union, *Dekorativnoe Iskusstvo SSSR* (*Decorative Arts in the USSR*), perhaps only exaggerated slightly when he described Thaw modernism as 'thoroughly authoritarian'.[23]

Efficiency, economy and speed

The attack on Stalinist aesthetics began more than twelve months before the momentous year of 1956. At the Soviet All-Union Confer-ence for Builders and Architects held in the Kremlin in December 1954, Khrushchev – then first Secretary of the Communist Party of Soviet Union – assailed Socialist Realism, the overblown aesthetic regime associated with the Stalin era. Well briefed by a lobby of Soviet architects, the Kremlin leader accused the architectural elite, by name, of acting in narrow self-interest, producing 'monuments to themselves'.[24] Monumental effects, expensive materials and excessive

ornament wasted precious resources. In emphasizing speed, efficiency and economy, Khrushchev introduced a new vocabulary into Soviet architectural discourse:

> Architects, like all builders, must make a sharp turn towards problems of construction economy... An architect, if he is to keep abreast of life, must know and be able to use not only architectural forms, ornaments, decorative elements; he must know the new progressive materials, reinforced concrete sections and parts and, most of all, must have an excellent understanding of construc-tion economy.[25]

In asserting the innate logic of industrial building methods, Khrushchev cast Socialist Realism – the dominant aesthetic of the Stalin years – as irrational. In this way, first architec-ture and then design were seized as symbolic fields in which the post-Stalinists could espouse their new-found commitment to a technocratic concept of progress.[26]

Although Khrushchev set new terms for architectural practice across the board, his attention was focused on housing. This sector lay at the heart of attempts to garner support for a renewed vision of socialism.[27] In July 1957 he set in motion an enormous building programme (which followed sen-sational promises made at the Twentieth Communist Party Congress in 1956 that each Soviet family would be housed in its own apartment). Housing conditions in the Soviet Union were at that time appalling: during the campaigns to collectivize agricul-ture and to industrialize the Soviet Union in the 1930s, countless thousands of peasants had been driven into towns and cities ill-prepared to house them; wartime devastation left numerous cities like Minsk and Kiev extensively damaged and innumerable people homeless. To meet the housing needs of even a small proportion of the poorly housed and homeless population, it was imperative to build quickly and cheaply. As a consequence, Soviet authorities turned to standardization and the prefabrication of building elements (5.6). The result was the construction of a new domestic landscape of squat five-storey apartment buildings in the 1950s known as *khrushchevki* after their patron in the

Kremlin and, in the 1960s, high-rise tower-blocks (so called *novostroiki* in Russian).

Khrushchev's directions for architects echoed throughout the Bloc. Most accepted the new line with little or no resistance. Unlike the Soviet Union, where Socialist Realism had been deeply embedded into the architectural and political culture since the early 1930s, in the people's republics the aesthetic had relatively shallow footings and was enthusiastically abandoned. In countries such as Czechoslovakia with a strong pre-war modernist practices, it was easy to present the 1948–55 period as an aberration in the inevitable trajectory of modernism.[28]

The industrialization of housing production represented a shift in the conception of the role of architect. Increasingly, architects – as technocrats – were required not to produce specific works of architecture but building 'types'. Housing design was effectively removed from the sphere of art to that of engineering.[29] Increasingly, it was practised within large building trusts (*kombinats*, as they were known in Poland and the German Democratic Republic) centred on panel construction factories. Modern architecture was, it was imagined, to be constructed with elements that could be manufactured off-site, many from reinforced concrete.

Prefabrication was increasingly applied not only to constructional elements of the building, but also to parts of the interior. Narrow design specifications were drawn up for windows, standard kitchen and bathroom fittings to be used in all new homes. Such apartments were to be filled with similarly standardized furnishings. Furniture designers were set the task of conceiving modular furniture systems, stripped of the mouldings and historicist embellishment, the preferred taste of the Stalin years. The Montagemöbel DW system of space-saving shelving and cupboards developed in the German Democratic Republic for apartments in the new *Plattenbauten* (high rises) is a typical example. First designed by Franz Erlich in the late 1950s, it was manufactured in six variations of colour, size and material.[30] Polish furniture factories produced an almost identical system – scaled to fit the standard dimensions of the apartment – which could incorporate desktops and foldaway beds into its framework.[31] Televisions and radios were in turn designed to fit the system's proportions. One critical commentator described the penetration of functionalism of this kind into the home as 'tasteful monotony ... only one degree better than the tasteless monotony of the past'.[32] To enter into a standard apartment furnished with standard furniture systems in standard colours and finishes was to experience the placelessness for which the Eastern Bloc latterly became notorious. Dissident playwright and future post-communist leader of Czechoslovakia, Václav Havel, described it thus:

5.6
Construction of residential quarter. Pencil, watercolour and ink on paper, 1953–5. This experimental scheme was constructed on Kousinena Street, Moscow, in 1957–9 to a design by Mikhail Posokhin, Ashot Mndoiants (architects), V. Lagutenko (engineer), A. Bartashevich (chief constructor) and S. Shkol'nikov (chief engineer). Schusev State Museum of Architecture (MUAR), Moscow

5.7
Aleksandr Vlasov,
perspective drawing entered
into the first round of the
competition to design
the Palace of the Soviets,
Moscow. Pencil, ink,
gouache and bronze powder
on paper, 1958. Schusev
State Museum of
Architecture (MUAR),
Moscow

A centralized furniture designer may
not be the most typical representative
of the totalitarian system, but as one
who unconsciously realizes its nihilizing
intentions, he may have more impact
than five government ministers together.
Millions of people have no choice but
to spend their lives surrounded by
his furniture.[33]

Experimental design

Whilst modern architecture and design in
Eastern Europe was later to attract – justly –
a good deal of criticism for its uniformity, the
industrialization of architecture was viewed
at first, by State, designers and the people,
with genuine optimism. The idea that the first
schemes were 'experimental' and, as such,
an anticipation of a new and better world,
was central to their appeal. Entire quarters like

Novye Cheremushki and Severnoe Chertanovo
in Moscow and Malaia Okhta in Leningrad
were, for instance, designated as 'experimental
districts'; central European cities also acquired
new 'experimental' housing schemes such
as Óbuda Housing Estate in Budapest (built to
test standard designs for one million apartments
which the regime had promised after the
Revolution had been crushed [34]); whilst the work
of Soviet fashion institutes divided between
models for the clothing industry and 'experimental' designs which encompassed what
in the West would be called 'haute couture'.

In the context of the ideological valoriza-
tion of science and technology (following
the July 1956 declaration of the 'scientific-
technological revolution' by the Central
Committee in the Soviet Union[35]), those
architects and designers who characterized
their schemes as 'experimental' were able

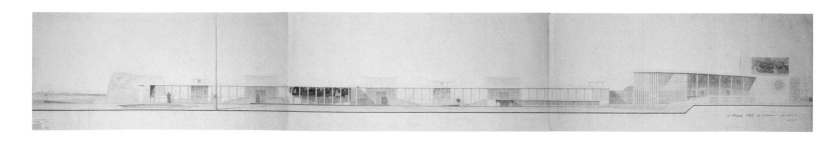

to draw on resources and expertise otherwise unavailable. They were supported by a considerable wave of new universities and research institutes, particularly in the Soviet Union. Western products, technologies and materials were no longer characterized as the efflorescence of a treacherous world, but a store of lessons which could be absorbed and applied to socialist conditions. This was not new: the rapid pace of Soviet industrialization before the Second World War had been achieved by contracting some of flagships of capitalism in the West including, most famously, the Ford Motor Company. But technology transfers from the West had been prohibited during the early years of the Cold War, with embargoes on both sides.[36] When East–West relations improved in the late 1950s, the Soviet Union put considerable diplomatic effort into securing protocols to gain access to those forms of technology it most lacked (alongside cultural exchanges from the West including reciprocal tours of the Philadelphia Symphony Orchestra and the Bolshoi Ballet, as well as the American National Exhibition and its Soviet equivalent in the Brooklyn Museum in 1959[37]). Sailing under the flag of 'peaceful coexistence', Khrushchev embarked on a series of missions to Western countries, including the USA, France and Austria, in 1959-60.[38] Soviet attention was focused on new industries such as chemicals, atomic energy and computing, as well as the manufacture of consumer goods.[39] American kitchens were, for instance, purchased and taken back to the Soviet Union for forensic examination.[40]

The term 'experimental' also represented a new kind of contract with the State on the part of architects. In taking on the role of researchers, they agreed to limit their sphere of interest to technical matters. The logic of design was now to be found within practice. A new architecture and design magazine in Poland, *Projekt* (*Design*), for instance, described itself as a 'militant publication for the advancement of art and technics'. The first editorial opened with a declaration: 'Theorizing will be avoided as far as possible, making way for practical demonstration ...'.[41] (Theory was here a code for Socialist Realism). Freed from the shackles of dogma, architects and designers came to see themselves as expert manipulators of form, materials and, above all, technology; in other words, as technocrats.

Despite the utilitarian rhetoric of standardization, economy and experimentation, a new set of architectural visions appeared in the Eastern Bloc during the Thaw which represented the genuinely creative face of experimental design. Some were polemical critiques aimed at the discredited aesthetics of the Stalin era: the Palace of Soviets project, a competition which had produced one of the icons of Stalinism, Boris Iofan's tiered Moscow tower capped with a monumental figure of Lenin, was revived in 1957-9. Never built, two rounds of competition nevertheless provided architects with an opportunity to assert new architectural and political values. Aleksandr Vlasov's 1957 design is a case in point (5.7): three oval-shaped halls were to be contained with a single glass-walled rectangular box. Horizontality and openness were claimed as new architectural values drawn – logically, according to the new modernist credo – from the essential qualities of building materials (steel and glass) and for a new Khrushchevist rhetoric of transparency. The project floundered over debates about the planned site on the periphery of the capital, with some critics arguing that a major public building required a prestigious location.[42]

Other landmark buildings were realized, albeit at considerable expense. The 'experimental district' of Cheremushki in Moscow, for instance, acquired a new facility, the Pioneer Palace (1959-62; 5.8).[43] Built in the shadow of Moscow University, one of the city's new high-rise blocks with a characteristic 'wedding cake' profile built to glorify Stalin, this cultural and educational centre for the Communist Youth Organization represented the new course in architecture. Low and irregular, with an organic plan that accommodated the topography and vegetation of its picturesque park setting, the building's many functions were articulated as distinct architectural components. A central axis was formed by a sequence of spaces connected by open internal bridges, and included a planetarium, a testimony to the importance of space in the age of the Sputnik, and a double-height winter garden contained within a glass-walled box. The young pioneers entered through the main entrance under a dynamic mosaic panel representing the world of the *Young Leninists* under a floating canopy supported by trim white piloti (5.9). In characteristic fashion, the building was presented to the Soviet public as a prototype for others that would be rolled out across the country. Within these democratic palaces, the minds and bodies of the country's youth (the people of the future) would be prepared for Communism (mankind's destiny).

Not all 'experimental' buildings of the Thaw period could declare their socialist credentials in this way. Supersam, for instance, a Warsaw supermarket which opened in 1962, was a striking architectural design based on ostentatious structural forms including a cantilevered concrete canopy over the entrance, aluminium panel walls and the funicular roof system of tensile cables and compressive arches (conceived by brilliant architectural engineer Wacław Zalewski; 5.10).[44] Following the Thaw blueprint, this landmark building was a dramatic statement of faith on the part of architects and the authorities in a technologically determined conception of modernity.

5.8
Early competition drawing
of the Pioneer Palace
on Lenin Hills, Moscow,
designed by Vladimir
Kubasov, Felix Novikov,
B. Palui, Igor Pokrovskii,
M. Khazhakian and I. Ionov
(engineer). Pencil, ink,
gouache and watercolour on
paper, 1958. Built 1959–62.
Schusev State Museum
of Architecture (MUAR),
Moscow

5.10
**Jerzy Hryniewiecki, Maciej
Krasiński and Ewa Krasińska**
with structural engineer
Wacław Zalewski, Supersam
supermarket, 1959–62,
Warsaw

5.9
Pioneers parading at the
official opening of the
Pioneer Palace on Lenin
Hills, Moscow, 1 June 1962

5.13
Assembly of Trabant 500 in Sackenring factory, Zwickau, East Germany, 1958. The car had a Duroplast body

5.14
Walter Ende, P70 coupé, Duroplast (plastic) body. Manufactured by VEB Automobilwerk AWZ, Zwickau, East Germany, 1954. Die Neue Sammlung, Munich

Thaw Modern: Design in Eastern Europe after 1956

in the first half of the 1950s, such 'functionalist' attitudes had been vilified as 'formalism' (see p.44). Emphasizing rationality and use, modern design in the GDR represented a high point in modernist asceticism. In this regard, modernist designers could characterize their disdain for ornament in politically correct terms:

> in the USA ... large amounts of plastics are produced. But they are made in the main into worthless, cheap and shockingly kitschy mass wares, into Woolworth products. Owing to their mania for ornamentation, these tend to be rendered quickly obsolete by something new and more fashionable.

Efficient, inexpensive and rational design of plastic goods had, by contrast, the potential to be 'useful and profitable'.[52]

Modernist designers in the GDR sometimes drew a harder line on questions of taste than prominent figures in government. This was apparent when East German leader Ulbricht turned on industrial design during an official tour of the Fifth German Art Exhibition, held in Dresden in 1962.[53] The exhibition had been mounted to broadcast the achievements of the Bitterfelder Weg (Bitterfeld Path), a cultural campaign launched in April 1959. Under its lead, writers, artists and photographers had been encouraged to go into factories to learn about industrial production at first hand. These encounters would, it was claimed, put the intelligentsia in contact with the working classes as well as overcome the separation of art and life.[54]

Reviewing the Bitterfeld achievements in Dresden, Ulbricht paused before the monochrome ceramic coffee pots and cups designed by Hedwig Bollhagen to bemoan their cylindrical forms and plain appearance (5.12). Scorn turned into a sustained criticism in October, when the Kulturkommission des ZK der SED (Cultural Commission of the Central Committee of the SED) met in the city. Speakers on the podium attacked industrial designers such as Bollhagen and Horst Michel of the Instituts für Innengestaltung (Institute of Interior Design) in Weimar for their formalist and elitist attitudes which ignored the tastes and demands of people and society.

Ulbricht took the stage, accusing designers of uncritically adopting Western formalist aesthetics in their desire to escape Stalinist historicism. What was required were not the spare cylindrical forms of Bollhagen's vessels, but bright colours and vivid forms to represent the optimism of socialism. Such designs were to resonate with popular desire, particularly in the unsettling months following the erection of the Berlin Wall. The ripple effects of this hardening of the official line were felt in the careers of individuals: Walter Heisig, director of the Institut für Angewandte Kunst (Applied Arts Institute) was replaced by Martin Kelm, a bureaucrat who defined industrial design first and foremost in narrow ideological terms and steered the Institute away from the quicksand of aesthetics.

Echoes of the Stalin years were unmistakable in this chain of events and, in fact, Ulbricht seemed to have dusted down speeches from the early 1950s when he attacked Bollhagen's designs. But the world had changed: 1962 was not 1952. Official censure was met with a confident defence of modernist design which was published in *Neues Deutschland* under the title 'Vases, tubes and ideology'. Gisela May, a singer and actress in Bertolt Brecht's famous Berliner Ensemble and a recipient of the Nationalpreis der Deutschen Demokratischen Republik (National Prize of the GDR), defended the designs: 'Harmless white vases were destroyed with an ideological hammer'. She argued for the freedom to exercise taste: 'We all love socialism. Our power, talent and everything we have learned comes from it. But let us have grey colours and white vases and ascetic chairs as well.'[55]

Bearing in mind this debate, which pitched high-minded modernists against populist politicians, it is appropriate that the emblem of East German design was not, however, the ascetic domestic 'tools' desired by the descendents of the Bauhaus, but the 'Trabant' (5.13). This car was supplied with a monocoque body fabricated from Duroplast, a composite composed of phenolic resin reinforced with Soviet cotton fibres (akin to Bakelite). First appearing in 1955 as the IFA F8 model, the car was claimed to be lighter, quieter and weatherproof and, as such, a superior object. In 1957, as production was extended, it was named the 'Trabant' (Satel-

lite) in homage to the launch of the Sputnik by the Soviet Union. Whilst this gesture was intended to assert its socialist modernity, the fact that early versions of the plastic car appeared in three models, including a coupé, suggests, as Colin Chant has noted, a market-minded sensibility (5.14).[56] Despite improvement in the design and the efficiency of the car's two-stroke engine and detailing, the automobile nevertheless became outdated, with the East German car industry unable to keep up with developments in the West (partly because of limits set by the Soviet Union through COMECON agreements). What had once been a symbol of East German 'competence, pride and progressivism' steadily became a notorious demonstration of the shortcomings of the SED's industrial policies.[57] It was also a hollow symbol of progress: it represented East German attempts to compete with the Federal Republic, but also the 'need to keep a dissatisfied population in check'.[58] Yet the East German regime – as the imposition of the Berlin Wall in 1961 made plain – was ultimately suspicious of the desire for mobility represented by the high demand for this car.

Designer bureaucrats

Sustaining innovation – as the case of the Trabant made increasingly clear – was an enduring problem in the design cultures of the Eastern Bloc. In the capitalist West the profession of the consultant designer secured a prominent place in the business in the course of the 1950s. Such celebrated figures as Raymond Loewy, Harley Earl and George Nelson provided American manufacturers with new and changing designs for their products. Fashion – generated in a cycle of desire and disavowal – was integrated into capitalist industry (with manufacturers increasingly seeking out flexible systems of production to accommodate change and variety). Obsolescence was promoted by American economists, designers and manufacturers of commodities such as automobiles as the solution to the 'problem' of 'underconsumption', and to stave off recession. Nelson, the designer responsible for the interiors of the pavilions at the American National Exhibition in Moscow, wrote an article in 1956 in which he claimed that obsolescence was not only the 'American way of design', but also the future: 'As other societies reach a comparable level [of consuming], similar attitudes will emerge'.[59]

During the Thaw years, Soviet leaders promised to overtake the USA precisely in the sphere of everyday consumption. But in the command economy – a managed system of production and distribution which sought to escape the volatile cycles associated with the capitalist marketplace – the questions of how to shape the modern products of industry and, ultimately, how to innovate, were difficult ones to answer. Specialist institutes were key instruments in the production of new designs (and in managing the thorny problem of quality and the growing issue of customer dissatisfaction).[60] Some were established in the immediate post-war period, whilst others were inventions of the Thaw: but all were given heightened importance in the economic reforms of the late 1950s and 1960s. The Instytut Wzornictwo Przemysłowe (Institute of Industrial Design) operated in Poland from 1950 (5.15), Iparművészeti Tanács (Council of Industrial Arts) in Hungary in 1954, and VNIITE, the All-Union Scientific Research Institute of Industrial Design (Vsesoiuznyi nauchno-issledovatel'skii institut tekhnicheskoi estetiki), was established in Moscow in 1962 under the auspices of the of the State Committee of Science and Engineering of the Council of Ministers of the USSR (Gosudarsstvennyi Komitet po nauke i tekhniki Soveta Ministrov SSSR).[61] Local branches were established throughout the Republics, often connected to local specialist industries (such as electronics in Latvia, where the Soviet authorities had nationalized the pre-war Vilnius Electrotechnical Works). Given the favoured status of a 'grade 1' institute which amounted to freedom to operate outside the requirements of the central plan, VNIITE was an instrument that accentuated the power of the centre in the Soviet Union. Alongside their research interests in ergonomics, materials and other forms of scientism, the primary function of such state bodies was to supply the nationalized industries with new prototypes for manufacture. As a rational mechanism for innovation, they were to generate new forms of socialist modernity.

Despite their bureaucratic origins, official design institutes commissioned original and

sometimes vivid designs. In 1956 Lubomir Tomaszewski, a sculptor employed by the Institute of Industrial Design in Warsaw, was commissioned to investigate the ideal ergonomic forms for tea and coffee sets, a typical brief. He set tight technical criteria for the design and manufacture of these products, but the resulting designs for the *Ina* (1961) and *Dorota* (1962) service were strikingly beautiful (5.16). Combining shell and tear-like forms, his organic cups and pots, in a monochrome glaze, achieved the spare plasticity which many leading designers on both sides of the East–West divide sought in the late 1950s. Tomaszewski's designs were widely reproduced in the popular press, but the designer was keen to assert the utility of his seductive design. Like Herbert Read, whose writings on aesthetics were widely translated in the Eastern Bloc after the Thaw, Tomaszewski drew a close connection between utility and beauty: 'If an object is made of appropriate materials to an appropriate design and perfectly fills its function, then we need not worry any more about its aesthetic value.'[62] In the Thaw context, Tomaszewski's abstract aesthetics were also a rebuttal of the taste for pseudo-luxury and pseudo-vernacularism characteristic of the Stalin years. Eugen Jindra's colourful music centre-lamp unit designed as part of suit for public music room ('*společesnská hudební interiérová sestava*'), exhibited at the Twelfth Milan

Triennale, was an extravagant experimental design produced as a prototype by the state furniture factory in Czechoslovakia (5.17).[63]

Raymond Hutchings – in a detailed commentary on Soviet industrial design written in 1968 – saw VNIITE as a bridgehead to Western fashions and preoccupations.[64] The foreign contacts of VNIITE and the other design institutes in the Bloc were rarely with manufacturers, but rather with a parallel rank of design educators and technocrats operating in the West.[65] It was the moderate aestheticism of Scandinavian design and, in the course of the 1960s, 'scientific operationalism' being promoted by the Hochschule für Gestaltung in Ulm (see p.91) which attracted the attention of Eastern Bloc modernists (and design theorist Tomás Maldonado visited Poland in 1963 to give lectures on his work at the Ulm school[66]). East and Western European design theorists – across the Cold War divide – shared a common disdain for the emotive effects of commercialism. Both saw the architect and the designer as members of kind of protective force, shielding mankind from the kitsch products of both consumer capitalism and authoritarianism by his deployment of rationality. In the Manichean world of the design expert, products could be 'good' (modest, functional, transparent, rational and enduring) or 'bad' (gauche, ambiguous, emotional and ephemeral). This viewpoint was ultimately conservative, lacking

5.16
Lubomir Tomaszewski, Ina coffee service. Porcelain, 1961. Manufactured by Ćmielów Porcelain manufacturer, 1964. National Museum, Warsaw

5.17
Eugen Jindra, table with music system and light. Wood, metal and upholstery, 1962. Museum of Decorative Arts, Prague

confidence in the individual's ability to form his or her own judgments about the world.

What is perhaps more surprising is the way in which Khrushchev's call to learn from the West also licensed an interest in Paris fashions. Although there had been some limited support for the idea of fashion in some corners of the Bloc (notably Czechoslovakia, which had initiated annual fashion competitions in the early 1950s that included not only evening wear, but also workers' overalls.[67]) Soviet ideologues had largely viewed fashion with disdain. Hutchings described the official line during the Stalin years thus:

> ... the Soviet Union kept or tried to keep itself aloof from sudden fashion changes. A sartorial aim of its rulers was to avoid capricious rises and falls in hemlines, just as an economic aim was to avoid booms and slumps in business activity. Thralldom to Paris fashions was viewed as hardly less irritating than thralldom to Wall Street ... Any new fashions were supposed to be introduced in an organized way.[68]

During the Thaw, fashion was drawn into the symbolic programme of modernization: as one writer in a Czech women's magazine put it: 'we do not wish to isolate ourselves from Western fashion and dress in some way other than people do everywhere else in the civilised world.'[69] Nevertheless, fashion writers and the official fashion institutes sought to walk a careful line between what was invariably claimed as 'beauty and taste' and the 'irrational' crazes emanating from the West. Invariably 'moderation' was claimed as the defining characteristic of socialist fashion.[70] What this meant in practice was an insistence on elegant eveningwear and matching coat, shoe and dress ensembles for daywear, that is, the most bourgeois apparel. As Djurdja Bartlett has argued, this 'transmitted' a 'very traditional idea of luxury' which prevailed long after more relaxed and youthful styles emerged in the West in the 1960s.[71] Although wrapped in contradictions, the upmarket designs promoted on the pages of Eastern Bloc fashion magazines and catwalk shows conformed to a key pattern of the Thaw: expertise was being used in an effort to regulate the practices of people.

Recognizing, as Eastern Bloc ideologues came to do during the Khrushchev years, that fashionability was legitimate was not the same thing as working out how to manage it in a command economy (as well as finding uses for the new synthetic fabrics, such as nylon and artificial fur, which were being promoted as agents of democratization of fashion). Soviet fashion designers from Moscow House of Clothing Design went to Paris in 1957, 1960 and 1965 in order to study the working methods of French haute couture houses producing bespoke garments for the wealthy.[72] Here was Khrushchev regime's oft-made call to improve upon the West in action. Conversely, Dior was invited to mount a catwalk show of the season's fashions in the rotunda of the Kryl'ia Sovetov (Soviet Wings), Moscow's air club, in June 1959 (5.18). Some 13,000 people watched these catwalk shows over five days (whilst, more impressively, the television audience was projected to be two million Soviet citizens).[73] A diplomatic gesture designed to cement Franco-Soviet relations (further extended by the exchange of major exhibitions in 1961), Dior had to accept the attention of several hundred Soviet manufacturers who inspected and sketched the clothes.[74]

Evidently fascinated by what they saw, these Soviet manufacturers were unable to transpose their findings in to the reality of garment production. Oriented to mass production and long production cycles, fashion was a luxury that the Soviet clothing industry was ill equipped to produce. Moreover, the five-year cycles of the central plan were hardly commensurate with the seasonal rhythms of haute couture. The achievements of this kind of Soviet fashion were largely impressionistic, appearing as prototypes in fashion shows and as images on the pages of the embryonic fashion press in the Soviet Union. In the summer of 1962, for instance, 9,000 items of fashion and footwear were exhibited at the Manège exhibition hall in Moscow.[75] Under a huge photomontage of the avuncular figure of Khrushchev greeting the Soviet visitors with wide arms and a slogan promising abundance ('All in the name of Man, for the benefit of Man'), the output of all the Soviet republics was put on display. The products were accompanied by profiles of the factory workers making them and

details of the extent of their production. A large proportion of the objects were described as 'prospective' on their labels, meaning that they had yet to be put into production (a detail which prompted Russian wags to comment that 'prospective' means 'planned for 1983').

As the case of the attempts to modernize Soviet fashion makes clear, Thaw modernism was often a revolution of images rather than of things. Few objects born on the drawing boards of the official design institutes ever went into production. Tomaszewski's organic tea and coffee sets were issued in minuscule numbers by the porcelain manufacturer Ćmielów in 1964. Despite the propaganda of success in which design wrapped itself, the official design institutes were never well integrated into the command economy, and State-owned industries were chronically disinterested in innovation.[76] Such objects were nevertheless widely reproduced and exhibited abroad. Jindra's combination table/music centre was exhibited at the Milan Triennale in 1962 as evidence of the sophistication of Czechoslovak culture. In other words, modern design gave Eastern Bloc socialism a liberal gloss.[77]

Serving the collective

Flicking through the pages of the design and architecture magazines produced in Poland and Czechoslovakia in the late 1950s and in the Soviet Union in the 1960s, the reader was presented with plastic furniture, vibrant decorative art, buildings with shimmering glass walls and sculptural concrete shells. Whilst these designs were evidently modern, how socialist were they? In form or materials, there was little to distinguish Eastern Bloc design from its Western counterparts. Thaw Modernism conformed to a paradox described by Györgyi Péteri, who has argued that the State socialist modernization project was marked by contradiction: it tried to create a form of modern civilization that was distinct from (and competing with) capitalism, and yet at the same time 'it accepted the economic and technological models' and 'standards of success prevailing in the advanced core area of the global system', that is, Western modernity.[78] In other words, socialist modernity looked just like that found on the other side of the East–West divide (a fact which, ironically, cemented the appeal of the West to Eastern Bloc societies[79]). The distribution of resources, however, remained a key aspect of socialist control. In the Soviet Union, Khrushchev and his allies set great ideological store by collective consumption and socialized services. They were to point to a specifically socialist route to higher living standards (and moderate the 'problem' of acquisitiveness). Thus Khrushchev, speaking to French journalists in March 1960, less than a year after the American National Exhibition in Moscow where all twenty-two annual models of automobiles produced in the USA had been on display, presented a Soviet alternative to private car ownership:

> Some people are wont to assess the standard of life in this or that country by the scale of production of motor cars … But it is precisely in this that we do not intend to compete with America, because we consider that human energy is spent none too wisely on the production of automobiles there…. In the future our

automobile production will develop in this way: We shall increase the output of cars, establishing a wide network of car rental garages … the system will be as follows: When anyone needs a car he will go to a garage, rent a car and go wherever he wants. … After using the car he will return it to the garage and will have no further cares. … it is irrational to have too many cars.[80]

VNIITE, the official industrial design institute in the Soviet Union, responded to Khrushchev's call for collective cars with new designs for taxis. Designer Iurii Dolmatovskii designed a single-body cab with a rear engine and an open interior (5.19). Whilst prototypes were produced and tested during the course of the 1960s, no such vehicle ever went into production.[81] The design was promoted internationally however, with Dolmatovskii even receiving recognition from the Mayor of New York in a competition for new taxi-cab design.

Dolmatovskii's teardrop taxi represented the official line because it was to be collective

5.19
Iurii Dolmatovskii, design for a new type of taxi, All-Union Research Institute of Industrial Design, VNIITE, 1966 (Source: *Tekhnicheskaia Estetika*, no.1, 1966, p.12)

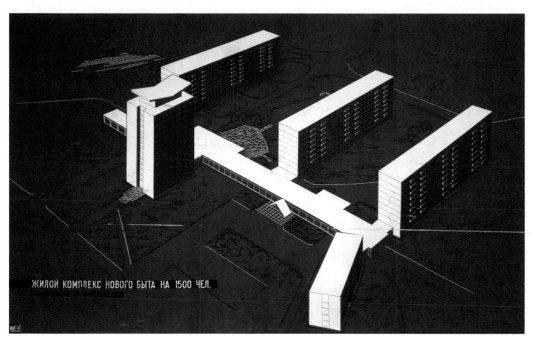

ЖИЛОЙ КОМПЛЕКС НОВОГО БЫТА НА 1500 ЧЕЛ.

5.20
**SAKB 2 (Special
Architectural-construction
Studio)**, housing complex for
1,500 people for the New
Cheremushki quarter,
Moscow. Ink and gouache
on paper, 1961. Schusev
State Museum of
Architecture (MUAR),
Moscow

property. Other loyalists in the Soviet Union
in the early 1960s imagined a world without
private property, the attachment to which
was seen as a brake on the advance towards
full Communism. This utopia was given
architectural form in model housing schemes.
Between 1962 and 1965 teams of architects
working for Mosprojekt 3 (the Institute of
Standard and Experimental Projects) explored
the possibilities of the Dom Novogo Byta
('House of New Life' – an unmistakably
utopian name) to be built as a new addition
to the Cheremushki district of Moscow. [82]
Evolving as a scheme over the course of the
early 1960s from the early concept represented here (5.20), the design settled into two
chevron-shaped residential slabs connected
by a low complex of communal building
containing a canteen, library, television rooms,
hairdressing salons, launderettes, cinema
and a sports centre with a gymnasium and
swimming pool. Some two thousand people
were to occupy the 812 small apartments
in the tall residential blocks. The aim was
to provide housing for young people and new
families, who would exchange the privacy
of the single flat for the benefits of communal
life. The quality of services available to the
occupant would mean that 'less time will
be wasted on domestic tasks and there will
be greater opportunities for the people to

develop themselves physically and morally,
to devote themselves to professional and
public activities'. [83]

Whilst their futurism was loudly
trumpeted, the debt that such schemes owed
to revolutionary housing schemes of the 1920s
in the Soviet Union was also acknowledged. [84]
Soviet architects in the 1920s had produced
visionary schemes for *doma kommuny*
(communal houses) which would accommodate hundreds of adults and children in
collective homes served by a single public
canteen and an on-site boarding school.
Minimal allowances of 'private' space were
to be provided in the design to foster the
kind of communalism lauded by communist
ideologues and inhibit the 'private' possession
of things. In fact, according to Marxist
futurology, the irrational desire for such things
was expected to disappear when all human
needs were satisfied by the perfect environment. When such concepts were revived
in the early 1960s, Soviet ideologues could
represent them as a return to the 'path'
established by Lenin, following the diversion
of the Stalin years. The promotion of modern
design – in the form of the House of New Life
in the 1960s – might be seen, therefore, as a
step closer to the communist paradise, a world
free of the friction caused by possessions. [85]

Such prestigious schemes were exceptional: but the concepts on which they were
based penetrated into everyday spaces of life
through extensive exhibitions promoting new
ideal apartments, domestic advice in literature
and articles in the press (5.21). [86] Vicariously,
citizens of the Soviet Union and the other
Eastern Bloc states could, in this manner,
witness the future that they would inherit.
In these celebrations of domestic modernity,
open-plan layouts which contained functional
'zones' in which householders could study
or play music; furniture which took on
the appearance of equipment or combined
a number of functions; and plain textiles
and wall coverings all served the aim of
'de-artefactualization', the 'elimination' of
possessions and, crucially, one's attachment
to them. [87] The reality was, as many commentators have noted, very different. [88] The new
apartments remained small, and it was not
unusual for three generations of a family to
share a one or two-room apartment. Moreover,
as Victor Buchli has suggested, the spatial

5.21
Cover of *Dekorativnoe
Iskusstvo* (no.1, 1962)
with a children's room
designed by the Experi-
mental Construction Studio
of the Soviet Socialist
Republic of Lithuania.
V&A/NAL: PP. 61. G

5.22
René Roubíček, *Blue
Glass Form*. Blown
and shaped glass. Made
by Borské sklo Glassworks,
Hantich branch, 1959.
V&A: C.21-1998

benefits and cultural associations of tasteful,
compact modern design had other, positive
connotations for householders, not least the
suggestion of spaciousness and an allegiance
to 'foreign' or Western style.[89]

Western style, for many Soviet citizens,
was not represented by American, French
or Italian designs; the 'West' was somewhat
nearer to home. The consumer revolution
in Central Europe went much further than
it did in the Soviet Union (and it was built
on foundations originating in pre-war capitalism). Writing of the popular taste for modern
design Iurii Gerchuk, editor of *Dekorativnoe
Iskusstvo* SSSR, the leading design magazine
in the Soviet Union, pointed out the appeal
of Czechoslovak, Polish and East German
commodities:

> Sluggish Soviet industry reconstructed
> itself only slowly, so that the demand
> for the new style had to be satisfied
> mainly by imports. These came primarily
> from Eastern Europe. The colour silk
> lampshades popular before the war
> became one of the symbols of 'philistine
> taste'. They were forced into extinction
> by multi-armed light fittings and double
> glass shades ... which were imported
> mainly from East Germany.[90]

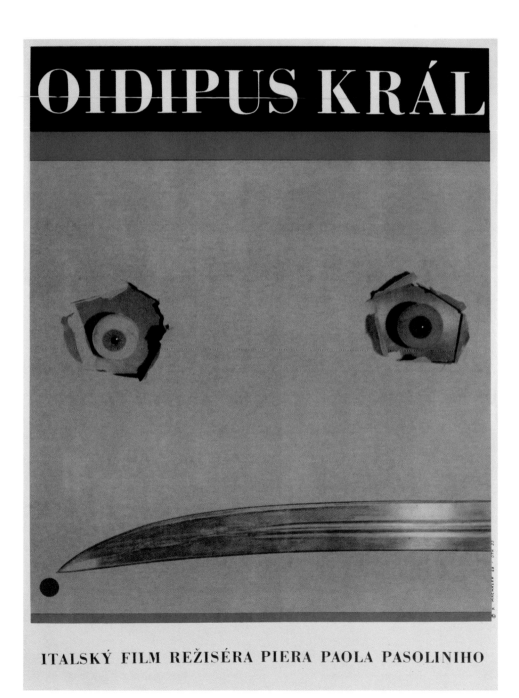

5.23
Karel Machálek, *Oidipus
král* (*Oedipus Rex*). Poster
promoting Pier Paolo
Pasolini's film, Czecho-
slovakia, 1968. Design
Archives, University
of Brighton

OIDIPUS KRÁL

ITALSKÝ FILM REŽISÉRA PIERA PAOLA PASOLINIHO

Even within the Soviet Union it was the
'inner abroad' represented by the Baltic States,
forcibly incorporated into the USSR during
the Second World War and with long traditions of contact with Scandinavia, that
represented another 'West'. The Estonian
magazine *Kunst ja kodu* (*Art and Home*) was
the first title to advocate the contemporary
style as the natural decor for the new small
flats in the industrially produced apartment
houses. First published in 1958, it was widely
read in Soviet Russia (and was published
in a Russian language edition in 1962).[91]

The preference for products of 'fraternal'
socialist nations was also shared, albeit for
different reasons, by the Soviet authorities.
When, for instance, they wanted to deflect
attention away from the spectacle of consumerism at the American National Exhibition in
Moscow in 1959, they mounted an exhibition
of Czech glass at the Manège with what
Oldřich Palata describes as 'unlimited funds'
(5.22).[92] One year earlier the display had been
one of the stunning successes of the Brussels
Expo. Combining expressive art glassworks
and useful wares in a highly theatrical
display – including a 'tree of life' dressed
with coloured glass leaves by René Roubíček –
the intention was to demonstrate the originality and modernity of these products by another
socialist nation, and thereby counter the
impact of the American consumer fantasy
nearby. The Soviet Union's 'need' to demonstrate the superior modernity of socialism
over its Cold War rival outweighed the
importance of maintaining the conventional
power lines of the Eastern Bloc.

Frictions

Whilst the technocratic contract between
designers and the communist state was
accepted by both parties without much
controversy, a small number of architects
and designers were critical of the dash to
modernize. An important vein of critique in
Central Europe was found in the maintenance
of surrealist aesthetics in poster design and
animation. Younger designers in the much-
celebrated Polish Poster School such as Jan
Lenica and Roman Cieślewicz and, a little
later, figures such as Milan Grygar and
Karel Machálek in Czechoslovakia, revived
the surrealist techniques of frottage and
collage in their posters for films and theatre

5.24
Still from **Walerian Borowczyk and Jan Lenica's** animated film *Dom*, produced by the KADR film studio, Poland, 1958

performances, often making use of glossy magazine imagery that had slipped in from the West (5.23).[93] Free of the commercial pressures operating in advertising in the West, these designers were able to generate 'personal' languages which, in their use of enigmatic and sometimes obscure symbols, escaped the attention of the censor. Already a démodé aesthetic in the West, the appeal of surreal images, which appeared to stress irrationalism and sexual desire or harked back to the past – often in the form of *belle epoch* imagery – to penetrate into the present was strong. In Eastern Europe, surrealist preoccupations of the 1920s and 1930s had not been subsumed into the spectacle of advertising as they had been in the West.[94] For many critics in the capitalist world, the avant-garde character of Surrealism had been fatally undermined by its spectacular qualities.[95] By contrast, the irrational and 'obsolete' images represented suppressed values in those socialist societies which endlessly trumpeted their rationalism and futurism. In Marxist-Leninism, the past was something to be overcome or, in the distortions of the historical record for which Eastern Bloc historiography was notorious, even repressed.

Surrealism penetrated deeply into experimental and animated films produced during the Thaw. *Dom*, a short animated film made in Poland by Jan Lenica and Walerian Borowczyk, is perhaps the most important work in this genre (5.24). Using an opening shot of a pre-war tenement as a metaphor for the mind, this short film is a series of investigations into domestic spaces of memory, desire and fear. Before each of the short episodes that make up this film, the camera focuses on a woman's face as she opens and closes her eyes. This gesture suggests the interior location of the scenes that we are about to witness. These include the stop-frame animation of hair seemingly consuming a meal; lingering panning shots over *belle epoch* photographs and antique postcards; and the compulsive repetition of a man entering a room countless times. In *Dom*, Lenica and Borowczyk's home had deep psychological, irrational reserves that could be tapped in photographs, in dreams and in sexual desire. These associations had little value in minds of the Party ideologues or, for that matter, of the rationalist design theorist.

Chill winds

Dom was a great international triumph. Winning the Grand Prix at the 1958 Brussels Experimental Film Festival (perhaps no surprise, with Man Ray on the jury), it caused a sensation for its combination of animation and real-time film of actors. But even as its makers were being fêted abroad, the political climate was beginning to change in Poland where a new conservatism took hold, particularly after the Third Congress of the Polish United Worker's Party, the prime communist organization in Poland, in 1959. Former Stalinists were reinstated in positions of influence in government, and the Central Committee gave a clear lead to the censors' office by challenging the freedoms exercised by journalists and film-makers.[96] Lenica, for instance, left for Germany in 1962 when film censors refused to allow the distribution of his next animated film, *Labyrinth*, despite the accolades that *Dom* had brought for Polish culture. Cieślewicz went on to become an art director for *Elle* magazine in Paris.[97]

Poland had been an exceptionally liberal environment during the Thaw. Nevertheless, a similar freeze set in elsewhere in the Bloc in the early 1960s. The most dramatic of these

5.25
Burt Glinn, Berliners
watching the Wall
go up, West Berlin,
West Germany, 1961

checks on freedom was, of course, the construction in August 1961 of the Berlin Wall, or what East German communist leader Walter Ulbricht called an 'Anti-Fascist protection barrier' (5.25). His purpose was largely to stem the tide of people fleeing East Germany for the West, a haemorrhage that threatened to bring the national economy to collapse.[98] The failure of the national economy to match the consumer boom in the West was blamed by the SED leadership in its communications with Moscow for the steady traffic of people heading West.[99]

In the visual arts, a key sign of the freeze was the so called 'Manège Affair' in Moscow in December 1962, during which Khrushchev made a direct attack on the modern works of art on display there, representing his views as those of the common Soviet man and woman.[100] Works by sculptor Ernst Neizvestnyi featured in the exhibition which were described by the Kremlin leader as 'disgusting', whilst a self-portrait by Boris Zhutovsky was described as 'a filthy mess which makes you sick to look at it'.[101] Cold War watchers in the West viewed this outburst as the sign of a sea change, marking the end of Khrushchev's reforms at home, and watched for signs of the chill setting in elsewhere in the Bloc.[102] Ulbricht's attack on Bollhagen's ascetic ceramics in Dresden in 1962 might be taken as a premonition of events in Moscow.

Such attacks on architecture and design were, however, rare. The course set in 1956 was largely maintained by Eastern Bloc states through the 1960s. Modern consumer goods, fashionable clothing, single-family apartments and other symbols of socialist achievement continued to be presented as entitlements of modern socialist life. As many commentators have noted, Eastern Bloc states raised expectations which their industries could not meet.[103] In the second half of the 1960s the opening of hard currency stores selling glossy Western consumer goods, and factories turning out new cars and stereos for domestic consumption and operating in partnership with Italian and Japanese investors, represented a second phase of the consumer contract.[104] Nevertheless, shortage not only remained the daily reality of most lives in the Eastern Bloc: it was increasingly understood as an injustice.[105] For idealist modernist designers and architects, the end of Thaw and the unabashed materialism of the Brezhnev years throughout the Bloc represented a different kind of disappointment.[106] Not only were the hopes of producing a rational world based on the principles of function and utility evaporating: the ambition of turning state socialism itself into a human design product was also being dashed.

Thaw Modern: Design in Eastern Europe after 1956

5.26
Perspective drawing of
the Pitsunda sanatorium
complex in Georgia. Pencil
and gouache on paper, 1962.
Built in 1962–7 to a design
by Mikhail Posokhin, Ashot
Mndoiants, B.Swirskii
(architects), S. Shkol'nikov
and B. Nikolaev (engineers).
Schusev State Museum
of Architecture (MUAR)
Moscow

'Our Kitchen is Just as Good': Soviet Responses to the American National Exhibition in Moscow, 1959

Susan E. Reid

5.27
Vice President Richard Nixon with USSR First Secretary Nikita Khrushchev during the 'kitchen debate' at the American National Exhibition, Moscow. 1959

On 26 July 1959 a photograph of a smiling Russian Everywoman, Zinaida, baking pies with her little girl in time for Dad coming home from work, appeared in the Soviet state newspaper *Izvestiia*.[1] Zinaida's kitchen boasts such step-saving conveniences as wall-mounted units and a rack for drying plates over the sink, while the sink has a mixer tap, indicating both hot and cold running water supplies, and is fitted into a continuous worktop: in short, it is a compact, modern, rationally planned, if rather modest kitchen. It was no coincidence that, just the previous day, the American National Exhibition had opened in Moscow's Sokol'niki Park. Purporting to represent 'a transplanted slice of the American way of life' in the heart of Moscow, the exhibition brought the ideal image of American mass consumption and domesticity vividly before the Soviet public on an unprecedented scale. 'Our kitchen', Zinaida asserts boldly in the caption, 'is just as good as the American one shown at the exhibition in Sokol'niki'.[2]

Much has been written about the American National Exhibition in Moscow (ANEM) in 1959. And one of the kitchens displayed there has gone down in history as the setting for perhaps the most iconic encounter of the Cold War: the notorious 'kitchen debate' between USSR First Secretary Nikita Khrushchev and US Vice President Richard Nixon (5.27). Amidst the gleaming appliances of the General Electric kitchen in the 'typical American home' on show there, the leaders thrashed out the competing claims of Communism and Capitalism to provide the best life for the greatest number of people.[3] The focus of this essay is Soviet responses to ANEM's representations of modern American domesticity and its technological apparatus in the form of kitchens. It should be noted, however, that while such displays were a key

part of the exhibition, they were not the only ways in which America represented its ideal self to its Cold War adversary; they took their place amidst important exhibits of fine art, books, cars, fashion, and the 'Family of Man' photographic exhibition. First we should take a brief look at the way the exhibition and its Soviet audience were conceived, and the impact it aimed to achieve. We shall then turn to the Soviet reception.

The exhibition and its aims

Not one but *four* state-of-the-art kitchens were installed in the heart of the Soviet capital under the auspices of ANEM. The American suburban kitchen was the supreme symbol of the imagined America, the chief site of individual family-based consumption, where the advances of modern science and technology were placed at the service of peaceful domestic life, and – in the rhetoric of the time – of 'making women happy'. There the full-time

housewife reigned supreme, keeping a serene home to which the male breadwinner could retreat from the nervous strains and alienation of the public sphere. With the effort and dirt of housework carefully hidden, everyday family life was constructed as a space of leisure and freedom from anxiety and work: a special enclave where 'Liberty and the Pursuit of Happiness' – sought since the Enlightenment and pronounced inalienable rights by the American Declaration of Independence – could be attained through individual consumption. The American housewife-consumer had been a potent propaganda weapon on the US home front during the Second World War, personifying the American dream, the life worth fighting for. In the global politics of the Cold War the Happy Housewife also did service as an advertisement for the benefits of 'people's capitalism'.[4] Conversely, her sister in the Communist Bloc was constructed by Western observers as her deprived, dowdy and work-

5.28
Scenes from the American
National Exhibition,
Moscow, 1959, clockwise
from top right: Cookery
demonstration in the
television studio; Coiffures
Americana demonstration
in the Beauty Kiosk; visitors
to the Exhibition; cake-
baking demonstration;
visitors to the Exhibition,
showing Buckminster
Fuller's Dome; Book
Exhibition in the Glass
Pavilion

5.29
Anne Anderson using
push-button panel in
the RCA Whirlpool 'Miracle
Kitchen' at the American
National Exhibition,
Moscow, 1959

worn antithesis, and her image, starkly contrasting with the glamorous hyperfemininity of the capitalist West, was deployed as an indictment of state socialism.

On the eve of the opening of the exhibition, the Communist Party Central Committee received anxious reports on the displays the Americans were about to unleash on the Soviet public, including a photo of a smiling housewife amidst an abundance of groceries and consumer goods, and film footage depicting an 'average' American housewife shopping for provisions and preparing a meal. The essence of these displays, the report warned, was to show 'what the simple person ("the average American") has in the USA', representing the American way of life as 'heaven on Earth'.[5] Co-ordinated by the US Information Agency (USIA), at a cost of $3.6 million of government funds in addition to large-scale investment from American business, ANEM's official purpose was to increase mutual understanding under the 1958 US–USSR agreement on cultural exchange. But for the American planners their exhibition in Moscow

was also an offensive weapon in the Cold War. A third front had joined the arms race and the space race: the living standards race.[6] To demonstrate the superiority of the American Way over the communist system, to instil envy, de-legitimate the regime and ruin the Soviet economy by raising demand among the Soviet population for products available only to Western consumers were among the exhibition's goals. 'By spurring the Russians to increase production of consumer goods we may be helping ourselves more than we are helping them', a special adviser to the exhibition predicted.[7] These aims accorded with what US sociologist David Riesman had dubbed the 'Nylon War' in 1951.[8] Significantly, the most powerful missiles in Riesman's conception of Nylon Warfare were consumer items targeted at women, such as vacuum cleaners and beauty aids. A 'universal feminine' desire to be a leisured consumer and to beautify herself and her home was presumed to transcend the Cold War ideological divide. These instincts, frustrated under Communism, supposedly rendered women

5.30
Viktor Koretsky, *From oil we take for the needs of our country a river of gasoline, oil and petroleum and in addition thousands of items for the home and for domestic comfort!* Poster, USSR, 1960. Private collection

ИЗ НЕФТИ МЫ БЕРЕМ ДЛЯ НУЖД СТРАНЫ СВОЕЙ ПОТОК БЕНЗИНА, МАСЕЛ И МАЗУТА, А К НИМ В ПРИДАЧУ ТЫСЯЧУ ВЕЩЕЙ ДЛЯ ДОМА И ДОМАШНЕГО УЮТА!

the weak link, susceptible to the allure of Capitalism.

The 1959 exhibition was to be a Trojan Horse of the American Way of Life. Penetrating the citadel of Communism, it was expected to capture the hearts of millions of Soviet Helens. The superiority of free enterprise over state planning was demonstrated most vividly and palpably in the model American dream-home, owned and occupied by a fictional 'typical' American family, the Browns. Split down the middle – hence its nickname, 'Splitnik' – the model house allowed Soviet visitors to walk through it, imagining themselves in the Browns' place. At $14,000, the modest, one-storey, prefabricated structure on a standard model, 'X-61', was allegedly affordable to the average US worker. Indeed, its architect, Stanley H. Klein, had already provided 'thousands of development homes' for ordinary Americans, the US press claimed: 'Possibly the star attraction, the American home on display has been mobbed from opening day.... X-61 is a Cold War celebrity.'[9]

All four American kitchens at ANEM were deployed amidst rhetoric of 'labour saving' and of 'liberating women' through the application of advanced science and technology to the domestic sphere. Their gadgets and conveniences represented a special gift for the housewife, two freedoms for the price of one: to the joy of freedom from drudgery was added the pleasure of free choice. A press release from Washington in advance of the opening spelled out the message: 'Soviet women soon will get a chance to see that American scientific progress is not limited to a man's world. Modern US inventions, they'll observe, also are making life easier for the housewife.'[10] The supreme realization of the dream of the easy life was the fully automated RCA Whirlpool 'Miracle Kitchen' or 'kitchen of the future' (5.29).[11] Its electronic 'brain' was operated, like a science fiction spaceship, from a central control panel by a lab-coated home economist who could prepare a complete meal without even leaving her seat, demonstrating 'how the domestic wonder takes the work out of cooking'.[12]

The General Electric kitchen of the model home also boasted the latest appliances. Nixon drew Khrushchev's attention to the panel-controlled washing machine: 'these are designed to make things easier for

our women'.[13] Khrushchev objected, 'your capitalist attitude to women does not occur under Communism'. But, cornered in the American kitchen, he was forced to defend the socialist system against claims for Capitalism on the terms set by his hosts: the capacity to satisfy citizens' needs and, specifically, to 'liberate' women. He bragged – as would Zinaida in the press the following day – that Soviet housewives already had kitchens that were just as good.[14]

Was Khrushchev's riposte pure bluff, or was there some substance to it? To be sure, if he had called the shots he might well have preferred to conduct his exchange with Nixon against a backdrop of space technology. In the cosmos, socialist science had proved its superiority with the launch of the first Sputnik on 4 October 1957, while the so-called 'Kitchen' missile currently under development was at the cutting edge of international rocket science.[15] The kitchen, meanwhile, and the wider problems of living conditions and consumption it stood for, remained the site of the Soviet system's humiliation on the world stage, and the symbol of its backwardness.[16] Nevertheless, Nixon was not wrong in assuming that he and Khrushchev shared the goal of 'making easier the life of women'. (And neither leader so much as entertained the possibility of achieving this by redistributing domestic labour to involve men: the home and its associated labour remained firmly gendered as women's domain and burden, even in spite of claimed and actual differences in the Soviet socialist approach.) In numerous pronouncements since coming to power Khrushchev had already pledged to 'help women' and linked the imminent transition to Communism to the attainment of high living standards for all (5.30). A number of policies were adopted with the explicit aim of freeing up women's time and energy to allow them to participate more equally in social-political life and in production, as well as measures intended to raise mass living standards across the board.

Among these measures the most fundamental was an intensive state campaign of mass housing construction, launched in 1957, with the aim of alleviating the acute housing shortage in the Soviet Union through the radical restructuring of building practices towards industrialized methods such as

standardization and factory prefabrication (see 5.6). This promised to change the life of millions, hitherto squashed into cramped and substandard accommodation. Khrushchev pledged to provide everyone with economical but well-appointed, modern apartments for single nuclear families, complete with 'central heating, a well-equipped kitchen, a gas stove, garbage chute, and hot water supply, bathroom, fitted cupboards ... and other conveniences'.[17] For Soviet women struggling to provide for their families in communal kitchens or on a single primus burner in the family's one room of a communal apartment, this also meant having their own kitchens for the first time, as well as running water and gas stoves. Zinaida's model modern kitchen might not yet exist on a mass scale in July 1959, but widely circulated images of domestic happiness in brand new flats were not just propaganda (5.31).

If the Soviet and American leaders agreed on the aim to alleviate women's domestic drudgery, and on technology as an important means to achieve this without restructuring gender roles in the home, they parted company over the ultimate purpose of liberation from housework. Khoziaika – 'housewife' – was only part of Zinaida's identity, not a full-time, surrogate 'profession'. The freedom gained through 'labour saving' was not freedom to be a leisured ornament, but to become a fully rounded person, and this entailed participation in social life and production outside the home.[18] Moreover, appliances for the individual home were neither the only means to women's attainment of a fully human, socially engaged and productive existence, nor the preferred one. Vacuum cleaners were not necessarily to be individually owned, but hired when needed, while mechanization of household tasks such as laundry could be more effectively and economically carried out by centralized provision.[19] The economic plan adopted in January 1959 made services and collective consumption the primary means to raise living standards and 'liberate women', promising the expansion of public childcare, laundries, various forms of public feeding, and cleaning agencies.[20] Thus socialist abundance would be distinguished from the capitalist model of prosperity by high-quality services, which were to be expanded and improved and, eventually, provided free. Communism would

5.31
Model kitchen
manufactured by the
'Standart' Experimental
Furniture Factory,
Soviet Socialist Republic
of Estonia, shown in
Dekorativnoe iskusstvo,
no.8, 1962
V&A/NAL: PP.61.G

provide the best life for the most people on the basis of social benefits: state housing, health care and sanatoria, education and services.[21]

Nevertheless, even as a distinct socialist way to the good life of abundance and ease was proclaimed and pursued in practice, the Soviet Union also entered into competition on terms set by US prosperity. The regime couched its promises of economic growth in terms of 'catching up with and surpassing America'. 'We Will Overtake America', ran the headline under which Khrushchev's speech at the official opening appeared in the press. 'We can learn something. We look at the American exhibition as an exhibition of our own achievements in the near future.'[22] Rather than a shop window, it was an instructive museum of the future from which to glean new processes and technologies on which to build Soviet, socialist prosperity.

Soviet responses

Daily attendance at the American National Exhibition in Moscow was estimated by US sources at 55–77,000 per day, totalling 2,700,000 over the six-week period.[23] How did Soviet citizens respond to the first mass encounter with the American dream on their own turf? According to American official reports, all four kitchens shown at the exhibition 'were jammed with admiring Soviet women from morning until night'. 'The crowds are wonderful', reported the cake-mix demonstrator for General Mills' convenience food kitchen, where Betty Crocker cookbooks were given away.[24] The American press reported Soviet people's awe before Splitnik's lemon yellow General Electric kitchen, where the Kitchen Debate took place: 'The labor-saving appliances in the kitchen are, for the most part, examined carefully, though in silence.'[25] Under the subheading: 'Kremlin worried?' *US News and World Report* found ANEM's consumer goods offensive to be having its desired effect: 'the curiosity about the American way of life as depicted at the fair is giving Soviet leaders concern that the Russian viewers will become discontented with their own lot.'[26] 'The available evidence leads to the conclusion that ... the exhibition was an overwhelming success.'[27] Other accounts were less sanguine, however. One of the American guides concluded her report after the exhibition: 'Did our

Exhibition jive with basic Russian impulses? No!' A USIA report on visitors' reactions, based on guides' accounts and overheard comments, also judged it at best a qualified success: the typical response was enjoyment marred by disappointment.[28]

The ambivalent Soviet popular response is also indicated in the visitors' comments books.[29] True, many were convinced by the American vision of domestic happiness and by its claims to set norms of progress and comfort towards which the Soviet Union must strive. 'As a housewife I want to thank you for your household appliances. I am deeply impressed by the quality of these products and also by how much they facilitate the work of a housewife. I wish that our housewives had the chance to own such things.' A teacher wrote: 'I liked the machines that facilitate the work of women. I especially liked the Miracle Kitchen. It would be nice if such kitchens were mass-produced. And if we could trade with you.'

But many comment writers were, or claimed to be, less impressed:

> We expected that the American exhibition would show something grandiose, some earthly equivalent to Soviet Sputniks. But you Americans want to amaze us with the glitter of your kitchen pans and the fashions which do not appeal to us at all.[30]

> And this is one of the greatest nations?? I feel sorry for the Americans, judging by your exhibition. Does your life really consist only of kitchens?

> The Americans have talked so much about their achievements that we wanted to see the exhibition. Having seen it, however, we have become convinced that you do not have anything special, and many things are better here with us. When you look at the Miracle Kitchen and similar things, you think of the many millions of unemployed who are not concerned with the Miracle Kitchen as they have to think about how they are going to live the next day.

America's achievements were also undermined directly on the territory of its

own claims to provide liberty, equality and happiness. The hollowness of promises of freedom through consumption was exposed. In particular, the claim to liberate women from kitchen drudgery through the purchase of an American kitchen replete with 'labor saving' devices became a central pillar of critique. Far from liberating women, some viewers objected that the American household technology was a source of further alienation and confinement. A construction engineer put this position eloquently:

> I am convinced that in the minds of more and more people, the idea 'kitchen' has become equivalent to the idea 'cage', with the only exception that kitchens are inhabited by women and cages by birds. In the Miracle Kitchen a woman is just as free as a bird in a miracle cage. The Miracle Kitchen shown at the exhibition demonstrates America's last word in the field of perfecting obsolete forms of everyday living which stultify women.[31]

This response was echoed by an authoritative condemnation of the Miracle Kitchen as a glorified coop published a few days later in *Izvestiia*, where Zinaida the Happy Soviet Housewife had made her appearance. The author, well-known writer Marietta Shaginian, welcomed some applications of technology to the home, in particular the mechanical garbage disposer that used electricity to grind the waste and wash it down the drain.[32] However, she rejected the appliance-saturated individual kitchens shown at ANEM. Far from liberating women, she argued, they represented a new form of bondage.

> The countless domestic conveniences of the Americans ... anchor to woman in perpetuity her mission as 'housewife', wife, and cook. They make this role easier for her, but the very process of alleviating individual housework as it were eternalizes this way of life, turning it into a profession for the woman. *But we love innovations that actually emancipate women* – new types of houses with public kitchens with their canteens for everyone living in the house; with laundries where vast machines wash clothes not just for one family alone.

The American kitchen and the version of liberty and happiness it offered were not for Soviet consumption, she concluded:

> On this matter the tastes and expectations of Soviet viewers depart from those of the American exhibition organizers ... A huge heaviness gradually descends upon the viewer. The abundance of objects for individual use creates a kind of power of things over man. Yet the organizers of the exhibition naively think that our Soviet viewer will be consumed by a thirst to possess 'property' ... The 'way of life' is a very individual matter; each people, each social system has its own tastes and ideals in this regard. The electric kitchen, for example, which the Americans promise in the future, appears to us a thoroughly cumbersome thing in private everyday life, but a very convenient one for public canteens and big restaurants.

Throughout, Shaginian's imagery opposes the millstone of fetishized private possessions to the emancipation of the person – and especially of women – which socialist relations were supposed to effect. Her account sets up vividly, from an orthodox perspective, the antithesis between the socialist and the bourgeois capitalist approach to the living standards race, opposing collective to individual consumption, communal servicing of everyday needs to that based in the segregated household and carried out by the isolated 'professional' housewife. Soviet domestic bliss was not simply to clone the American dream of consumption, comfort and convenience; it was necessary to foster a socialist attitude to things and to the home. Not a 'my-home-is-my-castle' mentality and consumer fetishism, but rational domestic living, satisfaction of reasonable needs, and the harmonization of individual desires with the greater good of the collective, were the path to a fully human life. Consumption, American-style, as epitomized in the individual kitchen, was not a path to freedom and happiness but to bondage and misery.

That the American kitchen would be the undoing of socialism was a central assumption of the Nylon War. And indeed, the Soviet authorities could not avoid competition with it and with its claims to 'make easier the life of women', least of all when it was thrust, fourfold, before the Soviet mass audience in Moscow. Selective appropriation and reverse engineering of American models cohabited with repudiation in the official response. The popular reception also indicates far from unequivocal enthusiasm. If the visitors' books are to be given any credence at all, the American kitchen did not march triumphant into the hearts and homes of Soviet citizens – even as an aspiration, let alone as an attainable reality.[33]

5.32
Boris Leo, *An Objective View*. Soviet cartoon from *Krokodil*, no. 22, 10 August 1959

6.1 **Raimund Abraham**, *Air-Ocean-City*. Photo and paper collage on cardboard, 1966. Deutsches Architekturmuseum, Frankfurt am Main

6 / The Hi-Tech Cold War

Jane Pavitt and David Crowley

In 1957, an earth-born object made by man was launched into the universe, where for some weeks it circled the earth according to the same laws of gravitation that swing and keep in motion the celestial bodies – the sun, the moon and the stars. To be sure, the man-made satellite was no moon or star, no heavenly body which could follow its circling path for a time span that to us mortals, bound by earthly time, lasts from eternity to eternity. Yet, for a time it managed to stay in the skies; it dwelt and moved in the proximity of the heavenly bodies as though it had been admitted tentatively to their sublime company.

(Hannah Arendt, *The Human Condition*, 1958)

On the morning of 4 October 1957, many awoke to hear the radio-broadcast 'bleep' of the first artificial satellite orbiting the Earth. Weighing 184lb and with a diameter of only 23in, the aluminium sphere known as 'Sputnik' continued to broadcast its signal for three weeks, until the radio gave out. The satellite itself stayed in orbit for 92 days.

Sputnik was the most public indication of the advancements made in Cold War science since the onset of East–West hostilities ten years earlier. It fired the imagination of a new space-conscious generation, whilst sending a chill into some hearts in the West. As philosopher Hannah Arendt observed in 1958, Sputnik signalled a modern desire to use human artifice by means of technology to escape our earthbound condition. Whilst some saw this as the shape of the future, for Arendt this escape into artifice represented the path to worldly alienation (6.2).[1]

The Sputnik represented the translation of science from fantasy to fact, accelerated by Cold War competition. In 1945 the science fiction writer Arthur C. Clarke had written a letter to a British journal anticipating the use of satellites for mass communication.[2] The USA had been researching orbital satellites since 1945, and in 1946 the techno-military think-tank, RAND Corporation, prepared a report entitled 'Preliminary Design of an Experimental World-Circling Space Ship', which was effectively a feasibility study for a satellite.[3] Although primarily concerned with its political and scientific benefits, the report also speculated on the future use of satellites to control airborne missiles. The report made clear that the development of space technology for weapons systems was the key to ensuring military dominance. The launch of a satellite, the report predicted, would 'inflame the imagination of mankind, and probably produce repercussions in the world comparable to the explosion of an atomic bomb'.[4] But of course it was the Soviet Union that achieved this watershed event.[5]

The extreme rivalry between the US and the USSR made defence, weaponry, security and intelligence the priorities of scientific research. Wartime research operations,[6] bolstered by massive injections of funds in the later 1940s, developed into a close-knit alliance of scientists, industrialists and the military which, in the West, would later be termed the 'military-industrial complex'.[7] Indeed, the boundaries between the 'open' and 'closed' worlds of scientific discourse were increasingly blurred. On one hand intense and necessary secrecy governed the scientific advancements of both East and West; on the other, the popularization of science had immense propaganda benefits, both as a show of strength to the opposite side and as a factor in the maintenance of public morale.[8] The higher moral and social purpose of science was also often asserted, amid claims that the internationalism of the scientific community could rise above party and state political divide. The much-publicized International Geophysical Year (IGY) of 1957/8 formed the backdrop to the launch of the first satellites.[9] Ostensibly the IGY was a sign of peaceful cooperation between nations (for the global study of geophysical phenomena), and the US offered to develop an artificial satellite which would gather geophysical data. But such initiatives were often little more than cover for more militaristic purposes.

If science was the pre-eminent tool in the race to the future, it is unsurprising that the visual and verbal culture of the Cold War became suffused with scientific allusions (6.3). The language of new technologies spilled over into everyday usage by the 1960s with terms such as 'networks', 'feedback', 'systems', 'software' and 'hardware' acquiring broader meaning beyond the bounds of their original usage. Cold War anxieties were frequently triggered by high-tech advances: the computer set off concerns about dehumanization; the fast spread of television led to discussion of the persuasive effects of new media; and global communication systems were imagined as instruments of surveillance.

The rapid permutation of society by electronic technologies in the 1960s produced a wealth of critical responses, particularly from the political left, including Herbert Marcuse's *One Dimensional Man* (1964) and J.K. Galbraith's *The New Industrial State* (1967). Such critiques of a bureaucratic and technocratic culture that subordinated freedom of thought and action to the interests of the corporation were matched by a counter-cultural response that preferred to stress the liberating aspects of technology. In a profusion of future scenarios, technology was perceived as the tool of both liberation and oppression, the framework of a hierarchical society as well as the means of its dissolution.

Marshall McLuhan was perhaps the most influential figure on this wave of technological euphoria.[10] A Canadian professor who broke

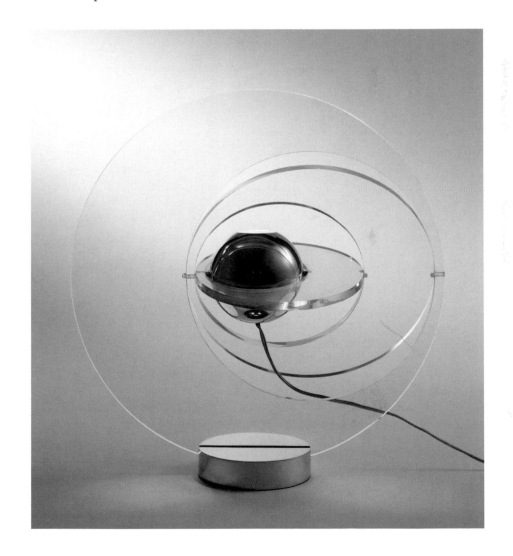

6.3
Yonel Lébovici, *Satellite* table lamp. Chrome-plated metal and colourless acrylic glass, edition made by Yonel Lébovici, Paris, 1965. Die Neue Sammlung, Munich

outside the narrow confines of academia, his aphoristic style of writing made him one of the most popular guides to the age. He seemed to provide explanations for the impact and effect of rapid technological changes, particularly in the field of communication. Easily understandable phrases like 'the medium is the message' and 'the global village' were rapidly assimilated and often recycled, not least by a new generation of architects and designers in the 1960s. Key to McLuhan's thinking was his explanation of the changing relationships between the body and technology. He repeatedly asserted that any successful new medium or technology constitutes an 'extension of man'. The information revolution of the second half of the twentieth century in the form of radio and electronic communications, for instance, prosthetically extended the nervous system of the body just as the first Industrial Revolution had physically extended the mechanical operations of the human body. Electronic communication promised to overcome the fragmenting effects of print media, producing a new type of consciousness. It would also produce a new planet or, in McLuhan's words, 'a global village'. In tracing dynamic relations between man and machine in which *both* were changed by their interaction, McLuhan was one of the chief popularizers of cybernetics, a product of Cold War science discussed in more detail below.

McLuhan's writings in the 1960s were marked by ambiguity. Whilst his fascination with a fast-changing world was evident, and he pointed to considerable social effects, he had relatively little to say about how industrial or communication systems were organized. In fact, his ideas seem to suggest the redundancy of ideology: technological progress had an inherent theocratic logic which would outlive particular political systems. He was not alone in this. For the most radical technophiles the challenge was to translate Cold War technologies away from narrow technocratic uses, 'efficiently' serving political systems, industry or business, to become genuine 'extensions of man' serving to extend his or her being in the world.

Closed worlds and open skies

At the heart of the vast post-war technocratic vision was the computer. Central to military strategy during the Cold War, the development

6.4
Ettore Sottsass Jr (designer) and Mario Tchou (engineer), Elea 9003 computer, Olivetti SpA, 1959. Associazione Archivio Storico Olivetti, Ivrea

of computing shaped (and was shaped by) the technological, political, institutional and social nexus which Paul N. Edwards has called 'the closed world'.[11] Military systems such as ENIAC (Electronic Numerical Integrator And Computer, 1946) and SAGE (Semi-Automatic Ground Environment, operating from 1956) were vital extensions of weapons and radar technology. SAGE, the early warning system covering the Arctic Circle, was the first command-control computerized system of the Cold War. It was the blueprint for the integrated defence and communications systems which became the infrastructure of the Cold War world, constituting what Edwards called 'a dome of global technological oversight'.[12]

The 1967–9 US Defense Department initiative known as ARPANET (named after ARPA, the Advanced Research Projects Agency), developed to facilitate resource-sharing between several massive research computers from four universities by means of a network, eventually gave rise to the Internet, the most global of networks. Corporations operated as partners in such schemes: IBM, for instance, provided the computing expertise for SAGE. The corporation's computers processed information relayed by these stations before being displayed on cathode ray screens. Operators bathed in their blue light would watch for aberrant patterns in the movement of aeroplanes and potential intercontinental weapons, while corporate partners in military research were able to apply hi-tech developments in the sphere of defence to the emergent world of business computing. The giant mainframes of the 1950s were given coherent visual identity by designers such as Eliot Noyes for IBM and Ettore Sottsass for Olivetti. Sottsass, conscious of the anxiety-inducing image of computing, gave the 1959 Olivetti Elea 9003 a colourful visual interface, and introduced a human scale to its monolithic components (6.4).[13]

The question of the proper relationship between computer and operative was not just a matter of sensitive industrial design. Since the early days of computing research in the 1930s and 1940s, the future role of the computer had been envisaged as something far beyond its function as a giant number-crunching device. Alan Turing's prediction in 1950 that computers would eventually become a form of 'artificial intelligence', developing the functions of sentient beings, stimulated a rich seam of science fantasy as well as predicting the direction that research would take.[14] In the United States this was aided by the development of a new theoretical framework for improving man/machine interfaces, the discipline of cybernetics.

Led by American mathematician Norbert Wiener, cybernetics grew in part from the study of anti-aircraft systems during the Second World War.[15] Wiener and his colleagues analysed the relationship between the human and mechanical components of the aeroplane and its on-board anti-aircraft apparatus.[16] By predicting patterns of behaviour of both gunner and pilot and modelling them using mathematical formulae, they found that, like computers, the air crew would regulate their behaviour according to repeat patterns of error and success. Elaborating this model, Wiener explored the man-machine relationship as one fed by a constant flow of information, based around interaction, the sending and receiving of messages and the consequent massing of data, calling this 'feedback'. In the aftermath of the Second World War, Wiener brought his new vision of human behaviour to a wider world.[17]

Wiener's faith in this vision of man as a self-regulating, computational being had its ideological aspect, too. Although it perhaps inevitably fuelled a dehumanized image of modern man, he saw such a model of human behaviour as benign, a system of human organization based on feedback and self-regulation which was infinitely preferable, in his view, to the state regulation of human activity as practised by Nazi and Soviet regimes. His accessibly written books were a popular success, and also helped to define yet another field of battle between East and West in a manner which was to demonstrate the extreme ideological pressures on science on the other side of the Iron Curtain.

In Stalin's USSR, Wiener's cybernetics were treated with scepticism, dismissed in the press as a 'pseudo-science' and part of a 'giant scale campaign of mass delusion' operating in the USA to promote the computer.[18] Any analogous comparison between human action or the human brain and the computer was viewed by the State as ideologically suspect, as it could be read as a proposal to replace human labour with machines: 'The process of production realized without workers! Only with machines controlled by the gigantic brain of the computer! ... what an enticing perspective for capitalism!'[19] Soviet computing research was conducted under conditions of strictest secrecy, as a key component of Soviet weapons development and the space enterprise, embarked upon by Stalin in an attempt to close the gap between American and Soviet capabilities. This policy did not change until after his death in 1953, when isolationism was cautiously abandoned by the Kremlin in favour of a highly visible campaign of technological modernity. Reducing the ideological temperature, the Soviet leadership then encouraged designers, engineers and scientists to research, adopt and improve upon innovations in the West.

The Scientific Technological Revolution announced by Soviet Premier Nikolai Bulganin in July 1956 was, in part, a means to exorcise the ghosts of Stalin's irrationalism and violence: it was also a programme intended to shape a new Soviet consciousness. A scientifically literate and technically expert society would be better able to conduct the 'peaceful competition' with capitalism declared by Nikita Khrushchev.[20] The chief symbols of the era – the Sputnik, atomic power and the industrialization of housing and other key sectors– were to represent the triumphant application of Soviet engineering and science.

The scientific complexes constructed in the late 1950s were important engines of Soviet modernization after Stalin. Akademgorodok, a new city in Siberia, was proposed by prominent figures in the Soviet Academy of Science in 1957 to explore, as Paul Josephson has shown, the newly licensed science of cybernetics and exploit the enormous resources of this undeveloped territory.[21] Far from other Soviet centres, this was to be a city relatively free from the interests of the ideologues and bureaucrats in Moscow. The conventional Cold War dichotomy between secrecy and openness was given an unexpected twist here. Never a closed city – of which many were built from the late 1940s to serve the Soviet nuclear weapons programme[22] – Akademgorodok was a remarkably free space for the large numbers of scientists and their families who came to live there in the 1960s. In their minds, it was an environment in which the hierarchical ranks of Soviet society were relaxed and real intellectual enquiry was possible.[23]

Soviet secret cities and research centres drew the attention of the new instruments of surveillance developed by Cold War technologists. At the Geneva Summit of 1955, President Eisenhower proposed an 'open skies' agreement which would allow the US and USSR to fly reconnaissance missions over one another's territories in order to assess their military capabilities. The proposed treaty was also a means of testing the post-Stalinist authorities and was, as expected, rejected by Khrushchev and Bulganin. In fact, the Open Skies proposal was used to provide cover for the CIA's high-altitude spy plane, the U-2, which was capable of flying in altitudes beyond radar detection, and was soon to be deployed in secret reconnaissance missions over the USSR. Furthermore, the Corona satellite system (ostensibly a technology facilitating research in the earth sciences) was also being developed; this was the US's first venture into secret photography from space (6.5).[24] This represented an extension of what writer Paul Virilio has called the 'military field of perception' from its conventional sphere, the battlefield, to the entire planet.[25] In the early 1960s constant surveillance from reconnaissance aircraft and spy satellites became a fact of life in the Cold War, despite the efforts made to keep this technology secret. In the Pentagon, Corona satellite imagery was analysed to gather information on secret research and military sites in the USSR.

Invisible eyes, flying overhead to record life below, became very visible in May 1960 when a US U-2 spy plane was brought down over Sverdlovsk in the Soviet Union and its pilot, Gary Powers, paraded before the world's cameras. Two years later, in October 1962, the Cuban Missile Crisis – which almost turned the Cold War into nuclear war – was triggered by American air reconnaissance of Soviet surface-to-air missile sites on the island. For a number of months that autumn the CIA had been gathering reports from refugees fleeing Cuba about the build-up of Soviet weapons there, despite loud USSR denials. What was as yet unclear was whether these missiles were defensive or offensive weapons.

Soviet Airfield (first image), 18 August 1960

6.5
First image captured by US Corona satellite of Mys Shmidta Air Field, USSR. Photograph, 18 August 1960

6.6
Cuban Missile Crisis: U-2 photograph of first intermediate-range ballistic missile site under construction, 17 October 1962

To establish this, President Kennedy ordered U-2 high-altitude flights over Cuba: using cameras with highly sensitive lenses and films it was possible to capture remarkable ground-level details from planes flying at 40,000ft (an achievement which would have been easily impeded had the Soviets camouflaged their work; 6.6). The resulting images proved that Soviet technicians were preparing offensive ballistic weapons capable of striking American cities. Kennedy took this information first to his allies in London and Paris and then, on 25 October, to the American public via a television broadcast. He announced his intention to impose a naval blockade, a move which would put the two nuclear powers on a war footing and triggered panic around the world. Three days later, at the United Nations, American ambassador Adlai E. Stevenson called the Soviet Union's bluff when he produced a series of reconnaissance photographs. Whilst these images required careful interpretation by specialists and careful labelling and indications of scale for public consumption, they appeared to be the product of an automatic or technical

operation, the unblinking eye in the sky.

In the mid-1960s Cold War military technologists – in both East and the West – began exploring the sinister possibilities of electronic warfare. US scientists at MIT and Harvard devised the necessary weapons, including directed-beam laser weapons, 'land-air dams' designed to watch enemy movements, and missiles fitted with video cameras so that ground controllers could home in on their targets from the safety of military bases. Some of this technology came into operation in the Vietnam War: by 1967 an electronic surveillance centre operating in Thailand could process and relay information from ground sensors in Vietnam back to US fighter-bombers overhead. In such networks, in Virilio's words, 'nothing distinguishes the functions of the weapon and the eye; the projectile's image and the image's projectile form a single composite. In its tasks of detection and acquisition, pursuit and destruction, the projectile is an image or signature on a screen, and the television picture is an ultrasonic projectile at the speed of light'.[26]

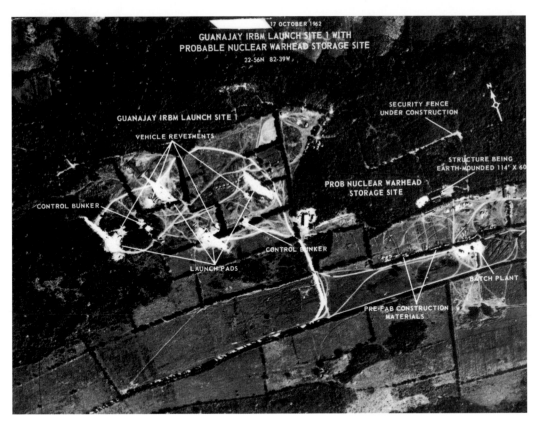

17 OCTOBER 1962

GUANAJAY IRBM LAUNCH SITE 1 WITH
PROBABLE NUCLEAR WARHEAD STORAGE SITE

22-56N 82-39W

GUANAJAY IRBM LAUNCH SITE 1

SECURITY FENCE
UNDER CONSTRUCTION

VEHICLE REVETMENTS

STRUCTURE BEING
EARTH-MOUNDED 114' X 60

CONTROL BUNKER

PROB NUCLEAR WARHEAD
STORAGE SITE

CONTROL BUNKER

LAUNCH PADS

BATCH PLANT

PRE-FAB CONSTRUCTION
MATERIALS

OK computer

I know you and Dave were planning
to disconnect me. And I'm afraid that's
something I cannot allow to happen.
(HAL, *2001: A Space Odyssey*, 1968)

The use of cybernetic systems to regulate
man's actions or, conversely, the level of
control exercised by man over advanced
technology, was the cause of much disquiet
in the 1950s and 1960s. The most important
expression of this was made in Stanley
Kubrick's 1968 film, *2001: A Space Odyssey*.
At the heart of the film is the spectre of
artificial intelligence, of machines beginning
to think as men and then utilizing this
capacity for destructive purpose. This was
already a popular theme amongst film-makers
eager to update the image of 'Frankenstein's
monster' for a Cold War audience. Kubrick
broke with science-fiction convention in his
depiction of HAL, the murderous computer
which could lip-read, recognize speech, play
chess and express emotion. Prior to HAL,
futuristic visions of man-machine hybrids

had usually taken the form of robots, with
their clanking imitation of human movement.
Unlike Robbie the Robot in *Forbidden Planet*
(1956), HAL is not a metal man but a system,
a complex architecture of abstract technologies, whose only physical human parallels
are the voice and the 'red eye' lenses with
which the computer scans the room. The
interior of the 'brain room', the only place
where the errant technology can be dismantled, is a minimal, modernist space, no mess
of wires and cables, only smooth surfaces
of metal, acrylic and light which are discon-
nected silently (6.7).

The fictional supercomputer as depicted
in the 1960s was sinister, corrupted and
capable of turning on its human operatives.
Not all, like HAL, were vulnerable. In the
film *Colossus: The Forbin Project* (1970), based
on a 1966 novel by Dennis Feltham Jones,
the American supercomputer built to direct
nuclear missiles joins forces with its Soviet
counterpart to assume global control, using
the nuclear missiles guided by computers
as threat against action. Constructed to
be impervious to attack, the computers are
found to be invincible when they seize power
from their creators. Often, the supercomputer
was presented as the tool of some shadowy
organization or regime intent on taking control
by nefarious means, as in Jean-Luc Godard's
Alphaville (1965) and Len Deighton's sequel
to *The Ipcress File* (1965), *Billion Dollar
Brain* (1967).

Despite the often ludicrous plot lines of
these films, the computers depicted strayed
very little in their design language from the
giant systems then in production by IBM,
Olivetti and other such leading corporations
in the field. For *2001: A Space Odyssey*,
Kubrick intended his vision of the future
to be grounded in what was considered
achievable technological advancement in
the mid-1960s. For this reason, the film was
'furnished' with commercially available
products such as Olivier Mourgue's Djinn
furniture (6.8), and peppered with recognizable brand-names such as Hilton Hotels
and Honeywell computers.[27] Over a hundred
experts were consulted during the film's
development,[28] from aerospace specialists
to industrial designers. Eliot Noyes' studio[29]
was approached to advise on the presentation
of electronic technologies.[30] As John Harwood

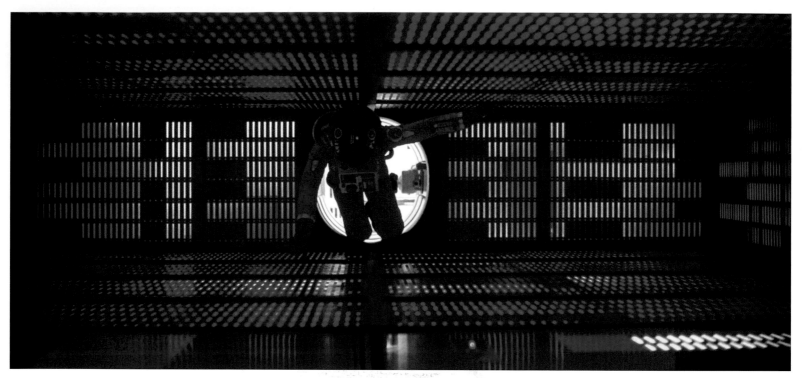

6.7
Astronaut Dave Bowman
(played by Keir Dullea)
inside the computer HAL.
Still from *2001: A Space
Odyssey*, directed by Stanley
Kubrick, 1968

6.8
Olivier Mourgue, chaise
longue of Djinn series. Steel
tube frame, polyurethane
foam upholstery and
stretch material, 1963,
manufactured by Airborne
International (1964).
V&A: Circ.201-1969

The Hi-Tech Cold War

explains in his essay (p.192 below), the appearance of IBM computers was part of a carefully managed exercise in building an understanding of computing through corporate identity, which extended from the design of graphical interfaces to the staging of multimedia events.[31] This visual language, the aesthetic epitome of technological modernity, also proved effective in giving the computer a more troubling identity in film. The buttons, dials and flashing lights, the whirring reels of magnetic tape, the clean, modular architecture of flush metal panels – all details which arose from the drive to make computer technology both comprehensible and user-friendly – were also employed by film-makers as a plausible language of techno-fear.

2001: A Space Odyssey considers the consequences of machines having an intelligence equivalent to or greater than man's. From its opening sequences, in which primitive man discovers how natural objects (bones) can be used as tools and weapons, Kubrick's film is concerned with technology as an 'extension of man'. But if HAL represents the point at which man's modification of technology threatens humankind, the film also suggests a final stage of transition from the human body into a kind of cosmic sublime intelligence with the mutation of Dave Bowman into the Starchild at the culmination of the film.

The film provoked widespread debate about its aesthetic significance. Film writer Gene Youngblood described it as 'a kind of cinematic Bauhaus' in its adherence to a minimalist aesthetic. Critical of the its portrayal of 'man/machine symbiosis as ominous or threatening',[32] he nevertheless lauded *2001* for its 'expanded' use of sophisticated cinematic technology, exemplified by the 'Star Gate' corridor sequence at the end of the film, achieved by its famous 'slit-scan' mechanical process in which a screen with a slit is mounted onto a moving stand between the camera and a light source, the effect of which is to produce a controlled blur of psychedelic light when filmed (6.9).[33]

Youngblood's influential writing on film (which married the philosophies of McLuhan,

Wiener and Buckminster Fuller to film studies) proposed a cybernetic understanding of film, video and television. 'Just as the term 'man' is coming to mean man/plant/machine', he wrote, 'so the definition of cinema must be expanded to include videotronics, computer science, and atomic light'.[34] Characteristic of a Cold War generation whose youth and political consciousness had been defined by television, Youngblood spoke as an advocate of the liberating potential of broadcast media. He was by no means alone in his enthusiasms. Young architects from the Archigram group in Britain to the Metabolists in Japan were fascinated by the potential of communications technology as architecture.

From hardware to software

In an essay of 1968 entitled 'The Triumph of Software', British architectural critic Peter Reyner Banham compared the use of technology in Kubrick's *2001* as 'all that grey plastic ... knobs and switches' to the 'software' of Roger Vadim's film *Barbarella* (1968), with its pneumatic heroine and inflatable sets: 'the living, breathing vision of a friendly, sexy, adaptable personal environment'.[35] If Banham's use of the terms hard/software was a creative abuse of computing terminology, it nevertheless served to reveal the extent to which computer language had permeated popular understanding. Ever alert to the latest fashions, it also underlined Banham's interest in the emerging aesthetic of temporary, inflatable and portable structures, in which services and gadgetry provide the essential components of architecture, and sound, light and video effects are used to furnish spaces.[36]

In the 1960s the home of the future was envisaged by young architects as 'plugged in' to the array of appliances which constituted the tools of everyday life – from air-conditioning to food and waste disposal, gadgets for housework, entertainment and environmental control. Banham summed up the changing role of the home, in an article published in *Art in America* in 1965, thus: 'When your house contains ... so many services that the hardware could stand up by itself without any assistance from the house, why have a house to hold it up?'[37] Indeed, as illustrated by François Dallegret (6.31), the accompanying images show Banham himself housed in an architecture which is little more than

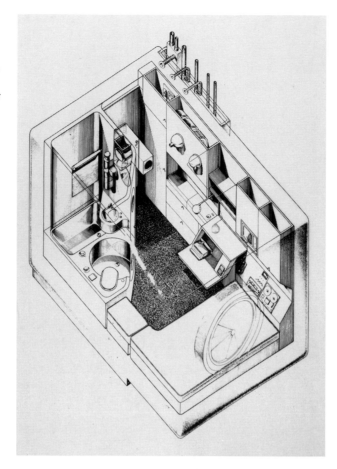

6.10
Kisho Kurokawa, *Nagakin-Capsule-Highrise*, isometric drawing of the interior of a capsule. Transparent reproduction on film, 1972. Deutsches Architekturmuseum, Frankfurt am Main

a transparent bubble inflated by air-conditioning output.

In the 1960s young Japanese architects associated with the Metabolist group went furthest in realizing the idea of the living capsules. Kisho Kurokawa's Nagakin 14-storey capsule tower completed in the Ginza district of the Japanese capital in 1972 was built to provide inexpensive accommodation for businessmen working late in central Tokyo during the week (6.10).[38] Each room is a one-person capsule based on the proportions of a shipping container with a circular window, a built-in bed and bathroom unit. Assembled in a factory and arriving on site complete with TV, radio and alarm clock, each room was hoisted into place by crane and fastened to the concrete core shaft. The units were designed to be detachable and replaceable (with the architect putting a 30-year expiry date on the units). The Nagakin Capsule Tower was most famous and widely reproduced realization of the Metabolists' vision of the

6.11
Raymond Loewy, design
for a stateroom in a
spacestation for NASA,
c.1968. Postercolour, pen,
ink and chalk on board.
V&A: E.3203–1980

future city fashioned from prefabricated elements. In an article of March 1969 entitled 'Capsule Declaration' Kurokawa declared: 'architecture from now will increasingly take on the character of equipment'. He used the cybernetic concept of feedback to conceive of an environment based on the flow of information:

> the capsule is a feedback mechanism in an information-oriented, a 'technetronic' society. It is a device which permits us to reject undesired information ... To protect us from the flood of information and the one-way traffic in information, we should have a feedback mechanism and a mechanism which rejects unnecessary information. The capsule serves as such a space.[39]

The spacesuit and space capsules – environments in which the body and technology are intimately connected – were, alongside cybernetics, key progenitors of such new architectural thinking. In 1966, NASA had begun to properly investigate the requirements for space habitation with its Skylab space station project (an offshoot of the Saturn-Apollo programme). The space station would

make possible the study of living in space over an extended period – and to this end a habitability programme was established to consider its physical as well as psychological effects. From 1967 until Skylab's eventual launch in 1973, NASA engaged Raymond Loewy as industrial design consultant. Loewy experimented with zero-gravity environments, and also proposed various products for use by astronauts (6.11).

The most spectacular examples of architectural 'software' of the period were derived from the spacesuits worn by astronauts in their trips into space and on the surface of the Moon (6.12).[40] Like small spacecraft, the suits had to supply the wearer with a supply of oxygen as well as control the temperature of his body and provide for the removal of waste. Electronic systems were used to monitor health and provide communication with Earth. Wearing their microenvironments, cosmonauts and astronauts came close to Manfred E. Clynes and Nathan S. Kline's conception of the 'cyborg', an enhanced human being who could survive in extraterrestrial environments. Clynes, an engineer and neuropsychologist, and Kline, a psychiatrist, developed the concept in studies of astronautics for NASA during the 1960s. As they wrote in 1960,

> The task of adapting man's body to any environment he may choose will be made easier by increased knowledge of homeostatic functioning, the cybernetic aspects of which are just beginning to be understood and investigated ... man in space, in addition to flying his vehicle, must continually be checking on things and making adjustments merely in order to keep himself alive, he becomes a slave to the machine. The purpose of the Cyborg, as well as his own homeostatic systems, is to provide an organizational system in which such robot-like problems are taken care of automatically and unconsciously, leaving man free to explore, to create, to think, and to feel.[41]

In the whirlwind of technological advance, it comes as no surprise that the spacesuit provided a possible model for a cyborg architecture. In his 1968 manifesto 'Alles ist Architektur', Hans Hollein described the

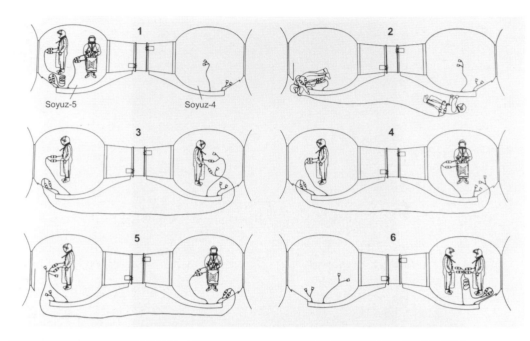

jet helmet, spacesuit and space capsule as
the ideal 'minimum dwelling'.[42] Archigram's
'Suitaloon', designed by Michael Webb
and exhibited at the 14th Milan Triennale in
1968 where it was described as 'full nomadic
unit', was a complete environment that could
be carried on the back (6.13).[43] Combining
a 'spine' (an armature) and a suit in the form
of an inflatable 'skin' containing food, water
supply, radio and acoustic apparatuses Webb
blurred the man-machine distinction further.
Ironic and spectacular, his project pointed
to underlying anxiety in the Cold War world:
what events on Earth would require humanity
to equip itself thus?

Teletowers

The swift translation of military and space-
race technological advances into mainstream
commercial applications was most evidently
seen in the field of telecommunications.
The development of microwave transmission
in the 1950s, which allowed for the relay
of telephone, television and radar signals
across continents, was used simultaneously
for civilian and military traffic. The British
network of relay stations, which included
the London Post Office Tower (built by the
Ministry of Public Building and Works in
1961–4; 6.14), served as a symbol of both
Harold Wilson's 'white heat [of] technology'
and a future based on global communications.[44] Furthermore, the breathless pace of
satellite successes since Sputnik had resulted
in Telstar, launched at Cape Canaveral on 10
July 1962, the world's first communications
satellite which was capable of transmitting
transatlantic telephone calls and live television broadcasts.[45] These developments meant
that television, the integration of which into
the American home was almost complete by
the end of the 1950s,[46] took on an international
dimension in the 1960s, a step towards that
'electronic interdependence' which McLuhan
said constituted the global village.[47]

The spate of television towers built
across the world in the 1950s and 1960s were
important gauges in Cold War competition.
Dependent on achievements in structural engineering and electronics, they demonstrated
the command of Eastern and Western states
over different bodies of technical knowledge.
Unlike the largely utilitarian radio masts of the
pre-war period which served the aural regimes

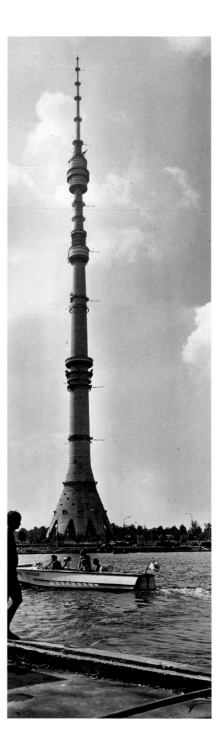

6.14
Ministry of Public Building and Works (chief architect Eric Bedford), the BT Tower, formerly the Post Office Tower, London, built 1961–4, opened 1965

6.15
Nikolai Nikitin (designer), Leonid Batalov and D. I. Burdin (architects), Ostankino Television Tower, Moscow, opened 1967

6.16
Karel Hubáček, Ještěd
telecommunications tower,
Liberec, 1968–73

6.17
Otakar Binar, dining room in
Ještěd telecommunications
tower and hotel, Liberec,
1968–73

of sound broadcasting, the teletowers of the 1950s and 1960s were knitted into the scopic regimes and information networks of the Cold War. Not only were they constructed to transmit television signals (see below); the visual effects of these enormous structures were an intrinsic part of their significance.

The first television tower was erected by Süddeutscher Rundfunk in Stuttgart, to Fritz Leonhardt's design (1954–6). In Eastern Europe, new towers followed in the wake of Bulganin's announcement of the 'Scientific Technological Revolution' during the Thaw. In 1959 the Soviet Ministry of Communications commissioned a new television tower to serve the Soviet capital. This decision represented the growing awareness that television would occupy a central role in socialist Eastern Europe, just as it did in the West.[48] Moscow's Ostankino Tower opened in 1967 to mark the 50th anniversary of the October Revolution, a moment of renewed futurism in the USSR (6.15). It was the hub of the all-Union network, then the world's largest broadcasting complex. Soviet television pictures – using Molniya satellites – were relayed across the eleven time zones and the sometimes mountainous terrain of the country.

By 1970 over 70 per cent of the population could receive a Soviet television signal.[49]

The fact that Moscow's new Tatlin Tower was, at 536m high, also the world's tallest structure when it opened amplified its propaganda value.[50] Unlike the prefabricated panel-constructed apartment buildings which were then being built in the Eastern Bloc to standard designs using mass-produced elements, these were bespoke structures which utilized the best design talents and precious resources. The Ostankino Tower drew upon the research expertise of 40 design and research institutes and dozens of Soviet construction organizations.

The telecommunications tower on top of the Ještěd mountain in Czechoslovakia is probably the most extraordinary architectural achievement of the period of communist rule in Central Europe (6.16, 6.17). Designed by a team of architects working in the local state architectural office (Stavoprojekt Office '7', later better known as Atelier SIAL) in the nearby city of Liberec in 1963, it is a piece of bravura engineering. The cone-shaped tower continues the profile of the mountain to a perfect vertical point. To construct the tower – combining telecommunications

station and hotel – on its site, a concrete core was sunk into the bedrock. This functioned as a 'pendulum' to counterbalance the damaging vibrations caused by the wind during the tower's construction. The tower's skin, above the accommodation level, is fashioned from fibreglass rods and panels – without a single metal element – to allow the unhindered transmission of radio and television signals. When in the late 1960s work on this difficult project on its inhospitable site slowed down, the chief architect, Karel Hubáček, appealed to the head of state, President Svoboda, for renewed support. This building was, as the architects stressed, at the forefront of the scientific and technological revolution.[51] Its national significance and socialist credentials were incontestable.[52]

Cold War television towers cannot just be understood as high-tech instruments or as symbols of Cold War competition: they were designed to attract the public to them. After all, they typically combined viewing towers, restaurants and hotels, features of the leisure economy. Roland Barthes, in a classic essay on the Eiffel Tower, emphasized the way in which this vertiginous triumph of nineteenth-century engineering and science cast an irrational spell over its age, becoming the focus of dreams and bodily pleasures.[53] A parallel can be drawn with the Cold War television tower, whose sculptural forms self-consciously referred to rockets and other contemporary fantasies of interstellar space travel. To realise this myth, for instance, both Ostankino Tower and the East Berlin Fernsehturm (6.18) were staffed by air hostesses dressed in synthetic uniforms (6.19). At Ještěd, Czech glass artists Stanislav Libenský and Jaroslava Brychtová were commissioned to produce glass meteorites which were then set into the building's concrete core as if they had crashed to Earth from space.

Teletowers were the focus of a dual fascination amongst architects: their hard-edged physical forms presented tremendous engineering challenges, yet at the same time they suggested the dematerialization of technology. By the early 1960s the Earth was becoming sheathed in an invisible cloud of electronic signals – what McLuhan memorably termed a 'cosmic membrane'. Many architects saw the future city as, in Kenzo

6.18
East Berlin
telecommunications
tower, 1965–9. Project
realization by Fritz Dieter
and Günter Franke after
a design by Hermann
Henselmann

6.19
Gera Wernitz, costume
designs for telecom-
munications tower staff
in East Berlin. Pen,
watercolour and sample
swatches, 1968. Stiftung
Stadtmuseum, Berlin

6.20
Archigram (Peter Cook),
Montreal '67 Tower, section
A–A with descriptions
of functions. Ink on
transparency, 1963.
Deutsches Architektur-
museum, Frankfurt
am Main

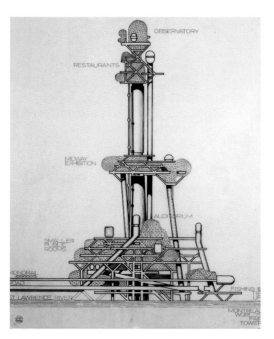

Tange's words, 'tied together by the invisible cords of a communication system'.[54] As early as 1963 Archigram suggested that electronic communication networks would invalidate fixed physical ones; architecture would become communication:

> The foreseeable rapid rate of change in transportation method may eventually make invalid the concept of a rigid mobile communications network as the main urban structure. A whole area of study is open for experiment of expendable systems and more flexible technology in terms of communication networks.... Large organizations will control their own visual communications network, allowing for a city center control with satellites dispersed in constant touch with the communication center, no longer dependent on physical communication.[55]

The fourth issue of Archigram's eponymous magazine (1964) included Peter Cook's prize-winning (but unbuilt) designs for an Entertainment Tower for Expo '67 in Montreal (6.20), which consisted of a central concrete core onto which temporary facilities, such as auditoria, could be suspended. Appearing as if Telstar had crash-landed into a NASA launch pad, the tower embodied the group's 'plug-in' ethos and paid homage to all of their technological enthusiasms, from geodesic domes to multi-media entertainment.

War in the airwaves

In 1964 McLuhan wrote: 'The "cold war" ... is really an electric battle of information and of images that goes far deeper and is more obsessional than the old hot wars of industrial hardware.'[56] He viewed television as the most significant weapon in a battleground where 'the dichotomy between civilian and military' had disappeared.[57] Its total penetration into ordinary homes in the USA in the 1940s and in Europe a few years later was decisive.[58] When 'the FBI and the CIA were looking in the rear view mirror for the revolutionary agents', the cathode-ray tube in the corner of the living room seemed like a bridgehead for anti-American forces.[59]

Writing in the 1960s, McLuhan was clearly casting a glance back at Senator Joe McCarthy's campaign conducted on and

against television to rid the USA of 'communist influences'.[60] But his attention was also drawn to the present. International diplomacy was increasingly conducted through the television screen. In fact, the famous Khrushchev-Nixon clash at the American National Exhibition in Moscow in 1959, where the two leaders argued over the capabilities of capitalism and state socialism to deliver the highest quality of life, one of their running exchanges took place in a television studio installed by the United States Information Agency (USIA) to demonstrate the USA's superior command of peaceful technologies.[61]

In 1961 Daniel Boorstin coined the term 'pseudo-event' to describe the way in which news was styled and timed for the hungry attention of the television cameras.[62] Television began to organize history. When Apollo 11 landed on the surface of the Moon in July 1969, astronaut Neil Armstrong's first task as he stepped down the ladder on to its surface was to switch on a television camera. An estimated audience of more than 600 million people watched the ghostly images it recorded of astronauts walking on the surface of the Moon (6.21). Soviet viewers were, however, denied the opportunity to be eyewitnesses to history. Their bill of fare on 21 July 1969 was a Soviet musical followed by a brief announcement of the moon walk in *Pravda*.[63]

Unhindered by international borders, television and radio broadcasts had – despite this lunar eclipse over the Soviet Union – important effects, particularly in those Cold War border regions where East met West. The purpose of the Voice of America, a wartime radio broadcaster, was renewed by Cold War tensions. Operating under the aegis of the USIA, it broadcast news and discussion to the rest of the World including, of course, the Soviet Union and her satellite states. Radio Free Europe was established in 1950 with a declared anti-communist brief. Funded by the American Congress, the radio station broadcast news and opinion pieces by émigrés. Its first short-wave signal was transmitted from a West German station in Czech, and its broadcasts soon extending to the rest of the Eastern Bloc. From the early days of the Cold War in 1948, Voice of America and Radio Free Europe broadcasts were met by specially emitted radio interference

as Budapest citizens rented rooms for the weekend to watch the television signal from Vienna, only fifty miles away.[67] Unable or unwilling to block television reception, the East German authorities invested considerable ideological energy in dismissing the news and images of everyday life tapped by East German rooftop antennae. A notorious weekly television programme, *Der Schwarze Kanal* (*The Black Channel*), was broadcast from 1960 (before the Berlin Wall was erected) by Deutscher Fernsehfunk, the state broadcaster. Playing clips of West German television with a disparaging commentary, the East Germans set out to reveal the 'lies' and 'errors' they contained.

McLuhan famously took the view that television was a 'cool medium', requiring much more conscious participation by the viewer than 'hot media' like radio.[68] GDR viewers were perhaps even more active than most: few appear to have been convinced by *Der Schwarze Kanal* and other attempts to counter the West German media.[69] Their preference for West German television stimulated an active imagination. By picturing life in the West as more beautiful and satisfying, according to Milena Veenis, citizens of the DDR – particularly late in the history of the East German State – could imagine that the world in which they lived was somehow illusory and unreal.[70]

In Western Europe, the *Internationale Situationniste* – the mouthpiece of sharp critics of the consumer society clustered around French writer Guy Debord – took a rather more disparaging view of television than McLuhan. It dubbed the box in the corner of the room 'the technology of isolation', which simulated sociality whilst producing alienated individuals. The editors of the journal were drawn to the following news item, which had appeared in the French press in 1962:

If you are a TV fanatic, you will definitely be interested in the newest, most extraordinary television set in the world: a TV that can go with you everywhere. Thanks to a totally new shape designed by the Hughes Aircraft Corporation in the USA, this television set is meant to be worn on the head. Weighing in at a mere 950 grams, it is actually installed on the type of headgear worn by pilots

from Soviet transmitters designed to make their signals inaudible.

The jamming of the airwaves was the cause of persistent anger in Central Europe. The electronic buzzing signal and, after 1964, speech and music (aural camouflage which sought to give the impression of atmospheric interference) may well have blocked Western broadcasts, but it transmitted one clear meaning: censorship. When Poles in Poznań rioted against the authorities in June 1956, during the period of political instability which followed Khrushchev's revelations at the Twentieth Congress of the Communist Party of the Soviet Union, one of their targets was a local radio station.[64] Their intention was not to broadcast, but to destroy. They smashed the jamming equipment there by hurling it out of the windows of the building.[65] When Władysław Gomułka's new regime took power in October 1956, it suspended jamming

to demonstrate its reform credentials. In the freeze-thaw pattern of communist rule in Eastern Europe, the jamming of Western radio broadcasts was a relatively good barometer of the political temperature. It reappeared in Poland after 1960, a clear sign that de-Stalinization was over.

Whilst Western radio broadcasts were frequently jammed throughout the Cold War period, television signals – a new presence in the atmosphere – were left unmolested. Blocking West German and Austrian television signals was not only technically more difficult, it would have also meant spoiling the reception of their domestic viewers, a matter which would have caused a diplomatic storm.[66] When Hungarians were able to purchase the first television sets in the late 1950s, they quickly tuned into Austrian programming. The town of Sopron becoming a centre of 'television tourism' around 1960,

6.21
Buzz Aldrin and the US flag
on the Moon. Photograph,
20 July 1969

6.22
Walter Pichler, TV helmet,
'Portable Living Room'.
Polyester, varnished white,
integrated TV monitor with
TV cable, 1967. Sammlung
Generali Foundation, Vienna

6.23
**Haus-Rucker-Co (Laurids
Ortner, Günter Zamp Kelp
and Klaus Pinter)**, photograph
of the artists wearing
'Environment Trans-
formers', 1968

and telephone operators. Thanks to a mount, its tiny round screen made of plastic and reminiscent of a monocle is kept at a distance of four centimeters from the eye ... You use only one eye to watch the image. With the other eye, according to the manufacturer, you can continue to look elsewhere, read, or engage in manual labor.[71]

In what had become already a standard Cold War pattern, the Hughes Aircraft Corporation, the producer of military technology, was looking for domestic applications for early 'Virtual Reality' helmets designed for high-altitude pilots. To the *Internationale Situationniste* this announcement revealed not only this technology's recent past but also its future as a sinister instrument turning viewers into automatons.

The idea of the television helmet stimulated sardonic responses from counter-cultural designers and artists in Vienna. In 1967, for instance, Walter Pichler conceived a 'Portable Living Room' (6.22), a missile-shaped helmet that included a television screen. Enclosed and with his or her senses triggered by electronic stimuli, the wearer was turned into a cyborg. Similarly, the early projects of Viennese group Haus-Rucker-Co included the 'Environment Transformer' helmets 'Flyhead', 'Viewatomizer' and 'Drizzler' (all 1968; 6.23). Each formed an entire environment, disengaging the wearer from his or her setting and repressing the senses so that the habitual ways of seeing or hearing might be broken and new imaginative capacities

discovered.[72] Like many counter-cultural schemes of the late 1960s, Haus-Rucker-Co's helmets offered an eccentric balance between utopia and distopia.

In 1969 Krzysztof Wodiczko was exploring similar themes, albeit with a very different effects, in the People's Republic of Poland.[73] Living in an environment in which the State engaged in the surveillance of society and controlled the supply of all resources, Wodiczko produced a communication device that inverted the libertarian aspect of Haus-Rucker-Co's helmets. Whilst the Austrian architects imagined switching off the world around the wearer, Wodiczko amplified it. At that time he was working as a designer for Unitra, the main state electronics conglomerate in Warsaw. He designed a series of artworks that he called 'products', some manufactured with expertise and equipment appropriated from the State. His 'Personal Instrument' (1969; 6.24), for instance, was a device worn on the head and hands. Responding to the movements of the wearer, the device allowed the individual to amplify or diminish the flow of sound from the environment. A sensor on the glove turned the hand into a microphone. The 'Personal Instrument' was an allegorical device that alluded to state surveillance of the individual. At the same time, the user excluded him/herself from the collective (a requirement, as Wodiczko specified that the 'Personal Instrument' was 'for the exclusive use of the artist which created it'). The extent to which Wodiczko's movements were his own remained uncertain, determined as they

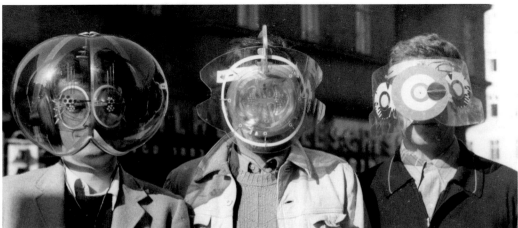

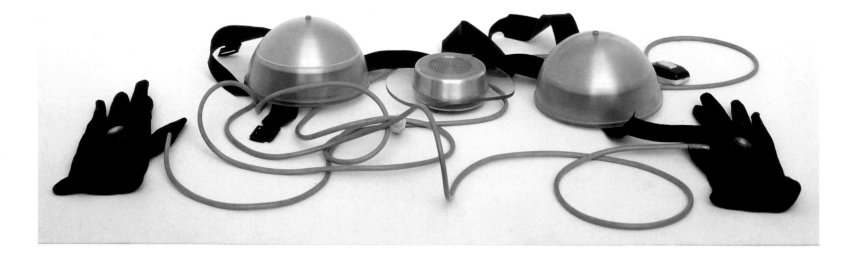

The Hi-Tech Cold War

were by the technology he was wearing.

The theme of freedom of action was also explored in a performance, *Bare Transmittors*, produced by Wodiczko at this time. One group of performers was instructed to press the buttons and dials on 12 transistor radios, following a 'score' written by Wodiczko and his collaborator Szabolcs Esztenyi, whilst a group of young musicians played classical music. Both groups were conducted by Esztenyi. Although the composition specified volume and tempo, each radio was tuned to a different wavelength so the result was cacophony. In this duel between music and noise, Wodiczko and Esztenyi reproduced the classified sounds of Eastern Bloc airwaves.

A blast on the senses

If broadcast television was criticized by some for its one-way flow of images, its manipulation of events and its isolation of the individual, other multi-media technologies were embraced for their potential to deliver synaesthetic and kinetic effects. The shift into multimedia environments was more than just a matter of designing novel spaces: architects and designers came to conceive their field of interest as not just the design of interiors, but the production of different kinds of embodied consciousness. And, as was so often the case during the Cold War, the technological innovation that made this potential realizable in the fields of film, television, video and computer-generated imagery was often the by-product of military-industrial research.

In 1958 the Californian computer artist and film-maker John Whitney, working in collaboration with his brother James, built an analogue computer to create the cosmic films of light, colour and music which he called 'liquid architecture'.[74] Whitney, who had worked at Lockheed Aircraft Co. during the Second World War, was familiar with the analogue systems used to operate anti-aircraft guns. Using a military surplus M5 anti-aircraft gun director as a platform (later supplemented with an M7) he built a computer (or 'cam-machine') that would allow him to plot graphics and make complex special effects. Developed from the type of apparatus on which Wiener had based his first cybernetic studies during the Second World War, the machine was one of the first examples of a cybernetic art-tool. Whitney used his

invention to create extraordinary optical landscapes, collected together in the 1961 film-reel *Catalog* (6.25), an influential forerunner of the 'mind-expanding' visual effects and sensory environments of the 1960s.[75]

Like his friends the designers Charles and Ray Eames, Whitney successfully combined his work on corporate and industrial projects with his experiments in the borderlands between art and technology. He made television commercials, title sequences for films (including the op-art opening to Hitchcock's *Vertigo* of 1958, with Saul Bass), even information films on guided missiles.[76] From 1966 to 1969 Whitney was the first artist in residence at IBM, and worked with the company to develop the creative use of the System 360 digital computers. His beautiful, cosmic, computer-generated films did not, like the Eames's work for IBM, seek to explain the computer, but rather contributed to the idea that the computer could be a tool of the imagination.

Whitney had worked with Charles and Ray Eames, pioneering figures in multisensory and multi-media techniques, on their

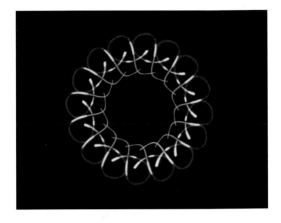

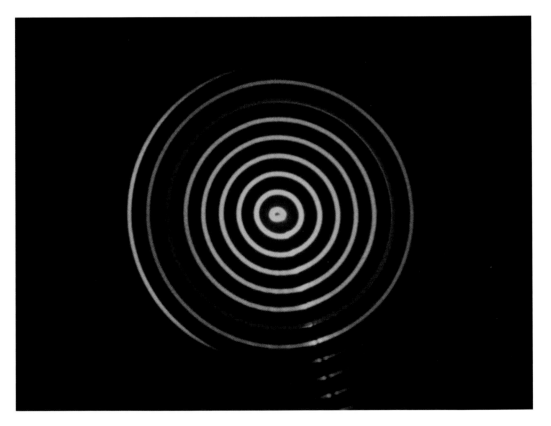

Varèse's music to produce moments of sensory dissonance. The angular interior of the pavilion sometimes functioned as a baffle dampening the sound, and at other points like a sounding-board amplifying resonance. The effect was, according to contemporary accounts, disorientating (a sensation hardly compensated for by the film's presentation of Le Corbusier's architecture as a remedy for the twentieth century's ills).

In the dualistic fashion characteristic of so much technological development during the Cold War, these visions of immersive, multimedia environments designed to restore human bodies and stimulate anaesthetized minds were accompanied by sinister doppelgängers. As Beatrix Colomina has pointed out, multi-screen presentation had long been a feature of both the government Situation Room and the military Control Centre.[85] Other parallels can be drawn between the new multimedia environments amongst designers in high fashion and the techniques of mind-control developed by the security services on both sides of the Iron Curtain.

In 1959 Hungarian anti-communist activist Lajos Ruff published his experience of treatment at the hands of his interrogators in Hungary six years earlier.[86] He described his cell as a new kind of cinema in which transparent furniture and a curved bed were designed to estrange the prisoner. Already deranged by drugs, he was made to watch projections of absurd and erotic films, mixed with other scenes recorded in the cell itself. Finally, in a *coup de grâce*, he was addressed by visitors as if he had participated in one of the adventure stories that he had been compelled to watch, confusing the boundary between art and life in this cinema-cell. Widely reported in the Western press, Ruff's experiences drew the attention of the *International Situationniste* journal. An article in the first issue (1958) reflected on Ruff's experiences to examine the potential of what it called 'ambient construction',[87] challenging 'progressive artists' to win 'the race [with] the police to experiment with and develop the use of the new techniques of conditioning'. Like a monstrous version of Bertolt Brecht's

epic theatre, updated with the new techniques of psychological warfare, this order of cinema promised a radical destruction of the subject. Such environments – whether repressive or 'liberating' – detonated the fiction of the 'humanist, artistic and juridical conception of the unalterable, inviolable personality'. This was something that the *International Situationniste* welcomed with characteristic zeal. 'Truly experimental cinema' would not restore sensation, let alone broadcast the achievements of American corporations: it would amplify the disruptive and 'destructive' effects of the new mechanical technologies of 'industrial cinema'.

Ruff's description of his experiences in a Budapest cell shared much in common with fictional representations of brainwashing in the early 1960s. Richard Condon's *The Manchurian Candidate* (1959), Len Deighton's *Ipcress File* (1962; 6.28) and Anthony Burgess's *A Clockwork Orange* (1962) took mind control as their central themes. Employing the part-Anglo-American, part-Russian language Burgess called 'Nadsat', his novel's dark hero

6.28
Kenneth Adam, design for
the brainwashing chamber
in the film *The Ipcress
File*, directed by Sidney
J. Furie. Ink on paper, 1965.
Sir Kenneth Adam, London

describes the State-sanctioned torture regime
designed to cure him of his addiction to
violence:

> I had truly done my best morning and
> afternoon to play it their way and sit
> like a horrorshow smiling cooperative
> malchick in the chair of torture whilst
> they flashed nasty bits of ultra-violence
> on the screen, my glazzies clipped open
> to viddy all, my plot and rookers and
> nogas fixed to the chair so I could not get
> away. What I was being made to viddy
> now was not really a veshch I would have
> thought to be too bad before ... But it was
> the throb and like crash crash crash in my
> gulliver and the wanting to be sick.[88]

One direct connection between the
multimedia environment and the disturbed
space of the torture chamber occurred in
1965 when Andy Warhol bought the rights
to make a film version of Burgess's novel.
Evidently fascinated by the brainwashing
scenes, Warhol ignored the moral aspect of the
original narrative in favour of a rapturous and
amphetamine-loaded celebration of sadomaso-
chism.[89] The resulting film, entitled *Vinyl* –
featuring Factory 'star' Gerard Malanga and
Tosh Carillo engaging in fantasy violence
dressed in leather – occupies a relatively
modest role in Warhol's oeuvre. In fact, the
film footage was rapidly absorbed into other
Warhol projects. It was, for instance, used
as a backdrop and over-projected with
psychedelic light effects and coloured gels
as well as performances by the Velvet
Underground at Warhol's Exploding Plastic
Inevitable (EPI) intermedia events in 1966–
7.[90] The audience for this barrage of sights,
sounds and visual effects was enveloped into
a disorienting and cacophonous experience
that failed to cohere into a narrative or
harmonize into information. Critics queued
up to issue their condemnations. One wrote:
'it is an assemblage that actually vibrates
with menace, cynicism and perversion.
To experience it is to be brutalized, helpless.'[91]
      Even though McLuhan chose to illustrate
the EPI in his popular visual primer, *The
Medium is the Message* (1967), to represent
his embrace of the synaesthetic and environmental effects of the electronic media, the
EPI did little to support his vision of the

subject extended by new technology. On the
contrary, Branden W. Joseph has characterized the EPI as a 'contradictory, experimental
space [that] trafficked in emergent technological forces still lingering on the threshold
before their complete subsumption within
the market'.[92] Moreover, in returning *Vinyl*
to source, the brainwashing chamber, Warhol
seemed to realize the disruptive and 'destructive' 'industrial cinema' called for by the
Internationale Situationniste in 1958.

Cybersyn

> Just as every fact is also metaphysical,
> every piece of hardware implies
> software: information about its existence.
> Television is invisible. It's not an object.
> It's not a piece of furniture. The television
> set is irrelevant to the phenomenon
> of television. The videosphere is the
> noosphere transformed into a perceivable
> state.[93]

Like the Situationists in Paris, Gene Youngblood was sharply critical of American
television's role in the production of media
spectacles.[94] But he imagined ways in which
the medium could be rewired – in social terms
– to shake the viewer out of his or her stupor.
Television's one-way flow of images, Youngblood argued, should be replaced by the
'videosphere', a cybernetic conception of
communications that imagined the central
nervous system of the body extended by
computers and video cameras.[95] Youngblood's
call to adopt television and video as revolutionary media had its advocates elsewhere. In
America, one model emerged around 1970
that was known by its protagonists as
'Guerilla Television'.[96] One of the early
exponents of Guerilla Television was Ant
Farm, an American collective of architects
who had given up their profession to organize
happenings, festivals and media activism.
They were early adopters of the Sony Porta-
pak, the first portable video recording device,
introduced by the Japanese manufacturer
in 1967.[97] Heavy and cumbersome by today's
standards, this 'studio in a box' nevertheless
allowed artists to record and instantly play
back their films, which facilitated the rapid
rise of video art from the late 1960s. Ant
Farm's multi-media spectacles, such as the

6.29
Ant Farm, *Space Cowboy Meets Plastic Businessman*. Photograph of a performance at Alley Theatre, Houston, 1969

6.30
Cybersyn Operations Room, 1971–3. Industrial design and information design by the Product Design Group at the Institute of Technological Investigation, INTEC, Santiago. Industrial designers: **Guillermo Capdevila, Alfonso Gómez, Fernando Shultz, Rodrigo Walker, Werner Zemp and Gui Bonsiepe** (coordinator). Graphic designers: **Pepa Foncea, Lucía Wormald, Eddy Carmona and Jessie Cintolesi**

1969 Houston 'Electronic Oasis', combined inflatables, television monitors, slide projections and other such props. The dress-up carnival character of their events included pop-cultural television references, from the Kennedy Assassination to Apollo missions, which formed the basis for performances, which were filmed and then played back on video (6.29).

Writing in 1970, the Marxist critic Hans Magnus Enzensberger viewed the technophilia of groups like Ant Farm and the Guerilla Television movement as being essentially apolitical. 'The Underground', he wrote, 'may be increasingly aware of the technical and aesthetic possibilities of the disc, of videotape, of the electronic camera, and so on, and is systematically exploring the terrain, but it has no political viewpoint of its own and therefore mostly falls a helpless victim to commercialism.'[98] The capacity of capitalism to neutralize critique by reworking it as fashion also, as many commentators noted at the time, absorbed the counter-culture. For the most part, the counter-culture may have imagined instances of 'expanded consciousness' through multi-media, performance and happenings, but rarely could these events be enacted beyond the bounds of an advanced capitalist system.

And yet, in a curious footnote to the hi-tech Cold War, there was one instance where revolutionary politics sought active engagement with cybernetic culture. In 1970, the British operations research scientist and cybernetician Stafford Beer received an extraordinary invitation. Beer had become known through the 1960s for his work on systems thinking and organizations, working as a consultant to large corporations, lecturing occasionally at the Architectural Association and publishing on the application of cybernetic thinking to management structures. A charismatic and radical thinker, Beer had, surprisingly, acquired a faithful audience for his work in Chile, centered on an engineering student, Fernando Flores, who had come across his books. When Flores became the government minister responsible for the nationalization of major industries, following the democratic election of the left-wing Unidad Popular ('Popular Unity') coalition led by marxist Salvatore Allende's party in 1970, he contacted Beer. Rejecting the Soviet model

of centralized industry, Flores persuaded Beer to develop a more radical communications system that would feed back on and regulate the planned economy. The result was Cybersyn, a system of telex machines linking Chile's factories to a central control-room where data sent daily could be analysed to map and regulate patterns of supply, distribution and worker productivity.[99] Beer's concept was that this system would eventually expand into a network of citizen feedback directed to the heart of government, encouraging the development of a sense of collective responsibility via a 'decentralizing, worker-participative and anti-bureaucratic' system.[100]

Although Cybersyn did have some tangible successes in the early years (in helping to maintain the distribution of food supplies during a truck drivers strike, for example), it was still encountering teething problems when the right-wing military coup of 1973 toppled Allende's government. His palace bombed, Allende is thought to have committed suicide. A futuristic control-room (6.30), built only in prototype by a team led by interface designer Gui Bonsiepe, was eventually destroyed and Cybersyn itself dismantled. Bonsiepe, formerly of the Hochschule für Gestaltung in Ulm, Germany,

had moved to Chile after the school's dramatic closure in 1968 and became closely involved with the Cybersyn project.[101] The criticisms that had targeted Cybersyn in its brief existence (it was accused of exerting a technocratic, dehumanizing influence over Chilean society) were perhaps well founded, given that in its application Beer and his colleagues had largely failed to communicate its supposed revolutionary potential to its operatives. Nevertheless, as an experiment in the harnessing of cybernetic thinking to the actual reorganization of social and political structures in the spirit of revolution, it was both singular and remarkable. For a short period, the claims of the superpowers on hi-technology were wrested out of their hands: cybernetic technology was to serve the cause of utopia.

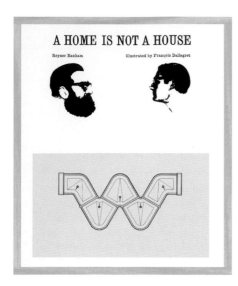

A HOME IS NOT A HOUSE

Reyner Banham   illustrated by François Dallegret

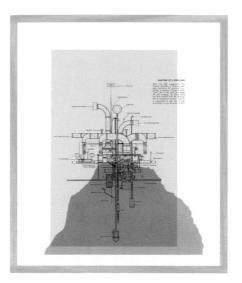

Dallegret's 20-20 hindsight and fore-
sight produced this historical capriccio
from the First Machine Age well before the present article was first
mooted. In the mode of its time, services are in a separate outhouse instead of being a mechanical clip-on.

SUPER-COUPE DE LONG-WEEK-END, 1927

Carrosserie Spéciale "La Parisienne"   Unité d'Habitation Grand-Confort, type Pullman   Cuisine et Bloc d'Eau, Marque "Révélation-Sanitaire"

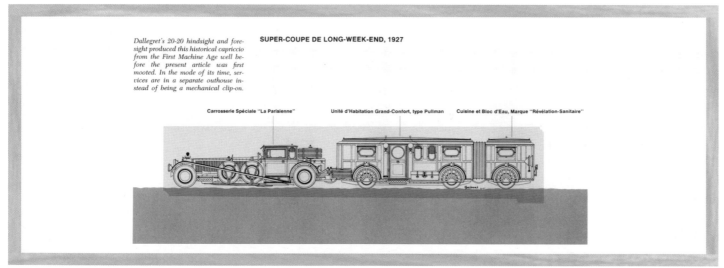

The present mobile home is a mess,
visually mechanically, and in its relationship to the permanent infrastructure of civilization. But if it could
be rendered more compact and mobile,
and be uprooted from its dependency
on static utilities, the trailer could ful-
fill its promise to put a nation on
wheels. The kind of mobile utility pack
suggested here does not exist yet, but it
may be no further over the hill than its
coming-attraction style would suggest.

TRAILMASTER GTO TRANSCONTINENTAL

Trailmaster GTO 2+2 with beefed rear axle and drive-train   Transcontinental "Instant Split-Level" trailer home   U-Tility Life-Support pack

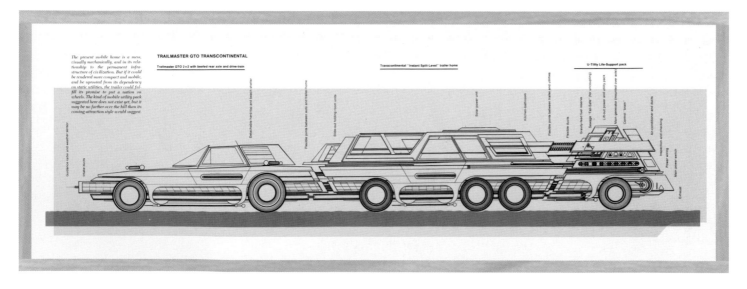

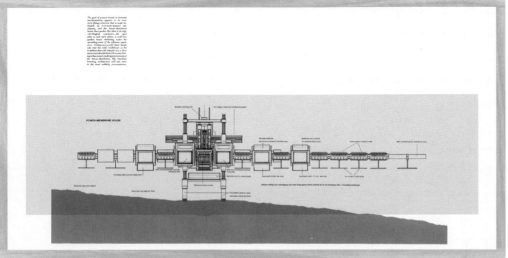

6.31
François Dallegret, *Un-house.
Transportable Standard-
of-Living Package. The
Environment Bubble*, from
Reyner Banham, 'A Home
Is Not a House', *Art in
America*, April 1965. Indian
ink on translucent film
and gelatin on transparent
acetate. Coll. François
Dallegret, Montréal

Imagining the Computer: Eliot Noyes, the Eames and the IBM Pavilion

John Harwood

6.32
**Eliot Noyes and Associates
and IBM Design Department**
(Poughkeepsie, NY), IBM
System/360, publicity
photograph, 1964

6.33
Eliot Noyes and Associates,
Selectric 1 golfball
typewriter, 1961.
Manufactured by IBM.
V&A: M.225:1–2007

... the machine that replaces your secretary and sets her free for full-time pre-marital sex will probably look less like a battery hen-house full of war-surplus W/T equipment than a tastefully two-toned filing cabinet with cooling louvres, discreetly wired to what appears to be a typewriter with ideas above its station. [Peter Reyner Banham].[1]

In 1960 International Business Machines Corporation (IBM) was teetering on the brink of financial insolvency.[2] The corporation – which had doubled its investment capital, facilities and employees over the previous five years in a move from typewriters and tabulators to computers – had just risked more than its net worth on the success of a new line of small, powerful, inter-machine compatible computers and peripherals called System/360 (6.32), finally launched on 7 April 1964. What was at stake in this gamble was the place of the computer within culture as a whole, and thus IBM's very identity. Could – and should – the computer become an indispensable part of everyday life?

Even before Edmund C. Berkeley published his heady exposé *Giant Brains, or Machines that Think*, in 1949,[3] the spectre of a machine that could mimic the activity of the human mind had haunted experts and laypersons alike. Fear and doubt reigned supreme: of oppressive technocracy, of 'depersonalization' and of accidental nuclear holocaust triggered by a callous, cross-wired machine.[4] In short, we once worried: what might a computerized world look like?

IBM recognized early that its problem of creating a mass market for computers was thus also one of visuality, space and experience – that is, of aesthetics. To solve the problem of the public's growing concern over the danger of computers, the company turned to the experts: architects, industrial designers and graphic artists. In 1954, coincident with its formal entry into the computer market, IBM President Thomas Watson Jr began to assemble a coterie of designers to help IBM redesign its 'corporate character'.[5] A formal design consultancy emerged in February 1956, headed by Watson's wartime friend, the industrial designer and architect Eliot Noyes. Noyes would collaborate with engineers on the design of all of IBM's products, and disburse architectural commissions for a dramatic expansion of the company's facilities. Paul Rand would handle graphics and advertising, and create design manuals for IBM employees; the critic and curator Edgar Kaufmann Jr and the designer and critic George Nelson would consult on the design of computers, and on sales and exhibition spaces.[6]

The consultancy began with the basics. Rand had redesigned IBM's logo in 1954 (and again in 1960), and in 1956 he mixed what would become Pantone 2718, the now familiar colour that earned IBM its nickname 'Big Blue'.[7] Noyes designed two new buildings for IBM's Poughkeepsie Campus – an IBM Education Center (1956–8) and a Research and Development Laboratory (1956–9) – that would serve as models for buildings commissioned from other architects across the globe.[8] Meanwhile, Noyes turned most of his attention to redesigning IBM's entire product line, using a peculiar strategy that has ever after conditioned the relationship between human beings and computers (6.33).

Describing the state of IBM's machines in 1954 as 'scattered and intricate',[9] Noyes deployed his understanding of modern architecture to solve the problem. To unite the computer's parts not only functionally but also aesthetically, he insisted instead that 'these machines should not be like a ranch house. They should be like a Mies house. They should have that much integrity and joy'.[10] Rather than assault the user with a mass of wires, transistors, and tubes, Noyes argued that the computer should be designed according to what became referred to as the 'parlour and coal cellar' principle. The inner workings of the computer, unpleasant and perhaps even dangerous to the user, should be hidden away in the 'coal cellar' behind panels, and the interfaces (such as keyboards, cathode ray tubes and instrument panels) should be conceived as furniture in the 'parlour'. Only the most minimal information about the inner workings of the computer would be revealed to the user in the parlour. This simple principle is today known as the interface of a computer, governing the form of those sites of interaction between computer and 'user'. The computer interface, first fully realized with the design of System/360, went some distance towards disarming the growing uneasiness about the ontology of the computer amongst experts.

The daunting task of rebuilding the public's understanding of the computer fell to another, exceptional contributor to the design programme, Charles Eames. As well as his prodigious reputation in the field of design, it was Eames's work in film that marked him out for the job. By way of introduction, Noyes presented Watson with a print of Charles and Ray Eames's short film, *A Communications Primer* (6.34), of 1953. The film offered, in lay terms, an explication of the basic tenets of information theory as laid out by Claude Shannon and his loyal popularizer Warren Weaver in *The Mathematical Theory of Communication* of 1949.[11] Combining live action footage with still photography and animation, the Eames' film playfully illustrated concepts such as coding and transmission

through the careful juxtaposition and overlapping of abstract shapes ('symbols' or 'bits') and photographic images of people, demonstrating how people 'naturally' use machines to create and transmit 'messages'. In *A Communications Primer*, the abstractions of the mathematical apparatus of communications theory were mapped directly on to the ostensibly concrete form of the human body, all set to a light-hearted jazz score by Elmer Bernstein and Charles Eames's own soothing narration.

IBM's interest in the film is easy to understand: Eames had given a friendly and human image to the abstract processes of communication, or data processing, that it sought to integrate into all aspects of modern life – from military planning to business management to everyday conversation. IBM bought several prints of the film to show to its employees, and invited Eames to deploy his strategy in greater breadth and depth; this relationship was to last until Eames's death in 1978. The Eames Office – particularly Charles Eames and his assistants Glen Fleck and Parke Meeke – went on to produce numerous additional films for IBM on cybernetics, astronomy, biology and the history of technology.[12]

But why was Eames, an architect and designer, interested in the mathematical logic of communication? The answer lies in his

incredibly ambitious agenda for reforming architectural theory – which he shared with many of his contemporaries, who saw themselves as heirs to the Bauhaus – by completing what he saw as the unfinished housework begun by the Modern Movement. The rigours of formal logic held a double appeal to the architect. On the one hand, they appeared to offer a truly objective basis for design, grounding it in scientific principle. On the other hand, Eames saw in information theory and cybernetics a means to expand radically the range of objects and problems to which architects could apply their expertise. Design became a generalized problem-solving technique, a practice that could be itself redesigned – along with every other human endeavour – into a pure, formal logical system. As the Italian critic Giulio Carlo Argan once wrote: 'The object teaches one how to act according to a plan for action: its human and social significance consists in the fact that, since behavior is a way of life, in designing objects one designs life itself.'[13] Eames condensed the sentiment into the pithy axiom 'Everything is architecture'.[14]

Yet if IBM was to overcome widespread misgivings about its abstract teletechnology, the company would need more than films and abstract theories of architecture. Watson and his executives determined to capitalize on the growing public interest in science and

6.34
Still from *A Communications Primer* directed by **Charles and Ray Eames**, 1953

6.35
Office of Charles and Ray Eames, 'Mathematica: A World of Numbers... and Beyond', California Museum of Science and Industry, 1961

technology in the wake of the Sputnik launch by intervening directly in the expanding realm of scientific education. The first of many such interventions was the Eames Office's museum exhibition 'Mathematica: A World of Numbers ... and Beyond', which opened at the California Museum of Science and Industry in March 1961 (6.35).[15] The exhibition translated the basic tropes of *A Communications Primer* into three-dimensional form and 'hands-on' experience. Images and models – many of them manipulable – arrayed in a loose configuration within a cage-like space, sought to demonstrate that the abstractions of mathematics do not just describe, but are present in every imaginable thing, from architecture and art to plants and planets, to the human body itself.

This mode of presentation – what Eames called 'a very special brand of fun'[16] – was also an effort to naturalize the computer at the most basic level of human understanding. The exhibition included a 'history wall', which

Imagining the Computer: Eliot Noyes, the Eames and the IBM Pavilion

presented the field of computer science as the culmination of the entire history of scientific endeavour. Animated 'peepshows' explained sophisticated mathematical concepts through children's storybook-like narratives played on 8mm film loops inside an old-fashioned viewfinder. The Eames Office sought to impregnate the human body with mathematics, fitting the display technique to the task. Serious concepts were blended seamlessly into games and inflected with the Eames's signature sense of humour and discovery. Notably, 'Mathematica' included a small section on 'The Man/Machine Interface', which featured witty anecdotes:

> Overheard in a recent conversation about computers: 'It's merely a matter of understanding what's taking place. I remember when we got our first TV set, my wife wouldn't undress in front of the screen.'

And:

> The mathematician [and computer scientist] John Von Neumann had amazing powers of rapid mental calculation. One of his associates said: 'Von Neumann was, of course, not human, but he had so carefully mastered the impersonation that most people believed him to be a member of the race.'[17]

Such jokes served a dual and contradictory function that proved essential to Eames's and IBM's strategy for naturalizing the computer. The first quote affirms the computer's status as a mere tool; the second implies the its basic humanity by playfully identifying the human being as a computer. Yet, despite the novel means of communication through design, IBM was unclear on what was actually being communicated.

The company's lack of clarity, however, was not for lack of effort. In 1960, as public

concerns about the uncanniness of the computer began to mount, IBM Vice President Dean R. McKay approached Noyes with commissions for two ambitious projects designed to counter such misgivings.[18] Noyes gave both projects to the Eames Office. One, for an 'IBM Museum' intended to provide the layperson with an intimate, hands-on introduction to the computer, consumed much of the Eames Office's attention over the next ten years, only to be cancelled due to funding constraints.[19] The second project, which came to fruition in the form of a pavilion for the corporation at the New York World's Fair of 1964–5 (6.36), marked the most complete realization of Noyes's, Eames's and IBM's strategy for naturalizing the computer. As a 1963 press release made clear, the pavilion would show that the business of IBM could be characterized as 'problem solving.'[20]

The basic *parti* of the pavilion was drawn from the idea of an informal garden or forest, in which plantings at ground level would almost seamlessly blend into naturalistic 'tree' columns of rolled steel, whose branches would meet at the top to form a translucent plastic-roofed canopy.[21] This open plan, the architects claimed, would allow visitors to move freely through the multiple exhibits. The absence of walls multiplied lines of sight, attracting visitors to the pavilion's carefully planned attractions and distractions. The pavilion was a syncretic mix of numerous building types, each selected for its more spectacular aspects, including references to cathedrals, theatres and follies.

The spectacular nature of this design was based on Eames's famous and rigorous interpretation of the visual and informational structure of the traditional circus:

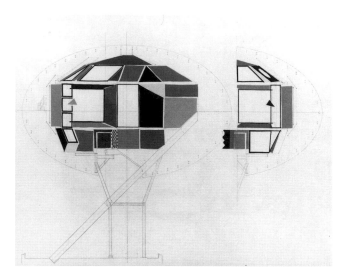

6.37
Office of Charles and Ray Eames and Eero Saarinen Associates, drawing of interior projection screens placement, IBM Pavilion, New York World's Fair, 1964. Eames Office LLC

> Everything in the circus is pushing the possible beyond the limit – bears do not really ride on bicycles, people do not really execute three and a half turn somersaults in the air from a board to a ball, and until recently no one dressed the way fliers do … Yet within this apparent freewheeling license, we find a discipline which is almost unbelievable…. The circus may look like the epitome of pleasure, but the person flying on a high wire, or executing a balancing act, or being shot from a cannon must take his pleasure very, very seriously. In the same vein, the scientist, in his laboratory, is pushing the possible beyond the limit and he too must take his pleasure very seriously.[22]

If the design of the pavilion was not carefully co-ordinated and disciplined, or the effects were not pleasurable enough, the bid to change public perception of the possibilities of computing would be lost. The whole experience had to convey the message that computers were natural but wholly magical extensions of human beings: 'Leaving the exhibit the visitor should feel that the aims of IBM are not foreign to his own.'[23]

Thus although the exhibits were made to appear chaotically pleasurable, they were rigorously and architecturally controlled. Advertised by Paul Rand's whimsical graphics, they included a hexagonal 'typewriter bar' where people could type out postcards on IBM typewriters; a series of 'puppet shows' about

computerizing the welfare state and the power of Boolean logic, each acted out by computer-controlled automata; a demonstration of automatic Russian language translation by character recognition software and hardware; and several exhibits borrowed from earlier IBM shows such as 'Mathematica'.[24] Accordingly, while each exhibit had its own internal spectacular logic, Eames and Kevin Roche (who took over from Eero Saarinen following his untimely death in 1961) gave the seemingly open and decentralized plan of the pavilion an invisible hierarchical spatial order of the strictest kind.

The centerpiece of the pavilion, lifted above the canopy of 'trees', was a giant ovoid theatre. This plaster-covered, steel-framed volume, nicknamed 'the egg' by its designers, provided an endpoint for a sophisticated *promenade architecturale* beginning at the pavilion's entrance. Although the pavilion could ostensibly be entered from any number of directions, ticket holders for the main event all entered at a point marked with a labyrinth inscribed in the pavement. From this metaphorical labyrinth, visitors were confronted with a confusing array of staircases to their left and right, with several possible entry points. They were encouraged by gaudily dressed strolling minstrels, clowns and jugglers to enter at any point they wished – indeed, it hardly mattered, since the seemingly aimless staircases all led eventually to the same point: the *People Wall*, an enormous set of bleachers perplexingly set in a rectangular pool of water. After the audience had been

funneled through to their seats, the tuxedoed host was lowered on a platform from the ovoid above and gave a brief welcoming statement. Then, beneath the bleachers a hydraulic lift powered up and the *People Wall* began to rise into the darkened interior of the theatre. When the wall stopped, the host, who had disappeared into the blackness, suddenly reappeared, spotlit on a balcony between the screens on the right-hand side. As an IBM promotional booklet described the beginning of the show:

> At the bidding of the host, information leaps at you from all directions. Just to show what the machine can do, he fills the screens with miscellaneous information about himself – his credit card, the change in his pocket, what he had for breakfast, what's inside his closet, even a little chat with his mother up in Schenectady.
> Another example, he announces – and suddenly you are in the roaring midst of a road race. *With all screens filled with action, you see far more than if you were actually on the spot: you are in many places at once*, on the curves, in the pits, with the onlookers, in the driver's seat, inches from the ground next to the front wheel…[25]

The spectators, one begins to suspect, were being taken on a kind of transcendental, quasi-religious journey. After passing over a symbolic labyrinth, and through a real one, bombarded with multimedia stimulus from every direction, the disoriented audience was placed in tidy rows and then lifted into a space of utter darkness. A moment of sensory deprivation, a comforting description from the host, and the bombardment begins anew, but now the terms have changed: this time no tactile journey through conventional space, no matter how odd; now, instead, a barrage of images structured precisely to deny any such sense of space. The viewers, gradually stripped of their spatial orientation, were now inside what Eames and IBM called 'The Information Machine', and were about to experience computerized consciousness, in the form of a 15-minute multi-screen projection, complete with voice-over and musical score (6.37). The screens, with no single focal point, no discernible hierarchy or order in which they should be viewed, fragmented the viewer's attention, as is clearly diagrammed in the Eames Office's plan of the ovoid theatre (6.38). This displacement and deprivation, combined with a sudden and radical extension of spatial perception, forms a perfect occlusion – both a total closure and an extreme absorption. This new form of attention, initially so shocking, was to be quickly alleviated by the comforting lessons of the 'Information Machine'.

In a slew of examples – ranging from planning a dinner party or a football game to designing a synthetic chemical compound or determining a missile trajectory – the host and the hyperactive images on the screens demonstrated that 'the method used in solving even the most complicated problems is essentially the same method we all use daily'. By identifying all forms of thought as arithmetical processes, and by bombarding the audience with imagery that represented the working of a computer's 'mind', the Eames Office and IBM pre-emptively deferred any question that might form in the audience's minds about the difference between an electronic brain and a human one. Put another way, if the computer can be described, as it was by its godfather Charles Babbage, as a 'Difference Engine',[26] the 'Information Machine', designed to foist the computer on the public at the World's Fair, was a homology engine. The paradox at the heart of Eames's design strategy is that in order to perform this work of homology, it had to present the

computer as both a wholly new and shocking force – a new way of seeing and foreseeing – and as a completely natural extension of everyday life. Under the sheer onslaught of contradictory claims and imagery, it is almost difficult to remember that it was in fact a metaphorical 'Information Machine' in the form of a building and a multi-media projection, and not a computer at all.

In the forty-odd years since IBM's pavilion was dismantled, its exhibits destroyed or relegated to museums, we have largely ceased to worry about the computer. Concerns about the threat to humanity posed by technologies such as 'artificial intelligence' have been replaced by nightmare scenarios of genetic manipulation (such as those swirling around the emerging pseudo-science of 'artificial life'); miniaturization, marketing and slick industrial design have ensured places for the PC, the MP3 player and the mobile phone in the most intimate spaces of everyday life, from the workplace to the

home. But the successful naturalization of the computer – of which we have seen but a handful of episodes in a long and intensive process – was not a question of granting true understanding to a sceptical public that just did not yet have all the facts. Noyes, Eames, and their fellow IBM designers recognized that, in order to naturalize the computer, it was necessary to present it to the public as simultaneously quotidian and magical. By oscillating rapidly between these two poles in their designs for 'Mathematica' and the IBM Pavilion, the Eames Office and IBM managed to suspend our fear of a machine just like us, and transpose it into something resembling wonder, if not joy.

Let us return, then, to our stunned spectators: 15 minutes after the show began, they were cast back into the glaring light of the earthly circus below, armed with the new knowledge that 'IBM's aims are not so foreign from [their] own'. Perhaps by then they were our own.

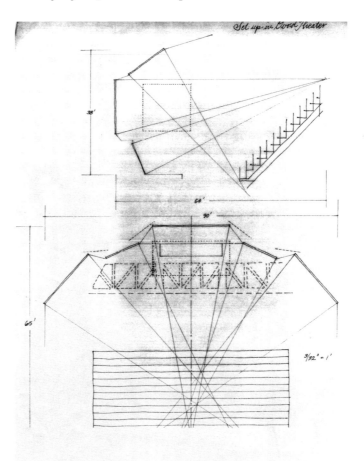

6.38
Glen Fleck (Eames Office), the Information Machine theatre. Sketch plan showing multiple sight lines. Drawing, c.1963

Expo '70 as Watershed: The Politics of American Art and Technology

Anne Collins Goodyear

Although the use of the arts for political purposes during the Cold War has been widely studied, less familiar, despite its critical importance during the 1960s, is the promotion of intersections between American art and new technology on the part of business and the federal government.[1] Nowhere more than at Expo '70 in Osaka, Japan, does the vitality of this connection in the years leading up to the fair make itself felt. A testament to its importance is the development of this theme at two American pavilions: that sponsored by the United States Information Agency (USIA) and that developed by Pepsi Cola. Although the American Pavilion and the Pepsi Pavilion were conceived independently, the concepts behind them reveal remarkable parallels, suggesting the willingness of government and business to adopt similar strategies to advertise their promises. However, the realization of these two projects provides a cautionary tale. These collaborations – undertaken in the late 1960s as innovative partnerships between art, technology, government, and corporate America – dissolved in the early 1970s as each was overtaken by social, political and economic tensions at home, undermining the very theme of unity the pavilions sought to project.

It is the demise of these collaborations that forms the focus of this essay. For it is precisely in examining the destructive misunderstandings that developed between artists and sponsors that a larger cultural transformation makes itself visible: the breakdown of the conviction that art constituted an independent sphere capable of using new technologies for purely aesthetic ends, a shift characteristic of the movement from the modern to the postmodern era.[2] The ideological and economic requirements of each of the pavilions under consideration demanded that art operate as an autonomous unit, analogous to but distinct from the technocratic institutions of government and business, capable of integrating new technological forms efficiently, apolitically and comprehensibly. However, as this essay seeks to demonstrate, although such mutually beneficial partnerships between art, technology, government and business seemed possible in the late 1960s, by the early 1970s, amidst an increasingly problematic war and an economic down-turn, art practice could no longer operate independently of political and economic concerns, and these ambitious collaborations collapsed.

The backdrop: art and technology as cultural partners

The immediate 'conditions of possibility' spurring collaborations between art and technology can be traced to the late 1950s and the launch of Sputnik. Early Soviet successes in the space race spawned an immediate rivalry with the USA, stimulating American investment in scientific research and education. In September 1958, President Eisenhower signed the National Defense Education Act into law, legislating increased training for American students in science and mathematics (as well as foreign languages).[3] Yet even from the earliest moment of a national push to encourage scientific and technological advances, concerns existed about the advisability of the exclusive pursuit of a technological agenda on the part of government.[4] As Miles Orville has noted, the 'traumatic reality of the Post-World War II world' consists in our awareness of the capacity of 'technology and science [to] astonish us with the magnitude of their destructive powers'.[5] It is no coincidence that C.P. Snow's famous advocacy of education as a tool to bridge 'the two cultures' of the sciences on the one hand and the arts and the humanities on the other drew an immense, and largely favourable, response. As Snow himself recognized, the 'flood of literature' that appeared in the wake of his publication of The Two Cultures in 1959 indicated two things. First, that his ideas were not unique to himself or his native England. Second, as he put it, that 'contained in them or hidden beneath them, there is something which people, all over the world, suspect is relevant to present actions'.[6] Indeed, by the early 1960s art came to be seen as a necessary complement to science and technology, intended to ensure that advances in those fields did not result in human devastation, and federal and corporate funding was directed to the arts on this basis.[7]

Rhetoric within the field of the arts helped promote such partnerships, suggesting not only that they were desirable, but indeed, mutually beneficial.[8] Reflecting upon artists' willingness to take advantage of such opportunities, Allan Kaprow noted wryly in 1964, '... if artists were in hell in 1946, now they are in business'.[9] On a more serious note, the organization Experiments in Art and Technology affirmed that positive things could come out of the access to industrial technology: '[I]t is essential for the artist to have permanent and organic access not only to existing technical facilities and materials but also to facilities for experimentation.... Only industry can give the artist what he wants.'[10] Leo Steinberg even suggested, somewhat warily, that contemporary critics were inclined to evaluate the success of new art in terms set forth by an economy wed to the encouragement of scientific and technological development:

> The dominant formalist critics today tend to treat modern painting as an evolving technology ... tasks set for the artist as problems are set for researchers

6.39
David, Brody, Chermayeff, Geismar, de Harak Associates, American Pavilion at Expo '70, Osaka. Photograph from *Life*, 13 April 1970

in the big corporations. The artist as engineer and research technician becomes important insofar as he comes up with solutions to the right problem. ... [T]he solution matters because it answers a problem set forth by a governing technocracy.[11]

In such an environment, the adoption of industrially or federally sponsored technology in no way appeared incompatible with the aims of avant-garde art.

The American Pavilion takes shape

By July 1967 the USIA had determined that the American contribution to Expo '70 would focus on what the agency described as 'topics dealing with Science, Technology, and the Arts'.[12] As the first World's Fair to be staged in Asia, the Japanese exposition, with its theme of 'Progress and Harmony for Mankind', promised the potential to wield great influence both internationally and at home.[13] As the USIA revealed in letters of invitation to potential participants, it was 'anxious that United States Participation in Osaka be characterized by, amongst other things, originality, daring, innovation, and imagination'.[14] The charge was reflected in, for example, the self-consciously futuristic structure designed by David, Brody, Chermayeff, Geismar, de Harak Associates for the American Pavilion. Featuring a prominent oval-shaped pneumatic roof, the enormous building – roughly the size of two American football fields – was regarded as an architectural milestone (6.39).[15]

the pavilion's courtyard (visible in the fore-ground of 6.40), and, at night, a light sculpture by Frosty Myers enclosed the architectural structure in a frame of white light. Inside, silver-suited hostesses provided guests with wireless handsets that enabled them to pick up audio signals from loops embedded in the floor. In another area, visitors could experience a display of 'visual sound', a combination of coloured lasers and avant-garde music envisioned by David Tudor and executed by composer Lowell Cross and physicist Carson Jeffries; they could also view inverted three-dimensional images created by a specially designed pneumatic hemispheric mirror (6.41, 6.42), masterminded by Robert Whitman, who, as noted above, had also installed a work with mirror-generated 'real' images at the American Pavilion. But perhaps most immedi-ately striking was a bank of fog that rested on the pavilion's dome (see 6.39). Conceived by Frosty Myers, the cloud was executed by the Japanese artist Fujiko Nakaya and the Californian cloud physicist Tom Mee. Intended in part to create a visual parallel with the fog-shrouded mountaintop of Mount Fuji, the fog produced by the team was so thick that local firefighters appeared on the scene after it was first unleashed.[33] Nearby vendors complained that it made them less visible, forcing E.A.T. to design a 'fog trap'.[34]

Breakdown and collapse

Despite E.A.T.'s remarkable ambition and forward-thinking approach to the develop-ment of the pavilion environment, the project proved far from an unqualified success. In a spectacular gesture Pepsi relieved E.A.T. of responsibility for running the pavilion on 25 April 1970, just five weeks after it had opened to the public. The most disputed area between the corporate patron and E.A.T. was financial. Given its grandiose goals for the pavilion, E.A.T. wanted no expense spared and, despite statements to the contrary, did not seem to appreciate that its sponsor had any real financial constraints. Although in E.A.T.'s early negotiations with Pepsi, Klüver had readily claimed that E.A.T.'s project could be kept to a cost of approximately half a million dollars, he showed no real willingness to operate within a budget. By the time Pepsi ended its relationship with E.A.T. the budget was approaching two million dollars, several

times more than what the company had intended to spend.[35] Other misunderstandings fuelled the fire. Perhaps most damning was the inability of Pepsi executives to locate markers of 'product identity' within the E.A.T. pavilion.[36] Each organization viewed its problems with the other in a totally different light: E.A.T. saw Pepsi as petty; Pepsi per-ceived E.A.T. as disorganized and unreliable.

The expensive and dispiriting debacle would lead Billy Klüver to declare several months later that 'art and technology was dead'.[37] While echoing modernist pronounce-ments of the death of painting, Klüver's dramatic remark, in retrospect, signals a broader cultural shift, and one that would have important implications for collaborations between art, technology, business and government. Most importantly, Klüver's comment reveals his recognition that art and technology could no longer operate as spheres autonomous from their historical, economic and political context.[38]

The prescience of Klüver's statement was born out by the experience of Maurice Tuchman in May 1971, when his full-scale 'Art and Technology' (A&T) exhibition opened at the Los Angles County Museum of Art, eight months after the conclusion of the World's Fair. Praised at Expo '70 for curating an exhibition 'embodying [President Nixon's] "bring-us together" philosophy', Tuchman received strong criticism for numerous failed collaborations between artists and various industrial partners sponsored by his art and technology programme. When A&T opened in May 1971 at the Los Angeles County Museum of Art only 16 collaborations had come to fruition, although 76 artists were listed as 'participating' in the programme.[39] As Tuchman's highly detailed exhibition catalogue, *A Report on the Art and Technology Program of the Los Angeles County Museum of Art, 1967–1971*, revealed, many companies experienced real discomfort at the presence of artists in their midst, much as Pepsi ultimately baulked at its partnership with E.A.T.[40]

Tuchman's catalogue (6.43), with its checkerboard pattern of faces of artists and businessmen, revealed a great divide between two new cultures: the establishment and the counter-culture, which would not be bridged for some time. Particularly problematic was

the reassessment of the meaning of technol-ogy itself, in the midst of the Vietnam War, as indicated by responses to Tuchman's exhibi-tion. Richard Serra, who participated in the show, made clear its violent association with death and destruction, asserting: 'Technology is what we do to the Black Panthers and the Vietnamese under the guise of advancement in a materialistic theology.'[41] Perhaps even more notable, however, was the documentable recognition, on the part of critic Amy Goldin, that art could no longer be seen to operate in a sphere independent of the political environ-ment in which it existed. As Goldin wrote: 'Making art is not simply esthetic behavior. It is bound into the social system in very specific ways. Ways that affect the kinds of meaning it makes available. Art plays its own part in our ecology – whether we like it or not.'[42]

Two striking points of commonality emerge in reviews of the exhibition by several art critics: first, attention to the historical moment in which A&T was undertaken; and second, a blanket condemnation of corporate America. The optimism fuelling collaborations between art, technology, government and industry had disappeared amidst the recogni-tion that none of the partners could operate independently of the other and that each infected the others with its own agendas. As critic, artist and historian Jack Burnham put it in 1971:

6.42
In the Mirror Dome of the Pepsi Pavilion, Expo '70, Osaka: a balloon draped with pink silk cloth for a performance by Remy Charlip, is positioned so that its image 'blooms' and fills the spherical mirror with pink. Standing to the right are Peter Poole and Remy Charlip

6.43
Art and Technology: A Report on the Art and Technology Program of the Los Angeles County Museum of Art, 1967–1971, edited by Maurice Tuchman (exhibition catalogue, Los Angeles County Museum of Art, 1971)

If presented five years ago, A&T would have been difficult to refute as an important event, posing some hard questions about the future of art. Given the effects of a Republican recession, the role of large industry as an intransigent beneficiary of an even more intractable federal government, and the fatal environmental effects of most of our technologies, few people are going to be seduced by three months of industry-sponsored art – no matter how laudable the initial motivation.[43]

If the business and federal interests on exhibit at the 1970 Osaka Expo were intended to showcase the benefits of collaborations between art, technology, business and government, the American Pavilion and the Pepsi Pavilion represented a delicate détente. The very fragility of these alliances may well have been apparent to American critics who attended the fair and found it a disappointment.[44] Perhaps most interesting of all was the response of architectural critic John Canaday, writing for the *New York Times*. Poking fun at the abundance of pneumatic architecture, which included both the American Pavilion and the Pepsi Pavilion's hemispherical mirror, with its three-dimensional images, Canaday reported: 'if you don't like the looks of the world of the future, the most effective weapon against

it would be an old-fashioned hat pin.'[45]

The metaphor of a bubble bursting was apt. The harnessing of art and technology for political and commercial ends proved more unruly than initially perceived by the organizers of these programmes, for ultimately distinctions between each of these entities could not be contained. If, on the one hand, artists of the era valued process even more than product, as suggested by Maurice Tuchman's 'Art and Technology' catalogue and the assessment of the Pepsi Pavilion later published by Klüver, this was not the real disconnect. Instead, the fracture between artistic interests and those of business and government represented a breakdown of mutual trust and respect due to fundamentally different ideas about the promotion of American ideals. No longer, as had largely been true for modern artists during the first half of the twentieth century, did an embrace of technology signal utopian goals, making a technologically oriented aesthetic attractive.[46] Instead, the application of technology to art became connected with the exploitation of new technologies by commercial and political interests.

Unwilling to risk cooperation with a technocratic system that appeared bent on destruction, art-world support for business and government-sponsored programmes eroded, while business interests, already compromised by a deepening recession, in turn shied away from the support of artists. And, while on paper federal expenditure on the arts increased throughout the Nixon presidency, in practice from 1970 on Nixon and his supporters strongly opposed governmental support of what he described as 'unintelligible art'.[47] Although exposure at Expo '70 had been eagerly sought by both Tuchman and E.A.T. in the late 1960s, as well as by the US government and Pepsi Cola, by the early 1970s such partnerships were no longer tenable. The American and Pepsi pavilions thus share an important – if unintended – legacy, marking the end of an era where the aims of business, government and high art appeared if not interchangeable, at least negotiable as distinct entities. In demonstrating this transition, these projects signal, through their very failures, the rupture of a modernist paradigm and the arrival of a new historical moment.

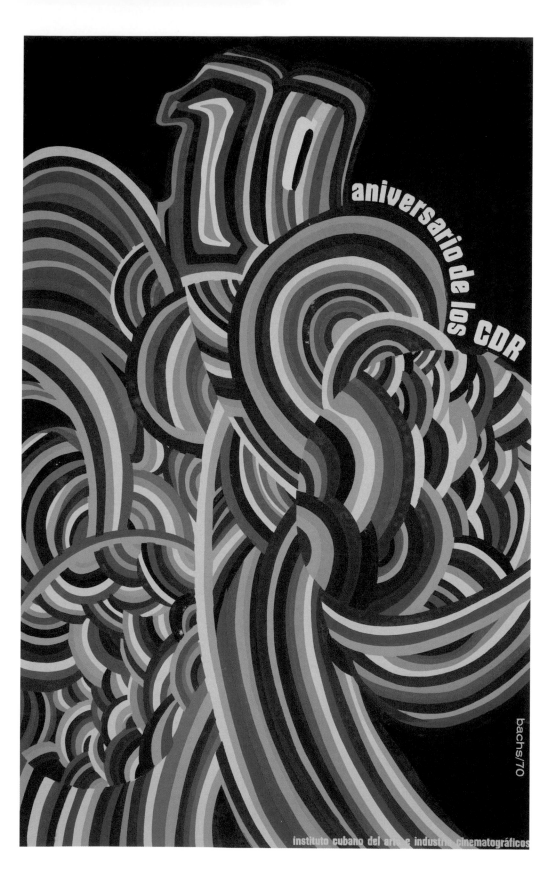

7.1
Eduardo Bachs, *10th anniversary of the Committees for the Defence of the Revolution*, poster issued by the Instituto Cubano del Arte e Industria Cinematográficos, Cuba, 1970. V&A: E. 770-2003

In the Image of Revolution

David Crowley

In 1967 Petr Sadecký, a young graduate of the Prague film school, left Czechoslovakia for West Germany. He carried a file of erotic drawings, which he intended to sell to publishers in the West. His plan worked and the images appeared in print four years later, creating a publishing sensation that drew the attention of the world's press.[1] Sadecký was not, however, the author of the drawings: they had been produced by other artists, including Zdeněk Burian, a well-established illustrator of popular adventure books in Czechoslovakia. In 1967 this fact did little to ensure their marketability in the West. The invasion of Czechoslovakia by Soviet-led forces in August 1968, however, presented a new opportunity for the young Czech émigré. Sadecký modified the drawings and created a gaudy explanation for their existence. Like a film editor, he carefully organized the few drawings in his possession to create new narratives in which a sexy superhero took centre stage.

A cartoon character with superhuman strength acquired in the crater of a radioactive volcano, she could travel anywhere in the world. She was a global revolutionary capable of enlisting native Americans to wreak political chaos in the USA, or flying to the aid of China to build its nuclear capacity. In this way 'Octobriana', a mythological figure representing 'the real spirit of the Great October Socialist Revolution' and scantily dressed in the manner of a Bond girl, was born (7.2). To satisfy the West's recent discovery of dissent in the Eastern Bloc, Sadecký credited authorship of these images to an underground group called Progressive Political Pornography (PPP), a network with cells in Soviet cities.

Amongst the many provocative actions of these artists, according to Sadecký, was the production of the samizdat (that is, self-published and, as such, uncensored and so illegal) comics in which Octobriana appeared. Far from being anti-communist, she was the expression of the authentic spirit of revolution.[2] In order to lend credibility to his tale, Sadecký supplied his publishers with a set of documentary photographs of the PPP engaged in clandestine activities in Kiev, their faces blacked out to emphasize the risky nature of their meetings. He also added an introduction from internationally acclaimed dissident author Anatoly Kuznetsov, then living in exile in London.

Sadecký's deception was exposed within days of the publication of his book, *Octobriana and the Russian Revolution*. He had modified the original drawings with sloganeering captions and red star motifs, and fabricated the documentary photographs. But this did little to diminish the appeal of his comic invention. Octobriana concentrated a diverse range of contemporary desires or, as Tomáš Pospiszyl puts it in his forensic investigation of the phenomenon, she was 'politically ambidextrous'.[3] Sadecký's right-wing publisher in Britain was drawn to the character as evidence of the moral bankruptcy of Soviet society whilst, one suspects, his youthful readers – drawn from the counter-culture – welcomed the comic's message about the 'real spirit' of revolution being found not in the Kremlin but in the bedroom. Octobriana was a Pop Art rendering of philosopher Herbert Marcuse's attempt to fuse Freud and Marx.[4] Sadecký's book also attracted the attention of socialist Czechoslovakia. There, the press took the episode as evidence of the West's desire to obstruct the march of progress initiated in Russia in 1917.[5]

Octobriana materialized in a phase of the Cold War when the idea of revolution had high currency around the world. 'We are living at the moment when the match is put to the fuse', observed Jean-Paul Sartre at the beginning of the 1960s.[6] In this chain of detonations, the non-Western world set the pace. The Soviet path – which the People's Republic of China had been following since 1949 – had led to bureaucracy, famine and economic crisis. Chairman Mao's answer to his own mismanagement was to launch the Great

7.2
Peter Sadecký, 'Octobriana'
montage including a still
from the Vasiliyev brothers'
film *Chapaev*, c.1968,
(Source: Peter Sadecký,
*Octobriana and the Russian
Underground*, London 1971,
p.118)

7.3
Hans Hillman, poster for
La Chinoise, directed by
Jean-Luc Godard, on its
release in West Germany,
1967. Private collection

Proletarian Cultural Revolution in 1966,
convulsing China in violent and radical
change.[7] A new revolutionary force – the Red
Guards – was unleashed on society to shake
the country off the 'capitalist road' (which it
was felt the Soviet Union had taken). Maoism
attracted its acolytes in the West, with the
image of Mao Tse-tung being paraded in
student demonstrations. Perhaps the most
famous of the Western Maoists was French
film director Jean-Luc Godard, whose
prescient film *La Chinoise* (1967) anticipated
the revolutionary manoeuvres in the French
capital in 1968 and commented on the
growing antipathy to both American and
Soviet power (7.3). Its narrative focuses on
an attempt to assassinate the Soviet Minister
of Culture when he makes an official visit
to France (an event represented by a brief
cut to a comic-book image of violence in the
manner of Sadecký's 'Octobriana'). But this
is not a work of high drama. Large sections
of the film are given over to debate – between
Maoist students in a chic apartment borrowed
for the summer – about the limits of revolutionary violence.

7.4
We Will Win (*Venceremos*),
anonymous student poster
from Mexico, c.1970.
V&A: E. 685-2004

The ideal revolutionary – in the minds of Western radicals – was to be a man or woman of thought and deed. Decolonization in Africa, the Algerian War of Independence, the Cuban Revolution and the Vietnam War threw up not only powerful images of societies undergoing dramatic transformation but, in some cases, charismatic revolutionary figures who combined philosophy with action. Sartre, after meeting Ernesto 'Che' Guevara in Cuba in 1960, called him 'the most complete man of his generation. He lived his words, spoke his own actions, and his story and that of the world ran parallel' (7.4).[8] The revolutionary was a medical doctor, a writer and a later government minister and, as such, a living refutation of alienation in the modern world.

Fragmented, with no control over his conditions of life, his fate or even his emotions, modern Western man seemed disadvantaged by comparison.

Europe was, of course, not exempt from the effects of this international wave of revolutionary sentiment. In 1968 European cities, most notably Paris, were filled with student protests (7.5). Expressing a wide range of frustrations, the student movement declared its opposition to the war in Vietnam, the bureaucratic structures of universities and the repressive environment that sought to mould social and sexual behaviour. The student protests in Paris were fixed upon the idea of spontaneous and direct action, often threaded with a strong libertarian ideology

7.6
Atelier Populaire, *The Police Speak to You Every Evening at 8 pm*. Screen-printed poster, 1968.
V&A: E.671-2004

calling for the emancipation of the imagination and of desire. These ideals were promoted by the Atelier Populaire, a loosely organized printing unit in the École des Beaux-Arts, with many posters and leaflets (7.6).[9] Avoiding conventional political demands, their designs were often capped with enigmatic and poetic slogans including, famously, 'Underneath the paving stones, the beach', or 'It is forbidden to forbid'. The student movement almost produced a major political crisis in de Gaulle's France, when in mid-May 1968 it triggered strikes across the country: on 13 May, ten million workers were on strike.[10] Perhaps more importantly, the *événements* of 1968 constituted a 'refusal' – by workers and students alike – to accept the order and roles assigned by Gaullist technocratic capitalism.[11] For a short period it seemed not only as if a stable Western European government was on the edge of collapse, but society was on the verge of wholesale change.

In the USA the Yippies (Youth International Party), founded in 1966, brought a carnivalesque approach to its protests against the war in Vietnam and corporate America. Yippie spokesman Abbie Hoffman called for 'Revolution for the hell of it'. Media-sharp, they adopted American television and the press as their weapons of choice. Spectacular Yippie pranks – such as dropping single dollar bills from the balcony above the trading floor of the New York Stock Exchange, thereby causing the brokers to scrabble on the floor with the effect of halting the trade in million dollar stocks – courted controversy:[12] when reported in the media, their actions were claimed as 'advertisements for revolution'.[13]

Eastern Europe was by no means untouched by this wave of revolution rippling around the world. In the spring of 1968 students and politicians in Czechoslovakia – many of whom were Communist Party members – attempted a 'revolution from within'. Their purpose was to break the hold of illegitimate power which had occupied the country since the late 1940s by ending censorship and installing democracy. The 'threat' of reform in the most westerly parts of the Eastern Bloc was stemmed by invasion of Soviet-led forces. As the joke 'Wake Up Lenin, Brezhnev's Gone Mad' daubed on the streets of Prague testified, whilst the Czech protestors might well have been

7.7
Roman Cieślewicz, cover
of *Opus International*
magazine, no.4, 1968

anti-Soviet, they were not necessarily anti-Marxist.[14]

The range of events and actions around the world described as 'revolutionary' in the late 1960s was wide and disjointed.[15] The advocates of wholesale political transformation across the globe shared neither common origins, common strategies nor common ambitions. One common ground, however, was an antipathy to the 'Cold War order', the East–West equilibrium which had settled by the late 1960s. America and the Soviet Union stood accused by radicals across the globe of exercising a destructive influence on the rest of the world and of betraying their own origins in revolutions governed by high ideals. This point was made graphically by Paris-based Polish artist Roman Cieślewicz in 1968 (7.7). He depicted two superpowers as mirror images of each other in his cover design for the French Paris-based left-wing art magazine, *Opus International*. 'Che' Guevara, a minister in Cuban government, made a similar point in a speech in Algiers in 1965 when he accused the Soviet Union and its allies in the Eastern Bloc of 'tacit complicity with the exploiting countries of the West'.[16] East–West trade deals in the Northern Hemisphere, which led to the manufacture of Fiat cars in the highly automated AutoVAZ factory operated under license with the Italian car company in the Soviet city of Togliatti and, in the 1970s, even to the opening of Holiday Inns in communist states, did nothing to improve the condition of the oppressed peoples in the underdeveloped South.[17] The challenge – as Che saw it in 1965 – was to rediscover and spread the 'spirit' of revolution. But where was this spirit to be found – in the first, second or third worlds?

1967

The fiftieth anniversary of the October Revolution in 1967 was seized by Aleksei Kosygin's and Leonid Brezhnev's regime as an opportunity to broadcast to the rest of the world the achievements of the Soviet Union in every sphere of human endeavour. Major state projects were timed to be completed in the run-up to the anniversary of the Revolution, and artists, architects, designers, film-makers and writers were commissioned to produce new works to celebrate this watershed event in world history. In Moscow, the Ostankino television tower, then the world's tallest building (6.15), and Novyi Arbat, a major thoroughfare flanked with international style modernist tower-blocks, including the headquarters of the COMECOM (Council for Mutual Economic Assistance), were opened to the public. This long avenue was also the site of Mikhail Posokhin and Ashot Mndoiants' new October cinema (7.8). The long mosaic panel wrapped around the first floor of this glass-walled box supplied an unmistakable Soviet pedigree to these international architectural symbols of modernity. Decorative artists Nikolai Andronov, A. Vasntsov, Viktor El'konin and L. Syrkin employed the planar and flattened style derived from the monumental aesthetic developed by the Mexican muralists before the Second World War, which had come to be the politically correct face of Socialist Realism in the Eastern Bloc by the 1960s.[18] Other great anniversary projects included the massive hydroelectric plant in Bratsk, south-eastern Siberia. Thirteen years in construction, the plant was put into full service in time for the October celebrations, and was, for a number of years, the world's largest single power producer. The gigantomania of these projects was to provide citizens at home and observers around the world with undeniable evidence of the Soviet Union's adventurous leap into the future.[19]

Soviet space technicians sought to achieve new triumphs in the cosmos that were worthy of this historic date. Early proposed accomplishments included raising a red flag on the surface of the Moon. When this proved beyond Soviet capabilities, the idea emerged to send a manned mission around the Moon, a 'lunar flyby'. Ultimately, the death of Soviet cosmonaut Vladimir Komarov on Soyuz 1 in April 1967, when his parachute failed on re-entry, put a hold on Soviet plans.[20] In the event, the cosmonauts were fixed by gravity to the tribune in Red Square to witness the march-past of intercontinental ballistic missiles, tanks and other military hardware (including 1917 vintage artillery[21]).

The figure of Lenin was placed at the centre of the 1967 commemorations. The anniversary was the trigger for a new wave of Lenin monuments. Matvei and Otto Manizer's 6m-high monument to the Bol-shevik leader installed in Odessa provided a model for numerous smaller Lenins in other Soviet towns.[22] His founding vision for the first socialist state and celebratory accounts of the heroism of the Bolshevik revolutionaries were to stir a renewal of Soviet-style social-ism. In this regard, 1967 conformed to a characteristic temporal pattern of Soviet modernity. Built on an ideology of rupture (with its insistence on revolution and dialec-tics), Soviet order was managed through returns, reiterations and rituals. A calendar of May Days and anniversaries of historic events had been instituted early in the post-revolutionary years to suggest an unbroken chain to the source of revolutionary virtue, Lenin.[23]

Declaring a 'return to Lenin' was a recurrent pattern in Soviet propaganda.[24] Eleven years earlier, Nikita Khrushchev had famously proclaimed the primacy of 'Leninist ideals' in his momentous 'Secret Speech' to a closed session of the Twentieth Congress of the Communist Party of the Soviet Union.[25] The superhuman figure of Lenin was the answer to the vicious and corrupt record of Stalin revealed during the Thaw. No doubt citizens of the Soviet Union had a strong sense of déjà vu when, a little over ten years later, in 1967, it was claimed that all spheres of life were to be revived – yet again – by the Leninist spirit. In this regard, film was given a key role. The original print of Sergei Eisenstein's portrait of the Revolution, *October* (1927) – itself a commemorative work when it was made – was restored and given a new sound-track by Dmitrii Shostakovich. It played to Soviet audiences throughout the republics in 1967. Reflection on the theme of the October Revolution was presented to film-makers in the USSR and throughout the Bloc as a duty to be rewarded with extensive budgets, staff and equipment. Aleksandr Askoldov, for instance, made *Commissar*, a film which explored the moral and political dilemmas of a Red Army soldier billeted with a Jewish family in the Ukraine during the Civil War (1918–22).[26] In its epic vision Askoldov's film evoked the heroic scale of Eisenstein's film of the 1920s. What the authorities commissioning this testimonial had not imagined, however, was that Askoldov would find moral and political complexity in events which had taken place 50 years earlier. His film explored the 'existential' choices facing the individual in terms of a dichotomy between the family and the State; it also explored the theme of anti-Semitism, an explosive matter at the time of the Arab-Israeli war. *Commissar* was subject to sharp criticism and was removed from Soviet screens (only to be screened again in the late 1980s, during the Perestroika years). As punishment for

7.8
Mikhail Posokhin and Ashot Mndoiants (architects), October Cinema, Kalinin Prospekt, Moscow, 1967

Boris Mikhailov, selection
from the 'Red Series'. Type-C
prints on paper, late 1960s/
early 1970s. Jane Voorhees
Zimmerli Art Museum, The
Norton and Nancy Dodge
Collection of Nonconformist
Art from the Soviet Union,
New Brunswick, NJ

his interpretation of a Soviet shibboleth, the director was sent into 'internal exile'.[27]

One conclusion to be drawn from the commemorative events of 1967 throughout the Eastern Bloc by observers in the East and the West, was that 'revolution' had become a kind of entropic concept, full of inflated symbolism but drained of vital meaning. The repeated incantation of progress masked considerable injustice. Such opinions were however rarely voiced within the Bloc. Only during the Prague Spring in 1968, for instance, could critics openly describe Soviet dissimulation (see p.221). According to one, Marx's 'critical thought [was] smothered in thicker and thicker clouds of the incense of faith and turned into an impotent dummy of May Day parades'.[28]

An early group of photographs by Boris Mikhailov known as the 'Red' series (1968–70) captured the sense of fatigue that ensued from 50 years of Soviet propaganda (7.9). At this early stage in his now fêted career, Mikhailov was still an amateur photographer living in Kharkov in the Ukraine. He used his camera to capture ordinary pleasures, producing intimate portraits of Soviet life (a matter of controversy when he was fired from his occupation as an engineer after his

nude portraits of his wife were discovered). In their fascination with the red horizon filling every sightline and the kitsch clutter of the parade, his 'Red' photographs were not openly critical of Soviet political culture; they were, however, darkly ironic.[29] The fossilization of revolutionary imagery by the late 1960s seemed a metaphor for the stagnant state of the communist project on its 'native soil'.

Revolution in the cosmos

Not all public events marking the 1967 anniversary of the October Revolution can be categorized as propaganda and dissimulation. A young generation of environmental artists and engineers operating within the spaces of official culture in the Soviet Union took advantage of rhetoric of revolution around 1967 to explore their interests: cybernetics, kinetic art and electronic music.

Some of these figures were attached to VNIITE (Vsesoiuznyi nauchno-issledovatel'skii institut tekhnicheskoi estetiki), the All-Union Scientific Research Institute of Industrial Design, which had been established in Moscow in 1962 under the auspices of the of the State Committee of Science and Engineering of the Council of Ministers of the USSR (Gosudarstvennyi

komitet Soveta Ministrov SSSR po nauke i tekhnike).[30] VNIITE was a network of research centres designed to provide the intellectual and creative resources to enable the Soviet Union to overcome the damage done by Stalinism to Soviet science and technology, and to realize Khrushchev's grand claims to overtake the West. By the time of the fiftieth anniversary of the October Revolution VNIITE had established 15 branches throughout the USSR and almost 200 design 'laboratories'. Alongside ergonomics and behavioural sciences (after ideological objections to the latter had been overcome), art played a central role in many, though by no means all, of these self-consciously experimental enterprises.[31] Located within the sanctioned sphere of research and off the radar of the Soviet art establishment, these artists escaped the attacks on abstraction which periodically featured in official proclamations on culture through the course of the 1960s.[32] Moreover, their official status meant that they enjoyed access to Western specialist publications where the work of kindred spirits like composer Iannis Xenakis or artist Nicholas Schöffer was reported.

The fiftieth anniversary of the October Revolution celebrations provided new opportunities for these young visionaries working in the interstices of art and science. Prometei (Prometheus), a group based in the Kazan Aviation Institute in Tatarstan, explored the borderlands between non-figurative art, cinema and architecture in their performances. Taking their name from a 1910 composition by Aleksandr Scriabin, the group self-consciously revived the tradition of synaesthetic 'light-music art' which had been an occupation of the Russian avant-garde before the First World War. In 1967 the group installed automatically controlled equipment in the historic tower of the Kazan Kremlin to synchronize beams of light with the chimes of the tower's clock (7.10). A metaphorical expression of the revolutionary 'spirit', this synaesthetic artwork was also based on a Russian idiom, 'crimson-coloured chime'.[33]

In 1967 Francisco Infante, a founder of the neoconstructivist group, Dvizhenie (Movement) and the subject of Jane Sharp's contribution to this book (p.234 below), was commissioned to create a kinetic sculpture

in the 'Exhibition of Scientific Creative Works of Youth' in Moscow's main exhibition grounds (VDNKh), an event which formed one of the many fiftieth anniversary celebrations. He installed a 2m-high crystalline structure entitled *Galaktika* in front of the gilded Stalin-era pavilions (7.11). This kinetic sculpture was fashioned from metal struts and synthetic string (a clothes line). Electric motors animated the heart of the structure, changing its angular forms to the accompaniment of music, and at night *Galaktika* was illuminated with coloured lights. The piece represented the aspiration of the group to imagine new models of public sculpture for the new urban centres being planned across the Soviet Union. On the eve of a visit

7.11
Francisco Infante-Arana,
Galaktika, kinetic construction at the 'Exhibition
of Scientific Creative Works
of Youth', Moscow. Metal,
clothes-line and electric
motors, with lamps and
speakers. October 1967.
Francisco Infante-Arana,
Moscow

from senior figures in the Moscow Party hierarchy, *Galaktika* was the subject of an 'ideological' inspection. Infante and his colleagues were judged to have gone too far in their enthusiasm for the abstract beauty of geometry, and were required to dismantle the artwork.[34] As this incident demonstrates, it is important to stress that whilst groups like Dvizhenie and Prometei were sometimes the focus of criticism from official quarters, they were not anti-communist. In fact, in its technophilia, their work might well be regarded as one of the last expressions of utopian faith in the communist project.

Rediscovering the avant-garde

Rediscovering the 'revolutionary tradition' in the Soviet Union did not necessarily mean an exclusively Marxist-Leninist one. The members of Dvizhenie and Prometei – along- side Czech and Polish artists in the mid-1960s – were early enthusiasts of suprematist art and the works of the visionary Soviet avant-garde of the 1920s.[35] The 1967 anniversary events – which Central European states had little choice but to celebrate – was a pretext for a spate of investigations into the 1920s. VNIITE had been not only the home for abstract artists but also for historians inter- ested in exploring the avant-gardism, includ- ing Selim Khan-Magamedov, the author of numerous pioneering studies on Rodchenko, Vesnin and other Soviet designers.[36] Close

contacts between Moscow and the people's republics in Central Europe meant that there was more expertise about the Soviet avant- garde in Czechoslovakia and Poland than anywhere else outside the Soviet Union in the 1960s. The fiftieth anniversary events provided a context for the exercise of this expertise. In 1967 Warsaw enjoyed a major exhibition on the 'Revolutionary Poster', curated by Szymon Bojko, a cultural appa- ratchik who was one of the first champions of Soviet design of the 1920s.[37] The chief Czech architectural magazine, *Architektura ČSR*, ran a special issue in 1967 which dedicated more words to the Soviet past than the overblown and often overrated architec- tural achievements of the Soviet present; the journal *Výtvarné umění*, meanwhile, used the events as an opportunity to publish the writings of Malevich, Gabo and El Lissitzky.[38]

Already, under Khrushchev, as Susan Reid has noted, 'practitioners and historians ... rehabilitated Constructivism and other modernist tendencies in disgrace since the early thirties, retrieving them as instructive precedents for contemporary architectural and design tasks ...'.[39] In the Thaw of the late 1950s this was a form of pragmatism: the engineer- ing aesthetic of the Modern Movement could provide models for cheap and efficient buildings in the hope of satisfying the desper- ate need for housing in the USSR. Moreover, cautious enthusiasm for the Modern Move-

ment also marked a symbolic break with the tainted aesthetic of Socialist Realism.[40] But by the mid-1960s much of the interest in the visionary schemes by Soviet artists – like El Lissitzky's *Prouns* and Kazimir Malevich's *Planet for Earth-beings* (*Planeta Zemlianitov*) of the 1920s – lay not in their potential as blueprints for a new material world but in their cosmic dimensions. Malevich was particularly important for his prophecies of flying satellite towns moving freely through space and circling the Earth.[41] These were early statements of faith in man's ability to escape from his earthbound condition. The launch of the first Sputnik and the Vostok had triggered off a new cosmic sensibility in Russian society. As Grigorii Revzin has noted, 'every native speaker of Russian language intuitively senses that after his short time in Orbit, Gagarin was more qualified to answer the question [of the existence of God] than anyone else alive on the planet'.[42] Revzin has detected in the landmark buildings of the 1967 anniversary a Cosmic vocabulary of radio-transmitting antenna (like the Ostankino television tower); flying saucers (such as the circus in Kazan, designed by Genadii Pichuev, another anniversary monu- ment opened in 1967) and the aerial view of the landscape, ordered as if to be read by visitors from space (the *microraion* or housing district). This was an apparently involuntary metaphysical response to man's first steps into space. Others were more explicit: in 1969 Czech sculptor Hugo Demartini, caught in the wave of fascination with Malevich, issued a sharp critique of the narrow pragmatists shaping the material environment: 'Today's utopias will be overridden through technologi- cal possibilities. Inhabitants of space stations, future towns on the sea, under the ground, suspended in space, cease to be a fantasy.'[43]

Reviewing the Warsaw exhibition of Soviet avant-garde posters in 1967, Camilla Gray accused Western art historians of misusing the term 'constructivism', applying it to any 'construction-type' sculpture and the work of Naum Gabo in particular.[44] Twenty years later, in a classic essay focusing on the career of Naum Gabo in the West in the post- war years, art historian Benjamin Buchloh argued something similar. Distanced from its radical origins and viewed from the Western side of the Cold War, 'the avant-garde

7.12
Burt Glinn, Fidel Castro
arriving in Santa Clara
during the Cuban
Revolution, 1959

tradition', he wrote, was 'reinstituted in such
a way that it would supply the radical aesthetic goods without the political strings originally
attached to the Dadaists and the Constructiv-
ists' work, especially that of their Productivist
followers'.[45] In one sense something similar
occurred in the Soviet Union and Central
Europe in the late 1960s, when figures like
Infante and Demartini retraced cosmic and
visionary contours of the avant-garde. The
critical difference was a matter of context.
Suprematism was valued for its transcenden-
talism, a metaphysical value then under
prohibition. This was a small protest against
the banal and instrumental uses to which
architecture and design were increasingly
being put in the Brezhnev years.

Cuba

In 1967 the French magazine *Opus International* claimed that Fidel Castro and Ernesto
'Che' Guevara had 'reinvented revolution'.[46]
This was a comment both on the ways in
which Castro's 26 July Movement had seized
power in the late 1950s, and on the influence
that Cuba continued to exert on the rest of the
world in the years that followed. The guerilla
war to oust the Batista dictatorship exploited –
like no other revolution before it – the power
of the image. Unlike the seizure of communist
power in Eastern Europe in the late 1940s,
'revolutions' achieved through murky machinations and menace, the Cuban Revolution
was highly photogenic (7.12). In fact, Castro
and his colleagues used the world's media
as weapon to destabilize Batista's regime.

7.13
Still from *I Am Cuba*,
directed by Mikhail
Kalatozov, shot on location
in Cuba, 1964–5

In February 1958, the 26 July Movement kidnapped world champion motor racing driver Juan Manuel Fangio and then released him unharmed, an event which drew attention to the general strike about to take place (and indirectly testified to the group's humanity when the driver described them as considerate and even friendly[47]). The Cuban revolutionaries, tiny in numbers, achieved the 'media effect' of amplification by performing horse-back parades and gun salutes for the cameras of the world's media.[48]

Once in power, the early actions of Castro's revolutionary government largely conformed to Soviet patterns. Key businesses and institutions were nationalized (the American-owned Havana Hilton was, for instance, taken into state ownership and

renamed the Habana Libre). A clearout of the capital's brothels and casinos, which under Batista had largely served American clients, was instituted. The barracks that had been occupied by Batista's hated militias were given new purpose as schools. In 1961 a campaign to eradicate literacy was mounted, conducted largely by an enormous cadre of student-teachers who were sent into the countryside. These actions not only spread literacy: they shared the new values of the regime. And the achievements were remark-able: one million people were taught to read in a year.[49]

With the arrival of Eastern Bloc economists and Soviet goods – machinery, newsprint, and above all, oil, all traded for sugar – it looked as if Cuba was to undergo

the structural transformation that Soviet Russia had experienced in the 1920s and 1930s, at express speed. But socialist Cuba was not – in its early years – being made in the exact image of Soviet Russia. Freedom of artistic expression, for instance, a right that Moscow was not prepared to concede to Soviet artists after the mid-1920s, was tackled by Castro early on. Reversing early intentions to impose Soviet-style socialist realist creed on artists, he famously announced his formula for art: 'within the Revolution, everything. Without it, nothing.'[50] By this he meant that any writer or artist who expressed support for the Revolution and its aims would be tolerated and even supported, without interference in the forms of expression that this espousal took. This point was put in Cold War terms when Castro later announced 'our enemies are capitalism and imperialism, not abstract art'.[51]

I Am Cuba

Castro visited the Soviet Union, his ally and patron, for the first time in April 1963. The momentum of Khrushchev's 1956 reforms had already faltered and the Soviet leader faced considerable problems at home.[52] The Caribbean country was charged with the mythical elixir of 'revolution' and seemed capable of re-energizing Soviet-style socialism. Castro was genuinely popular amongst Russians and the peoples of the Soviet republics that he visited on his five-week trip, and Cuba was the subject of a widespread craze that seemed to unite all orders of Soviet society. When Castro escaped the attention of his Soviet hosts in Moscow and strolled into Red Square, crowds swarmed around him.[53] To tap the wave of enthusiasm for Cuba, Mosfilm (the Soviet film production agency) signed an agreement to make a film with ICAIC (Cuban Institute of Cinematic Art and Industry/Instituto Cubano de Arte e Industria Cinematográficos).[54] The resulting film, I Am Cuba (1964–5), drew upon the talents of director Mikhail Kalatozov and Thaw poet Evgenii Evtushenko, leading lights in the reform of Soviet culture in the late 1950s (7.13).[55] Along with production designer Evgenii Svidetelev they toured Cuba for three months, accompanied by Cuban poet Enrique Piñeda Barnet, scouting out film locations and talking to leading figures in the Revolution,

including Castro himself. Svidetelev's drawings dwell on the monuments of the Americanization of Cuba under Batista in the 1950s: high-rise hotels, drive-in cinemas, nightclubs and billboards. In the film these locations form a landscape of privilege and corruption, which is rejected by Cuban society as it acquires a revolutionary consciousness. Four life-stories are metaphorically woven together in the moment of triumph that concludes the film when Castro's troops sweep across the island from their mountain strongholds.

Director Kalatozov and his cinematographer Sergei Urusevskii developed a filming technique which they described as 'emotional'.[56] Long passages of the film were shot with a mobile hand-held camera, a technique that had the effect of seeming to propel the viewer into the centre of the action. In some passages the camera even appears to leave the expert hands of the film-maker to be passed around by the actors, whilst in others it takes flight, floating down the sheer elevations of tall buildings and even diving underwater. Urusevskii also employed wide-angle lenses and oddly tilted angles to distort the images of the characters, a technique indebted to Expressionist cinema and the lighting effects employed in Eisenstein's aborted Mexican film Que Viva Mexico, shot in 1931. To achieve the high contrast between the brilliant white sand of Cuba's beaches and the island's liquid skies, Urusevskii used infra-red film stock.[57] At the emotional climax of the film – the murder of a young revolutionary by one of Batista's henchmen – the image dissolves into lachrymose clouds. The film, though fêted for its technical achievements, was damned by Soviet critics for its fascination with misery and oppression under the Batista dictatorship. The film-makers were mesmerized by the lifestyle of American capitalists, even if they represented them as signs of imperial order.[58] These criticisms also reflected a changed climate in Moscow. By the time the film was screened, Khrushchev was no longer in power and warming Sino-Cuban relations troubled the Moscow's ideologues. The film was withdrawn from circulation, only to be rediscovered in the 1990s.[59]

I Am Cuba represented the Cuban Revolution in unmistakably sensual terms. In the opening sequence, the island 'speaks' in a woman's voice in a first-person narration

offering herself to the viewer. Almost all sympathetic characterizations of the new Cuba in the early 1960s were keen to emphasize its emotional qualities (often drawing implicit comparison with the rigid and partisan forms of cultural expression demanded by Eastern Bloc states of their artists).[60] Such views of Cuban emotionalism may well have been built on older European fantasies about this 'exotic' island, but it was a mythical association also promoted by prominent Cuban artists and designers.[61] Painter Wilfredo Lam, who had left the island in the 1920s, was presented to the world as an uncommissioned ambassador (even though he had declined the position of Minister of Culture). His surrealist canvases, in their combination of African and Cuban religious and cultural references as well as their sensuous themes, were received as the output of a liberated spirit.[62] Similarly, Ricardo Porro's School of Plastic Arts (1960–65) is based on an anthropomorphized architectural form that has clear sexual reference to a woman's body. Whilst these fleshy forms were neither exclusively Cuban (echoing the carioca style of Oscar Niemeyer and Affonso Reidy's designs in Brazil) nor socialist, they were associated with the permissive image of the revolution on this Caribbean island.[63]

The poster – one of the island's most successful cultural exports in the 1960s – reinforced the conception of the Cuban Revolution as the site of pleasure. Issued by the COR (Commission of Revolutionary Orientation), the main ideological watchdog of the Cuban Communist Party, ICAIC and OSPAAAL (Organization of Solidarity of the People of Asia, Africa and Latin America), Cuban posters from the mid-1960s drew warm praise around the world for their vivid fields of colour and uninhibited designs (7.14).[64] They were produced in straitened circumstances: paper supplies were limited and early posters were usually screenprinted by hand (rather than lithographically printed, as was the practice in Europe and North America). The diversity of styles was, it seems, a living proof of Castro's 1961 contract to withdraw from questions of artistic form, in exchange for Party control of content. Although American writer Susan Sontag argued that undisciplined aesthetics could not be truly revolutionary, she did see the contours of freedom in

7.14
Niko, *The Tenth Anniversary of the Victory at the Bay of Pigs*, poster commissioned by the Instituto Cubano del Arte e Industria Cinematográficos, Cuba, 1971.
V&A: E.760-2003

their hedonism. Perhaps alluding to the Soviet Union, she wrote these words in 1970:

> These posters give evidence of a revolutionary society that is not repressive and philistine ... a culture which is alive, international in orientation and relatively free of the kind of bureaucratic interference that has blighted the arts in practically every other country where a communist revolution has come to power.[65]

Sontag, like many Western commentators drawn to the island, accepted the discipline and even violence from which revolutions are made.[66] Some of the most strikingly lyrical Cuban posters represented the complete loyalty to the revolution which Castro demanded of all Cubans. Eduardo Bachs' commemoration of the ten-year anniversary of the establishment of the network of Committees for the Defense of the Revolution (Comités de Defensa de la Revolución) in 1970, for instance, represented the network of informants and party workers operating at the ground level of Cuban society as a rippling wave of energy. This network worked in close collaboration with the Ministry of the Interior to repress opposition on the island, as well as managing such benign matters as vaccination campaigns (7.1).[67]

Exporting revolution

Cuba's international reputation as a dynamo of revolution increased during the 1960s. The survival of this David in the face of considerable opposition from its Goliath neighbour, the USA, as well as superpower brinkmanship during the Cuban Missile Crisis in October 1962, lent Cuba considerable importance in Cold War geopolitics. But this Caribbean island was not just a battleground for Cold War competition between the superpowers.[68] Castro's revolutionaries had, as we have already noted, become adept players of the international media in their own right. Fully aware of the impact of his appearance on television, Minister of Industries Che Guevara, for instance, spoke at the United Nations before the world's cameras in December 1964, dressed in uniform as if ready for combat. He presented himself as the personification of revolution. A self-appointed spokesman for 'oppressed peoples', Guevara launched into a vigorous attack on 'Yankee' imperialism. New York was one stop on what was a remarkable world tour that over the winter of 1964–5 took in the People's Republic of China, Algeria, Congo-Brazaville, Tanzania, Ghana and Guinea, as well as the United Arab Republic (Egypt). Che's trail followed a series of simmering fault-lines in the Cold War. The Cold War 'order' – which had settled into place in the 1950s – was increasingly being disturbed by the effects of decolonialization in Africa; the rise of the Non-Aligned Movement, formed by states which refused to side with one superpower or the other; and marked Sino-Soviet tensions. [69] The so-called 'Third World' increasingly protested its exploitation.

Cuba's loudly voiced declaration to spread revolution to Latin America and Africa was realized, albeit temporarily, when Guevara led Cuban fighters to the Congo in 1965 and Bolivia in 1967, where he met his death. The image of the revolutionary prepared to take up arms to fight injustice was, it seems, as attractive to those living in the affluent West as it was to those living in the underdeveloped world. Guevara's portrait, usually in the memorable form of Alberto Korda's iconic photograph taken in March 1960, became a generic symbol of political change in the West, appearing on banners and t-shirts at every demonstration and rally.[70] As a number of left-wing critics pointed out, his image was just as easily adopted by capitalism as it was by the new left. As Sontag noted in her discussion of the vogue for Cuban posters in the West, consumption in capitalist societies is based on severing things from the context of their production: 'counter-revolutionary societies ... [have] a flair for ripping any object out of context and turning it into an object of consumption.'[71]

Paris-based Icelandic artist Erró's (Gudmundur Gudmundsson) series of paintings *American Interiors* (1968) addressed a similar theme, that of the penetration of third-world revolution into the consciousness of the West (7.15). In each, a desirable 'American' interior appears to be surrounded by monumental 'freedom fighters' from China or Vietnam. Some fighters appear in the floor-to-ceiling mirrors in these chic interiors; others appear to have invaded the room itself. In addressing consumerism and revolutionary politics, the series represents a European response to the cool and conventionally apolitical aesthetic of Pop Art in the USA. Despite the title, the setting is not necessarily in the USA. As described by Greg Castillo (p.66 above), American interiors had long been a Cold War instrument to produce loyalty and envy in Europe. In their deadpan style, Erró's paintings bring two opposing representational languages, consumer advertising and the highly graphic variant of Socialist Realism produced in China during the Cultural Revolution, face to face, amplifying their antagonisms. These works are clearly comments on different orders of propaganda, but Erró's message is ambiguous. Should the viewer read the image as the West encircled by its enemies? Or should the image of the freedom fighter on the wall or in the mirror be judged as a commentary on what Raoul Vaneigem, writing in 1967, called 'radical chic'?[72]

For Hans Magnus Enzensberger, Marxist media critic, encountering the image of Che

7.16
Unknown designer, *Down with US Imperialism, Down with Soviet Revisionism,* poster produced during the Cultural Revolution in China, 1967. Private collection

7.17
Li Zhensheng, public humiliation of local officials during the Cultural Revolution, Harbin, China, c.1967

打倒美帝打倒苏修

1967 年西安交通大学反到底兵团三二四纵队

in capitalist advertising was not a reason for radicals in the West to give up on the media.[73] Opponents of capitalism, he argued, should emancipate television and the press from its 'repressive' role by encouraging consumers to become producers. New developments in the electronic media – like the emergence of portable video cameras, which had just come on the market – had, he claimed, great potential. The determining change was not technical but social: 'The campaign against illiteracy in Cuba broke through the linear, exclusive, and isolating structure of the medium of the book.'[74] The fact that the campaign brought peasants and students into new social relations was as important as the words that they learned to read.

In a similar vein, Enzensberger claimed, perhaps naively, that 'In the China of the Cultural Revolution, wall newspapers functioned like an electronic mass medium'. Like many Western commentators observing Mao's Cultural Revolution at a distance, this Marxist critic – like others, including Jean-Luc Godard, director of *La Chinoise* – imagined a world where the alchemy of revolution transformed the relations between power and people (7.16).[75] Of course, the reality of the Cultural Revolution was appalling violence and chaos (7.17). In towns and cities throughout the country libraries and Buddhist temples were destroyed; officials were dragged before enormous crowds to be mocked and beaten; and different factions engaged in pitched battles in towns and cities. In this living nightmare, the streets became a frenzied battleground without clearly defined fronts. Moreover, buildings, squares and even pavements were dressed with enormous calligraphic posters – known as *dazibao* – which declared the aims of the Cultural Revolution and denounced its opponents. In the provincial city of Harbin, official photojournalist Li Zhensheng captured the advance of propaganda as it consumed not only the city but also its citizens.[76] Regional party leaders were forced to stand for hours in the central square wearing *dazibao* around their necks or as dunce's caps, to broadcast their 'crimes' to the world. Far from being a sign of a liberated society, the wall newspaper represented the distorted values of the Cultural Revolution.

1968

For a few short days in 1968 the cities of Czechoslovakia came to resemble those in Mao's China. Jindřich Marco, observing the scenes in Prague immediately following the invasion of the Warsaw Pact forces in late August 1968, wrote:

> with the speed of lightning, Prague was transformed into a huge newspaper. The shop windows in the centre of the town, and not only the centre, were one next to the other papered with posters. The inhabitants of Prague stood in front of them and bitterly amused themselves.[77]

The tone of many of these paper protests was mocking irony. Amongst the many banners, cartoon and slogans encountered by Warsaw Pact armies occupying the streets of Prague and other Czechoslovak cities, they faced banners in Russian bearing the message 'Soldiers Go Home, there is no counter-revolution in our country!' (7.18). This was a response to Soviet attempts to cast the movement to reform socialism in the Czechoslovak Socialist Republic as a conspiracy by 'imperialists' and 'anti-socialist forces'.

Nothing could have been further from the truth. Some of the most prominent figures in the reform movement that had gathered pace in the Socialist Republic of Czechoslovakia over the course of 1967 and 1968 had been Party members. They were joined by others who demanded democratic entitlements and freedom of expression, as well as the right to travel and live abroad. Writer Milan Kundera, for instance, had told the fourth Congress of Czechoslovak Writers six months earlier: 'I am sometimes frightened that the present civilisation is losing that European character which lay so close to the hearts of the Czech humanists and revivalists ... in our case, the guarding of frontiers is still regarded as a greater virtue than crossing them.'[78]

The reform movement – to 'install socialism with a human face' – had, in fact, been growing since the mid-1960s as Czechoslovakia enjoyed a 'late thaw'. De-Stalinization after 1956 – which had been felt as an earthquake in Poland and Hungary – had barely registered on the Richter Scale in Czechoslovakia. The Communist Party, keen to demonstrate its loyalty to Moscow, exercised a strong command over the economy and culture until the mid-1960s. Profound economic crisis, which prompted consider-

able reforms, growing international exchange and the efforts of artists, writers and film-makers to test the limits of censorship and dogma, put pressure on the capacity of the State to control society.

Czechoslovak culture in the mid-1960s was remarkably animated in ways that eschewed the narrow roles prescribed for artists, writers, film-makers and designers by the Party. Former youthful supporters of the regime in the 1950s – like the writers Milan Kundera and Ludvík Vaculík – set out to liberalize culture, often drawing on the resources provided by official culture. Works of modern art, posters and, above all, feature films tested the limits of authority though metaphor and allusion. At the same time the public learned to read between the lines. The cinema became a ground for social observation, frank eroticism, surreal absurdism and formal experimentalism in movies that drew tremendous praise (and some degree of envy) amongst Western critics. For example, Miloš Forman's *Lásky jedné plavovlásky* (*Loves of a Blonde*, 1965), which explores an error of socialist planning in which women outnumber men in a small Czech town, was described – in its bitter humour – as being far more 'authentic' than the *cinéma vérité* which was then in vogue in the West.[79] Similarly, Vera Chytilová's *Sedmikrásky* (*Daisies*, 1966) – a film that follows the chaotic lives of two 'spoiled' teenage girls and eschews narrative – stretched, according to one reviewer, the intellectual muscles of even the most ardent enthusiast of underground cinema.[80] Here was evidence of a genuinely popular culture that met high modernist artistic criteria. The late 'thaw' in Czechoslovak culture represented by such films was a prologue to the Prague Spring. Metaphor and allusion were to become redundant in the tidal wave of explicit demands and frank criticisms issued by the sweeping reform movement.

Viewed from Prague, 1968 was a year of sharply rising hopes and anxieties. The strident calls for reform from radicals as well the attempts by Alexander Dubček's regime, under pressure from Moscow, to hold expectations in check, were charted in streams of print. Words ricocheted like bullets in the street. Declarations in the student press and on the stages of conferences by writers,

7.18
Josef Koudelka, protests against the invasion of Warsaw Pact troops at the St Wenceslas monument, Prague, August 1968

film-makers and other intelligentsia groups were met by counter-declarations in the official daily press. The ideological culmination of this war of words was '2,000 words to Workers, Farmers, Scientists, Artists and Everyone', a manifesto written in June 1967 by young novelist Ludvík Vaculík and signed by more than 70 public figures from the arts, education, sports and agriculture.[81] But in the fast turn of events, the unstable line between State and opposition became unclear: in March 1968, for instance, the censorship board, a committee stacked with communists, called for its own dissolution.[82]

The Czechoslovak 'Revolution' was strikingly literary in character. Artist-poet Jiří Kolář – whose primary medium was collage – chose to incorporate this flow of words into his 'diary', a cycle of images produced in 1968. The results were extraordinary commentary on the media effects of living in a country where public opinion had too long been sequestered by the interests of the Party; Louis Aragon described them as 'an insistent reminder written on the world's conscience'.[83] These highly idiosyncratic journals capture the thrilling excitement and pleasures of the Prague Spring, and the tribulation of its suppression through allusion and metaphor. Kolář here deployed many of the numerous collage techniques he had developed and labelled since the early 1950s, including 'crumplage', 'chiasmage' and 'intercollage', as well as reproductions of his own earlier pieces.[84]

The exuberance in the early phases of the 1968 diary reflected the changed circumstances in which the artist-poet found himself. Kolář had been imprisoned in 1953 when the police raided the house of a literary critic and discovered a manuscript that compromised him in the eyes of the State. In the decade that followed, his opportunities to publish and exhibit his work had been sharply circumscribed. Censorship became a kind of muse. During these years he produced 'silent' concrete poems using the punctuation marks – full stops, commas and colons – on a typewriter. Similarly, his collage works of the early 1960s destroyed the flow of words, paragraphs and pages as printed sentences in different languages and staves of music were cut up, folded, pasted or crumpled to form a commentary on the condition of language

7.19
Jiří Kolář, *Diary 1968: Entrée*. Collage, 1968. Neues Museum – Staatliches Museum für Kunst und Design, Nuremberg

7.20
Jiří Kolář, *Diary 1968: Mladý Svět 24.8.1968.* (*Young World*). Collage, 1968. Neues Museum – Staatliches Museum für Kunst und Design, Nuremberg

in communist Czechoslovakia. In one image in the 1968 series captioned 'Deliver Us From Evil', Kolář turns to the absences and silences in the official historical record. During the Prague Spring, the Party had been put under great pressure to reveal the truth about the show trials of the 1950s in which loyal communists had been prosecuted and then executed on trumped-up charges.[85] In 'But Deliver Us from Evil' the Czech artist reproduces three sets of twinned images over a circular musical motif. Each pair of contrasting images reveals the crooked practice of Soviet historiography in which inconvenient figures were 'disappeared' in the dark room.[86] Soviet history was not driven by Marx's dialectic: it was shaped by the Stalinist principles of décollage.

Kolář's 1968 cycle includes works dedicated to the *événements* in Paris in May (7.19). Although the motives for the student-led conflict with de Gaulle's France were poorly understood in Czechoslovakia, in *Entrée* his treatment points, perhaps intuitively, to a carnavalesque revolution: here the dominating elements are a reproduction of Pop artist Robert Indiana's canvas *Love* and tickets for the Metro and tourist sites.[87]

The mood of the collages produced in the aftermath of the occupation in August is very different. Drawing on the output of the anti-Soviet media, Kolář reduced his collage poetics to dark accusations. In *Young World* he laid a page from an 'independently printed' student magazine depicting the site of a murder of a teenage boy, strewn with flowers and his blood-stained clothes, over larger newspaper pages in which scraps of reports of Soviet 'diplomacy' could be read (7.20). The metaphoric language that Czech artists, not least Kolář, had developed so effectively under the period of communist rule was – for this short, confused period of protests and violence – not needed.

With the invading forces struggling to find figures who could form a government loyal to Moscow, Czechoslovakia found itself in a strange position in the days that immediately followed the invasion. The anti-Soviet media continued to broadcast and publish, and ordinary people refused to collaborate with the invading forces by, for instance, effectively closing down the railway system. The Czechoslovak Communist Party

7.21
**Jaroslava Brychtová and
Stanislav Libenský**, *The River
of Life*, glass sculpture on
display at Expo '70, Osaka,
1970

continued to declare its support for Dubček, then under arrest in Moscow. But resistance was steadily eroded. Only exceptional incidents, such as the suicide by self-immolation by student Jan Palach in Wenceslas Square in Prague in January 1969, broke, temporarily, the drift back into Stalinism. Palach eventually died three days later and his funeral became a mournful national protest against the suppression of reform. When in May 1969 the pro-Soviet communist leader Gustáv Husák assumed full control of the country, it was clear that the reform movement was truly over.

Protest in Czechoslovakia was increasingly forced underground or back to the Aesopian language of metaphor. In one illustrative episode, Czech glass-artists Stanislav Libenský and Jaroslava Brychtová, long protected by the State as symbols of Czechoslovak progress, were commissioned to represent the nation at Osaka '70 World's Fair. They produced a free-standing glass wall entitled *The River of Life*, an apparently anodyne and universal theme that seemed serve the new regime's empty rhetoric (7.21). However, the Czech artists also cast the impression of booted footprints into the swirling river, its movement ceasing as water froze into ice. The allusion to military forces trampling on the Prague Spring was unmistakable to all, including the ideological commissars who inspected the national display. Libenský and Brychtová were obliged to watch the footprints being erased by a glass-grinder flown in especially for this task and were expelled from the Party on their return to Prague.[88]

Prague in Moscow

During the turbulent months of the Prague Spring, President Brezhnev had been unable to countenance the possibility of a democratic socialist state breaking ranks. An article in *Pravda* in September 1968 made the brutal logic of what became known as the 'Brezhnev Doctrine' clear to all: 'The weakening of any of any link in the world socialist system has a direct effect on all the socialist countries, which cannot be indifferent to this.'[89] The ugly suppression of the reform movement in Czechoslovakia was designed, above all, to safeguard Soviet interests, not least by maintaining the borders keeping NATO far

away from the Soviet Union. The Brezhnev Doctrine made it clear to reform-minded politicians in the rest of the Bloc what might occur should they conflict with Moscow's interests. Even Castro, who had presented Cuba as the friend of small nations living in the shadow of aggressive neighbours, came out against Czechoslovak autonomy.[90] Brezhnev's *rappel à l'ordre* ultimately did little to secure the Bloc. The resentment of an entire nation was a powerful motivator twenty years later when the Czechoslovaks mounted the 'Velvet Revolution' against communist rule.

In the USSR, the suppression of the reform movement had, as many commentators have noted, a significant impact on attitudes to socialism. The invasion seemed, finally, to extinguish the hope – first raised by Khrushchev – that the Soviet project could be regenerated, and that the revolution could be put back on a progressive path. This was one of the assaults on utopia that marked the late 1960s. For the Soviet intelligentsia, the loss of faith in the longer-term aims of socialism was marked by a withdrawal into a kind of privatized cosmos, as Boym puts it, 'minor private retreats from the public li[f]e'.[91] Kuznetsov, the Russian dissident who escaped to London in 1969, recalled the atmosphere when news broke of the Warsaw Pact 'defence' of Czechoslovakia:

People were forced to turn up at meetings so that the newspapers could demonstrate to the world the 'unanimous, nationwide, approval' of the aggression. These were strange dreary meetings at which people listened with sad, worried faces to the official speakers reading prefabricated texts of resolutions that approved the actions of 'our wise Communist party and Soviet Government'.[92]

For a few citizens of the USSR the suppression of the reform movement in Czechoslovakia was, however, a trigger to action. In late August 1968 seven courageous protestors, some of whom were already engaged in a campaign against the Soviet treatment of prisoners of conscience in labour camps, led a demonstration against the invasion in Moscow's Red Square.[93] Sitting with banners and Czechoslovak flags (echo-

ing, on a modest scale, the streets of Prague), they took great care not to be arrested for public order offences: this was a protest, not a revolt. Like nuclear scientist Andrei Sakharov, they drew a connection between the suppression of the Prague Spring and the suppression of human rights in the USSR.[94] The Red Square protestors were met with a swift response from the KGB (Komitet Gosudarstvennoi Bezopasnosti), the Soviet Secret Police. Put on trial, five members of the small group were given sentences of detention in forced labour camps or 'internal exile'; the other two were declared insane and spent time in 'special psychiatric hospitals' organized by the KGB. This demonstration was one of the least spectacular events of 1968, yet it was no less significant: it marked early steps in a long and costly – in personal terms – campaign of dissent that ultimately contributed to the end of the USSR 23 years later.[95]

Back to October

When Sadecký's Octobriana appeared in print in 1971 she was, it seems, already *démodé*. At the time of her birth four years earlier, the world seemed to be on the threshold of dramatic, even revolutionary, shift. But by the beginning of the 1970s the plate tectonics of the Cold War were shifting back into place. What is more, the 'spirit of revolution' that she was supposed to encapsulate and which had long been claimed as the engine of modernity, seemed enervated in the West as well as in the East. The idea that the world could be 'cleansed' by violence, that tradition could be overhauled in a radical shift in power, or even that the future could be made through a radical rejection of present conditions, no longer seemed tenable, except for the few who turned to guerrilla activism and terrorism in the 1970s.[96] The myth of revolution that had catalysed modernity since the mid-nineteenth century seemed, finally, to be exhausted.

7.22
Josef Koudelka, *Prague 1968*, gelatin silver print, 1968.
V&A: PH.1442-1980

Josef Koudelka took this photograph in Wenceslas Square in Prague on 22 August 1968, a day when a mass demonstration against the suppression of the reform movement had been called. When the citizens of the city learned that the Warsaw Pact forces which had invaded the country would meet protest with violence, the event was cancelled. Koudelka captured the emptiness of the square at the time when the rally should have been at full strength. The Prague Spring was over.

Protest by Design: Giancarlo De Carlo and the 14th Milan Triennale

Paola Nicolin

Exhibitions are like castles made out of paper, it takes very little to make them collapse[1]

Shortly after the 14th Milan Triennale closed, the Italian architect and chief organizer of the exhibition, Giancarlo De Carlo, wrote to Japanese architect Arata Isozaki to thank him for his participation. Isozaki had contributed a dramatic installation on the theme of the future city in ruins entitled 'Electric Laby-rinth'.[2] Isozaki's installation was, however, never to be seen by its intended audience. On the day of its inauguration, 30 May 1968, the entire exhibition was occupied by a group determined to interrupt the opening.[3] In the heat of the events of 1968, following riots in Paris and demonstrations in Italy in the early spring, the Triennale, the premier design event in Europe, was brought to a sudden halt by the actions of protestors. In his letter to Isozaki, De Carlo reflects on the role he played in the organization of the exhibition and the thinking that lay behind it:

Dear Arata,
I think you can understand that: I did a lot of work as an organizator [sic] (which is not my work) in the hope that the Triennale could be a good opportuni-ties [sic] for a large scale confrontation of new ideas the Italian people should know. The result was a miscarriage from many points of view: not all the architects I had called to work on the Greater Number exhibition give their best to suggest new proposal and some of them have been only involved in giving a very personal description of themselves; an ambiguous occupation did the rest and destroyed all possibilities for a peaceful and useful debate.

De Carlo continues by considering the motives of the protestors in the context of the wider revolt against the academic and institutional system, characteristic of the Italian cultural scene at the end of the 1960s:

Perhaps everything is violent today and the violence is the only way to clarify the involved situation in which we live. And instead of doing work for cultural institution it is inescapable to fight on political terms. I am not against this conclusion ... but the occupation of the Triennale gave me the demonstration that the measure of political terms is very easy and can mystify everything. I don't know if you realized that the first wave of the occupants was composed by angry painters and sculptors excluded from the exhibition: I didn't invite them because they believe that their art is a sacral metaphysical and uncontami-nated matter for restricted elite. I believe on the contrary that this XIX century idea of art is definitively dead and that our time needs new relationships between art and people, which means a radical transformation (perhaps the destruction) of art.[4]

His distress at the events in Milan of May and June 1968 was less to do with the destruction of the design fair than with the frustration of having his intentions misunderstood. From the outset, the 1968 Triennale had been conceived as a form of social and cultural critique. Seeing in architecture the means to formulate an alternative vision for the future of the world, De Carlo and the curators of the exhibition invited a range of designers, chosen for their ability to design not so much an object as an environment. As well as Isozaki, the list of participants included

Hans Hollein, who coordinated the Austrian Pavilion 'Austriennale' which he conceived as a critical reflection on mass consumerism and a space for public interaction (7.23).[5] The British group Archigram presented their 'Milanogram', reflections on the theme of personal choice in one's living environment, which included various inflatable structures (7.24).[6] Others included the Italian group Archizoom, the NER Group from Moscow, and from the USA Saul Bass, George Nelson and Gyorgy Kepes, as well as American-born Shadrach Woods, former assistant to Le Corbusier, who was responsible for the 'Urbanism is Everybody's Business' display with artist Joachim Pfeuffer. De Carlo also invited many of his associates from the breakaway architectural group Team 10, including not only Woods but also the Dutch architect Aldo van Eyck, and Peter and Alison Smithson from Britain.[7] As a final factor, public attendance was itself seen as an intrinsic aspect of 'the Greater Number'. Moreover, this was the first Triennale to consider the enjoyment of the public as a political factor and a criterion to establish the quality of the show itself.

This agenda marked an extension of the Triennale's ambitions. Since its move from Monza to Milan in 1933, the Triennale had been an important showcase for new trends in the decorative and industrial arts.[8] After the war, successive curators used the event to explore social and cultural propositions for architecture and design. However, it was between 1965 and 1968 that a group led by De Carlo had devised an exhibition for the 14th Triennale which strongly aimed at involving and informing a wider public of the changes and transformations of the age.[9] The 1968 Triennale was to represent the optimism of the economic boom and the rise of the consumer society on the one hand, and the

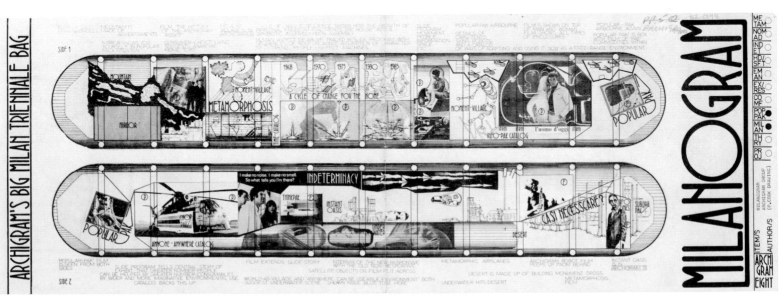

anxiety of the individual lost in a system of nascent globalism on the other. The committee eventually settled on the idea of 'The Greater Number' as an exhibition theme through which to explore this polarity.[10] For De Carlo in particular, this was a reflection of his personal architectural philosophy and his fiercely held political beliefs, forged in the turbulent years of Italy's reconstruction following the Second World War. De Carlo, who had fought with the anti-fascist Partisan movement and then became involved with the anarchists shortly after the war, was a close friend and colleague of Ernesto Nathan Rogers, the architect and post-war editor of *Domus* (1946–7) and *Casabella* (1953–65), who led the call for a socially responsible modern architecture in the late 1940s. As well as being a member of Team 10, De Carlo was also in touch with a wide range of architectural writers and urban theorists from Europe and the USA.[11]

A structure renewed
The Triennale of 1968 was intended to be a different sort of exhibition, bringing together the calls for reform that had exercised the Executive Council since its 1948 revival. There were many new factors: from 1964 to 1968 the Triennale's research body, called the Centre of Studies (Centro Studi), took a more central role in orchestrating the event.[12] Also, the exhibition needed to change from being what was essentially a commercial display of luxury goods to a thematic show that engaged with contemporary cultural debate. In order to recapture the attention of the wider public the exhibition layout underwent substantial modification. It was no longer to be divided into the three traditional areas of architecture, art and production. Instead, the curators proposed a thematic arrangement, laid out on two floors of the Palazzo dell'Arte, bringing together the traditional sections into one continuous circuit in order 'to represent with greater clarity the reciprocity of the relationships between them'.[13] Participants from different disciplines were to be brought together with the objective of exploring concepts over forms, engaging with the ongoing debate about alternative means of exhibition presentation in architecture and art, and on the synthesis of the arts (which had, in fact, been a feature of the Triennale since the

'De Divina Proportione' conference of 1951, held at the 9th Triennale[14]).

Organized by a team led by De Carlo, the 1968 exhibition was to unite architecture, design and art through novel means of exhibition and communication. Participants would be invited to develop research projects that reflected on the modern city and its transformation, on population growth, on the birth of mass society and the behaviour of social groups, on large-scale communication and transport systems and, at the same time, on the effects of all this on the individual. For De Carlo the architectural exhibition as a cognitive structure (or, as Umberto Eco would write at the time, 'architecture as mass communication'[15]) was to fulfil the purpose of being a proper research and investigative tool: it would therefore examine the exhibition concept itself, and the ways in which the ideas contained within it were communicated.

With the theme of 'the Greater Number', the Centre of Studies aimed to stress how much the old formula of simply displaying the exhibits had lost its value, and that a new way of communicating with the huge audience was needed. Author and Journalist Dino Buzzati summed up the change in attitude:

> The Milan Triennale, after a long period of self-imposed isolation due to its snobbish and technological outlook which has led to the majority of the Milanese ignoring its existence, may finally this year turn out to be welcoming and popular … the Greater Number, as the exhibition ascertains, means in fact something very straightforward: it means the obsession, the neurasthenia, the vertigo but also the imagination, the intoxication, the impulsive enthusiasms of the world of today and tomorrow, standardized, mechanized and made uniform.[16]

However, it was more than clear that by developing a more critical and enquiring stance for the exhibition the organizers were responding to the same frustrations that fuelled the protest which eventually consumed the event. Inside its institutional walls, the Triennale committee attempted to introduce an element of doubt about its own history and existence and to engage the public in

debate. It wished to open a more direct channel of communication with the social sciences and with new technologies, which were beginning to become the new realities for architecture – or better still, its new primary material. To some extent, the exhibition was intentionally making a protest itself, choosing to express its message by quite clearly discarding all notions of discipline and handing over to the public the tools for discussion and debate on the project.[17]

This critical intention was to be clear to the visitor from the outset. It began with a room entitled 'The Mistakes' curated by De Carlo, Marco Zanuso and Vittoriano Viganò. In the entrance hall of the Palazzo dell'Arte a series of photographs of crowded places had been put together in order to show how the environment 'in which the man of today lives, is used, in most cases inappropriately and therefore with dangerously inadequate and damagingly crowded results, which are often chaotic and sometimes completely negative'.[18] Images of such 'mistakes', printed in black and white, were shown one after another on a strip of plexiglas hung from the ceiling. The strip was threaded at the ends between wooden rollers, illuminated from within, which projected light alternately downwards and upwards. The photographs showed chaotic views of great metropolitan centres, including Milan, Hong Kong, Paris and London, their station terminals, underground trains and traffic. The other displays mounted by De Carlo are discussed below, but it is important to establish here the changing character of Italian society at the time. A general climate of contradiction pervaded Italy in the second half of the 1960s. Modernization was uneven: increasing prosperity for many was accompanied by marked social imbalance; a booming economy built on low salaries meant increased tension between employers and unions; at the same time, the extension of the education system was beginning to bring about profound changes in the old social and political networks. In this context the Triennale takes on a significance not only because of the topicality of its architectural themes, but also because of the occupation of the protestors itself.

The need to protest was felt throughout the social and political fabric of Italy under the fourth government of the post-war Republic (1963–8). Dissent ensued from social unease that had built up during the course of the 1960s. In many ways Milan was a mirror of rapid developments in the Italian economy between the end of the 1950s and the early 1960s. All the characteristics and contradictions of a country undergoing change could be found there, in terms of the city's rapidly modernizing infrastructure and the social impact of economic migration from the south of the country to the northern industrial cities. Student unrest flared up in the city in the spring of 1968 with the occupation of three of Milan's universities: the Università Cattolica, the Università Statale and the Politecnico. And then in May, protest infected the Triennale.

No entry: protest at the Triennale

On 30 May, according to contemporary reports, a little over a hundred people – students, critics and intellectuals – gathered in front of the Palazzo dell'Arte. Among the demonstrators were several artists, including Giò Pomodoro, Alik Cavaliere, Gianni Dova, Ernesto Treccani and Enzo Mari, all members of the Associazione Pittori e Scultori (Association of Painters and Sculptors) (7.25). The situation degenerated in the early evening. De Carlo tried to talk to the demonstrators until Dino Gentili, the president of the Triennale, agreed to let them in to the theatre hall to hold a discussion about the reasons for the protest. As soon as they entered, the demonstrators made for the exhibition

The Personal Visions and Public Spaces of the Movement Group (Dvizhenie)

Jane A. Sharp

Writing about the Movement Group (Dvizhenie) today is a delicate matter. First there is the measure of cultural-historical difference – gaps in context that viewers in the West are bound to feel as they look at unknown images which at first seem familiar. We see clear parallels between works produced by Francisco Infante-Arana, Viacheslav Koleichuk and Lev Nussberg and those produced in roughly the same period by members of the German 'Zero' Group, Heinz Mack and Otto Piene and Guenther Uecker, for example. Yet the creation of such images and objects in the Soviet Union of the 1960s and 1970s was an undertaking of a different order and scale, and – given the possible negative consequences – ambition. To create art out of the bounds of Soviet art academies (especially if one had received the privileged status of student in any one of them) was to acquire the reputation of pariah in an exclusive social network of artists, historians and functionaries – or to cultivate a deeply personal, often isolated, world shaped by viewers who were chosen among a select few trusted friends. Such work would be limited to underground venues that had little public and (until recently) historical impact. During the Thaw, a period framed by Khrushchev's denunciation of the Stalin cult of personality at the Twentieth Communist Party of the Soviet Union Congress in 1956 and the trials of writers Andrei Siniavsky and Yulii Daniil in Moscow in 1966, Socialist Realism was still dogma, its 'policemen' among the most manipulative and brutal figures in Soviet public life. Valentin Serov, President of the USSR Academy of Arts and First Secretary of the Artists' Union, led the charge at one hopeful moment of official-unofficial art world integration during the notorious 'Manege' ('Manezh') exhibition in 1962, just as the artists who formed Dvizhenie were completing their education. In his debate with unofficial artists, Khrushchev famously declared their work to be 'shit', and that they were more deserving of labour camp sentences than studios and stipends.[1]

Secondly, the accounts that exist of unofficial art in the Soviet Union do not adequately represent the scope of Dvizhenie, nor do they attempt to reconstruct or interpret individual contributions within any meaningful framework. Because artists needed to bond together to produce public projects, no matter what the motivation, to gain expanded public access, Movement Group artists, like many others east and west of the Iron Curtain, had a great deal at stake in the positions expressed in collective manifestos. This measure of achievement, like so much else in Russian avant-garde art history, is left first to the artists themselves to define. Ilya Kabakov and Andrei Monastyrski were not alone in creating archives that need to be addressed as part of their oeuvre. Yet despite all this – and, I would argue, because of it – the ideas that Movement Group artists generated, whether individually or as a group, constitute one of the most vivid creative events in the post-Second World War era. The projects they planned, whether realized or left as diagrams and paintings, are a unique phenomenon in the history of post-war Russian and Soviet modernism. The concern to address optimistically a world seen whole again from a vantage point outside the post-Second World War geopolitical spheres of influence resonated with other collective ventures in Europe of the 1960s. And though this in itself distinguishes Movement Group activities from other unofficial and official ventures, the artists and their projects are only now receiving recognition that is long overdue.[2]

Dvizhenie: shared interests and rival histories

The question of Dvizhenie's historical impact is further complicated by the turbulent internal politics among former members of the group, few of whom agree on its benchmark moments, especially the innovations and collaborations of its founders. The debate centres on a distinction insisted on by Infante and elided by Nussberg in their respective accounts of the group's organization and composition. Infante has explained that towards the end of 1962, artists who knew each other from Moscow art schools in the late 1950s began to constitute what he calls an as yet unnamed 'association of friends' (*sodruzhestvo*) based on shared professional interests. They included: Infante, Nussberg, Mikhail Dorokhov, Rimma Zanevskayia (later Sapgir), Anatolii Krivchikov, Viktor Stepanov and Viacheslav Shcherbakov; Viacheslav Koleichuk participated in some projects and public events.[3] For Nussberg this moment simply marks the beginning of their history as the collective he claims to have named at that point 'Movement Group', and whose aims he codified in a manifesto drafted in 1965 and published in 1966.[4] The association's goals as a collective were more formally defined by Nussberg in the latter months of 1964 (by December), the date accepted as the 'founding' of Dvizhenie by these early members, including Infante.

This manifesto, which calls for the creation of a world institute of kineticism, reveals great sensitivity to the moment as one of precarious idealism when, amid the rumblings of the arms race and the space race, Russian artists could still hope for global integration – to be achieved by their generation through the union of art and science:

We are pioneers.
We unite the WORLD to KINETICISM!
    KINETICISM?
TODAY'S man is torn apart, sick.
    'Man, are you not tired of
    destruction?'
TODAY'S child is already the cosmic
    generation.
The stars have come nearer. Then let
    ART draw people together through
    the breath of the stars![5]

By this time the composition of the group had changed and included Viktor Akulinin; later still, Aleksandr Grigoriev, Galina Bitt, Natalia Prokuratova and Tatiana Bystrova would join. Over the course of 1966 the first members of the association gravitated away from Nussberg (Infante left the group in 1968) to found other associations: Infante's ARGO (Authors' Working Group) was founded in 1972 and Koleichuk's Mir (Peace/World) in 1968.

There is no doubt that Nussberg was the main organizer and promoter of public events, even if the individual authors of projects shaped their visual appearance and executed the critical components themselves. For this reason it is nearly impossible to speak generally or theorize about the nature of their 'collective work'. Collaborations began as advice and hands-on assistance among individuals working on their own sculptures and installations, or as exhibitions where each artist presented his or her work as individually authored. Early significant exhibitions were: an exhibition of 'Ornamentalists' (a name Nussberg devised) held at the Moscow House of Art Workers for a few days in 1963; followed by the exhibition 'On the Path to Synthesis in the Arts' held at the Dzerzhinskii Regional Committee Club of the Komsomol in 1964, also in Moscow. During the period preceding the naming of the Movement Group as Dvizhenie, and an explicit commitment to kinetic art, they adopted the term 'Synthesis and Movement' to describe their shared goals. In the mid- to late-1960s the artists made several television appearances, notably in Moscow in 1964 and in Kazan three years later. Early collective projects were Nussberg's 1967 installation in the Finland Station Square in Leningrad for the celebration of 'Fifty Years of Soviet Power', while in Moscow

Infante created and for the most part executed an installation entitled *Galaktika* at VDNKh (the Exhibition Grounds for Economic Achievements), a project discussed by David Crowley in this book (p.214).

But there were a few early collaborations in the larger sense – discussed, co-created and planned by at least two artists. Evidence of this lies in some key works, notably Nussberg and Prokuratova's *Altar for the Temple of the Spirit (Sketch for the Creation of an Altar at the Institute of Kinetics)*, 1969–70 (7.27). This work speaks to the goals expressed in the manifesto, and represents the underlying motivation for much Movement Group art of that period: the synthesis of art and science in order to foster a 'new relation to the world ... [and] bring life close to the world of dreams and imagination'. In this photo-collaged work the artists create a hybrid imaginary-documentary place that viewers are meant to understand as potentially existing in the future. Here individuals control their own material and cosmic environments, united in shared purpose under a construction that merges inner and outer space. A number of other works authored by Nussberg are later projections of interactive kinetic spaces

7.27
Lev Nussberg and Natalia Prokuratova, *Altar for the Temple of the Spirit (Sketch for the Creation of an Altar at the Institute of Kinetics)*. Tempera and photo collage on paper, 1969–70. Jane Voorhees Zimmerli Art Museum, The Norton and Nancy Dodge Collection of Nonconformist Art from the Soviet Union, New Brunswick, NJ

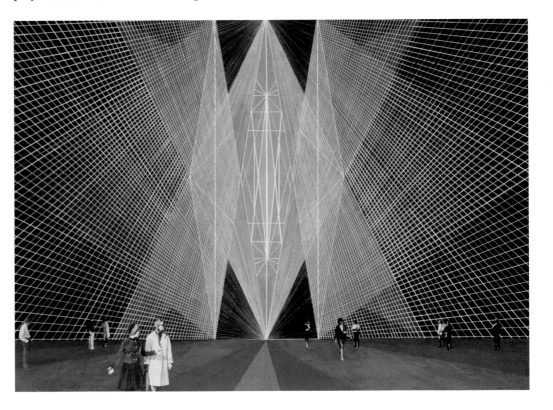

7.28
Lev Nussberg, *Night Visions (Fantastic Artificial Project for a Cybernetic Environment)*. Tempera on paper, 1966. Jane Voorhees Zimmerli Art Museum, The Norton and Nancy Dodge Collection of Nonconformist Art from the Soviet Union, New Brunswick, NJ

7.29
Francisco Infante-Arana, *Scheme for the kinetic illumination of the old architectural buildings in the Moscow Kremlin (the Spasskaya, Nikol'skaya towers, the Kremlin wall, the cathedral of Basil-the Blessed) and the mausoleum on the Red Square*. Tempera and Indian ink on cardboard, 1968. Francisco Infante-Arana, Moscow

that were never intended to be realized.

Nussberg's work prior to his kinetic period was, like Infante's, Koleichuk's and Akulinin's, drawn from geometrical principles. However, he eventually grounded his theory and images in research on cybernetics, creating imaginary animated figures endowed with psychological and emotional characteristics, which he called 'Bion-kinetic' (*Bionkin*; 7.28).[6] Nussberg's futurological rhetoric also no doubt owes much to the 1960s novels of Stanisław Lem, especially *Solaris* (1961). But for Nussberg motivation also lay in the rediscovery of the historical Russian avant-garde of the 1910s and 1920s through objects and images that remained in the home of the artists' descendents and a few visionary collectors, like George Costakis. Particularly the works produced by Kazimir Malevich, El Lissitzky (*Prouns*), Gustav Klucis and Vladimir Tatlin, and the constructivist sculptures of Alexander Rodchenko (such as the oval *Spatial Construction* of 1920) amassed in Costakis's Moscow apartment, presented a model of creative freedom – of social inclusion and transformation – that while still suppressed, appeared newly relevant in the Thaw era.[7] Infante's response to the historical Russian avant-garde was more personal and less programmatic. He professes to have preferred Mondrian over Malevich and recalls his interest specifically in the abstract work of Ivan Kliun and Lissitzky on display in Costakis's apartment.[8] Nussberg and others connected to the Movement Group sought to match this earlier generation's ambitions and achievements (however limited its actual realization) in order to integrate individual creative gestures into a unified collective political and social space – to create great public works.[9]

Yet unlike parallel ventures in the West, the constructions and installations created in 1960s Soviet Russia were sited not in museums or galleries but in scientific and other public institutions, such as the Kurchatov Institute of Atomic Energy, the Moscow House of Architects and, indeed, VDNKh. These institutions were a legacy of the artistic-intellectual traditions that had made Russia a front runner in the sciences even prior to the revolution. Yet there can be no doubt as to the tremendous investment of materials, money and prestige that the Soviet Union and its leaders conferred on scientists at the end of the Second World War by subsidizing these particular institutes. At the moment when visionary practice in the visual arts went underground, experimental activities in research institutes expanded, and permitted (even encouraged) sponsorship of compatible creative endeavours. Thus the elaboration of a kinetic interior space could function both as an individual installation and an evocative backdrop for the futurological programme of the State (realized by

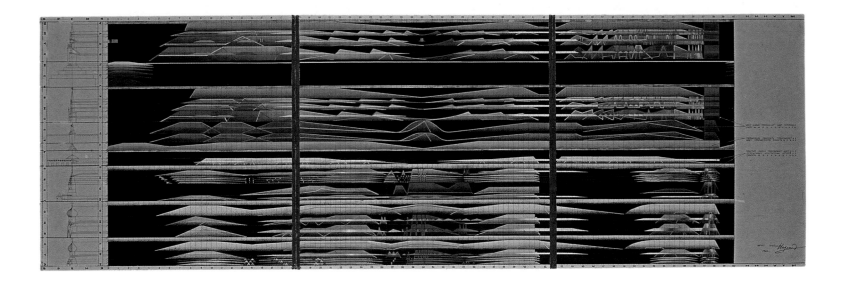

its leaders in science). For artists, scientific institutes became official spaces that provided financial backing and audiences for work otherwise overlooked or censored.

This congruence of site and artistic project created an unusually compelling utopian vision – one that, because of its physical location, might be imagined by viewers as achieved. Such consonance of motivation and realization of an avant-garde project was an unintended result of official censorship: abstract work had to be presented in scientific or industrial spaces in order to be neutralized as high art and bypass competition or confrontation with official Socialist Realism. If Movement Group projects evaded censure as art, they would be appreciated in the terms provided by their display context. Thus many kinetic installations and design projects are genuinely ambiguous. Undeniably concerned with and derived from the visual arts traditions of avant-garde abstraction, they are also technically, scientifically informed, attuned to the inventive feats and ambitions of Soviet engineering. Unfortunately this ambivalence was echoed in the corridors of institutional power and relatively few large projects were realized.

A stunning example of official approval – followed by bureaucratic mismanagement – of a Movement Group era project was Infante's proposal for the kinetic illumination of the Moscow Kremlin.[10] A project he originated in 1968 in the chief Moscow architectural office

(Mosproekt), Infante's work made it to the model stage, complete with electronically timed lights (using a primitive computer; 7.29). According to Infante, his presentation to the Kremlin directors of the project was pre-empted by his superiors who signalled their intention to claim authorship. Rather than see his work co-opted, Infante destroyed it. He believes to this day that a competing project of a light projection from the roof of the state store (GUM) opposite the Kremlin was positioned to win the commission – which, in the end, it did. Indeed, it is difficult to imagine a more unlikely scenario: a dynamic display of pure colour flashing in musically timed sequences across the Kremlin towers and walls – produced by an artist already known for his abstract constructions.[11]

Historical photographs are all that remain of the few kinetic installations that were realized, although one sequence of illuminated interior windows created by Infante in 1965 survives to this day in the building that houses the Institute of High Temperatures in Moscow. Made of coloured filters pressed between two layers of glass, the windows expand the geometric studies that document his earliest attempts to visually resolve the paradox of fixing infinite sets. For the most part, Movement Group projects remain on paper and, as is true for the early twentieth-century Russian avant-garde, they thereby remain visionary – material and ideological constraints in a competitive,

future-oriented Soviet Union ironically guaranteeing their utopian qualities. Clearly many were designed with that seemingly limited goal in mind. For to realize a metaphorical construct in real three-dimensional space might not adequately express its motivation, which, as Infante frequently argued, ideally remains within the realm of metaphysics.

A key work that demonstrates the intellectual/metaphysical impetus of his early Movement Group projects is Infante's multiple series, *Reconstruction of the Firmament* (1965–7; 7.30). Having arrived at the idea that the infinite expansion of the cosmos might be addressed in forms both abstract and representational prior to 1965, in the course of the next two years Infante produced over sixty individual images, all created in tempera on paper, of various speculative 'reconstructions' of star patterns in the night sky. They range from graphic signs and geometrically ordered sequences to more random patterns, and are painted with such a high degree of illusionistic detail that in reproduction they might easily be read as photographs documenting something actually seen.

On one level, the series represents a fascination with space generated by the 'race to space' that followed the Soviet Union's successful launch of the first Sputnik satellite in 1957. Throughout the 1960s a constant battery of articles in the press, public television programmes, and the popularization of scientific discourse that accompanied

7.30
Francisco Infante-Arana,
Star Rain, from the series
*Project of the Reconstruction
of the Firmament*. Airbrush
and gouache on paper, 1968.
Jane Voorhees Zimmerli
Art Museum, The Norton
and Nancy Dodge Collection
of Nonconformist Art
from the Soviet Union,
New Brunswick, NJ

rocket launches in Russia and the US made
theories about deep space more available
and certainly more appealing to the mass
public in both cultures. Human travel into
the cosmos was no longer a theory; it was
a demonstrated accomplishment that made
even more fantastical ventures in the future
seem inevitable.

Infante's infinite sequences

Infante's preoccupation with the notion
of 'infinite' space, and its implications for
the human experience of time, pre-dates his
joining the Movement Group and is recorded
in numerous interviews, as well as in his first
major series of images of geometric shapes,
vertical progressions, intersecting squares,
circles and eventually spirals (1961–4).[12]
The spiral underwent many transformations
and continued to preoccupy the artist through
the 1960s. It is linked to a reconceptualization
of cosmic space in the series of *Twists* (*Vitki*)
and *Beads* (*Busery*) that culminated in the
1971 image of the Earth encircled in a
necklace of interwoven spirals as if viewed
from a point in outer space (*Ozherel'e: Vid iz
kosmosa*).

Reconstruction of the Firmament* marks
a crucial point in Infante's development of
these concerns, which are subsumed in his
use of the term 'infinity', as represented on a
two-dimensional surface. In his founding text
on the *Projects for the Reconstruction of the
Firmament*, dated 1965, Infante muses on the
appropriate medium for the representation of
various definitions of infinity, cosmic space
and human awareness of it. He observes that
two-dimensional 'sign constructions' (*znako-
vye konstruktsii*) convey the infinite character
of space better than three-dimensional ones:
'It is apparent that cosmic depth reaching into
infinity swallows up space which becomes
similar to a canvas or a sheet of paper. In this
too, we see the traces of the metaphysical
nature of infinity and its realization as signs.'
Whereas the trace on paper succeeds in
expressing a motivated relationship of concept
to visuality – the flatness of the material
surface directs the viewer to cosmic speculation – Infante argues that three-dimensional
forms 'prevent the realization of the metaphysical dimension'. A construction is not
metaphysical, he concludes, because 'it is
too object-like ... It is space itself'. Yet objects

do play an important role in moving thought,
and art, forward, to 'new horizons' where
new metaphysical concerns might arise
'from as yet unknown positions'.[13]

Infante's series was envisioned, but never
installed, in its entirety in circular formation,
each work placed against a dark ground. In
such an arrangement the viewer would be
physically encompassed by 'sign systems'
and experience the perpetual contradiction
that underpins metaphysical speculation on
the cosmos. When in the physical presence
of such an accumulation of its signs, abstract
sensations of infinity might be experienced
by individuals (particularly Infante) as union
or rupture with a cosmic dimension. The
viewer's encounter with *The Reconstructions
of the Firmament* would allow for an immediate apprehension of self in relation to the
infinite depth of space, as well as providing
a set of diagrams pointing to the larger
abstract order of the cosmos. But one also
senses Infante's equivocation in their multi-
plicity. As in the spiral series, the repetition
of so many geometric patterns speaks on the
one hand to a constant state of self-awareness
in relation to the infinite scale of the universe,
and on the other to the individual's incompre-
hension of its origins and purpose.

Infante attempted to realize the potential
of the hand-manufactured three-dimensional
object and its two-dimensional representation
in his earlier drawings and 1971 installation
of a crystal-like interior. The crystal, like
his series of spirals, is among Infante's most
significant realizations in various material
forms of his effort to understand the sensation
of infinity. He attributes his earliest independent gestures as an artist to these works
and their motivation: the aim to explore and
to reconcile through art the paradox of life
understood as unbounded, spatially and
temporally unlimited, but experienced through
concrete events and in art, visualized as
geometric figure or pattern. His many texts
on the crystal and the spiral record a persistent
need to manifest and demonstrate these
experiences through organic forms as well.
Crystal reveals the slippage in much Movement Group work between representational
systems that suggest rational, even mechanically reproducible forms and their utopian,
fantastical potential. These two interdepend-
ent aspects of Infante's work are what make

7.31
Francisco Infante-Arana,
*Space – Movement – Infinity
(Project for a Kinetic Object)*.
Tempera and ink on paper
mounted on fibreboard,
1963. Jane Voorhees
Zimmerli Art Museum, The
Norton and Nancy Dodge
Collection of Nonconformist
Art from the Soviet Union,
New Brunswick, NJ

his projects compelling as art rather than as simple decoration or installation design.

The work at the centre of the series is a drawn diagram entitled *Space – Movement – Infinity* created in 1963 (7.31). Though the image resembles a crystal in terms of the mathematical progression of scale, it describes a virtual cube, a purely spatial rather than material form created through the implied intersections of two-dimensional planes. Their interstices are articulated by drawn lines that suggest an infinite (imagined) number of other planes turning in space. Movement is thus implied both through the repetition of the projected planes and the lines that link and distort them. Because of its inherent contradictions, this image is one of Infante's most successful early works. Like a document or plan it diagrams a concept of immateriality, as if the expanded form could be materially reconstructed in real space. It is rendered in a simulation of isometric perspective – a convention used by architects to enable the exact physical construction of the two-dimensional design. All lines can be measured and understood mathematically in relation to

each other so that a builder could recreate the correct proportions or ratios by simply measuring each line. But the drawn artefact eschews this sense of its realization: all planes are implied as luminous, coloured space, not materially fixed. It is unclear when looking at the drawing exactly what kind of construction – or object – the artist has proposed: what part is form, what part is space?

Related to this image are works that remain in the artist's collection: a kinetic, illuminated sculpture of the same form (a crystal) and its preparatory drawing, both from 1963–5. Soon after the object was produced it was photographed both as a demonstration of kinetic principles and as a 'sculptural' object in its own right. In the dark, the motorized movement and electrical illumination of metallic rods that frame each plane light up an ever-changing abstract form, a series of spherical spaces emerges that escapes geometric description. A different group of photographs conveys the perceptual distortions that the form achieves when realized as an interactive space. Such a space was created in Moscow's VDNKh exhibition

Francisco Infante-Arana,
plan for 'Artificial Space,
Crystal'. Tempera on paper,
mounted on paperboard,
1971. Jane Voorhees
Zimmerli Art Museum, The
Norton and Nancy Dodge
Collection of Nonconformist
Art from the Soviet Union,
New Brunswick, NJ

grounds with the title *Artificial Space, Crystal* by the ARGO collective in 1971 (7.32, 7.33), and it extended the problem articulated in the drawings.[14] The seemingly endless replication of faceted planes and their boundaries, both material and illusory, embed the viewer in their infinite refractions, creating a true, real-time equivalent for theoretical speculation on the dissolution of fixed positions in space. A later, even more elaborately detailed representation of an artificial space draws on the experience of moving through these kinetic projects. Infante's *Project for an Artificial Space* (1973) merges the faceted forms of the crystal with the magnified coils of a spiral, into which the viewer/participant

is suspended. Here the integration of contrasting forms expresses the energetic rhythms of space and the sensation of movement through it.

If these geometric forms seem to be generated by algorithms, this is not accidental. Infante acknowledged a kinship in his distinction, especially in his spiral sequence, between positive and radical infinity (his terms) and the theories of the nineteenth-century mathematician Georg Kantor, who described a distinction between 'potential' and 'actual' projections of infinity.[15] He lists the drawings of *Space – Movement – Infinity*, the *Reconstruction of the Firmament* and his spiral series as evidence of his early

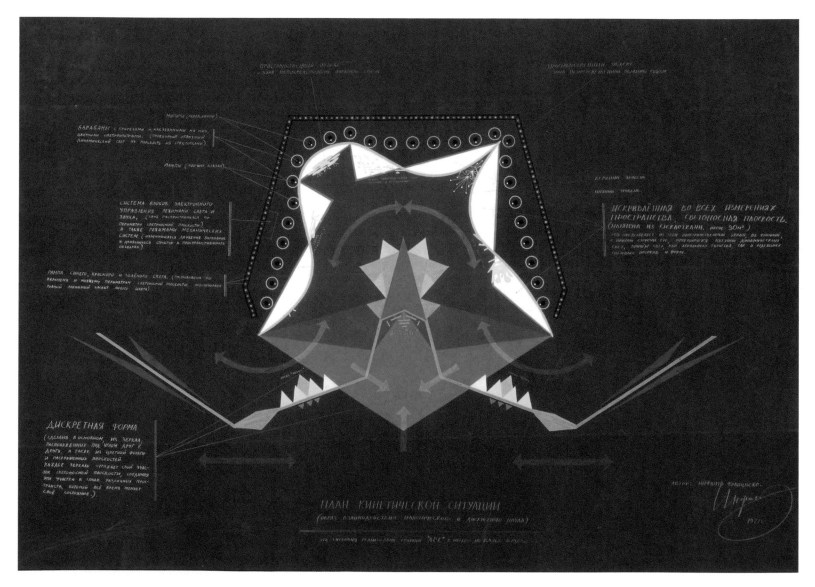

interest in this recurrent problem of fixed points in infinite sequences, which he described in 1965:

> In space, line is distorted, that is it is characterized by the properties of space itself. Consequently, in its natural sense, it never intersects with another line at an angle of 90 degrees. Although (and this is the paradox!) spatial lines of an infinite multitude of points must intersect precisely at a right angle. To observe this, one must find an ideal point of view (thus symbolic space is incorporated into natural space) which is coordinated with the ideal schematic structural essence of the form. But as soon as this ideal point is found, the lines forming the cross immediately roll up into a point, and, moreover, in all their infinite proximity these lines transform into the point.

For Infante this mathematical-spatial paradox permeates all forms of life and human experience; it is the source of metaphysical knowledge.

> What is characteristic for the form of a spiral, namely the alteration of directional tendencies of the point – due to the discrete momentum – is characteristic also of countless other forms of life. Mass alternates with emptiness, bad with good, living with dead, etc. And even being [existence] itself evidently does not escape this predetermination. Crossing over into the point of an inverted state, in a discrete manner, it turns into non-being.[16]

These images are driven by speculations on space, human existence, and the relationship between individual and collective agency. On this metaphysical level they resolve the fundamental dilemma of art practice in the Soviet era. Infante's projects, like Nussberg's and Koleichuk's, renew the significance of public address that was crucial to Soviet artists whatever their aesthetic stance, by attuning high-art practices to the philosophical and practical consequences of 'progress'. In this sense they share in the wider optimism of 1960s' explorations in science and technology. Yet Infante's series do so in the very private realm of self-perception set within this larger whole. Remarkably, for at least a decade, in an environment of drastically reduced access to alternative art and knowledge about the world outside, this group of Soviet artists managed to create work that pressed beyond traditional boundaries of display; their installations and designed interiors are meaningful as painting/sculpture and architectural frameworks for social action. Now, viewed in their global context, we can fully appreciate how these projects bridge the Cold War gap that isolated visionary practices in the Soviet Union from those initiated in the West.

7.33
Installation photographs of 'Artificial Space, Crystal' by the ARGO collective in 1972, VDNKh exhibition grounds, Moscow. Jane Voorhees Zimmerli Art Museum, The Norton and Nancy Dodge Collection of Nonconformist Art from the Soviet Union, New Brunswick, NJ

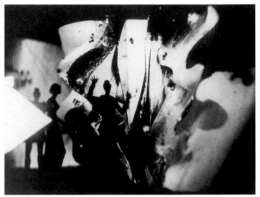

Architecture or Revolution? – Vienna's 1968

Jana Scholze

7.34
Hans Hollein, 'Aircraft Carrier City in Landscape' project, exterior perspective. Cut-and-pasted printed paper on gelatin silver photographs mounted on board, 1964. The Museum of Modern Art, New York

A country road cuts through rolling fields punctuated with bushes and haystacks: in the middle of this romantic landscape stands a giant, dark aircraft carrier. This disturbing scene is, in fact, a collage by architect Hans Hollein from 1964 called *Aircraft Carrier City in Landscape* (7.34). The city proposed in this monumental design is dark, colossal and dense: it is more of a defensive fortification or a strange totemic sculpture than a habitat for human life. Typical of the *Transformations* series (1963–8), of which this collage forms a part, Hollein's image uses art to question the character of the modern city. His aim was 'absolute architecture', a concept that he defined for an exhibition at the Galerie St Stephan, an influential Viennese gallery, in 1963, where works including *Aircraft Carrier City in Landscape* were on display. In the exhibition catalogue, he wrote: '… this point in time when an immensely advanced science and perfected technology offer us every means possible, we build what and how we will, we make an architecture that is not determined by technology but utilizes technology, a pure, absolute architecture.'[1]

Hollein organized the exhibition, entitled 'Architektur' ('Architecture'), with artist Walter Pichler.[2] The pair displayed new designs which took a critical position against the rational and functional logic of contemporary architecture. In their emphatic statements and new visual concepts they not only claimed back the emotional, sensual and spiritual side of architecture, but also brought to it a more disquieting and even threatening approach. These putative constructions establish strong connections to high technology and, in their brutality, to the military, yet at the same time they embody the magic and mystery associated with archaic forms and shapes.[3] Never just buildings, they are models for autonomous cities or, as Reyner Banham later called them, 'megastructures'.[4]

This novel conception of architecture could, it seems, only be realized within the context of art. Galerie St Stephan– a hotbed of the avant-gardism of the city during the 1950s and 1960s – was probably the only location in Vienna at the time where the boundaries of Austrian provinciality were being broken down and international developments in the art world discussed.[5] In 1963 Hollein and Pichler extended the gallery's activities towards architecture, thus creating an important reference point for the younger generation of Austrian visionary architects later in the decade.[6]

If Hollein and Pichler's exhibition was the trigger for what British architect and founder member of Archigram Peter Cook once called the 'Austrian Phenomenon', a 'strong architectural tradition' as well as 'Austria's characteristic decadence' were at its root.[7] The visionaries of the 1960s – including the groups Zünd-Up, Haus-Rucker-Co and Coop Himmelblau – emerged from a situation of individual discontent and opposition to a predominantly conservative society. The post-war generation had grown up with an awareness of an unresolved, silent relationship with the dark Nazi past of their parents' generation.[8] Pre-war and monarchic values and related traditions were much celebrated, and the decisive influence of the Catholic Church remained unbroken. At the same time, the teaching structure in Austrian universities was still hierarchical and authoritarian. The growing mood of opposition among those young Austrians was first expressed as artistic protest in a number of angry manifestos, performances and exhibitions as early as the 1950s.[9] In the following decade, the violent action art movement, called Viennese Actionism,[10] formed the hub of a youthful culture of protest that developed in various forms of individual rebellious and uncompromising

artistic manifestations, often expressed in performances or actions. The conservatism and, increasingly, the growing affluence of Austrian society offered a fertile ground for generational conflict. However, unlike Prague and Paris, this culture of dissent did not spread into mass protest in the late 1960s but remained solely within artistic circles.

Pop groups

Architectural thinking in Austria in the 1960s was marked by conservativism, inhibited by 'the notorious time lag',[11] as historian and architectural critic Friedrich Achleitner once described it. With regard to architecture, he continued: '... the international reaction to modern academicism (for example, the successors of Mies van der Rohe) coincided with the first efforts of Austrian Constructivism, the first wave of New Brutalism with the beginning of interest in urbanism.'[12] Individuals like Hollein and Pichler were rare when they mounted their 'Architektur' exhibition. But 1963 was also the year when Professor Karl Schwanzer and his assistant Günther Feuerstein started their highly praised teaching programme at the Technische Hochschule (TH) in Vienna, giving a central space to fantasy in the design process and opening discussion of the international architectural scene. Characterized by a 'strong feeling of cynicism', the young generation of architects – some still students – were, in the course of the next few years, to imagine 'some of the most advanced environmental ideas ... which explode into fascinating dissertations on pneumatics, plastic structures, flexible structures and the most curious formal combinations'.[13]

Graduates of Vienna and Graz, the key figures of the Austrian architectural avant-garde of the 1960s were Raimund Abraham, Friedrich St Florian, Günther Domenig, Eilfried Huth, Peter Noever and Gernot Nalbach, among others.[14] Collaboration was a striking feature of their activities, prompted in part by the intertwining of the architectural scene with the art world. It was also stimulated by the exciting mass-media phenomenon of the age, the pop group. The engagement with popular culture signalled antagonism with the technocratic figure of the specialist: 'They all declared that they wanted to explore entirely new constructs and communication

7.35
Coop Himmelblau (Wolf D. Prix and Helmut Swiczinsky), photograph of installation 'Soft Space', 1970

forms for architectural imagination, keeping well away from social and specialist constraints.'[15] The names selected by groups signalled their interest in critique and transformation. Zünd-Up (founded by Michael Pühringer, Timo Huber, Bertram Mayer and Hermann Simböck in spring 1969) translates as 'lighting up and setting fire', but also refers to a famous brand of German motorbike 'Zünd-app'; 'Hausruck', the root of Haus-Rucker-Co (founded in 1967 by Laurids Ortner, Günther Zamp Kelp and Klaus Pinter), is the name of a mountain range in upper Austria and describes the act of shifting houses; and 'Coop-Himmelblau' (formed by Wolff D. Prix, Helmut Swiczinsky and Michael Holzer in 1968) means literally 'Coop-Skyblue', stressing the idea of the cooperative, collective endeavour towards an 'architecture with fantasy, as buoyant and variable as clouds'.[16]

Architecture in an expanded field

The main characteristic that connects most of the Austrian projects of the 1960s is the manipulation of perception. One of the leading terms employed by Haus-Rucker-Co in this period was *Bewußtseinserweiterung*, literally 'mind expanding'.[17] Their aim was '... the

creation of visual principles and the design of environments, which function as breeding ground of those developments at the same time. It starts with a mini-environment, worn on the human body, and ending with the all-encompassing, all-formative: the city'.[18] Such interventions within the existing environment were either physical, in the form of performance, or material, employing different kinds of construction. The latter were often temporary spaces or covers for the body including, most famously, helmet-type objects designed to produce powerful effects by interfering with the receptive functions of the eye, ear and nose.[19] Coop Himmelblau, for example, designed the 'Face Space' (also known as 'Soul Flipper') in 1969 in which facial emotions and tactile qualities are transmitted, that is, translated into colours and sounds. Their subsequent projects, 'Hard Space' and 'Soft Space' (both 1970), extended the zone of interference to the whole body. Both projects transformed an environment within minutes, 'Hard Space' by creating a space through a series of explosions triggered by the heartbeats of the artists, and 'Soft Space' by covering a Viennese street in foam in ten minutes (7.35). The mostly unprepared and disgruntled public reacted with surprise if not shock at the new spatial experience within a familiar environment. These experiments extended the boundaries of common spatial perception and defined architecture in the widest sense. Similar experiments by colleagues like Hans Hollein[20] and Friedrich St Florian[21] followed, all of them attempts at imaginary, ephemeral and immaterial architecture anticipating virtual reality.

Somewhat closer to built structures were Coop Himmelblau's pneumatic prototypes, which were presented by the group as archetypes for architecture beyond rationalism, a material critique aimed at commercial grid-architecture and consumerist industrial design. Their approach centred on the human scale and body and its ways of communicating with the environment. Air – reinterpreted as a new building material in the 1960s – enabled them to materialize their dream of a 'design for an architecture that is as variable as a cloud'.[22] One of the first key projects was 'Villa Rosa' ('The Pink Villa', 1968), a prototype for a pneumatic living unit (7.36).[23] Here, pneumatic architecture conveyed an impression of a dream, flotation and illusion, while at the same time demonstrated mobility as well as ephemerality. 'Villa Rosa' was composed of three spaces for an inflatable travelling habitat. Its core was a load-bearing structure accompanied by a mixture of tubes onto which balloons were fastened. The three spaces were described by the group as follows:

> The pneumatic prototype is composed of three units: The pulsating unit with the revolving bed, projection and sound program. Through the ventilation system appropriate fragrances accompany the changing audiovisual program. The pneumatic transformable space. 8 inflatable balloons vary the size of the units space from minimum to maximum volume. The space in the suitcase – mobile space. From a helmet-shaped suitcase one can inflate an air-conditioned shell, complete with bed.[24]

The 'Villa Rosa' anticipates projects for flexible constructions like Hollein's 'Mobile Office' (1969),[25] which was a response to what the architect saw as society's new flexibility and mobility. Mobile and portable architectural environments were among the key ideas of the 1960s. Permanently changing society should, it was claimed, be reflected in space and building, city and landscape. In this spirit, Coop Himmelblau claimed in 1968: 'Our architecture has no physical ground plan, but a psychic one. Walls no longer exist. Our spaces are pulsating balloons. Our heartbeat becomes space; our face is the façade.'[26] The inhabitant of these environments was to be the urban nomad. Pneumatic architecture offered a light, portable and provisional home that could be equipped with a complex system of responsive technologies. Furthermore, such projects clearly show the influence of the space age, with capsules designed for space travel or as life-support systems which act as extensions of the body. In fact, in order to emphasize its futurism, Coop Himmelblau promoted its ideas for 'Villa Rosa' to NASA for use as virtual environments for astronauts.[27]

Techno-frictions

A second characteristic shared by these groups was a common enthusiasm for technology, although it must be stressed that their early fascination for the possibilities offered by the new communication and construction technologies soon gave way to a more complex view of progress laced with a dystopian sensibility. The project that best conveys this ambiguous fascination with technology is 'The Great Vienna Auto-Expander' by Zünd-Up (1969; 7.37). This was Zünd-Up's provocative response to a design brief issued at the Technische Hochschule that asked for a solution to traffic congestion in the centre of Vienna.[28] Their 'solution' was a gigantic monument on Karlsplatz, in the centre of the city, in the shape of a transformed pinball machine. In the design a machine was to be made from pipes that would break though the city's buildings from Karlsplatz to Stephansplatz and its famous Stephansdom forming a kind of drag-racing course. The cars travelling along this fantastic track would be beautified with decoration, becoming racing cars, and then be pulverized in a 'destruction-game'. Compressed into small parcels, they would then be taken home and buried. This project was an unmistakable confrontation with the myths of car-owning democracy: it spoke to the social and cultural impact of consumer and, more specifically, car culture on daily life and city architecture in particular.[29] Dennis Hopper's film *Easy Rider*, released in 1969, seems to have served as a source of inspiration, not only in terms of its theme but also in the way in which the scheme was promoted. When it was presented as a multimedia performance in the appropriate location of an underground car park, a group of forty Harley-Davidson and Norton Motorbike club members were invited to watch the event. The fascination generated by their powerful American and British motorcycles could easily have been mistaken for the central message of the project, which

7.36
Coop Himmelblau (Wolf D. Prix and Helmut Swiczinsky), drawing of *Villa Rosa,* M 1:20. Black ink on tracing paper, Letraset, 1968. Collection FRAC Centre, Orléans

7.37
Zünd-Up (Bertram Mayer,
Michael Pühringer, Hermann
Simböck and Timo Huber),
photomontage of instal-
lation 'The Great Vienna
Auto-Expander. Standort
Karlsplatz, Vienna, 1969.
V&A: E.469-2008

focused in fact on evaluating and critiquing the effects of car culture on society. In the minds of Zünd-Up, aggression was necessary and the act of destruction at the heart of the project was in the end aimed at the relationship between confrontational architecture and conventional society. As Zünd-Up made clear in the texts and manifestos accompanying the project, destruction was seen as a positive process in which new freedoms could be secured to encourage innovation.[30]

After 1970 the techno-futurism of schemes produced by Haus-Rucker-Co was increasingly underscored by a growing sense of anxiety over the effects of modern technology on the environment. The symbolically named 'Oasis No. 7', for instance was an inflatable structure realized by the group at documenta V in 1972 (7.38). A transparent balloon 8m in diameter emerged from a second-floor window of the Fridericianum, stabilized by a standard steel tube armature which also provided a tunnel entrance. Inside the balloon were two palm trees, a hammock, some artificial ferns and a little red flag with the number '7' written on it. Selected visitors were invited inside to enjoy a transformed view of the familiar world, albeit rendered strange by the immediate surrounding of an artificial beach. With the balloon Haus-Rucker-Co intended to enhance and increase awareness and alter perception of a familiar public space, thereby suggesting the possibility of experimentation and change. It is difficult to describe the effects of a mini-environment like 'Oasis No. 7', as one has to engage with the space physically and psychically in order to experience the intended effect. As Dieter Bogner once said: 'The actual work is defined … neither through the outer structure nor the coloured space but is constituted only when used through expanding into the immaterial space of a user's consciousness.'[31]

'Oasis No. 7' was the last pneumatic architectural work realized by Haus-Rucker-Co. It marks the turning point from the group's experimental and playful attitude towards a more critical approach; Haus-Rucker-Co became the only group in Austria to raise environmental concerns in the early 1970s. One of its most successful and widely discussed projects was an exhibition in the Museum Haus Lange in the German city of Krefeld in 1971, entitled 'Cover: Überleben in verschmutzter Umwelt' ('Cover: Survival in a Polluted Environment'; 7.39, 1.18). The location was well selected, as it was in the Ruhr area, famous for coal mining. A giant air-inflated tent covered the museum that had been designed by Mies van der Rohe as a family house for the director of the silk weaving mill, Hermann Lange, and built between 1928 and 1930. The exhibition's subtitle, 'Survival in a Polluted Environment', revealed its focal point: the relationship between the natural landscape and artificial environments, disturbing the conventional perception of inside and outside; interior and exterior; and landscape and architecture. Haus-Rucker-Co's 'Cover' was not only protection and shelter for the house, but also for nature itself in the sense that it defined it as an area for special

attention. This new environment – a space capsule with its own microclimate – was to be self-sustaining, albeit only with the help of essential technology. Quartz iodine lamps provided 'sunlight', and optical and acoustic devices simulated 'natural' changes in landscape and weather. Illusion substituted forgotten or unfamiliar experiences, as if they could only be felt within the restricted space of this synthetic microcosm. Haus-Rucker-Co seemed to point to a situation where the polluted environment had become a threat to the survival of humanity. 'Despite massive campaigns against pollution', they wrote, 'the continuity of the process and the permanent assimilation with the progressively bad conditions evade an intuitive awareness of the extent of the threat. One does not die from environment as fast as from an h-bomb but with the same efficiency'.[32] The exhibition inside the house showed predominantly large-scale installations as mini-residences dealing with the artificial recovery of natural elements such as air and water, which had thus far been seen as unlimited natural resources. However, nowhere in the exhibition were direct links to or illustrations of the polluted environment displayed. Only a display of the effects of pneumoconiosis, a lung disease caused by inhaling coal dust, pointed towards the real danger. Everywhere else, visitors were allowed to playfully experience the alternative spaces of the numerous installations in clean and colourful PVC materials. As irony was always a crucial component of Haus-Rucker-Co's work, the exhibition did not aim to provide 'solutions' but rather to raise questions and encourage discussion. In contrast to positive utopias of the age, this was a negative one, reminiscent of Noah's Ark, the last retreat in a contaminated environment. The aestheticized vision of an imminent synthetic environment brought upon us by global ecological devastation provoked not only headlines in contemporary newspapers ('Life in synthetic reservations', Forest air from the plastic bag', '15,000 in shock', 'Three artists raise alarm'),[33] but debates on the reality of man-made urban landscapes and the effects of unlimited development and extreme industrialization on the environment.

Revolution withdrawn?

In the context of conservative Vienna of 1968, the performances and happenings conducted by radical architects were not understood by the public as experiments with space and perception, or even as architectural projects, but simply as provocations. This response was, however, welcomed by the architects. Indeed, Coop Himmelblau designed 'shock therapies' to revolt against the conservative and constrained approach to architecture in relation to the individual and to society.[34] Like their friends the Zünd-Up group, Coop Himmelblau made aggressive interventions

7.38
Haus-Rucker-Co (Laurids Ortner, Günter Zamp Kelp, Manfred Ortner and Klaus Pinter), photograph of installation 'Oasis No. 7' at documenta V in Kassel, 1972

7.39
Haus-Rucker-Co (Laurids Ortner, Günter Zamp Kelp and Klaus Pinter), 'Haus Lange, Covered', 1971

in 'Alles ist Architektur' Hollein presented a radical redefinition of architecture, removing all boundaries to connect it with other art disciplines, but above all revealing its psychological and emotional level and linking it with diverse areas of contemporary culture. In addition, Hollein addressed the radical implications of information technology and immersive environment. By including non-material architecture determined by light, smell, temperature, chemicals and drugs in his reflections, Hollein was calling for nothing less than a definition which embraced the entire environment. The purpose of architecture was no longer to shelter or symbolize, but rather to be a connective support system. Hollein presented his manifesto in the form of a collage of 27 pages of images accompanying a single page of text, supporting the character of the manifesto as an expression of a transitional moment which defined succinctly and directly the state of Austrian architecture in 1968.

The years around 1968 in Austria, and especially Vienna, were a period of anger, criticism, social concern, political engagement and protest. But despite strong interest in the 1968 student movement in Paris and Berlin and events in neighbouring Prague, Viennese political activism generally did not aim at revolution. Criticism and social concerns were not articulated directly, but were themselves aesthetically transformed. Artistic public performances rather than political demonstrations triggered little more than irritation and complaint on Austrian streets. Crossovers were commonplace between the art disciplines, but unheard of outside them. Nevertheless, with regard to art and architecture, this period of protest, critique and discontent made a significant contribution to the future of Austrian as well as international architecture. Hollein and his contemporaries chose visionary projects, performances and commentaries on architecture as the means by which their own revolutionary gesture could be made.

into urban space in the late 1960s and early 1970s: 'we decided to have our actions in the street in order to avoid being urged into a museum. At first our actions in Basel and Vienna were friendly. But surprisingly they caused such strong aggression from the public that our actions became more aggressive.'[35] Antagonism did not equate with agonism. In fact, Zünd-Up, despite being the youngest of the various radical design groups in Austria, was the most politically engaged. Many of the group's architectural projects were presented as angry happenings and pointed at the deep-seated crisis of a comfortable and mute society and its consumerist culture. Without following a clearly defined ideology, all Zünd-Up works nevertheless display a rigorous social critique. However, not being affiliated with the international political student movement or radical group, their work always remained within the parameters of architecture and

art.[36] Despite sharing inspiration from rock music, especially the Rolling Stones, Jimi Hendrix and Frank Zappa, and a common fascination with performance, the members of Zünd-Up distanced themselves from Haus-Rucker-Co and Coop Himmelblau, criticizing their work as too aesthetic, apolitical and not provocative enough.

Sensing the moment, and with a desire to articulate its unrestricted thinking, Hans Hollein wrote an architectural manifesto in April 1968, which he titled 'Alles ist Architektur' ('Everything is Architecture').[37] He published the manifesto in the seminal Austrian magazine *Bau* (1965–71), an advocate of new trends in architecture, art and society. Following in the footsteps of his predecessor Le Corbusier with his *Tout est Architecture* (1931) and anticipating Joseph Beuys' claim at documenta V in 1972 that 'Everything is Art and Everyone is an Artist',

8.1
Unknown designer, *Save Our Planet, Save Our Cities*, poster produced by Olivetti featuring Richard Buckminster Fuller's 'Dome over Manhattan', USA, 1971. V&A: E.137–1972

8 / Looking Down on Spaceship Earth: Cold War Landscapes

David Crowley

In his 1963 *Operating Manual for Spaceship Earth* visionary American engineer Richard Buckminster Fuller asked his readers to imagine the planet from space:

> I'm sure that you don't really sense yourself to be aboard a fantastically real spaceship – our spherical Spaceship Earth. Of our little sphere you have seen only small portions. However, you have viewed more than did pre-twentieth-century man, for in his entire lifetime he saw only

one-millionth of the Earth's surface. You've seen a lot more. If you are a veteran world airlines pilot you may have seen one one-hundredth of Earth's surface. But even that is sum totally not enough to see and feel Earth to be a sphere – unless, unbeknownst to me, one of you happens to be a Cape Kennedy capsuler.[1]

Fuller saw 'Spaceship Earth as an integrally-designed machine which to be persistently successful must be comprehended and serviced in total'.[2] This 'machine' was not supplied with an inexhaustible supply of fuel.

The Earth was, he argued, approaching the critical point of over-consumption that would lead to its eventual extinction. The competitive conditions of Cold War politics hastened the crisis:

> Paradoxically, at the present moment our Spaceship Earth is in the perilous condition of having the Russians sitting at one set of the co-pilot's flying controls while the Americans sit at the other. France controls the starboard engines, and the Chinese control the port engines, while the United Nations controls the passenger operation.

The vision of the Earth from space described vividly by Fuller in 1963 became available to the world five years later following the return of NASA's Apollo 8 mission to map the surface of the Moon for possible landing sites. The astronauts' Hasselblads captured one of the most widely reproduced images of the century, *Earthrise*, the view of the Earth as NASA's craft came from behind the Moon after a lunar orbit insertion burn (8.2). The contrast between the luminous and indisputably living surface of the blue planet swathed in clouds and the dusty surface of its satellite prompted a wave of sentiment, with commentators stressing the fragility of the Earth in an age when militarism and affluence, twin buttresses of the Cold War order, prevailed. The protective atmospheric layer that supported life on Earth was evidently thin when compared with the dark vacuum of endless space. One only had to look at the dead surface of the Moon to realize this. Others pointed to an image of the planet that was not inscribed with borders or political divisions: Africa, a 'forgotten' continent conventionally reduced in scale by the Mercator Projection used to represent the globe on maps, loomed much larger than many had imagined it. American counter-culture activist Michael Shamberg wrote: 'It's ironic that NASA, probably the greatest government agency produced by America, has killed patriotism. National boundaries are simply not a motivating image when we have photographs of the Whole Earth.'[3] In this image lay, for some, the possibility of discovering a new and just world.

8.2
Earthrise, photograph taken during the NASA Apollo 8 mission around the Moon, 1968

8.3
Isamu Noguchi, *Memorial to Man* (later retitled *Sculpture to Be Seen from Mars*). Sand on board, 1947. The Isamu Noguchi Foundation and Garden Museum/ARS, New York

As this image-event suggests, the ways in which the planet was imagined were changed as a consequence of the Cold War. Electronic communications, environmental pollution, the prospect of nuclear war as well as the explicit intention of extending the limits of what was described on one side of the Cold War divide as the 'free world' and on the other as the 'fraternity of peace-loving nations', all contributed to new kinds of global consciousness. Marshall McLuhan's cheerful phrase 'the global village' was joined during the course of the 1960s by rather more troubling descriptions, including 'Spaceship Earth' and the 'fragile planet'. In this final chapter, I set out to explore the different ways in which the landscapes of the planet itself were reconsidered during the last waves of Cold War modernism. The duality that was shot through Cold War modernity – the dialectics of progress and disaster and of utopia and distopia – became evident during the late 1960s when visionary architects, engineers and planners came to conceive their work literally on a global scale.

In the dust

Most commentators reflecting on the Apollo 8 *Earthrise* image were also drawn – inevitably – to reflect soberly on the dusty surface of the Moon. As an environmentally minded editorial in the *New York Times* warned, 'unless this flowering home planet (the Earth) remains a haven of life, the entire solar system may become as devoid of life as are now the mountains of the moon and the polar regions of Mars'.[4] The Moon-watchers were, of course, gazing at another order of Cold War landscape, the desert. The image of a desolate environment in which the world had been reduced to dust had been a potent symbol of distopia for over twenty years. The image of Hiroshima and Nagasaki as perished earth and ruins had a tremendous impact on post-war culture, seeping as after-images into numerous films, novels and artworks. Japanese-American sculptor Isamu Noguchi, for instance, produced an early work in this genre in 1947, *Memorial to Man* (later retitled *Sculpture to Be Seen from Mars*; 8.3). This 'sketch', fashioned with sand on board, was photographed without any indication of scale to give the illusion of being seen from a great distance. Noguchi imagined it as a prototype for a large earthwork that would be sited 'in some desert, some unwanted area'.[5] The work suggested a face as if partially buried in sand or earth. With the appearance of a slanted pyramid, the nose would have been a mile across and only visible through a super high-powered telescope on Mars. This was a place that one could not visit, let alone recognize on Earth. Noguchi's image was strangely elegiac, capturing the archaeological remains of a long-lost civilization, mankind. The scale of the catastrophe was to be gauged in the archaeology signifying ordinary human existence before the Fall. The image presented a vertiginous sense of the distant past, like the ruins of Romans or the Incas. Made in the year that the world seemed to be falling into a new East–West conflict, Noguchi's model sculpture suggested a disturbing prophesy.

In the years that followed, the image of the nuclear desert was drawn in numerous

apocalyptic visions. From the B-movie desert of *Them!* (1954), with its cast of gigantic ants, the mutant by-product of nuclear weapon tests, to J.G. Ballard's haunting *Terminal Beach* (1964), artists and film-makers drew a connection between the wilderness and the existential anxieties thrown up by push-button destruction. The end of civilization has, of course, been a long-established theme in the history of art and literature. Ruins have been employed as allegorical forms to chart the irresistible force of time, with the weeds that thrive in their cracks testifying to the slow but inevitable triumph of nature over culture.[6] The post-apocalyptic landscape that filled the imagination after Hiroshima did not lend itself to this kind of aestheticism. As Japanese architect Arata Isozaki recalled, the ruins in Japan 'were created before my very eyes, instantaneously'.[7] They could not function as what Georg Simmel called, in his classic essay on the ruin, a 'naturalized artefact', because their origins lay in man-made catastrophe.[8]

In the course of the 1960s the metaphor of the planet as desert was drawn into new relations with modernity, largely under the influence of the emergent environmental movement. Environmental activism in the USA – focused on the effects of industrial pollution and the use of pesticides in agriculture – gathered pace (though the movement was relatively undeveloped when compared to Canada). The 'desecration of America' was, as numerous commentators have remarked, closely connected to the relentless pursuit of economic growth. The 'American way of life' – producing an urbanized and motorized high-consumption society – was indicted for its effects on the natural landscape at home and abroad.[9]

The most vociferous criticism of American industry came from the counter-culture. Anti-war protestors, for instance, publicized the 'ecocide' in Vietnam, that is, the strategic use of arsenical herbicides to destroy the crops and farm animals necessary to maintain civilian life.[10] Others saw the adventure on the Moon as the first steps in man's pollution of the cosmos: 'They are trying to go out into the planetary system and spread their cancerous spirit of asphalt and concrete there. But we're not going to the Moon, we're staying right here and we're going to reclaim the

Earth.'[11] Theodore Roszak, self-appointed spokesman for the counter-culture, described America as a 'technological wilderness' that had pursued the holy grail of 'progress' at great social, psychological and environmental cost:

Nothing too big, too bizarre, too mind-boggling to be dared. Matter, we have learned, is a vibrant jelly of energy; the universe a burst balloon of galactic fragments; thought itself a mere feedback in the cerebral electronics; life a chemical code soon to be deciphered; all seeming law nothing but the large-scale likeli-hoods of basic chaos. No absolutes. Nothing sacred. Any day now homuncu-lus in a test tube – cyborgs made to order – interstellar tourism – the doomsday bomb. Why not? What is possible is mandatory ...[12]

8.4
Robert Leydenfrost, *Earth Day*, poster promoting environmental awareness-raising events with a photograph by Don Brewster, USA, 1970. V&A: E.329-2004

8.5
Arata Isozaki, *Re-ruined Hiroshima*, perspective. Ink and gouache with cut-and-pasted gelatin silver print on gelatin silver print, 1968. The Museum of Modern Art, New York

By the end of the 1960s environmentalism had become a mass movement in the USA. The celebration of 'Earth Day' for the first time on 22 April 1970 in the form of 'teach-ins' in American colleges and universities, carnivalesque parades and public art projects was its coming out. Initiated by American senator Gaylord Nelson, it attracted the support of Hollywood as well as prominent artists and designers. They designed propaganda for the cause, in some instances producing chilling images of the globe viewed from space (8.4).

Environmentalism was not just a product of uneasy American consciences. The fast industrialization of Eastern Bloc states had destructive effects on nature. In the Soviet Union, the post-Stalinist regime's plans to exploit the 'virgin lands' of Western Siberia to feed the nation and to tap the region's natural resources threatened the ecological balance of the untouched environment. In the years that followed, Soviet rivers were poisoned by chemicals discharged by industry and the air quality in cities plummeted to unhealthy levels. A remarkably vigorous environmental movement operated throughout the history of the Soviet Union, initially within the 'professional' spheres of science and nature protection where limited criticism of official policy could be voiced. As Douglas Weiner has shown, bold ecologists and

biologists criticized the activities of the Soviet ministries and defended the *zapovedniki* (nature reserves), 'rare physical and social spaces … that had largely escaped the juggernaut of Stalin's "Great Break"'.[13] By the mid-1960s something like a popular movement emerged when these specialists were joined by ordinary citizens and journalists to protect Lake Baikal in Southern Siberia, the world's largest reservoir of fresh water, the existence of which was threatened by unchecked logging practices and plans to build a massive pulp and resin complex to serve the paper industry and the needs of the military (particularly for high-quality cord for aircraft tyres). Protests and attempts to declare the region a *zapovednik* had little effect (except, perhaps, to consolidate environmentalism as putative 'movement' in the Soviet Union), and the Baikalsk plant was subsequently built.

The twin faces of the desert as a post-nuclear terrain and as the landscape of post-industry disaster were brought together in one of the most haunting visions of the post-Second World War period, Isozaki's *Re-ruined Hiroshima* (1968; 8.5) This photomontage was the centrepiece of his 'Electric Labyrinth' installation at the 14th Milan Triennale, which opened, albeit briefly, during the turbulent summer of 1968 before being closed by protesting students. The Triennale, the major European design fair of the post-war

era, had taken the 'greater number' as its theme, a loosely sociological concept that alluded to over-population, a growing pre-occupation of architects and designers.[14] It was a tacit acknowledgement, under pressure from the emergent counter-culture and environmental movement, that the design boom in the West during the 1960s had been built on over-consumption. Projecting two megastructures – the architectural form on which Isozaki's already considerable reputation was built – on to a large panoramic photograph of the city in ruins in 1945, the Japanese architect seemed to suggest that Hiroshima had undergone a second devastation. The burned-out skeletons of a metal frame haunted the charnel city. The viewer was left to reflect uncomfortably on what had triggered this new desolation. In a key work in what had become an important architectural genre in the course of the 1960s, the visionary scheme, Isozaki seemed to point to a dark shadow behind the dream of utopia. The challenge, he appeared to suggest, was how to balance mankind's tremendous and hitherto only imagined potential to transform the world with its mighty destructive capacities.

Spanning the world
In the late 1950s and 1960s a number of architects around the world, including Isozaki, came to imagine a new scale of architecture

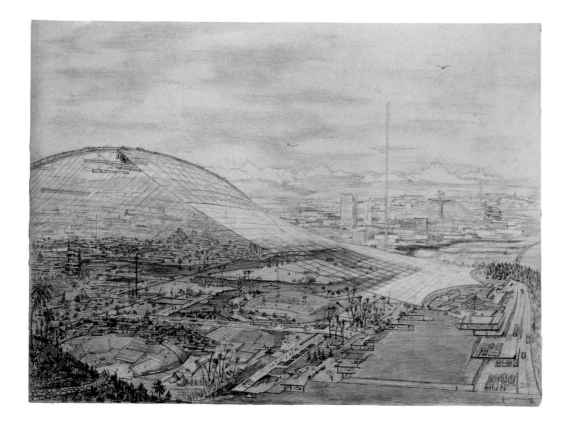

8.6
Frei Otto, *Roofed Futurist City*. Pencil on cardboard, 1963. Deutsches Architekturmuseum, Frankfurt am Main

8.7
Ron Herron (Archigram), *Walking City, Walking Cities in the Desert*. Airbrushed ink and paper collage on board, 1973. Deutsches Architektur-museum, Frankfurt am Main

for environments that had hitherto been overlooked or dismissed as inhospitable to mankind. Schemes for floating and mountain-top megastructures, and the designs of massive arctic, submarine and underground cities, constituted an important face of an international 'movement', albeit one that coalesced in retrospect.[15] Architects such as the Metabolists in Japan, who issued their first manifesto in 1960; international alliances such as the Groupe d'Espace et de l'Architecture Mobile (GEAM), founded by Yona Friedman in 1957; the Archigram collective in Britain; the NER (New Element of the Urban Environment/Novye elementy rasseleniia) Group in the Soviet Union; and individuals including Buckminster Fuller and Frei Otto created schemes for new cities, typically in the form of massive frameworks supporting building 'elements' (8.6).[16] Unlike the zoned conception of the modernist city represented by CIAM's Athens Charter (drafted in 1933 but first published 1942 and a guiding vision for much urban planning in the post-war years), these new habitats sought to achieve a new density in a single multi-functional structure that was labelled as

a 'megastructure'. Stimulated by the prospect of new materials and building techniques, some architects imagined the habitats they designed as evolving or growing structures, even as organisms capable of auto-generation (for instance, Kurokawa's Helix Structures of 1960–61, which resemble giant DNA structures[17]). Unreservedly futurist, such schemes were indifferent to history and tradition (although in some one can find traces of pre-modern patterns of settlement). In this regard, the megastructuralists repre-sented the high-water mark of modernist urbanism in the twentieth century.

Amongst the achievements of the new visionaries of the 1960s was their tremendous ability to visualize their schemes in compel-ling drawings and graphic images. The technique of photomontage – hitherto little more than an occasional practice amongst architects – was seized and thoroughly renewed by this generation.[18] It allowed, perhaps more than any other medium, entirely new architectural scales to be visualized. Mechanical elements were blown up to city-size proportions and landscapes were dwarfed by domestic objects and mechanical

components wrenched from their familiar settings and turned into enigmatic monuments of modernity. Archigram's Ron Herron was the master builder of this aesthetic. His various schemes for a 'Walking City' produced from 1964 were disturbingly mechanical, an effect amplified by the inclusion of photomechanical reproductions of his own architectural automata (8.7). These enormous itinerant pods, augmented with turrets, towers and gunnels, resembled alien craft just landed on the planet. Herron described the 'Walking City' as:

> a world capital [that] consists of a series of giant vehicles, each housing elements that collectively made up a metropolis. The vehicles roam the globe forming and reforming. Moscow, a desert, New York Harbour, a pacific atoll, and the Thames Estuary, any place and every place, a world capital of total probability.[19]

Whilst Herron's vision was evidently and ironically grotesque (though apparently not to all who saw these works[20]), other city-scale schemes – produced by busy studios engaged in the business of construction like that run by Kenzo Tange – were serious-minded proposals.[21] Nevertheless, viewed collectively these paper projects constituted a new variety of the 'technological sublime', an aesthetic that, according to historian David E. Nye, describes the changed scale of human relations with the machine in modernity.[22] Whilst the 'natural sublime' had implied human limits, he argues in his study of nineteenth- and twentieth-century America, the technological sublime undermines all ideas of limitation. The pace and scale of technological development in the twentieth century, amplified by Cold War competition, produced a new ratios between man and the machine, as well as between man and nature. Nye's observation that in America the 'awe induced by seeing an immense or dynamic technological object became a celebration of the power of human reason' was no less true in the Soviet Bloc (or even in the developing world, where massive projects like the Aswan Dam in Egypt and Islamabad, the new capital of Pakistan, were constructed with expertise and funding from Cold War superpowers).[23] Commenting on this new spirit, Hans Hollein and Walter Pichler announced:

> Today, for the first time in human history, at this point in time when an immensely advanced science and perfected technology offer all possible means, we build what and how we will, we make an architecture that is not determined by technology but utilizes technology, a pure, absolute architecture.[24]

Alongside its enthusiasm for high-gear ratios, another key feature of this putative movement was its internationalism. In Cold War terms, by the mid 1960s an interest in megastructures spanned the East–West divide in what one commentator has called an 'orbital flow of ideas'.[25] Although the lines of contact were sometimes indirect and fragmentary, with few Eastern Bloc architects being able to travel to conferences or participate in exhibitions, magazines and occasional publications played a crucial role in the exchange of ideas. The architectural press in Western Europe in the mid-1960s kept a fair-weather eye on developments in the East. At the same time architects and designers in the socialist bloc were keen followers of developments in the West,

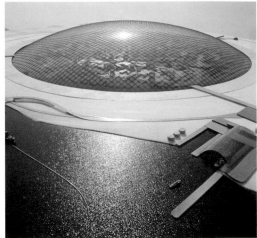

8.11
Frei Otto with Ewald Bubner, Kenzo Tange and Ove Arup, model of a proposed city in the Arctic, 1971. Atelier Frei Otto, Warmbronn

8.10
Arata Isozaki, *Cluster in the Air*, model. Wood, cork and metal on laminated chipboard, 1962. Deutsches Architekturmuseum, Frankfurt am Main

The city would be served by its own atomic power station (the hot water derived from the generation of electricity would be drained into the sea to keep the harbour ice-free). The environment inside would be an Arctic paradise in which every open space and roof would be covered with vegetation. The effects of the long Arctic winter on the inhabitants and the plant-life would be offset by a massive artificial sun moving on tracks suspended below the surface of the dome.

The frozen lands above the Arctic Circle had particular strategic and symbolic importance for the Soviet Union.[44] In the mid-1960s plans were published for massive triangular blocks to house the workers in the nickel processing plants of Norilsk, a closed city in the Krasnoiarsk Territory of Northern Siberia, on the Taimyr Peninsula. The area contains about a third of the planet's nickel reserves and 40 per cent of the planet's reserves of platinum, as well as significant amounts of cobalt and copper.[45] Even before new megastructures were planned for Norilsk, it was already one of the largest Soviet cities in the permafrost zone. It had been designed along

formal socialist realist axes in the 1940s by Leningrad architects who had been imprisoned in the nearby gulag, and completed with prison labour and loyal Soviet volunteers. After the gulag closed the city was singled out for expansion. High wages and even higher praise were offered to workers prepared to move east to work in its mineral extracting and processing plants.[46] A new vision for life in the city was envisaged by A. Shipkov and E. Shipkova in the form of monumental 26-storey tetrahedral 'cities'. Enormous glazed structures would operate like greenhouses with a central courtyard at their core.[47] Sufficiently large to allow trees and shrubs to grow inside, these internal parks would frame the public facilities of the new socialist habitat. Norilsk's glass pyramids were not built, though the industrial expansion of the region was swift, with devastating consequences: by the end of the Soviet Union Norilsk had acquired the unenviable reputation of having the worst air and water pollution in Russia, a country itself widely accused of wholesale ecocide.[48]

8.12
Ettore Sottsass Jr, *The Future of Architecture; Buckminster Fuller, Stranded* from his series *Planet as Festival*. Zinc lithograph and crayon on paper, 1973. Deutsches Architekturmuseum, Frankfurt am Main

8.13
Alex Mlynarčik, Ĺudovít Kupkovič and Viera Mecková, *Heliopolis* project. Architectural model, c.1970. VAL, Žilina

The end of utopia

By the beginning of the 1970s critics – many of whom had once been keen advocates of megastructures – were queuing up to announce their demise.[49] The fact this planetary habitat had been domesticated, in the form of new-built projects for multi-lane motorways and megastructure housing estates, diminished its utopian credentials. Utopia, after all, is an ideal; to build is to compromise. For influential critic Manfredo Tafuri, the neo-avant-garde credentials of groups like Archigram were undermined by the fact that their schemes appropriated existing technologies that had been generated largely by capitalism.[50]

Reflecting on what he called 'the end of utopia' in 1971, GEAM member Manfredi Nicoletti pointed to the rise of three paths being followed by architects who wished to press their radical credentials.[51] The first was to continue the 'vague' ambitions of the megastructure 'movement' even as it fell into convention, becoming, in Nicoletti's words, the '*academicism d'avant garde*'. Another path was to eschew all architectural ambitions in favour of catalytic images that might stimulate reaction. Nicoletti did not illustrate his point, but he might have had in mind the work of Superstudio (see below) or Ettore

Sottsass – a central figure in the international fashion for chic Italian design in the late 1950s and 1960s. The Milan-based furniture designer effectively withdrew from industry for a short period at the beginning of the 1970s to produce 'schemes' for structures that guaranteed their visionary status by being unbuildable. His *Planet as Festival* (*Il Planeta come festival*) series of drawings of the early 1970s represented the liberation of life on Earth (8.12). Gone were the banks, offices and factories, the instruments of technocratic modernity. In their place were new 'superinstruments' that would release repressed sexual and emotional sensibilities.

Clear intellectual and aesthetic parallels can be drawn with the work of Slovak artist Alex Mlynarčik and architects Ĺudovít Kupkovič and Viera Mecková, members of VAL (Voies et Aspectes du Lendemain/Ways and Aspects of Tomorrow), who imagined a new city perched like a bird's nest on the tops of mountains (8.13).[52] Their Heliopolis Project, a ring-shaped megastructure at 2,150m above sea-level that could house 60,000 people, was a mechanism to protect the natural environment from its greatest threat, man. The project took shape when it was proposed to hold the Olympics in the Tatra mountains. Floating high in the peaks of the mountains and

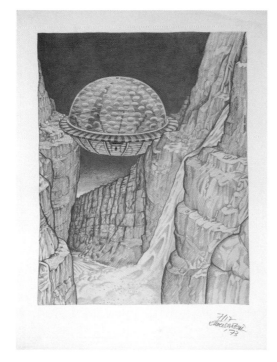

crossing the Polish-Czechoslovak border (which only recently had been the entry point for Soviet-led forces suppressing the Prague Spring), the untouched landscape would be left pristine below. And in fact two of the six zones specified by the architects in their scheme were to be left untouched and inaccessible, a natural 'counter-monument' to man's destructive capacities. Like the expressionist projects designed by members of the Gläserne Kette (Glass Chain) group, such as Bruno Taut in Germany in the years after the First World War or El Lissitzky's *Prouns* produced in the Soviet Union in the early 1920s, this architecture was a gesture of impossible perfection.[53] The relationship of utopian architecture built from the distopian logic of environmentalism was particularly provocative in the setting of the Eastern Bloc, where to question the limits of the feasible was to issue a challenge to official state doctrine, Communism.

In his diagnosis of the state of utopianism Nicoletti described the third trend as 'Psycho-Social Mysticism', which, he wrote,

> aims to a sort of primitive state, a come-back to the origin, a naturality now forbidden by the rhythm of life. It is a genuine reaction against the stereotyped sterility of the environment ... the search for a richer ambience where mystery and plasticity arise hidden memories of a lost Eden.[54]

Communes, 'Buddhist Economics', the bricolage aesthetic of 'adhocism' in the early 1970s, 'Digger' activism in San Francisco and Provo activism in Amsterdam, the production of 'People's Parks' by community action and even the hippy trail to India represented a search for alternatives to what Herbert Marcuse, in his influential early critique, called 'technological rationality'.[55] All operated on a different scale to the grand, even revolutionary schemes to create utopia in the world. This trend reached its apogee in the commune movement that took hold throughout North America and Western Europe in the late 1960s.[56] The participants in these experimental social communities acted with a range of different motivations: some were guided by Kropotkin's anarchism, whilst others were engaged in a search for transcendental

experience (and both strains were combined in the 'primitive' Christianity promoted by some American communes). Other communes indulged in 'back to the land' romanticism, with a fascinated writer in *Life* magazine describing their members as 'refugees from affluence'.[57] Many of these diverse groups expressed their antagonism to mainstream lifestyles by turning to unorthodox architectural forms (when judged by the standards set by Western housing), including domes derived from Buckminster Fuller's inventive futurism as well as yurts and other traditional nomadic tents (8.14). From Nicoletti's perspective, this trend was ill equipped to stave off its commercialization that was, as he wrote, already converting opposition into another a lifestyle option. He imagined the commune in its dome as a variation of the weekend cottage, which gave 'a bourgeois clientele, absorbed all year in the push-button adventure of the metropolis ... a quick jump into a primeval world giving

a ready-made identification with forgotten genuine values'.[58]

A postdiluvian world?

The most widely reported commune of the period, Drop City, near Trinidad, Colorado, would – on first inspection – appear to fit Nicoletti's characterization of the commune movement as back to the land romantics (8.15). A fluid group of between 14 and 20 people built and lived in the homes and communal buildings erected there between 1965 and 1969 (with the site being abandoned by 1973). The desert location matched its experimental nature (and that of many other communes established in Colorado, Nevada and New Mexico in the late 1960s). Deserts have long been represented as extraterritorial spaces:[59] to enter into them is to set aside the 'normal' conditions that govern life. In this respect they are natural laboratories in which many different of kinds of experiment have been conducted. (After all, this was the reason why atom bomb tests had been carried out in the 'empty' deserts of the American Southwest in the 1940s and early 1950s.) If the desert was a place to escape modern America, it was also, however, a setting for its revival. The Western wildernesses carried deep messianistic associations in the American consciousness.[60] In this sense, the counter-cultural commune was a continuation of the 'New World' tradition. Following a strange doubling effect, life in Drop City paralleled America's nineteenth-century pioneers as well as that of survivors after a future apocalypse.

Drop City's own residents represented life there as a form of twentieth-century tribalism: 'There is no political structure in Drop City. Things work out; the cosmic forces mesh with people in a strange complex intuitive interaction … When things are done the slow intuitive way, the tribe makes sense.'[61] And reflecting the counter-culture's preoccupation with the alienating effects of modernity, life in Drop City was mythologized as a kind of pure communism in which man and woman took equal pleasure in all their efforts: 'digging a ditch carries no less status than erecting a sculpture; in fact the individual often discovers he is happier digging a ditch, sculpting a ditch. Life forms and art forms begin to interact.'[62]

This elision of the pre- and post-modern was also found in the materials used to fashion Drop City. The small cluster of homes and communal structures was made from the debris and waste that its founders, artists Clark Richert and Gene and JoAnn Bernofsky, acquired from local farmers and junkyards. The salvage aesthetic of Drop City's structures was frequently interpreted as a critique of consumerist excess. Writing in 1970, Peter Cook described it as 'a highly rhetorical gesture (with some organic overtones) of opportunism: the beaten-out parts of automobiles and other thrown-away bits are heaped up into Fuller-like domes to house a drop out community'.[63] Some of the structures on site were freely derived from Buckminster Fuller's ideas about lightweight self-supporting structures. His geodesic principles, widely employed as exhibition and industrial structure and even given military uses, were reinvigorated by the growing Drop City commonwealth. The first building to be erected, known as the 'Great Pumpkin', was a dome 5.4m in diameter, with a timber structure. Its pentagonal windows were fashioned from the windscreens of cars and sealed with cement and tar. Drop City's artist-constructors were highly inventive in their junk aesthetic. Steve Baer, a temporary resident in Drop City, brought his idea of the 'Zome', a geometric structure created by slicing off the top of car with axes and building a polyhedra on the base.[64] Even Detroit's products could be fashioned into counter-cultural forms.

What is equally striking is that Drop City was widely reported – by the media of the global village – as a reply to the untrammelled technophilia of the age.[65] When, for instance, Neil Armstrong made his moon walk, according to Richert, network television news planned to cut to Drop City to provide a sharp contrast with this momentous event (though this televisual montage never occurred).[66] In fact, the founders of Drop City, like wide elements of the West Coast counter-culture, were keen enthusiasts for new media and other state-of-the-art technologies. One Drop citizen announced in 1967:

> We want TV videotape recorders and cameras. We want computers and miles of color film and elaborate cine cameras and hundreds of strobes and tape decks and amps and echo chambers and everything. We want millionaire patrons. We want to use everything, new, junk, good, bad, we want to be able to make

limitless things. We need the most up to date equipment in the world to make our things. We want an atomic reactor.[67]

It is clear that for some environmental activists in the loose ranks of the counter-culture, the retreat into an Edenic existence before capitalist industrialization was a delusion. Making a reference to Henry David Thoreau's famous 'experiment with simplicity' in the 1840s, one wrote that we cannot 'run back to Walden Pond: it has to share its oxygen with the Con Ed Plants in New York City'.[68]

The *Whole Earth Catalog*

The theme of the interconnectedness of the planet was also central to the *Whole Earth Catalog*, a remarkably successful quarterly publication that first appeared in 1968 (8.16). It was triggered, in part, by a visit by its founder, Stewart Brand, to Drop City. The *Whole Earth Catalog* was a modified version of a long-established commercial medium in America, the mail-order catalogue. Alongside eccentric texts from Buckminster Fuller's writing, the *I-Ching* and reports from self-builders in Colorado and New Mexico, the catalogue reviewed products and services that would make possible the environmentally attuned lifestyles desired by many (8.17).

Readers could use the catalogue to order a wide range of goods from their manufacturers – from moccasins to self-assembly geodesic domes, and even IBM computers. Imagined as a service to the communes (and, in fact, a Whole Earth Truck Store travelled between isolated communities until its driver gave up the road to follow his guru, Baba Ram Dass[69]), the catalogue became an international success, attracting readers around the world. Like the megastructuralists, who had imagined a ribbon network of cities linking to girdle the planet, the *Whole Earth Catalog* suggested an interconnected planet. Brand and his friends had, however, little interest in assuming the global proportions of a multinational corporation or in providing the lattice skeleton of a new megastructure. The catalogue had little to say about the right form for new patterns of life (though the critique of consumer modernity was apparent). It did not sell the products described on its pages, nor in fact did Brand and his friends write the reviews that it published. Readers were encouraged to recommend and review those products and services that might serve the counter-culture. It was, in other words, an exchange-point in an information network. The fact that the *Whole Earth Catalog* anticipated the future shape of the Internet is not, as many commentators have

8.16
Stewart Brand, cover of the *Whole Earth Catalog*, autumn 1969

8.17
Pages from the *Whole Earth Catalog*, autumn 1969

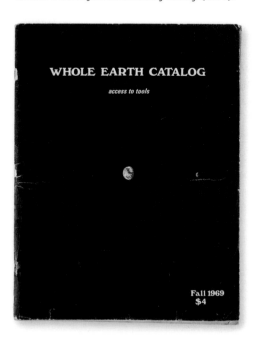

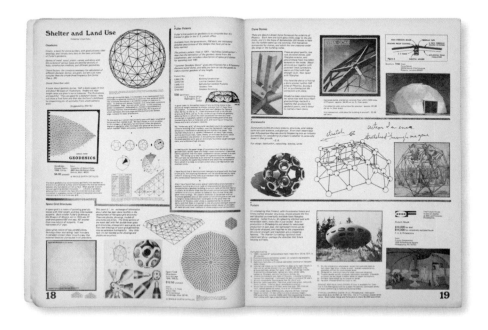

noted, a coincidence.[70] The network of comm, communes and alternative technology projects that emerged in California in the late 1960s and 1970s were eventually connected in the 1980s by the Whole Earth 'Lectronic Link', a San Francisco Bay-area bulletin-board system, a civilian precursor of the Internet. Silicon Valley was populated by computing pioneers and hackers with personal histories in the counter-culture.

Moreover, the products and services on its pages represented a wish to assert control over the material and intellectual environment of life. 'We are as gods and might as well get used to it', wrote Stewart Brand, in a statement that appeared in issues of the *Whole Earth Catalog* after 1969. 'So far,' he continued,

> remotely done power and glory – as via government, big business, formal education, church – has succeeded to the point where gross defects obscure actual gains. In response to this dilemma and to these gains a realm of intimate, personal power is developing – power of the individual to conduct his own education, find his own inspiration, shape his own environment, and share his adventure with whoever is interested. Tools that aid this process are sought and promoted by the WHOLE EARTH CATALOG.

The concept of the 'tool' was central to Brand's thinking. The catalogue was not selling commodities – items that seduced would-be consumers with their aesthetic qualities and associations of prestige: it provided tools, that is, instruments that amplified the powers of the individual or community to shape their world (and, as such, were unlike machines of industry, which tend to assimilate the worker). Once operating as 'extensions of man', modern technology had been, according to one influential writer in the period, transformed into a force *above* man.[71] Mankind needed to abandon its Olympian assurance and imagine a new scale of 'technology for life'.

Like the founders of Drop City, Stewart Brand and his *Whole Earth Catalog* were by no means opposed to technological advances or even to 'progress'. And like their guru, Buckminster Fuller, they judged technologies in terms of scale and of their effects. The environmentalist voices in the counter-culture, as Fred Turner has argued,

> saw the large-scale weapons technologies of the cold war and the organizations that produced them as emblems of a malevolent and ubiquitous technological bureaucracy.... as they played their stereos and dropped LSD many came to believe that small-scale technologies could help bring about an alternative to that world.[72]

Viewed like this, the *Whole Earth Catalog* was one of the most visible symbols of an emergent movement in the West that sought to re-scale life in just proportions.[73] In the face of the 'unholy infinities of desire: to produce and devour without limit, to build big, kill big, control big',[74] critics of the consumerism and militarism at the heart of the Cold War saw beauty in smallness.[75] Smallness did not necessarily mean isolation or withdrawal. In a spirit shared with the environmentalism movement with its slogan, 'Think globally, act locally', they took the view that no action – benign or malign – was without consequence on Spaceship Earth.

The world as a game

Buckminster Fuller was the author of the 'World Game', one of the most ambitious attempts to illustrate the interconnectedness of the planet in the era. Invited to design the American Pavilion at the Expo held in Montreal in 1967, Fuller tried unsuccessfully to persuade his commissioner, the United States Information Agency, that it should fill this spherical structure with an international-ist vision of the planet.[76] Visitors on raised platforms would be presented with an accurate spherical representation of 'Space-ship Earth' depicting all the cities of the world, suspended at the heart of the spherical pavilion. At the beginning of the game, this miniature earth would unfold, forming an enormous map on the floor below. This would be one of Fuller's trademark dymaxion maps in which the planet was represented as 13 equally proportioned triangles (8.18).[77] In this way the viewer had the possibility of seeing the entire world as a single entity. Fuller's dymaxion vision was a rejection of what had long been the dominant view of the planet in which the Northern Hemisphere was exaggerated in scale and positioned at the 'top' of the planet.

The map on the ground was to be threaded with banks and tracks of lights controlled by a supercomputer in the pavilion's basement. These illuminated points were to represent all the world's resources, including energy, water, foods and population. Pulsing on and off, they measured production and consumption. The computer was programmed with data that Buckminster Fuller had been gathering to support his futurology since the 1940s.[78] Whilst markets might judge resources in commercial terms and politicians might measure importance in terms of national security, Fuller ordered the world's common resources according to their availability: oxygen was, for instance, 'available in sufficient quantity to sustain human life only within two miles above the Earth's spherical surface', whereas other elements, such as helium, were 'not publicly available because used entirely by industry'.[79] In the 'World Game', all the world's resources were freed from private and national interests to be made available to the player.

For its audience the 'World Game' was not just to be a spectacle of the living planet: it was to be played by visitors to the pavilion, individually or in teams. They were to instruct the computer to expend all the world's resources for the benefit of all people on the planet. It was in the command of the players to move entire cities or redirect all communication flows. What if, Fuller speculated, electricity was delivered on a planetary grid rather than a series of wasteful national ones? The load over the course of a day would be more even and therefore more efficient: peaks in demand would pass from continent to continent in relation to the diurnal rotation of the Earth.[80] The planet was revealed – like one of Fuller's self-supporting 'tensegrity' structures – as a network through which the forces of energy flow. The currents of resources, people and information were interconnected in the 'World Game' just as they are in life. The task for the players was to improve these global synapses.

In this game without competitors Fuller wanted to inculcate a sense of partnership amongst its players. He declared its objective to be 'to explore the ways to make it possible guarantee total comfort' (8.21). Life in the new society eschewed products or refuse. But the 'Supersurface' as a high-tech habitat did not a mean a return to a primitive condition. This was to be post-consumerist one, in which quality of life would measured by psychic and emotional values rather than status symbols. Objects had to be returned, argued Superstudio member Adolfo Natalini, 'to the condition of neutral and disposable elements'.[86]

The 'Continuous Monument' perhaps on first inspection looked like an attempt to rehabilitate the architectural fashion of the day, that of the megastructure. It was also tuned into the counter-cultural dream of communal life. Both visions were utopian and both, as the Superstudio scheme made clear, produced paradoxes. The image of the hippies on the high-tech grid illustrates Superstudio's technique of *demonstratio ad absurdum*, the exaggeration of a concept to the point of absurdity.[87] In other words, it was a critical essay on the limits of utopia. Following the

perspectival logic of the grid (the device employed by the group as its trademark aesthetic), the 'Continuous Monument' took Modernism to its vanishing points. Like the vision of the Earth from dark space which opened this essay, the 'Continuous Monument' issued a check on the utopian rhetoric of unceasing progress, of 'dematerialization', orbital flows and of benign globalization that had accompanied Cold War modernity.

8.21
Superstudio, *Life: The Encampment (Vita: L'Accampanento)*, photomontage, 1971–2. Musée nationale d'art moderne, Paris

8.22
Footprint left by an astronaut on lunar soil during the Apollo 11 lunar mission, in which astronauts Neil Armstrong and Buzz Aldrin took a walk on the Moon's surface

Notes

1 / INTRODUCTION

1
Hamilton provided a discussion of his sources in 'An exposition of $he', *Architectural Design* (October 1962), p.30.

2
Christopher Booker, *The Neophiliacs* (London 1992), pp.134-5

3
This event is widely discussed in many sources; see Walter L. Hixson, *Parting the Curtain: Propaganda, Culture and the Cold War, 1945-1961* (London/Basingstoke 1997); Karal Ann Marling, *As Seen on TV: The Visual Culture of Everyday Life in the 1950s* (Cambridge, MA, 1994); Robert H. Haddow, *Pavilions of Plenty: Exhibiting American Culture Abroad in the 1950s* (Washington, DC, 1997), pp.104-68; David Crowley, 'Making the Post-War Home in Eastern Europe', in Mark Pittaway (ed.), *Globalization and Europe* (Milton Keynes 2003) pp.249-89.

4
Nixon, cited in 'The Two Worlds: A Day-Long Debate', *New York Times* (25 July 1959), p.1.

5
See Greg Castillo, 'Domesticating the Cold War: Household Consumption as Propaganda in Marshall Plan Germany', *Journal of Contemporary History*, vol.40, no.2 (April 2005), pp.261-89; see also Robert A. Haddow, *Pavilions of Plenty: Exhibiting America Abroad in the 1950s* (Washington 1997), and S. Jonathan Wiesen, 'Miracles for Sale: Consumer Displays and Advertising in Postwar West Germany', in David Crew (ed.), *Consuming Germany in the Cold War* (Oxford/New York 2002), pp.151-78.

6
Mary Anne Staniszewski, *The Power of Display: A History of Exhibition Installations at the Museum of Modern Art* (Cambridge, MA, 1998).

7
Ivan T. Berend, *Central and Eastern Europe, 1944-1993:*

Detour from the Periphery to the Periphery (Cambridge 1997), p.216.

8
The literature on the cultural politics of the Cold War is extensive. For a thoroughly researched recent survey see David Caute, *The Dancer Defects; The Struggle for Cultural Supremacy during the Cold War* (New York 2003). For a detailed but very US-centred perspective see Richard Alan Schwartz, *Cold War Culture: Media and the Arts, 1945-1990* (New York 2000).

9
For discussion of the planning and architecture of Expo '58 see Mil de Kooning and Rika Devos, *L'Architecture Moderne à l'Expo '58* (Brussels 2006); M. Kint, *Expo '58 als belichaming van het humanistisch modernisme* (Rotterdam 2001).

10
'In the Western world ... there is a rough consensus among intellectuals on political issues: the acceptance of a Welfare State; the desirability of decentralized power; a system of mixed economy and of political pluralism. In that sense, too, the ideological age has ended': Daniel Bell, *The End of Ideology: On the Exhaustion of Political Ideas in the Fifties* (Harvard 1962), p.373.

11
Cf. Adam Rome, '"Give Earth a Chance": The Environmental Movement and the Sixties', *Journal of American History*, vol.90, no.2 (September 2003), pp.525-54.

12
This phrase is borrowed from Susan Buck-Morss' thoughtful account of what she calls 'mass utopia', the vision of the commonwealth that lay at the heart of the Marxist project, in *Dreamworld and Catastrophe: The Passing of Mass Utopia in East and West* (Cambridge, MA, 2000).

13
Paul Edwards, *The Closed World: Computers and the Politics of Discourse in Cold War America* (Cambridge, MA, 1996).

14
See Adrian Forty, 'Cold War Concrete', in Mart Kalm and Ingrid Ruudi (eds), *Constructed Happiness: Domestic Environment in the Cold War Era* (Tallinn 2005), pp.28-45. See also Paul R. Josephson, *Red Atom. Russia's Nuclear Power Programme from Stalin to Today* (Pittsburgh 2000), pp.81-108. Wayne D. Cocroft and Roger J.C. Thomas, *Cold War : Building for Nuclear Confrontation 1946-89*, ed. P.S. Barnwell (London 2003).

15
For recent scholarship on Modernism in the post-war period see various essays in Hubert-Jan Henket and Hilde Heynen (eds) *Back from Utopia: The Challenge of the Modern Movement* (Rotterdam 2002).

16
See, for example, Eva Cockcroft, 'Abstract Expressionism: Weapon of the Cold War', *Artforum*, vol.12 (June 1974), pp.38-41; Francis Frascina (ed.), *Pollock and After: The Critical Debate* (1st published 1985, rev. edn with new introductory essay, Routledge 2000); Serge Guilbaut, *How New York Stole the Idea of Modern Art: Abstract Expressionism, Freedom, and the Cold War* (Chicago 1983).

17
Christin J. Mamiya, 'We the People: The Art of Robert Rauschenberg and the Construction of American National Identity', *American Art*, vol.7, no.3 (summer 1993), pp.40-64.

18
The literature on the political history of the Cold War is enormous and ever-growing. For recent accounts, see John Lewis Gaddis, *The Cold War: A New History* (Harmondsworth 2005); John Lewis Gaddis, *We Now Know: Rethinking Cold War History* (Oxford 1997); Odd Arne Westad (ed.), *Reviewing the Cold War: Approaches, Interpretations, Theory* (London 2000). Martin Walker's *The Cold War: A History* (New York 1993) remains a very valuable overview of the period. Jussi M. Hanhimäki and Odd Arne Westad (eds), *The Cold War: A History in Documents and Eyewitness Accounts* (Oxford 2004) provides an excellent

selection of primary documents and accounts.

19
Eric Hobsbawm, *Age of Extremes. The Short Twentieth Century 1914-1991* (London 1995), pp.225-37.

20
For a discussion of the long history of the Iron Curtain metaphor, see Patrick Wright, *Iron Curtain: From Stage to Cold War* (London 2006).

21
For an authoritative account of the effects of the Cold War on international relations around the world, see Odd Arne Westad, *The Global Cold War: Third World Interventions and the Making of Our Times* (Cambridge 2005).

22
See Ronald Taylor, *Berlin and its Culture: A Historical Portrait* (New Haven/London, 1997); Alexandra Richie, *Faust's Metropolis. A History of Berlin* (New York, 1998); Brian Ladd, *The Ghosts of Berlin. Confronting German History in the Urban Landscape* (Chicago/London 1997).

23
Ann and John Tusa, *The Berlin Airlift* (Boulder, CO, 1998).

24
See Frederick Taylor, *The Berlin Wall: A World Divided, 1961-1989* (London 2007).

25
Robert Burstow, 'The Limits of Modernist Art as a "Weapon of the Cold War": Reassessing the Unknown Patron of the Monument to the Unknown Political Prisoner', *Oxford Art Journal*, vol.20, no.1 (1997), pp.68-80.

26
See Niels Gutschow and Barbara Klain, *Vernichtung und Utopie. Stadtplanung Warschau 1939-1945* (Hamburg 1994); Wim Beeren (ed.), *Het Nieuwe Bouwen in Rotterdam 1920-1960* (Delft 1982).

27
On the activities of the Deutsche Werkbund after 1945, see Paul Betts, *The Authority of Everyday Objects* (Berkeley, CA, 2004).

28
Hildtrud Ebert (ed.), *Drei Kapitel Weißensee (Dokumente zur Geschichte der Kunsthochschule Berlin-Weißensee, 1946-1957)* (Berlin 1996).

29
The EXAT 51 manifesto, signed by Bernado Bernadi, Zdravko Bregovac, Ivan Picelj, Božidar Rašica, Vjencelsav Richter, Aleksandar Srnec and Vladimir Zarahovič, appears in *EXAT 51 1951-1956*, exh. cat., Centro Cultural de Cascais (Cascais 2001), pp.22-3.

30
See Jasner Galjer, *Design of the Fifties in Croatia: From Utopia to Reality* (Zagreb 2004).

31
On the pessimistic mood in architectural discourse after 1945, see Barry Curtis, 'The Heart of the City', in Jonathan Hughes and Simon Sadler (eds), *Non-Plan: Essays on Freedom, Participation and Change in Modern Architecture and Urbanism* (Oxford 2000) pp.52-65; various essays in Sarah Williams Goldhagen and Réjean Legault (eds), *Anxious Modernisms: Experimentation in Postwar Architectural Culture* (Cambridge, MA, 2001).

32
See Mil de Kooning and Rika Devos, *L'Architecture Moderne à l'Expo '58* (Brussels 2006); M. Kint, *Expo '58 als belichaming van het humanistisch modernisme* (Rotterdam 2001).

33
Expo '58, news release no. 2 (undated) (British Library SA 60/28).

34
For example, designer Raymond Loewy was singled out for criticism. See Paul Betts, *The Authority of Everyday Objects: A Cultural History of West German Industrial Design* (Berkeley/Los Angeles 2004), pp.87-9.

35
Asger Jorn, letter to Max Bill cited in Joan Ochman (ed.), *Architecture Culture 1943-1968* (New York 1993), p.173.

36
Asger Jorn, 'Arguments apropos of the International Movement for an Imaginist Bauhaus, against an Imaginary Bauhaus; and its Purpose Today (1954)', in Joan Ochman (ed.), *Architecture Culture 1943-1968* (New York 1993), p.173.

37
See Richard Barbrook, *Imaginary Futures: From Thinking Machines to Global Villages* (London 2007).

38
Newsweek (May 1943), cited in Steven Phillips, 'Plastics', in Beatriz Colomina, Annmarie Brennan and Jeannie Kim (eds), *Cold War Hothouses: Inventing Postwar Culture from Cockpit to Playboy* (New York 2004), p.97.

39
See Jeffrey L. Meikle, *American Plastic: A Cultural History* (Chapel Hill, NC, 1995), pp.212-13.

40
The authors extend their thanks to Krystyna Łuczak-Surówka for alerting them to the existence and history of this chair and its designer.

41
Ghyczy's chair has a curious history. When the licence to produce it was quietly sold to an East German producer in 1971 it developed two parallel identities: as both an iconic 'pop' product in the West, and a symbol of manufacturing innovation in the East. New research into the history of this object, acquired by the V&A, has been undertaken by Jana Scholze.

42
This theme has been the subject of much academic debate, for example: Joel Mokyr, *Lever of Riches: Technological Creativity and Economic Progress* (Oxford 1992).

43
President Eisenhower made reference to the 'unwarranted influence' of the military-industrial complex in his 1961 farewell speech.

44
John Kenneth Galbraith, 'The Cold War and the Corporations', *Progressive*, vol.31, no.7 (1967), pp.14-18; David F. Noble, *America by Design: Science, Technology, and the Rise of Corporate Capitalism* (New York 1977); Diane B. Kunz, *Butter and Guns : America's Cold War Economic Diplomacy* (New York 1997).

45
Raymond Hutchings, 'Soviet Design: The Neglected Partner of Soviet Science and Technology', *Slavic Review*, vol.37, no.4 (1978), p.569.

46
As Györgyi Peteri has noted, 'Out of fifty major technical advances that were made during the post-war era and still shape our lives today, only three appeared first in a socialist country'. See 'Nylon Curtain: Transnational and Transsystemic Tendencies in the Cultural Life of State-Socialist Russia and East-Central Europe', *Slavonica*, vol.10, no.2 (November 2004), p.118.

47
Václav Cigler a Absolventi Oddelenia Sklo v Architektúre na Vysokéj škole výtvarných umění v Bratislavě 1965-1979, exh. cat., Galérie Porkorná, Prague and Slovenská Národná Galéria, Bratislava (2003).

48
See Marc Dessauce, *The Inflatable Moment: Pneumatics and Protest in '68* (Princeton, NJ, 1999), p.50.

49
Hobsbawm 1995, pp.286, 403-32.

50
In 1977 Charles Jencks famously identified the moment of the 'death' of modern architecture as 3.32pm on 15 July 1972 (the date when the Pruitt-Igoe social housing district in St Louis, Missouri, USA, was demolished due to the extensive social problems faced by its residents). See Charles Jencks, *The Language of Post-modern Architecture* (New York 1984 edn), p.9.

51
John Thackara (ed.), *Design after Modernism, Beyond the Object* (London 1988).

52
Frederic Jameson, *Post Modernism, or, The Cultural Logic of Late Capitalism* (Durham, NC, 1991); David Harvey, *The Condition of Post Modernity* (Cambridge, MA, 1990), particularly 'The passage from modernity to postmodernity in contemporary culture', pp.3-112.

From Monuments to Fast Cars: Aspects of Cold War Art, 1946-1957

1
The Comintern (Communist International), founded in Moscow in March 1919, was committed to an international Soviet republic and worldwide proletarian revolution. When the USSR became our allies (after the Nazi invasion in 1941) its dissolution in 1943 became inevitable. The Cominform (Communist Information Bureau) was set up in September 1947, in the wake of the US Marshall Aid plan for Europe and the fall of the 'Iron Curtain' to coordinate Stalinist foreign policy; it was dissolved in 1956.

2
There is some suggestion it was offered to Warsaw. A. Rotula and P. Krakowski, *Rzeźba Wspőłczesna* (Warsaw 1980), p.132.

3
See Sylvain Lecombre and Helena Staub, *Ossip Zadkine, l'oeuvre sculpté* (Paris 1994), no.403, pp.437-61, including all quotations above.

4
John Berger, *Permanent Red: Essays in Seeing* (London 1960), pp.116-18 (originally published in the *New Statesman*, 2 February 1959).

5
'The Unknown Political Prisoner', Tate Gallery, 14 March - 30 April 1953. See Robert Burstow, 'Butler's competition project for a monument to "The Unknown Political Prisoner"? Abstraction and Cold War politics', *Art History*, vol.12, no.4 (December 1989), pp.472-96; Joan Marter, 'The Ascendancy of Abstraction for Public Art: The Monument to the Unknown Political Prisoner Competition', *Art Journal*, vol.53, no.4 (winter 1994); *Sculpture in Postwar Europe and America, 1945-59*, pp.28-36; Robert Burstow, 'The Limits of Modernist Art as a "Weapon of the Cold War": Reassessing the Unknown Patron of the Monument to the Unknown Political Prisoner', *The Oxford Art Journal*, vol.20, no.1 (1997), pp.68-80; and Axel Lapp, 'The Freedom of Sculpture – The Sculpture of Freedom: The International Sculpture Competition for a Monument to the Unknown Political Prisoner, London, 1951-3', *Sculpture Journal 2* (1998), pp.113-22.

6
For an extensive discussion of commission and reception, including quotations by Gabo, see Joan Pachner, 'Zadkine and Gabo in Rotterdam', *Art Journal* (December 1994), pp.79-85.

7
'...alternatively, 'professing a "laical Judaism" perhaps Gabo could not have cared less'; see John E. Bowlt, review of Martin Hammer, Christina Lodder, *Constructing Modernity, the Art and Career of Naum Gabo* (London 2000) *Burlington Magazine*, vol.143, no.1178, p.304.

8
Zadkine, catalogue raisonné, no.313, p.344: *Christ*, 5.25m high, loaned by the French National Museum of Modern Art to the church of Arques, the village where Zadkine spent much time prior to leaving for New York.

9
'The geometry of fear' was how Herbert Read characterized the work of sculptors such as Edouardo Paolozzi, Reg Butler, and Lynn Chadwick, British Pavilion, Venice Biennale, 1952.

10
See also theologian Paul Tillich's *Shaking of the Foundations* (New York 1948); he would preface the exhibition 'New Images of Man' at the Museum of Modern Art, New York, in 1959.

11
See A. Honneth, H. Kocyba and B. Schwibbs, 'Fieldwork in Philosophy' (1985) and Cheleen Mahar, 'Pierre Bourdieu: the Intellectual Project', in Derek Robbins (ed.), *Pierre Bourdieu* (London/Thousand Oaks, CA/New Delhi 2000), vol.1, pp.1-27, 32-47ff.

12
See Gertje R. Utley, *Picasso, the Communist Years* (New Haven 2000); Gérard Gosselin and Jean-Pierre Jouffroy, *Picasso et la Presse, un peintre dans l'histoire* (Paris 2000). Zadkine sculpted portraits of André Gide and François Mauriac - both notoriously anti-Soviet - in New York and set up a school for GI bill artists in Paris.

13
For Willi Münzenberg and the Comintern see Stephen Koch, *Double Lives: Spies and Writers in the Secret Soviet War of Ideas Against the West* (New York/Ontario 1994).

14
See Michael O'Mahony, *Representations of 'Fizkultura' in official Soviet culture from the First Five Year Plan to the Great Patriotic War, 1929-41*, Ph.D. thesis, University of London, 1988, and *Sport in the USSR: Physical Culture-Visual Culture* (London 2006).

15
A.A. Zhdanov, 'On the International Situation', in Giuliano Proccacci et al., *The Cominform. Minutes of the three conferences, 1947, 1948, 1949* (Milan 1994), p.225 (reproduced in *Cahiers du communisme* [November 1947], p.1150).

16
The Cominform, minutes of the third conference, 16-19 November 1949, pp.687, 723.

17
The exhibition 'L'Art et La Paix', organized by the Comité lyonnais pour la défense de la Paix in April 1950, involved over three hundred artists.

18
See André Fougeron: 'David et nous', *Arts de France*, no.31 (1950); Louis Aragon, *L'Exemple de Courbet* (Paris 1952); Hélène Parmelin, *Le massacre des Innocents* (Paris 1954), published, like Paul Eluard's highly ideo-

logical *Anthologie des Ecrits du l'Art* (3 vols, 1952-4) by the communist publishers Cercle d'Art, Paris.

19

On 24 October 1950 René Pleven attempted to launch a European army to include German forces, the C.E.D. (Communauté Européenne de Défense); the project was defeated in August 1954.

20

See Sarah Wilson, *Art and the Politics of the Left in France, c.1935-1955*, Ph.D. thesis, University of London, 1992, pp.281ff. and pp.352-3 (a source for much of this essay).

21

See Sarah Wilson, 'The Picasso Files', *Tate Magazine*, issue 2 (1994), pp.28-32.

22

For the CIA funding story, first exposed in 1967, see Francis Frascina, *Pollock and After: The Critical Debate* (New York 1985) and Frances Stonor Saunders, *Who Paid the Piper: The CIA and the Cultural Cold War* (London 2000).

23

Various authors, *Picasso w Polsce* (Cracow, 1979) and Dominique Desanti, *Nous avons choisi la Paix* (Paris 1949).

24

Jean-François Laglenne, 'L'Art au Congrès de la Paix', *Arts de France*, no.34 (January 1951).

25

De Marx à Staline, Maison de Metallurgie, Paris, 14-31 May 1953, first analysed in Pierre Bourdieu's journal by Jeannette Verdès-Leroux, 'L'Art de Parti. Le Parti Communiste et ses Peintres, 1947-1954', *Actes de Recherche en Sciences Sociales*, no.28 (June 1979).

26

See James Hyman, 'A "Pioneer Painter", Renato Guttuso and Realism in Britain', *Renato Guttuso*, exh. cat., Whitechapel Art Gallery (London 1996), pp.39-53; John Berger's monograph on Guttuso was published in Dresden only, in 1957.

27

See Frances K. Pohl, 'An American in Venice: Ben Shahn and American Foreign Policy at the 1954 Venice Biennale', *Art History*, vol.4 (March 1981), pp.80-113.

28

Following Cold War exhibitions and catalogues of the 1970s, such as *Italienische Realisten, 1945 bis 1974*, Neue Gesellschaft für Bildende Kunst und Kunstamt, Kreuzberg (Berlin 1974). See Christopher Duggan and Christopher Wagstaff, *Italy in the Cold War: Politics, Culture and Society, 1948-58* (Oxford and Washington 1995); Victor Zaslavsky with E. Agarossi, *Togliatti e Stalin. Il Partito comunista italiano e la politica estera sovietica* (Bologna 1998); Lara Pucci, *Picturing the Worker, Guttuso, Visconti, De Santis and the Partito Communista Italiano, 1944-1953*, Ph.D. thesis, University of London, 2007.

29

See Philippe Régnier, *La propagande anticommuniste de Paix et Liberté, France, 1950-1956* (Brussels 1986); for 'Paix et Liberté' posters, Laurent Gervereau and Philippe Buton (eds), *Le Couteau entre les Dents* (Paris 1989); for concentration camps, David Rousset, who then published the Soviet Penal code in November 1949 in the *Figaro Littéraire*, followed by several publications on the gulag through the 1950s, e.g. *Pour la vérité sur les camps concentrationnaire* (Paris 1951) and, with Paul Barton, *L'Institution concentrationnaire en Russie, 1930-1957* (Paris 1957).

30

The emigré Berthold Lubetkin's monument to Vladimir I. Lenin, unveiled in London by the Soviet ambassador in 1942, was a rare but short-lived exception. It was soon removed because of repeated attacks by anti-Communists.

31

See *Les Lettres Françaises* for 24 January 24 1952 and subsequent articles: Aragon's discussion of the crisis of contemporary French monumental sculpture in 'Il y a des sculpteurs à Moscou', 31 January 1952; 'Avez-vous lu Victor Hugo', 28 February 1952.

32

See Giles Scott-Smith, *The Politics of Apolitical Culture: The Congress for Cultural Freedom, the CIA and Post-War American Hegemony* (London 2002); while the festival was mainly musical, 'L'Oeuvre du XXe siècle' involved artworks selected by James Johnson Sweeney; see also *Preuves*, 15 May 1952. A more concerted push followed: 'Twelve American Painters and sculptors' (April – June 1953); 'Contemporary American drawings' (October – November 1954); 'Fifty years of Art from the United States', 1955; 'The New U.S. Painting', 1959.

33

See Aragon, *Avez-vous lu Victor Hugo?* (Paris 1952), p.37.

34

Kristin Ross, *Fast Cars, Clean Bodies, Decolonization and the reordering of French Culture* (Boston, MA, 1996); see also Richard F. Kuisel, *Seducing the French: The Dilemma of Americanization* (Berkeley, CA, 1993).

35

James Burnham, *The Managerial Revolution* (London 1941), trans. as *L'ère des organisateurs* (Paris 1947). Aron's extensive series of pro-American articles in *Le Figaro* on the Cold War, together with *Le Grand Schisme* (Paris 1948), *Guerres en chaine* (Paris 1951) and finally *L'opium des Intellectuels* (Paris 1955), were key for the pro-American intelligentsia. See Denis Boneau, 'Raymond Aron, avocat d'atlantisme', www.voltairenet.org/article15295.html.

36

Alexis de Tocqueville, *De la Democratie en Amérique*, 2 vols (Paris 1835, 1840).

37

'Art Méxicain du précolombien à nos jours' had been held from May to July 1953, at the Musée d'Art Moderne. Aragon published extracts from Georgi Malenkov's report from the 19th PCUS congress (October 1952) in April 1953, requiring more satire and stigmatization of vice. For the Fougeron-Picasso scandal around the latter's obituary 'Stalin portrait' and more detail including 'self-criticsms' and aftermath, see Wilson 1992, chap.6, final pages.

38

See Foucault, 'Nietszche, Genealogy, History', in D.F. Bouchard (ed.), *Language, Counter-Memory, Practice* (New York 1977), p.161.

39

From Aragon's *Pour un réalisme socialiste*, 1935, to his praise of Soviet shock-brigade paintings and Stalin-Prize works in *Les Lettres Françaises*, 10-17 April 1952.

40

Elsa Triolet, *Le Monument* (Paris 1957) appeared in *Les Lettres Françaises* from 4 April 1957, illustrated by Jacques Englebert. See Wilson 1992, chap.6, note 160.

41

See Martin Zec, 'Destiny of the Nation - Sculptor Otakar Švec', Art Wall Gallery, Letná Park, Prague, 4 April - 5 May 2006; Benoit Humeau, 'La triste histoire d'Otakar Švec, sculpteur de Staline et victime de son époque', www.Radio.cz/fr/edition/79600.

Modernism between Peace and Freedom: Picasso and Others at the Congress of Intellectuals in Wrocław, 1948

1

Max Frisch, *Sketchbook: 1946-1949* [1950], trans. Geoffrey Skelton (New York/London 1977), p.211.

2

Vladimr Kemenov, 'Aspects of Two Cultures', *VOKS Bulletin* (Moscow 1947, pp.20-36), reprinted in C. Harrison and P. Wood (eds), *Art in Theory 1900-1990: Anthology of Changing Ideas* (London 1992), pp.647-9; David Caute, *The Fellow-Travellers: A Postscript to the Enlightenment* (London 1973), p.289; Tony Judt, *Past Imperfect: French Intellectuals, 1944-1956* (Berkeley/Los Angeles/Oxford 1992).

3

For such a view, see James Thrall Soby, 'Postwar Painting: In the Shadow of "Guernica"', in *America and the Mind of Europe*, intro. L. Galantière (London 1950), pp.105-15; Arthur M. Schlesinger Jr, 'The Politics of Freedom' (1950), in C. Harrison and P. Wood (eds), *Art in Theory 1900-1990*: *An Anthology of Changing Ideas* (London 1992), p.659.

4

There is no comprehensive monograph of the Wrocław Congress, but the primary source is the official publication of the proceedings, *Congrès Mondial des Intellectuelles pour la Paix, Wroclaw – Pologne, 25-28 Aout 1948, Compte-rendu presenté pour le Bureau du Secretaire General* (Warsaw 1949). On the Congress of Cultural Freedom, see Frances Stonor Saunders, *The Cultural Cold War: The CIA and the World of Art and Letters* (New York 1999) and Giles Scott-Smith, *The Politics of Apolitical Culture: The Congress for Cultural Freedom, the CIA and post-war American hegemony* (London/New York 2002).

5

Donald D. Egbert, *Social Radicalism and the Arts – Western Europe: A Cultural History from the French Revolution to 1968* (London 1970), pp.340-46; Gertje R. Utley, *Picasso: The Communist Years* (New Haven/London 2000), pp.101-33.

6

Critical accounts of the Congress were published by Martin Kingsley in *The New Statesman and Nation* (4 September 1948, pp.187-8) and Julian Huxley in *The Spectator* (10 September 1948, pp.326-7), who later sharpened his negative opinion about the Congress in his memoirs, *Memories II* (Harmondsworth 1973), pp.57-9; for the most vitriolic attacks, see A.J.P. Taylor in the *Manchester Guardian* (1948), as well as in his autobiography, *A Personal History* (London 1983), and Kathleen Burk, *The Troublemaker* (London 2000), pp.191-5. See also J.M. Richards, *Memoirs of an Unjust Fella* (London 1980), pp.198-200. Many books refer to Taylor's account and Caute's interpretation as the major sources of information about the Congress: see C.H. Rolph, *Kingsley: The Life, Letters and Diaries of Kingsley Martin* (London 1973), pp.320-21; Scott-Smith 2002, pp.87, 93-4, and notes; John Jenks, 'Fight Against Peace? Britain and the Partisans of Peace, 1948-1951', in M.F. Hopkins and M.D. Kandiah (eds), *Cold War Britain, 1945-1962: New Perspectives* (Basingstoke 2003), p.57. According to the hegemonic discourse, the Wrocław Congress initiated the process which made 'peace a dirty word' (Jenks, op. cit., pp.53, 66).

7

For a detailed analysis of Picasso's reception in Poland, see Piotr Bernatowicz, 'Picasso w Polsce zaraz po wojnie', *Artium Quaestiones* (2000), no.11, pp.155-220, and for his reception in Eastern Europe in 1945-70, Piotr Bernatowicz, *Picasso za Żelazną Kurtyną: Recepcja artysty i jego sztuki w krajach Europy Środkowo-Wschodniej w latach 1945-1970* (Cracow 2006).

8

For information about the origins and the organization of the Congress, see Dominique Desanti, *Nous avons choisi la paix* (Paris 1949); Emmanuel Auricoste, 'Les artistes et la paix', *Arts de France*, nos 23-4 (1948), pp.63-4; Ivor Montagu, *What happened at Wroclaw*, preface by Dr J.G. Crowther (London 1949); Dominique Desanti, *Les Staliniens (1944-1956): une expérience politique* (Paris 1975), pp.94-124; Pierre Daix, *J'ai cru au matin* (Paris 1976), pp.217-51; Dominique Desanti, 'Sartre, une hyène dactylographe', in *Ce que le siècle m'a dit: Mémoires* (Paris 1997), pp.346-65; Pierre Daix, 'Le Congres de Wrocław', in *Tout mon temps: mémoires* (Paris 2001), pp.217-25; also Zygmunt Woźniczka, 'Wrocławski Kongres Intelektualistów w Obronie Pokoju', *Kwartalnik Historyczny*, vol.95, no.2 (1988), pp.131-57; Józef Laptos, 'Le pacifisme apprivoisé: Le congrès des intellectuels pour la défense de la paix en 1948', in M. Vaïsse, *Le pacifisme en Europe des années 1920 aux années 1950* (Brussels 1993), pp.325-38; Zygmunt Woźniczka, 'Pisarze polscy w Ruchu Obrońców Pokoju 1948-1956', in S. Zabierowski and M. Krakowiak (eds), *Realizm Socjalistyczny w Polsce z perspektywy 50 lat* (Katowice 2001), pp.27-49. I am grateful to Stanley Mitchell for sending me a manuscript of his unpublished paper 'The Wrocław Congress', given at the *Cold War Culture* conference held at University College, London, in 1994. For the World Peace Council and Peace Conference (Paris/Prague [1949], Sheffield/ Warsaw [1950], Vienna [1952], Helsinki [1955], Stockholm [1958]), see J. Ślusarczyk, *Powstanie i działalność ruchu obrońców pokoju w latach 1948-1957* (Wrocław 1987), and, in a British context, Lynda Morris, 'Painting Picasso Red', *The Guardian*, 12 September 1981, p.9; Ivor Montagu, 'The Peacemonger', in B. Swann and F. Aprahamian (eds), *J.D. Bernal: A Life in Science and Politics* (London/New York 1999), pp.212-34; and Andrew Brown, *J.D. Bernal: the sage of science* (Oxford 2005), pp.318-41, 412-34.

9

Norman Davies and Roger Moorhouse, *Microcosm: Portrait of a Central European City* (London 2003), pp.1-12.

10

Montagu 1999, p.218; Ivor Montagu was elected chairman of the British Peace Committee.

11

He also received Stalin Peace Prize awarded to him by the Second Peace Congress in Warsaw, in November 1950. Picasso's support of the Stalinist regime was to be harshly criticized by the Polish poet in exile Czesław Miłosz in an open letter to the artist, which was first published in June 1956 in *Preuves*, the French organ of the Congress for Cultural Freedom, and republished in American *Dissent* (Czesław Miłosz, 'A Letter to Picasso', *Digest*, vol.3, no.4 [autumn 1956] pp.340, 438-50), just before the outbreak of the Hungarian Revolution - and not, as claimed by virtually all authors referring to this letter - in response to it. For various accounts of Picasso's visit to Poland, see Mieczysław Bibrowski, *Picasso w Polsce* (Cracow 1979); Françoise Gilot and Carlton Lake, *Life with Picasso* (Harmondsworth 1966), pp.211-12; Dorota Folga-Januszewska, *Picasso – Przemiany*, National Museum in Warsaw (Warsaw 2002).

12

Le Corbusier belonged to the Polish-French organizational committee of the Congress; see Woźniczka 1988, p.137; his caricature, drawn by Mieczysław Piotrowski, was published in a weekly magazine *Kuźnica*, nos 34-5 (22-9 August 1948), p.32.

13

Desanti 1997, p.348.

14

For the Soviet assessment of the Congress, see Ilya Ehrenburg, 'The World Intellectuals Congress for Peace', *Novy'e Vremia*, no.38 (15 September 1948).

15

For the full list of British delegates see *Congrès Mondial des Intellectuelles pour la Paix* (1949), pp.215-16. Reports on the Wrocław Congress were published in Marxist journals *Our Time* (1948) and *Modern Quarterly* (see J. D. Bernal, 'Wroclaw and After', *Modern Quarterly*, vol.4, no.1 [winter 1949], pp.5-27), as well as in a brochure, *What happened in Wroclaw*, written by Ivor Montagu and published under the auspices of the newly established British Cultural Committee for Peace, with a solid bibliography of articles about the Congress which appeared in Britain and the Soviet Union (London 1949).

16

Kingsley Martin, 'Hyenas and other reptiles', *The New Statesman and Nation* (4 September 1948), pp.187-8; see also Peter Blackman, 'Letter to an English Intellectual', *The New Statesman and Nation*, vol.36, no.927 (11 December 1948), pp.519-20.

17

Feliks Topolski, 'Confessions of a Congress Delegate' (London 1948), republished with some omissions in Feliks Topolski, *Fourteen Letters* (London 1984).

18

Ironically, Topolski's book passed without notice in the mainstream British journals, but it received two reviews in *Our Time*: Peter Blackman, 'Delegate's Dilemma', *Our Time*, vol.8, no.3 (March 1949), pp.78-9, and Paul Hogarth, 'The Artist-Reporter', op. cit., p.79.

19

Frisch [1950] 1977, pp.206-23.

20

Ibid., pp.219-20.

21

For British impressions of the Exhibition of the Lands Regained, see J.G. Crowther, 'A New Unity is Born (1)', *Our Time*, vol.7, no.13 (October 1948), p.339; Martin 1948, pp.187-8; Richard Hughes, 'Polish Impressions', *The Spectator*, vol.181, no.6273 (17 September 1948), p.358; Montagu 1949, p.4; J.M. Richards in 'Round the Table: Round the World', *The Architects' Journal*, vol.109, no.2815 (20 January 1949), p.74. See also Frisch [1950] 1977, p.207. The most detailed account of the exhibition to date is given by Jakub Tyszkiewicz, *Sto wielkich dni Wrocławia: Wystawa Ziem Odzyskanych we Wrocławiu a propaganda polityczna ziem zachodnich i północnych w latach 1945-1948* (Wrocław 1997).

22

Hryniewiecki articulated his ideas on exhibition design in his article which, written on the occasion of the International Fairs in Poznań in July 1948, referred to the 'Exhibition of the Land Regained' as an experimental ground for testing those new ideas: 'In the same way in which Cassandre's poster exposed the masses to cubism, or advertisement slogans, widely used, popularized the language of futurism, exhibition design should win the working classes to the new architecture. To a degree, we will test those ideas at the Exhibition of the Lands Regained' (Jerzy Hryniewiecki, 'Język wystawy', *Katalog oficjalny Wystawy Ziem Odzyskanych* [Wrocław 1948], pp.2-3).

23

Bożena Kowalska, *Polska Awangarda Malarska 1945-1980: Szanse i mity* (Warsaw 1988), pp.62-4.

24

Jerzy Hryniewiecki, 'O naszym wystawiennictwie', *Projekt*, no.2 (1956), pp.20-35; on the survival of Modernism in studio crafts during the Stalinist period, see David Crowley, 'Stalinism and Modernist Craft in Poland', *Journal of Design History*, vol.11, no.1 (1998), pp.71-83.

25

For Guttuso at the Congress, see Desanti 1949, pp.111-14. His drawing *Le rovine di Wrocław ditto gridano al mondo: Pace!* was published in *L'Unità*, 28 October 1948. The Congress certainly helped to launch Guttuso's eventful Eastern European career: his articles legitimizing the unconditional demise of 'over-aesthetisized, elitist and mouldy' formalism for the sake of the courageous gesture of realism, served much better the Soviet understanding of 'anti-formalism' than the proposals of Picasso, Borejsza and Hryniewiecki. Guttuso won the Lenin Peace Prize twice, as well as other awards such as that of the Polish State given to him in Warsaw in 1951. He had a retrospective exhibition in the Zachęta Gallery in Warsaw and in Katowice in 1954. For more information, see recently Joanna Kordjak-Piotrowska, 'Wstęp', in *Andrzej Wróblewski 1927-1957*, National Museum in Warsaw (Warsaw 2007), p.80.

26

Christian Zervos, *Pablo Picasso*, vol.10: *Oeuvres de 1939 et 1940* (Paris 1959), no.158.

27

Jean Marcenac, 'Malarstwo francuskie na kongresie wrocławskim', *Odrodzenie*, vol.3, no.34 (1948): on the exhibition of French paintings in Wrocław and Warsaw, see Katarzyna Murawska-Muthesius, 'Paris from behind the Iron Curtain', in S. Wilson et al., *Paris: Capital of the Arts* (London 2002), pp.255-6.

28

Bernatowicz 2006, pp.193-200.

29

On the eclipse of Picasso's fame by Fougeron in Poland at the end of the 1940s and the beginning of the 1950s, see Katarzyna Murawska-Muthesius, 'How the West corroborated Socialist Realism in the East: Fougeron, Taslitzky and Picasso in Warsaw', *Biuletyn Historii Sztuki*, vol.65, no.2 (2003), pp.303-29.

30

Ibid.; on the turmoil created by the *Massacre of Korea* in America, see Serge Guilbaut, 'Postwar Painting Games: The Rough and the Slick', in S. Guilbaut (ed.), *Reconstructing Modernism: Art in New York, Paris, and Montreal 1945-1964* (Cambridge/London 1990), pp.69-73.

31

Hanna Onoszko, 'Dekoracje festiwalowe', *Przegląd Artystyczny*, nos 3-4 (1955), p.70; Bernatowicz 2006, pp.201-7.

32

According to the curators of the National Museum in Warsaw Joanna Kordjak and Anna Żakiewicz (verbal communication in August 2006 pointing to an unpublished diary of the Polish sculptor Stanisław Kulon), the copy of the *Massacre in Korea* was turned into a kind of shrine of the martyrdom of the Hungarian nation, with people lighting candles in the evenings, bringing flowers and collecting money for the victims of the Soviet aggression.

2 / EUROPE RECONSTRUCTED, EUROPE DIVIDED

1

Syrkus's oeuvre is reviewed in a long discussion of her career that occupies most of the July 1957 issue of *Architektura*. She was also the author of *Społeczne cele urbanizacji. Człowiek i środowisko* (Warszaw 1984). For an analysis of her speech see Hilde Heynen, 'The Jargon of Authenticity. Modernism and its (non)-political position', in Mart Kalm and Ingrid Ruudi (eds), *Constructed Happiness. Domestic environment in the Cold War Era* (Tallinn 2005), pp.10-27.

2

Helena Syrkus, '[Art Belongs to the People]', in Joan Ochman (ed.), *Architecture Culture 1943-1968* (New York 1993), p.120.

3

A. Zhdanov, speech delivered at a conference of representatives of a number of communist parties held in Poland in the latter part of September 1947. The speech was itself a response to Truman's declaration of 'Two Worlds'. See Geoffrey Roberts, *The Soviet Union in World Politics: Coexistence, Revolution and Cold War, 1945-1991* (London 1999), and 'Moscow and the Marshall Plan: Politics, Ideology and the Onset of the Cold War, 1947', *Europe-Asia Studies*, vol.46, no.8 (1994), pp.1371-86.

4

New Times (11 July 1947), cited in Richard B. Day (ed.), *Cold War Capitalism. The View from Moscow, 1945-1975* (New York 1995), p.50.

5

In December 1947, for instance, the editors of the British magazine *The Architectural Review* received an angry letter from the Soviet Embassy in London. Signed by three leading Russian architects, it accused the editors of making 'slanderous and groundless attacks on the whole of Soviet architecture and the Soviet people' in its reports of reconstruction in the Soviet Union.

6

Handbuch für Architekten, Hrsg. von der Deutschen Bauakademie (Berlin 1954), cited by Anders Åman, *Architecture and Ideology in Eastern Europe during the Stalin Era. An Aspect of Cold War History* (Cambridge, MA, 1992), p.251.

7

Karl Liebknecht, *Die nationalen Aufgaben der deutschen Architektur* (Berlin 1954).

8

Endre Prakfalvi, 'Sztálinváros. The paradigm of Stalinist Town planning in Hungary', *Ars*, 2-3 (1993), p.185. On another Stalin era new town, see Ruth May, 'Planned city Stalinstadt: a manifesto of the early German Democratic Republic', *Journal Planning Perspectives*, vol.18, issue 1 (January 2003), pp.47-78.

9

The last phase of Jiří Kroha's career in the Stalin years in Czechoslovakia is, for instance, put under the spotlight in Marcela Macharáčková (ed.), *Jiří Kroha (1893-1974) - architekt, malíř, designer, teoretik- v proměnách umění 20. Století* (Brno 2007).

10

Eric Mumford offers an excellent discussion of the attitudes expressed at Bergamo (and their subsequent reporting in the years that followed). See *The CIAM Discourse on Urbanism, 1928-1960* (Boston, MA, 2000), pp.179-97.

11

Ernesto Nathan Rogers, 'Ricostruzione: dall'oggetto d'uso alla città, Conferenza tenuta a Zurigo il 3 novembre 1946 per invito dello Schweizerischer Werkbund', *Domus*, no.215 (November 1946), pp.2-5.

12

For an excellent study of debates about monuments and reconstruction in post-Second World War Germany see Rudi Koshar, *From Monuments to Traces: Artifacts of German Memory, 1870-1990* (Berkley, CA, 2000), pp.143-224; and for the case of the Polish capital, see David Crowley, *Warsaw* (London 2003), chap.1.

13

See Philip Ursprung, 'Continuity: Max Bill's public sculpture and the representation of money', in Charlotte Benton (ed.), *Figuration/Abstraction: strategies for Public Sculpture in Europe 1945-1968* (London 2004), pp.236-7.

14

Reuben Fowkes, 'Soviet War Memorials in Eastern Europe', in Benton 2004, pp.11-33; Sergiusz Michalski, *Public Monuments: Art in Political Bondage 1870-1997* (London 1998), pp.126-7; Michael Ignatieff, 'Soviet War Memorials', *History Workshop Journal*, vol.17, no.1 (1984), pp.157-63

15

Hans Gunther (ed.), *The Culture of the Stalin Period* (New York 1990); David Crowley and Susan E. Reid (eds), *Socialist Spaces. Sites of Everyday Life in the Eastern Bloc* (Oxford 2003); Christel Lane, *The Rites or Rulers? Ritual in Industrial Society: the Soviet Case* (Cambridge 1981).

16

For discussion of the 'totalitarian paradigm' in political discourse see Achim Segal (ed.), *The Totalitarian Paradigm After the End of Communism* (Amsterdam 1998).

17

Gregor Paulsson, in a contribution to a symposium entitled 'In Search of A New Monumentality', published in *Architectural Review* (September 1948), pp.123. Others invited included Henry-Russell Hitchcock, William Holford, Sigfried Giedion, Walter Gropius, Lucio Costa and Alfred Roth.

18

Ibid., p.126. Giedion's article had in fact already been given as a lecture at RIBA, London, in July 1946.

19

On Socialist Realism in Soviet architecture see Boris Groys, *The Total Art of Stalinism* (Princeton, NJ, 1993); Alexei Tarkhanov and Sergei Kavtaradze, *Stalinist Architecture* (London 1992); Catherine Cooke, 'Socialist-Realist Architecture', in Matthew Cullerne Bown and Brandon Taylor (eds), *Art of the Soviets. Painting, sculpture and architecture in a one-party state, 1917-1992* (Manchester 1993); Catherine Cooke, 'Beauty as a Route to "the Radiant Future": Responses of Soviet Architecture', *Journal of Design History*, vol.10, no.2, pp.137-60.

20

Tarkhanov and Kavtaradze, *Stalinist Architecture* (London 1992), pp.120-32.

21

The scheme was not abandoned during the war (Iofan's studio was evacuated to Sverdlovsk, where it continued work on the Palace) and was being discussed as late as 1956. See Tarkhanov and Kavtaradze 1992, p.118.

22

Henri Lefebvre, *The Production of Space* (Oxford 1991), p.361.

23

See Sarah Bradford Landau and Carl W. Condit, *Rise of the New York Skyscraper* (New Haven, CT/London 1996), pp.381-91.

24

See Sona S. Hoisington, 'Soviet Schizophrenia and the American Skyscraper', in Rosalind P. Blakesley and Susan E. Reid (eds), *Russian Art and the West. A Century of Dialogue in Painting, Architecture, and the Decorative Arts* (Deklab 2006), pp.166-8.

25

Edmund Goldzamt, *Architektura Zespołów Śródmiejskich I Problemy Dziedzictwa* (Warsaw 1956), pp.329-30.

26

This point was illustrated, somewhat oddly, by Goldzamt with the Secretariat Block of the United Nations Headquarters of 1947-53. It was perhaps chosen because it was the first major post-war office building to use a full-height curtain wall suspended off the structure.

27

Goldzamt 1956, p.331.

28

Pavel Halík, 'Architektura padesátých let', in Rostislav Švácha and Marie Platovská (eds), *Dějiny českého výtvarného umění 1939-1958* (Prague 2005) pp.295-9. See also Radomíra Sedláková, 'Sorela. Česká architektura padesátých Let', in *Sorela*, exh. cat. (Prague 1994).

29

See T. Toranska, *Oni* (London 1987) pp.305-6.

30

Stolica (22 February 1953), p.2.

31

Anon., 'Odwiedziny u budowniczych Palacu', *Stolica* (1 November 1953), p.7.

32

The best source on the Sovietization of Central European architecture remains Anders Åman, *Architecture and Ideology in Eastern Europe during the Stalin Era. An Aspect of Cold War History* (Cambridge, MA, 1992).

33

See David Crowley, 'Paris or Moscow? Warsaw Architects and the Image of the Modern City in the 1950s', *Kritika* (forthcoming); Werner Durth, Jörn Düvel and Niels Gutschow, *Ostkreuz: Personen, Pläne, Perspektiven: Architektur und Städtebau der DDR*, vol.1 (Frankfurt 1998), pp.142-73.

34

Stefan Muthesius, 'International Modernism or National Style. Warsaw Architecture of the early 20th century', *Architectural History* (2000), pp.233-50.

35

Stanisław Jankowski (ed.), *MDM. Marszałkowska 1730-1954* (Warsaw 1955).

36
Greg Castillo, 'Henselmann and the Architecture of German Socialist Realism', *Slavonica*, vol.11, no.1 (April 2005), p.36.

37
An important exception was the Hauptstadt Plan competition announced by Berlin Senate in 1957, which provocatively ignored the East-West divide, much to the anger of the East German authorities. See Stephen Rosenberg, 'Berlin and the "Hauptstadt Berlin" Competition', *Architect's Yearbook*, no.9 (1960), pp.68-94.

38
'Sixteen Principles for the Restructuring of Cities', in Ochman 1993, p.128.

39
See 'New Berlin Strike reported Planned', *New York Times* (8 July 1953), p.6.

40
See Jean-Louis Cohen and Hubert Damisch, *Scenes of the World to Come: European Architecture and the American Challenge, 1893–1960* (Paris/Montreal 1995).

41
For a discussion of the use of international tours to 're-educate' German architects, see Greg Castillo, 'Design Pedagogy Enters the Cold War. The Reeducation of Eleven West German Architects', *Journal of Architectural Education* (May 2004) pp.10-18.

42
Michel Écochard, cited in Cohen and Damisch 1995, p.171.

43
Op. cit., p. 164.

44
Hans Ibelings (ed.), *Americanism: Dutch Architecture and the Transatlantic Model* (Rotterdam 1997), p.28.

45
Dennis Doordan, 'The Curious Case of Frank Lloyd Wright and American Cultural Diplomacy in the early Cold War Era', lecture, Victoria and Albert Museum, London, January 2007.

46
Edgar Kaufmann, Jr, *What is Modern Design?* (New York 1950), p.8. Kaufmann's views were contested by other influential commentators, not least Elizabeth Gordon, editor of *House Beautiful*, who wrote: '[If] we can be sold on accepting dictators in matters of taste and how our homes are to be ordered, our minds are certainly well prepared to accept dictators in other departments of life ... So you see, this well-developed movement has social implications because it affects the heart of our society – the home. Beyond the nonsense of trying to make us want to give up our ... conveniences for what is supposed to be a better and more serene life, there is a threat of total regimentation and total control' ('The Threat to the Next America', *House Beautiful* [April 1953], pp.126-31). I would like to thank Greg Castillo for this reference.

47
See Adrian von Buttlar, '"Germanic" Structure Versus "American" Texture in German High-rise Building', *German Historical Institute Bulletin Supplement*, vol.2 (2005), p.78.

48
Paolo Scrivano, 'Signs of Americanization in Italian Domestic Life: Italy's Postwar Conversion to Consumerism', *Journal of Contemporary History*, vol.40 (April 2005), pp.321-2.

49
Exceptions include the architecture of American diplomacy. SOM built the American consulates in Bremen and Düsseldorf employing glass façades, an architectural language that was associated with transparency and democracy in West German architectural discourse. See Deborah Ascher Barnstone, *The Transparent State. Architecture and Politics in Postwar Germany* (London 2005).

50
Annabel Jane Wharton, *Building the Cold War: Hilton International Hotels and Modern Architecture* (Chicago 2001), p.35.

51
Le Corbusier, *The Modulor* (London 1951), p.52.

52
Marcel Lods, 'Retour d'Amérique' (1946), in Ochman 1993, p.81.

53
See Paul Damaz, 'Quelques nouvelles techniques de construction aux Etats Unis', *L'Architecture d'Aujourd'hui* (December 1953), pp.134-56.

54
Alexander Sedlmaier, 'Berlin's Europa-Center (1963-65): Americanization, Consumerism, and the Uses of the International Style', *German Historical Institute Bulletin Supplement*, vol.2 (2005), pp.87-100.

55
See Tim Benton, 'Unité d'Habitation, Marseilles', in *Le Corbusier, Architect of the Century*, exh. cat., Hayward Gallery (London 1987), pp.220-22.

56
These elevated 'streets' were not very successful. The delivery of supplies was difficult and the shopkeepers complained about the lack of trade. See D. Tomkinson, 'The Marseilles experiment', *Town Planning Review*, vol.25 (1953-4), p.208.

57
Kenneth Frampton, *Modern Architecture. A Critical History* (London 1980), p.227.

58
Jean-Louis Cohen, *Le Corbusier and the Mystique of the USSR* (Princeton, NJ, 1992).

59
See Victor Buchli, *An Archaeology of Socialism* (Oxford 1999).

60
Le Corbusier 1951, p.52.

61
Ibid., p.123.

62
Reyner Banham credits this term to Le Corbusier in *The New Brutalism* (London 1966), p.16.

63
Simon Richards, *Le Corbusier and the Concept of the Self* (New Haven 2003), pp.254-5, note 37.

64
William J.R. Curtis, *Le Corbusier: Ideas and Forms* (London 1992), p.164.

65
Max Bill, contribution to plenary session of 7th CIAM congress (29 July 1949), reproduced in *Documents: 7 CIAM Bergamo* (Neneln 1979), p.9.

66
Ibid.

67
Charles Jencks, *Modern Movements in Architecture* (Harmondsworth 1973), p.15.

68
Ibid., p.18.

69
Manfredo Tafuri, *Modern Architecture*, vol.2 (Milan 1976), p.317.

70
Le Corbusier 1951, p.123.

71
I am indebted to Joe Kerr for making this observation with regard to post-war London.

72
Henry-Russell Hitchcock, cited in 'In Search of A New Monumentality. A Symposium', *Architectural Review* (September 1948), p.119.

73
Wim Beeren et al., '1947-1957: Ten years of "Opbouw"', in *Het Nieuwe Bouwen in Rotterdam 1920-1960* (Delft 1982), p.147.

74
Cornelius Wagenaar, 'Jaap Bakema and the Fight for Freedom', in Sarah Williams Goldhagen and Réjean Legault (eds), *Anxious Modernisms: Experimentation in Postwar Architectural Culture* (Cambridge, MA, 2000), pp.261-78.

75
Barry Curtis, 'The Heart of the City', in Jonathan Hughes and Simon Sadler (eds), *Non-plan: Essays on Freedom, Participation and Change in Modern Architecture and Urbanism* (London 1999), p.52.

76
See Sarah Williams Goldhagen, 'Freedom's Domiciles: Three Projects by Alison and Peter Smithson', in Goldhagen and Legault 2000, pp.79-83. More generally on Team 10 see Max Risselada and Dirk van den Heuvel (eds.), *Team 10, 1953–1981: In Search of a Utopia of the Present* (Rotterdam 2005).

77
Max Bill (ed.), *Le Corbusier and P. Jeanneret. Oeuvre complète 1934-38* (Zurich 1939).

78
'Die Mathematische denkweise in der kunst unserer zeit', *Das Werk*, no.3 (1949), reproduced in Eduard Hüttingered (ed.), *Max Bill* (Zurich 1978), pp.105-17.

79
Max Bill, 'Concrete Art' (1936), in *Max Bill*, exh. cat. (Buffalo 1974), p.47.

80
Max Bill, 'A Monument' (1952), in Hüttinger 1978, p.118.

81
Herbert Read, 'Introduction', *International Sculpture Competition: The Unknown Political Prisoner* (London 1953), p.1.

82
Bill, 'A Monument' (1952), in Hüttinger 1978, p.122.

83
Bill, 'Die Mathematische denkweise...', in Hüttinger 1978, p.108.

84
Bill cited in Godehard Janzing, 'National division as a formal problem in West German public sculpture: Memorials to German unity in Münster and Berlin', in Benton 2004, p.129.

85
For overviews of the development of Interbau, see Stefanie Schulz and Carl-Georg Schulz, *Das Hansaviertel – Ikone der Moderne. 50 Jahre Interbau* (Berlin 2007); Frank-Manuel Peter, *Das Berliner Hansaviertel und die Interbau 1957* (Erfurt 2007); Gabi Dolff-Bonekämper and Franziska Schmidt, *Das Hansaviertel. Internationale Nachkriegsmoderne*

the Italian Fashion Industry (New York 2000).

47
Robert Lumley, *States of Emergency, Cultures of Revolt in Italy from 1968-78* (London 1990), Part 1: *Origins of the Crisis of 1968-9*, pp.9-46.

48
Lumley 1990.

49
The history of the Italian Radical Design Movement has been documented by one of its chief protagonists, Andrea Branzi, in his book *The Hot House: Italian New Wave Design* (London 1984). See p.78.

50
Included in David Riesman, *Abundance for What? And Other Essays* (New York 1964).

51
De Grazia 2005.

52
The practices of streamlining in design and product obsolescence also came under attack in the USA, with designers such as George Nelson protesting against 'superficial' design practices. For a discussion of this see Stanley Abercrombie and George Nelson, *The Design of Modern Design* (Cambridge, MA, 1995), chap.3. Loewy's autobiography, *Never Leave Well Enough Alone* (New York 1950), was translated into German in 1952, entitled *Häßlichkeit verkauft sich schlecht* ('Ugliness Doesn't' Sell'). Betts 2004, p.87.

53
Raymond Loewy, *Never Leave Well Enough Alone*, rev. edn 2002, Introduction by Glenn Porter; quoted, p.xxiv.

54
See Greg Castillo, *Cold War on the Home Front: Midcentury Design in the Service of Cultural Revolution* (Minneapolis, forthcoming).

55
The idea was indebted to the early activities of the German Werkbund, and had parallels with Max Bill's concept of 'Gute Form'. See Terence Riley and Edward

Eigen, 'Between the Museum and the Marketplace: Selling Good Design', in John Elderfield (ed.), *The Museum of Modern Art at Mid-Century At Home and Abroad*, Studies in Modern Art, vol.4n(New York 1994), pp.150-79.

56
Summary of French Press Reactions to '50 Ans d'Art aux Etats-Unis', 1 May 1956, p.8, Museum of Modern Art Archives: IC/IP Exh. Records (ICE-F-24-54: Paris): Box 11.1. Quoted in Helen M. Franc, 'The Early Years of the International Program and Council', in Elderfield 1994, p.126, n.60. For an account of the exhibition in France, see also Gay McDonald, 'Selling the American Dream: MoMA, Industrial Design and Post-War France', *Journal of Design History* vol.17, no.4 (2004), pp.397-412.

57
The Eames worked with the Evans Products Company on the military contract, which also led to the development of several other experimental applications, such as a stretcher and plywood pilot seats. For an account of the Eames plywood experiments, see Pat Kirkham, *Charles and Ray Eames: Designers of the Twentieth Century* (Cambridge, MA, 1998), pp.203-21.

58
Donald Albrecht et al., *The Work of Charles and Ray Eames: A Legacy of Invention* (New York 1997), p.86.

59
A programme of experimental private housing instigated by John Entenza, editor of *Arts and Architecture* magazine, in 1945. The houses were widely known in Europe through journals. See Reyner Banham, 'Klarheit, Ehrlichkeit, Einfachkeit ... and Wit Too! The Case Study Houses in the World's Eyes', in Elizabeth A. T. Smith (ed.), *Blueprints for Modern Living, History and Legacy of the Case Study Houses* (Cambridge, MA, 1999) pp.183-95.

60
B. Colomina, *Domesticity at War* (Cambridge, MA, 2007), pp.30-31.

61
Kirkham 1998, p.113.

62
See Castillo in this book, p.67.

63
Betts 2004, p.99.

64
The theme of transparency and architecture in relation to German architecture is discussed in Deborah Ascher Barnstone, *The Transparent State: Architecture and Politics in Postwar German.* (London/New York 2005).

65
Paul Betts discusses the concept of 'honest living' in Betts 2004, p.191.

66
'The German Section at the 1958 Brussels Expo', news release, no.17 (undated, unpaginated).

67
These critical voices came together in the planning of a major exhibition (and accompanying publication) of Italian design at MoMA in 1972. For example, see Alessandro Mendini, 'The Land of Good Design', in Emilio Ambasz (ed.), *Italy: The New Domestic Landscape* (New York/Florence 1972), pp.370-89.

68
I am indebted to the recent scholarship by Greg Castillo and Paul Betts on West German modernism and the Ulm school in particular. See Betts 2004; Greg Castillo, 'The Bauhaus in Cold War Germany', in Kathleen James-Chakraborty, *Bauhaus Culture: from Weimar to the Cold War* (Minneapolis 2006).

69
Betts 2004, p.146.

70
René Spitz, *hfg ulm, The view behind the Foreground: The political history of the Ulm School of Design, 1953-1968* (Fellbach 2002). pp.60-63.

71
Scholl published an account of the group's activities in 1952. Inge Scholl, *Students Against Tyranny: The Resistance of the White Rose, Munich, 1942-3*

(rev. edn, Middletown, CT, 1970).

72
Inge Scholl was also imprisoned, over eighty members were eventually taken into custody and there were three further executions.

73
Max Bill, *Form: A Balance-Sheet of Mid-Twentieth-Century Trends in Design* (Basel 1952); and Max Bill, *Die Gute Form* (Wintherthur 1957).

74
An early, important interpretation of Ulm was offered by Kenneth Frampton, 'Apropos Ulm: Curriculum and Critical Theory', *Oppositions*, vol.3 (1974). Significant studies have been written by former staff and students, including Herbert Lindinger (ed.), *Ulm: die Moral der Gegestände*, exh. cat., Bauhaus Archive, Berlin; Centre Pompidou, Paris, Wilhelm Ernst & Sohn (Berlin 1987) and Heiner Jacob, 'HfG Ulm: A Personal View of an Experiment in Democracy and Design Education', *Journal of Design History*, vol.1, no.3/4 (1988), pp.221-34. More recent analyses have explored the wider political context, namely Spitz 2002, Betts 2004, Castillo, 2006.

75
For discussion of McCloy's involvement with the school, see Castillo in Kathleen James-Chakraborty 2006, pp.182-8, and Betts 2004, pp.144-5. See also Thomas Alan Schwartz, *America's Germany: John J. McCloy and the Federal Republic of Germany* (Cambridge,MA, 1991).

76
This phrase was used by Otl Aicher in 1948, quoted in Betts 2004, p.144 and p.294, note 33. Rathgeb discusses the use of the terms 'spiritual Marshall Plan' and 'spiritual ERP' in various documents by Scholl and Aicher of 1949. Rathgeb, 2006, pp.70-71.

77
Castillo discusses Gropius' intervention, and quotes a letter from Bill to McCloy, distancing the school from any taint of communist sympathy. Castillo, in James-Chakraborty 2006, pp.184-5.

78
Paul Betts has observed that when Gropius addressed students protesting the school's closure in 1968 (when they attempted to compare it to the Nazi closure of the Bauhaus), he urged them not to mix design education with politics: Betts 2004, pp.250-51.

79
Max Bill, letter to McCloy, 15 April 1952, quoted in Markus Rathgeb, *Otl Aicher* (London 2006), p.43.

80
Spitz 2002.

81
Quoted in Betts 2004, p.162.

82
This took place at the Milan Triennale of 1954, and in correspondence between the two. For discussion of the debate, see Joan Ockman (ed.), *Architecture Culture 1943-1968: A Documentary Anthology* (New York 1993), pp.172-5; Guy Atkins, *Asger Jorn 1986, The Crucial Years, 1954-64*, vol.3 (London 1986).

83
Asger Jorn, *Notes on the Formation of An Imaginist Bauhaus*, trans. Ken Knabb (1957): see Situationist International Online, www.cddc.vt.edu/sionline/presitu/bauhaus.html.

84
Leaflet, quoted in Nathalie Aubert, '"Cobra after Cobra" and the Alba Congress: From Revolutionary Avant-Garde to Situationist Experiment', *Third Text* , vol.20, no.2, p.264.

85
Asger Jorn, *Opening Speech to the First World Congress of Free Artists in Alba, Italy (September 1956)*, trans., Thomas Y. Levin: see Situationist International Online, www.cddc.vt.edu/sionline/presitu/opening.html.

86
Castillo in James-Chakraborthy 2006, pp.186-7.

87
Betts 2004, pp.167-77.

88
Spitz 2002, pp.302-97.

89
Quoted in Rathgeb 2006, p.73.
See Claude Schnaidt, 'Architecture and Political Comment', *Ulm*, vol.19, no.20 (1967), pp.26-34.

90
Rathgeb 2006, pp.72-5.

91
Edgar Kaufmann, *What is Modern Design?* (New York 1950), p.8.

Cold War Front Lines: The Architecture of Defence

1
Tom Vanderbilt, *Survival City: Adventures among the Ruins of Atomic America* (New York 2002).

2
Ibid., p.39.

3
Lewis Mumford, *From the Ground Up* (New York 1956), p.164, quoted in Vanderbilt 2002, p.16.

4
See also Sarah A. Lichtman, 'Do-It-Yourself Security: Safety, Gender, and the Home Fallout Shelter in Cold War America', *Journal of Design History*, vol.19, no.1 (2006), p.39.

5
Vanderbilt 2002, pp.17-18. For more on the architectural firm SOM, see Richard Gid Powers, 'The Cold War in the Rockies: American Ideology and the Air Force Academy Design', *Art Journal*, vol.33, no.4 (summer 1974), pp.304-13.

6
The Manhattan Project was America's nuclear weapons research and development programme that had been initiated at the end of the 1930s and climaxed in the explosions over Hiroshima and Nagasaki. It was so named because Manhattan was the first home of what later became an extensive and secret network of atomic cities - i.e., secret research and production sites - across the USA.

7
'Atom City', *The Architectural Forum* (October 1945), p.103.

See also '"Atom City": Oak Ridge, Tennessee', *Builder* (April 1946), pp.404-8; George Anderson, 'America's no.1 Defense Community: Oak Ridge, Tennessee', *Progressive Architecture* (June 1951), pp.63-84.

8
See F. Robert Naka and William W. Ward, 'Distant-Early-Warning Line Radars: The Quest for Automatic Signal Detection', *Lincoln Laboratory Journal*, no.2 (2000), p.1.

9
See *The Dew Line Story: Western Electric Company*, n.d., in P. Withney Lackenbauer, Matthew J. Farish and Jennifer Arthur-Lackenbauer, *The Distant Earl Warning (DEW) Line: A Bibliography and Documentary Resources List* (Calgary 2005).

10
Martin Pawley, *Buckminster Fuller* (London 1990), p.132.

11
Alex Soojung-Kim Pang, 'Dome days', in Francis Spufford and Jenny Uglow (eds), *Cultural Babbage. Technology, Time and Invention* (London/Boston 1996), p.168.

12
Pawley 1990, p.138.

13
Felicity D. Scott, 'Media Ecology', in Eava-Liisa Pelkonen and Esa Laaksonen (eds), *Architecture + Art: New Visions, New Strategies* (Helsinki 2007), p.147.

14
Felicity D. Scott, 'Acid Visions', *Grey Room*, no.23 (spring 2006) pp.22-39.

15
See Caroline Maniaque, 'Hard French versus Soft America: Les alternatives nord-américaines vues de France', *Les Cahiers de la recherche architecturale et urbaine* (Paris 2002), pp.37-48.

16
See Caroline Maniaque, 'Walter Bird', in Antoine Picon (ed.), *L'art de l'ingénieur* (Paris 1997), p.84, and Caroline Maniaque, 'In Search of Lightness', in Marie-Eve Mestre (ed.), *Celebrating Air-Air, Monaco* (Monaco 2000), pp.118-49.

17
Roger N. Dent, *Principles of Pneumatic Architecture* (London 1971), pp.178-9.

18
Richard Hewlett and Jack M. Holl, *Atoms for Peace and War 1953-1961. Eisenhower and the Atomic Energy Commission* (Berkeley 1989), p.565.

19
Ibid., p.565.

20
Dent 1971, p.44.

21
Walter Bird, 'Air Structures - Early Development and Outlook', *LSA (Lightweight Structures in Architecture)*, no.86 (Sydney 1986), Proceedings, vol.1, pp.545-63.

22
See Michel Guillou, 'La technologie américaine à Pleumeur-Bodou, ou la rencontre d'une ambition nationale avec des projets internationaux', *Coloquium Pierre Mazin*, Pleumeur-Bodou (13 October 2005).

23
A darker legacy of the DEW line that surfaced after the handover to Canadian custody was the question of what would be done with the abandoned stations. Fierce political controversy raged over whether the United States or Canada was responsible for the clean-up and dismantling of the stations. Finally an agreement was reached in 1996, with the United States contributing $100 million toward the clean-up. Meanwhile, proposals have been made to preserve at least one DEW line station intact as a museum. See Mark Wolverton, 'The DEW Line', *Invention and Technology Magazine*, vol.22, issue 4 (spring 2007).

24
See, for example, 'The DEW Line Sites in Canada, Alaska and Greenland', http://www.lswilson.ca/dewline.htm (date of consultation 3 March 2007).

4 / THE BOMB IN THE BRAIN

1
The first Soviet nuclear test, of a plutonium bomb code-named 'First Lightening', was on 29 August 1949. In the West it was nicknamed 'Joe-1' after Josef Stalin.

2
Rosalind J. Marsh, 'Soviet Fiction and the Nuclear Debate', *Soviet Studies*, vol.38, no.2 (April 1986), p.252.

3
The phrase is actually a mistranslation from the Hindu Scripture. Oppenheimer recalled how the quotation had occurred to him in a documentary for US television made in 1965. There is no evidence he spoke these words at the time.

4
Speech given to the General Assembly of the United Nations on the peaceful uses of atomic energy, 8 December 1953 (www.atomicarchive.com/Docs/Deterrence/Atomsforpeace.shtml, accessed 13 September 2007).

5
For a history of Eisenhower's initiative and the formation of the Atomic Energy Agency, see David Fischer, *History of the International Atomic Agency, The First Forty Years* (Vienna 1997).

6
For an exploration of the impact of atomic imagery on American art and design, see B.K. Rapaport and K.L. Stayton, *Vital Forms: American Art and Design in the Atomic Age, 1940-1960* (New York 2001). The architecture of the Brussels Expo is explored in R. Devos and M. de Kooning, *L'Architecture Moderne a L'Expo 58 'Pour un Monde Plus Humain'* (Brussels 2006).

7
Steven Heller, *Design Literacy: Understanding Graphic Design* (New York 1999), pp.419-21.

8
Peter B. Hales, 'The Atomic Sublime', *American Studies*, no.32 (spring 1991), pp.5-31.

9
Time published the Alamogordo photographs on 17 August 1945, and *Life* magazine included colour images on 19 November 1945.

10
Only when the exhibition was transferred on its tour to Tokyo was Steichen persuaded to include photographs of atomic bomb victims. Even then, their inclusion caused public consternation, and such images were either concealed or removed during visits by the Japanese imperial family. Tessa Morris-Suzuki, *The Past Within Us: Media, Memory, History* (New York 2005), pp.114-15.

11
Kenneth D. Rose, *One Nation, Underground: A History of the Fallout Shelter* (New York 2001).

12
Enrico Baj, quoted in Tristram Sauvage (aka Arturo Schwartz), *Nuclear Art* (Gallery Schwartz, Milan), trans. John A. Stephens (Milan 1962), p.19.

13
Jackson Pollock, in a 1951 radio interview, quoted in Rapaport and Stayton 2001, pp.82-3.

14
Stephen Petersen, 'Explosive Propositions: Artists React to the Atomic Age', *Science in Context*, vol.17, no.4 (2004), pp.579-609.

15
Petersen 2004, p.591.

16
Sauvage 1962, p.30.

17
Interplanetary Art (Naples, January 1959), quoted in Sauvage 1962, p.211.

18
The observations were made by the critic Lisa Ponti, daughter of Gio. Petersen 2004, p.591.

19
Peter Galison, 'War Against the Center', *Grey Room*, no.4 (summer 2001), pp.5-33.

20
Michael Quinn Dudley, 'Sprawl as Strategy: City Planners Face the Bomb', *Journal of Planning*

26
Alec Nove, *Stalinism and After* (London 1975), p.142.

27
See Blair A. Ruble, 'From khrushcheby to korobki', in William Craft Brumfield and Blair A. Ruble (eds), *Russian Housing in the Modern Age: Design and Social History* (Cambridge 1995), pp.232–70; Susan E. Reid, 'Khrushchev Modern: Agency and Modernization in the Soviet Home', *Cahiers du Monde Russe*, vol.47, nos 1–2 (2006), pp.227–68.

28
Cf. Radomíra Sedláková's introductory essay to *Sorela. Česká architektura padesátych let*, exh. cat., Národní Galerie (Prague 1994), pp.5–19.

29
Architects were organized into large centralized architectural offices. For instance, two major offices operated in Prague in the 1960s (Stavoprojekt 1 serving the capital and Stavoprojekt 2 for all schemes in Central Bohemia).

30
Anna Minta, 'The Authority of the Ordinary: Building Socialism and the Ideology of Domestic Space in East Germany's Furniture Industry', in Mart Kalm and Ingrid Ruudi, *Constructed Happiness. Domestic Environment in the Cold War* (Tallinn 2005), p.114.

31
See Jan Pańkowski, 'Meble do małych mieszkań', *Wiadomość IWP*, vols 3–4 (1963), pp.12–25; Danuta Wróblewska, 'Nowe typy umeblowania', in *Projekt*, vol.2 (February 1963), pp.9–11.

32
Raymond Hutchings, 'The Weakening of Ideological Influences upon Soviet Design', *Slavic Review*, vol.27, no.1. (March 1968), p.84.

33
Václav Havel, 'Stories and Totalitarianism', in *Open Letters. Selected Prose 1965–1990* (London 1990), p.343.

34
András Ferkai, *Housing Estates* (Budapest 2005), pp.55–8.

35
Robert Vincent Daniels, *The Rise and Fall of Communism in Russia* (New Haven 2007), p.341.

36
See Michael Mastanduno, *Economic Containment: CoCom and the Politics of East–West Trade* (Ithaca 1992).

37
J.D. Parks, *Culture, Conflict and Co-Existence: American-Soviet Relations, 1917–1958* (Jefferson, NC, 1983), pp.172–3; see also David Caute, *The Dancer Defects. The Struggles for Cultural Supremacy during the Cold War* (Oxford 2003).

38
See Rósa Magnúsdóttir, '"Be Careful in America, Premier Khrushchev!": Soviet perceptions of peaceful coexistence with the United States in 1959', *Cahiers du Monde Russe*, vol.47, nos 1–2 (2006), pp.108–30.

39
Antony C. Sutton, *Western Technology and Soviet Economic Development, 1930 to 1945* (Stanford, CA, 1971), pp.411–15.

40
Karal Ann Marling, *As Seen on TV: The Visual Culture of Everyday Life in the 1950s* (Cambridge, MA, 1993), p.254.

41
'Od Redakcji', in *Projekt*, no.1 (May–June, 1956), p.2.

42
Andreï Ikonnikov, *L'architecture russe de la période soviétique* (Moscow 1990), p.290.

43
See Susan E. Reid, 'Khrushchev's Children's Paradise: The Pioneer Palace, Moscow, 1958–1962', in Crowley and Reid 2002, pp.141–81.

44
Anon., 'Supersam w Warszawie', in *Architektura*, vol.9 (September 1962), pp.343–9.

45
Jan Michl, *Institutional Framework Around Successful Art Forms in Communist Czechoslovakia* (Budapest 1999), p.5.

46
Reid 2002, p.162.

47
Ulbricht cited by Paul Betts, 'The Twilight of the Idols: East German Memory and Material Culture', *Journal of Modern History*, vol.72, no. 3 (September 2000), p.756.

48
Raymond G. Stokes, *Constructing Socialism: Technology and Change in East Germany, 1945–1990* (Baltimore/London 2000), p.85.

49
Judd Stitziel, *Fashioning Socialism: Clothing, Politics and Consumer Culture in East Germany* (Oxford/New York 2005), p.46.

50
Stokes 2000, p.86.

51
Eli Rubin, 'Plastics and Dictatorship in the German Democratic Republic: Towards an Economic, Consumer, Design, and Cultural History', *German Historical Institute Bulletin*, vol.38 (spring 2006), p.92. See also E. Rubin, 'The Form of Socialism without Ornament Consumption, Ideology, and the Fall and Rise of Modernist Design in the German Democratic Republic', *Journal of Design History*, vol.19, no.2 (2006) pp.155–68; and 'The Order of Substitutes: Plastic Consumer Goods in the Volkswirtschaft and Everyday Domestic Life in the GDR', in David Crew (ed.), *Consuming Germany in the Cold War* (Oxford/New York 2003), pp.87–121.

52
Redeker cited in Stokes in Reid and Crowley 2000, p.75.

53
This discussion is indebted to Hein Köster, 'Schmerzliche Ankunft in der Moderne. Industriedesign auf der V. Deutschen Kunstausstellung', in *Neue Gesellschaft für Bildende Kunst, Wunderwirtschaft. DDR-Konsumkultur in den 60er Jahren* (Cologne/Weimar/Vienna 1996), pp.96–103.

54
See David Bathrick, *The Powers of Speech. The Politics of Culture in the GDR*, (Lincoln, NE, 1995), pp.109–28.

55
'Vasen, Röhren und Ideologie, Volksaussprache zum VI. Parteitag der SED', *Neues Deutschland* (4 January 1963), p.3. Eli Rubin has shown that similar enthusiasms for modernist design were expressed by the public in defiance of criticisms of 'formalism' published in the East German press. See Rubin 2006, pp.93–4.

56
Colin Chant, 'Cars, contexts and identities: the Volkswagen and the Trabant', in Mark Pittaway (ed.), *Globalization and Europe* (Milton Keynes 2000), p.222.

57
Raymond Stokes, in Reid and Crowley 2000, p.72.

58
Jonathan Zatlin, 'The vehicle of desire: the Trabant, the Wartburg, and the end of the GDR', *German History*, vol.15, no.3 (1997), pp.358–80.

59
George Nelson, 'Obsolesence', in *Industrial Design*, vol.6 (1956), p.82.

60
Numerous commentators identified the problem of unwanted and unconsumed goods filling the shelves of stores. See, for instance, Radio Free Europe research report, 'New Pricing System for Hungarian Goods' (24 August 1965), p.2 - OSA archives.

61
On the formation of these bodies see David Crowley, '"Beauty, everyday and for all" – The Social Vision of Design in Stalinist Poland', in Judy Attfield (ed.), *Utility Reassessed* (Manchester 1999), pp.58–72; Gyula Ernyey, *Made in Hungary* (Budapest 1993), p.194; Dmitry Azrikan, 'VNIITE, Dinosaur of Totalitarianism or Plato's Academy of Design?', *Design Issues*, vol.15, no. 3 (autumn 1999), pp.45–77.

62
Read's *Art and Industry* (London 1934) was published in Warsaw as *Sztuka a przemysł* in 1964.

63
50. Léta Užité Uměni a Design, exh. cat., Uměleckoprůmyslové Muzeum (Prague 1988), n.p.

64
Raymond Hutchings, 'The Weakening of Ideological Influences upon Soviet Design', *Slavic Review*, vol.27, no.1 (March 1968), p.81.

65
See for instance Frank Height, 'Design in the Soviet Union', in *Design*, vol.228 (December 1967), pp.28–33. The Council of Industrial Design also sent a touring exhibition to Poland in 1963: see DW,'Brytyjskie wzornictwo przemysłowe', in *Projekt*, vol.39 (June 1963), pp.20–22.

66
At the second ICSID (International Council of Societies of Industrial Design) Congress in 1960, Maldonado is reported to have claimed that the only opportunities for keeping a check on the usefulness and pertinence of design in the future would be found in the socialist half of Europe. A. Pawłowski, *Inicjacje: O sztuce, projektowaniei kształceniu projektowaniu* (Warsaw 1989), p.28.

67
See Konstantina Hlaváčková, *Czech Fashion 1940–1970: Mirror of the Times* (Prague 2000), p.52.

68
Hutchings 1968, p.73.

69
Unidentified author writing in *Žena a Moda* (1957) in Hlaváčková 2000, p.42.

70
Ol'ga Vashstein, 'Female Fashion. Soviet Style: Bodies of Ideology', in Helena Goscilo and Beth Holmgren (eds), *Russia Women Culture* (Bloomington, IN, 1996), p.69.

71
Djurdja Bartlett, 'Let Them Wear Beige: The Petit-Bourgeois World of Official Socialist Dress', *Fashion*

Theory, vol.8, no.2 (June 2004), pp.137-8.

72
See Larissa Zakharova, 'Dior in Moscow: A Taste for Luxury in Soviet Fashion under Khrushchev', in David Crowley and Susan E. Reid (eds), *Pleasures in Socialism: Leisure and Luxury in the Eastern Bloc* (forthcoming).

73
'Dior House to take Fashion to Russians', *New York Times* (13 May 1959), p.17.

74
Gloria Emerson, 'Dior Models held in Awe by Russians', *New York Times* (29 June 1959), p.26.

75
Anon., 'Clothing Exhibit Popular in Soviet', *New York Times* (24 June 1962), p.14.

76
Cf. Heinz Hirdina, *Gestalten für die Serie: Design in der DDR, 1949-1985* (Dresden 1988), p.126.

77
For a parallel discussion of the uses of modern art by Eastern Bloc states to broadcast their apparent liberalism, see Miklos Haraszti, *The Velvet Prison. Artists Under State Socialism* (Harmondsworth 1989).

78
Györgyi Peteri, 'Nylon Curtain: Transnational and Transsystemic Tendencies in the Cultural Life of State-Socialist Russia and East-Central Europe', *Slavonica*, vol.10, no.2 (November 2004), p.114.

79
A point made by Nordica Nettleton, 'Driving towards Communist Consumerism AvtoVAZ', *Cahiers du Monde Russe*, vol.47, nos 1-2 (2006), p.152.

80
TASS report (1 April 1960), cited in 'The Quotable Khrushchev', a report written by Radio Free Europe (Munich) Evaluation and Analysis Department (30 September 1960), Open Society Archives report 58-2-1. For a discussion of Khrushchev era attitudes to car consumption, see Jukka Gronow and Sergey Zhuravlev, 'Soviet Luxuries from Champagne to Private Cars', in Crowley and Reid forthcoming.

81
On the expansion of the private car market in the Soviet Union see Lewis H. Siegelbaum, 'Cars, Cars and More Cars: The Faustian Bargain of the Brezhnev Era', in L. Siegelbaum (ed.), *Borders of Socialism: Private Spheres of Soviet Russia* (Houndmills 2006), pp.83-106.

82
Nathan Osterman, 'Le Habitat de l'Avenir' and 'I.S.D. Novye Tchérémouchka Kvatal', in *L'Architecture d'Aujourd'hui* (December 1969-January 1970), pp.94-9 and 100-101 respectively; See also Monica Rüthers, *Moskau bauen von Lenin bis Chruscev. Öffentliche Räume zwischen Utopie, Terror und Alltag* (Cologne, 2007), pp.248-61.

83
Unacknowledged writer in *Architektura* (30 May 1965), cited in Anatole Kopp, *Town and Revolution* (New York 1970), p.236.

84
Milka Bliznakov, 'Soviet housing during the experimental years, 1918 to 1933', in William Craft Brumfield and Blair A. Ruble (eds), *Russian Housing in the Modern Age: Design and Social History* (Cambridge 1993), pp.85-149.

85
See Susan E. Reid, 'Destalinisation and Taste, 1953-1963', *Journal of Design History*, vol.10, no.2 (1997), pp.161-75; V. Buchli, 'Khrushchev, Modernism and the Fight against *Petit-bourgeois* Consciousness in the Soviet Home', *Journal of Design History*, vol.10, no.2 (1997), pp.161-75.

86
See Susan E. Reid, 'Khrushchev Modern. Agency and modernization in the Soviet Home', *Cahiers du Monde Russe*, vol.47, nos 1-2 (2006), p.234.

87
On the zoning of domestic space, see Anatole Kopp, *Town and Revolution* (New York 1970), p.237, and Reid 2006, p.255.

88
Steven E. Harris, 'In Search of "Ordinary" Russia: Everyday Life in the NEP, the Thaw, and the Communal Apartment', in *Kritika: Explorations in Russian and Eurasian History*, vol.6, no.3 (summer 2005), pp.675-88.

89
Victor Buchli, 'Khrushchev, modernism, and the fight against petit-bourgeois consciousness', *Journal of Design History*, vol.10, no.2 (1977), pp.161-76. See also Victor Buchli, *An Archaeology of Socialism* (Oxford/New York 1999).

90
Yuri Gerchuk, 'The aesthetics of everyday life during the Khrushchev Thaw in the USSR (1954-64)', in Reid and Crowley 2000, p.91.

91
Andres Kurg, 'Almanahh "Kunst ja Kodu" 1973-1980', in *Kunstiteaduslikke Uurimusi*, vol.2, no.13 (2004), pp.110-42. Tallinn was a significant centre of modernist and experimental art during the Soviet period with strong contacts to the Moscow nonconformist artists. See Ami Liivak (ed.), *Tallinn-Moskva/Moskva-Tallinn, 1956-1985*, exh. cat., Tallinn Art Hall (Tallinn 1996). For a parallel discussion of Lithuanian modern design see Lolita Jablonskienė, 'A Brief History of the "Art into Everyday Life: Movement"', in 'David Mabb, *Menas Kasdienybei*, exh. cat., Contemporary Art Centre (Vilnius 2006), pp.34-43.

92
Oldřich Palata, 'Czechoslovak Glass: A Subtle Weapon in the Superpowers: The Czechoslovak Glass Exhibition, Moscow, 1959', in Helmut Ricke (ed.), *Czech Glass 1945-1980: Design in an Age of Adversity* (Stuttgart 2005), pp.104-11.

93
See Martá Sylvestrová (ed.), *Česky plakát 60. let*, exh. cat., Moravské Galerie (Brno 1997).

94
In fact, Lenica commented on the incorporation the primitive and the uncanny by the banal 'Alice in Wonderland' world of advertising in the West in the 1960s. See Jan Lenica, 'Le plus important c'est l'oreille', *Opus* (April 1968), p.105.

95
In a generally favourable review of *Dom*, American film critic Parker Tyler wrote: 'it is sometimes a little smart on the smart magazine lay-out side and resembles the advertising décor influenced by the Bauhaus and by Surrealism'. Tyler Parker, *Underground Film* (New York 1969), p.172.

96
Tomasz Goban-Klas, *The Orchestration of the Media* (Boulder, CO, 1994), p.119.

97
See Margo Rouard-Snowman, *Roman Cieślewicz* (London 1993); Anna Grabowska-Konwent (ed.), *Roman Cieślewicz 1930-1996* (Poznań 2006).

98
Frederick Taylor, *The Berlin Wall: A World Divided, 1961-1989* (London 2007).

99
Jeffrey Kopstein, *The Politics of Economic Decline in East Germany, 1945-1989* (Chapel Hill, NC, 1996), p.44.

100
Susan E. Reid, 'In the Name of the People: The Manege Affair Revisited', *Kritika*, vol.6, no.4 (autumn 2005), pp.1-43; see also Priscilla Johnson and Leopold Labedz, *Khrushchev and the Arts: The Politics of Soviet Culture 1962-1964* (Cambridge, MA, 1965).

101
Khrushchev, cited by Colin Mason, 'Youth and Age in Moscow Today', *The Guardian* (16 March 1963), p.6.

102
Dorothy Miller, 'Movement on GDR Cultural Scene', report written for Non-Target Communist Area Analysis Department, Radio Free Europe/Munich (18 March 1965), Open Society Archives report 24-7-225.

103
Katherine Verdery, *What was Socialism and What Comes Next?* (Princeton 1996).

104
See J.L. Kerr, 'Hard Currency Shops in Eastern Europe', Radio Free Europe / Research RAD Background Report/211 (27 October 1977); Jonathan R. Zatlin, *The Currency of Socialism: Money and Political Culture in East Germany* (Cambridge 2007), esp. chap.6, 'Consuming ideology'; Nordica Nettleton, 'Driving Towards Communist Consumerism', *Cahiers du Monde russe*, vol.47, nos 1-2 (January-June 2006), pp.195-226. See also Jeremi Suri, 'The Promise and Failure of "Developed Socialism": The Soviet "Thaw" and the Crucible of the Prague Spring, 1964-1972', *Contemporary European History*, vol.15 (2006), pp.133-58.

105
See Ferenc Fehér, Ágnes Heller and György Márkus, *Dictatorship over Needs: An Analysis of Soviet Societies* (Oxford 1984); János Kornai, *Economics of Shortage*, 2 vols (Amsterdam 1980).

106
Douglas Crimp, Rosalyn Deutsche and Ewa Lajer-Burcharth, 'A conversation with Krzysztof Wodiczko' in *October 38* (autumn 1986), p.33.

'Our Kitchen is Just as Good': Soviet Responses to the American National Exhibition in Moscow, 1959

1
Photograph by V. Biriukov, *Izvestiia* 26 July 1959. A longer version of this essay is to appear in Ruth Oldenziel and Karin Zachmann (eds), *Kitchen Politics in the Cold War: Americanization, Technology, and European Users* (Cambridge, MA, 2009).

2
G. Zimmerman and B. Lerner, 'What the Russians Will See', *Look* (21 July 1959), p.54.

3
For the American context of the exhibition and 'kitchen debate' see Elaine Tyler May, *Homeward Bound: American Families in the Cold War Era* (New York 1988), esp. pp.16-20 and chap.7; Karal Ann Marling, *As Seen on TV: The Visual Culture of Everyday Life in the 1950s* (Cambridge, MA, 1994), pp.243-83; Walter L. Hixson, *Parting the Curtain:*

48

Kristin Roth-Ey, 'Finding a Home for Television in the USSR, 1950-1970', *Slavic Studies*, vol.66, no.2 (2006), pp.278-305.

49

John Downing, 'The Intersputnik System and Soviet Television', *Soviet Studies*, vol.37, no.4. (October 1985), p.468.

50

It was overtaken by the CN tower in Toronto, 1973-6.

51

The letter is reproduced in Jiří Jiroutek, *Fenomenen Ještěd* (Liberec 2005), p.66; see also 'Excerpts from an interview with Karel Hubáček', in *Mašinisti*, exh. cat., Fragner Gallery (Prague 1996), p.138.

52

SIAL continued to enjoy patronage of the State during the period of normalization in the early 1970s when the communists restored their hold over Czechoslovak society. Hubáček' adopted the 'party speak' demanded by the authorities whilst government minister Šupka, in charge of new technology, acted as an advocate for the group in the face of attempts to have it disbanded. See 'Excerpts for an interview with Karel Hubáček', in *Mašinisti*, exh. cat., Fragner Gallery (Prague 1996), p.138.

53

Roland Barthes, 'Eiffel Tower', *The Eiffel Tower and Other Mythologies* (New York 1982), p.5.

54

Quoted in Wigley 2001, p.105.

55

Archigram, 'Living City', *Living Arts*, no.2 (June 1963), as cited in Peter Cook (ed.), *Archigram* (London 1972), p.21.

56

Marshall McLuhan, *Understanding Media* (London 1967), p.361.

57

Marshall McLuhan, *War and Peace in the Global Village* (Corta Madera 2001), p.134.

58

Karal Ann Marling, *As Seen On TV: The Visual Culture of Everyday Life in the 1950s* (Cambridge, MA, 1996).

59

McLuhan 2001, p.134.

60

See also Cornelia Vismann, 'Tele-Tribunals: Anatomy of a Medium', in *Grey Room*, vol.1, no.10 (January 2003), pp.5-21; Stephen J. Whitfield, *The Culture of the Cold War* (Baltimore 1991), chap.7. Thomas Doherty argues the reverse in *Cold War, Cool Medium: Television, McCarthyism, and American Culture* (New York 2004).

61

See Walter L. Hixson, *Parting the Curtain: Propaganda, Culture and the Cold War, 1945-1961* (Basingstoke 1997), chap. 6.

62

Daniel Boorstin, *The Image* (New York 1961), chap.1.

63

'Soviet TV Viewers Catch Up', *New York Times* (21 July 1989).

64

Tony Kemp-Welch, 'Dethroning Stalin: Poland 1956 and its Legacy', *Europe-Asia Studies* no.58 (2006), pp.1261-84.

65

Michael Nelson, *War of the Black Heavens. The Battles of Western Broadcasting in the Cold War* (Syracuse 1997), pp.70-71.

66

David Marks, 'Broadcasting Across the Wall: The Free Flow of Information Between East and West Germany', *Journal of Communication*, vol.33, no.1 (March 1983), pp.46-55.

67

Open Society Archives (OSA), 300-40-4/23d., item no. 5279/59, p.2.

68

McLuhan 1967, pp.31-43.

69

Michael Meyen and Ute Nawratil, 'The Viewers: Television and everyday life in East Germany', *Historical Journal of Film and Television Studies*, vol.24, no.3 (August 2004), pp.355-64.

70

Milena Veenis, 'Fantastic things', in *Experiencing Material Culture in the Western World*, ed. Susan M. Pearce (London 1997), pp.154-74.

71

Journal du Dimanche, 29 July 1962, cited in 'The Technology of Isolation', *Internationale Situationniste*, no.9 (August 1964).

72

For a description of the project, see Heinrich Klotz (ed.), *Haus-Rucker-Co 1967 bis 1983* (Braunschweig/ Wiesbaden 1984), pp.86f.

73

See Łukasz Ronduda, 'Krzysztof Wodiczko - projektowanie i sztuka', *Piktogram*, no.7 (2007), pp.12-27.

74

Kerry Brougher et al., *Visual Music, Synaesthesia in Art and Museum Since 1900* (London/ New York 2005).

75

The output of films from the machine were issued as a sample reel in 1961, entitled 'Catalog'; see Brougher et al. 2005, p.260.

76

Youngblood 1970, pp.207-10.

77

Pat Kirkham, *Charles and Ray Eames, Designers of the Twentieth Century* (Cambridge, MA, 1995), p.323.

78

Kirkham 1995, chap. 7; Beatriz Colomina, 'Enclosed by Images: The Eameses' Multimedia Architecture', in *Grey Room*, no.2 (winter 2001), pp.6-29; Ben Highmore, 'Machinic Magic: IBM at the 1964-65 New York World's Fair', in *New Formations*, no.51 (winter 2003) pp.128-48.

79

Highmore 2003, p.145.

80

John Neuhart, Marilyn Neuhart and Ray Eames, *Eames Design: The Work of the Office of Charles and Ray Eames* (New York 1989), p.177.

81

Michael Bielicky, 'Prague: A Place of Illusionists', in Jeffrey Shaw and Peter Weibel (eds), *Future Cinema: The Cinematic Imaginary after Film* (Cambridge, MA, 2003), p.99.

82

Youngblood 1970, p.348.

83

Ibid., p.359.

84

See Marc Treib, *Space Calculated in Seconds* (Princeton 1996).

85

Beatriz Colomina, 'Enclosed by Images: The Eameses' Multimedia Architecture', *Grey Room*, no.2 (winter 2001), pp.6-29.

86

See Lajos Ruff, *The Brain-washing Machine* (London 1959).

87

'In and Against Cinema', *Internationale Situationiste*, no.1 (June 1958), available on-line at http://www.cddc.vt.edu/sionline/si/situ.html.

88

Anthony Burgess, *A Clockwork Orange* (Harmondsworth 1972), p.89.

89

The moral aspect had already been abused by Burgess's American publisher, W.W. Norton, who had required that he drop the optimistic final chapter in which represents the redemption of his 'space-age hooligan'. Kubrick's 1971 film also overlooked this material in favour of a more pessimistic ending. The 'missing' chapter featured in all other editions of the book.

90

A vivid *Boston Broadside* review of an Exploding Plastic Inevitable performance appears in Clinton Heylin (ed.), *All Yesterdays' Parties* (Cambridge, MA, 2006), pp.24-8.

91

Cited by Branden W. Joseph, '"My Mind Split Open": Andy Warhol's Exploding Plastic Inevitable', in *Grey Room*, no.8 (summer 2002), p.91.

92

Ibid, p.97.

93

Youngblood 1970, p.78.

94

Ibid., p.46.

95

Ibid.

96

Michael Shamberg and Raindance Corporation, *Guerrilla Television* (New York 1971).

97

'Interview with Ant Farm', in C.M. Lewallen (ed.), *Ant Farm 1968-1978* (Berkeley 2004), p.59.

98

Hans Magnus Enzensberger, 'Constituents of a Theory of the Media', *New Left Review* (November–December 1970), p.19.

99

Cybersyn is described in detail in the transcript of a lecture by Stafford Beer: 'Fanfare for Effective Freedom, Cybernetic Praxis in Government', the 3rd Richard Goodman Memorial Lecture, delivered at Brighton Polytechnic, Mouslecoomb, Brighton, 14 February 1973 (www.williambowles.info/sa/FanfareforEffectiveFreedom.pdf, accessed 30 October 2007).

100

For a full account of the Cybersyn experiment, see Eden Medina, 'Designing Freedom, Regulating a Nation: Socialist Cybernetics in Allende's Chile', *Journal of Latin American Studies*, no.38 (Cambridge 2006), pp.571-606.

101

Bonsiepe, who had established close links with Latin America in the 1960s, moved to Chile as consultant to the International Labour Organisation (ILO) to work on an industrial development project. He became an influential figure in Chilean design before moving to Argentina after Allende's death. See James Fathers, 'Peripheral Vision: An Interview with Gui Bonsiepe Charting a Lifetime of Commitment to Design Empowerment', *Design Issues*, vol.9, no.4 (autumn 2003).

Imagining the Computer: Eliot Noyes, the Eames and the IBM Pavilion

1

Reyner Banham, '(Thinks): Think!', *The New Statesman* (11 October 1965), pp.109–18, repr. in R. Banham, *Design by Choice*, ed. Penny Sparks (New York 1981), pp.115–16.

2

For an extremely thorough historical account of IBM's financial strategems and its various legal entanglements during the second half of the twentieth century, see Fisher et al., *I.B.M. and the U.S. Data Processing Industry: An Economic History* (New York 1983).

3

E.C. Berkeley, *Giant Brains, or Machines that Think* (New York 1949).

4

The haywire computer that triggers Armageddon is, of course, a deeply resonant theme in science fiction after the twin inventions of the computer and nuclear warfare during the Second World War. Classics of the genre include Nevil Shute's *On the Beach* (New York 1957), Philip K. Dick's *Time Out of Joint* (Philadelphia 1959), Eugene Burdick and Henry Wheeler's *Fail-Safe* (New York 1962), Stanley Kubrick's *Dr Strangelove: Or, how I learned to stop worrying and love the bomb* (1963), James Cameron's film series *Terminator* (1984) and *Terminator 2: Judgment Day* (1991), Herman Kahn's *On Thermonuclear War* (Princeton/London 1960), and Harrison S. Brown, *Must Destruction Be Our Destiny?* (New York 1946).

5

Eliot Noyes, quoted in Scott Kelly, 'Curator of corporate character ... Eliot Noyes and Associates', *Industrial Design*, no.13 (June 1966), p.43.

6

The most complete account of Noyes's work is given in Gordon Bruce, *Eliot Noyes: A Pioneer of Design and Architecture in the Age of American Modernism* (London/New York 2006). My dissertation, *The Redesign of Design: Multinational Corporations, Computers and Design Logic, 1945–1976* (New York/Ann Arbor 2006), offers an alternative account and interpretation of Noyes's work for IBM and Westinghouse. On Rand's work for IBM, see: Stephen Heller, *Paul Rand* (London 1999); Paul Rand and IBM, *The IBM Logo: Its Use in Company Identification* (Armonk, NY, 1982); *IBM Trademark Manual*, n.d. [1960], IBM Corporate Archives, F47; and the very valuable materials preserved in the Paul Rand Collection, Yale University Archives, New Haven, CT, box 22.

7

As related by Christine Quain (IBM Armonk) to Reinhold Martin, 22 April 1998. I am grateful to Reinhold for supplying a copy of this letter.

8

On Noyes's buildings for the IBM Poughkeepsie campus see: 'Clarity, Cohesiveness, Good Detail', *Architectural Record*, no.126 (September 1959), pp.199–204; 'IBM Engineering & Development Laboratory in the Northeast', *Architectural Record*, no.118 (September 1955), pp.210–11.

9

'Brain Center: A new machine, a new showroom dramatize IBM design policy', *Industrial Design*, vol.2, no.3 (July 1955), pp.36–41, esp. p.36.

10

Hugh B. Johnston, 'From Old IBM to New IBM', *Industrial Design*, vol.4, no.3 (March 1957), pp.48–53, esp. p.51.

11

Claude Shannon and Warren Weaver, *The Mathematical Theory of Communication* (Urbana, IL/Chicago 1963).

12

Descriptions of all of the Eames Office's films may be found in John Neuhart, Marilyn Neuhart and Ray Eames, *Eames Design: The Work of the Office of Charles and Ray Eames* (New York 1989).

13

Guilio Carlo Argan, 'Ideological Development in the Thought and Imagery of Italian Design', in Emilio Ambasz (ed.), *Italy: The New Domestic Landscape, Achievements and Problems of Italian Design* (New York/Florence 1972), pp.358–69, esp. p.359.

14

Eames, handwritten notes, Charles and Ray Eames Collection, Library of Congress, box 217, folder 9, 'Burns. Lecture Tour, 1970'.

15

On *Mathematica*, see Charles and Ray Eames Collection, boxes 156–9.

16

Quoted in Neuhart, Neuhart and Eames 1989, p.255.

17

Both quotations, though unpublished, are legible in the Eames family's private collection of photographs and slides of the exhibit. My thanks to Eames Demetrios for allowing me to see these photos.

18

See Eliot Noyes to Paul Rand, 15 August 1960, Eliot Noyes Archive box 62, folder 'IBM Project 1964'.

19

On the IBM Museum project, see Harwood 2006, chap.6.

20

Department of Information, International Business Machines Corporation, 'A Profile of *International Business Machines Corporation*', press release, 15 December 1963, p.1 (IBM Corporate Archives, World's Fair box 20, folder 6, 'NY 64/65 Press Releases').

21

Diagrams of the building, and many of the Eames Office's and Saarinen and Roche's early designs (including facsimiles of drawings and photographs of models) for the pavilion are presented in a report by Eero Saarinen and Associates, 'New York World's Fair for 1964: IBM Building Report' (5 January 1962), IBM Corporate Archives, World's Fair box 20, folder 8, 'Architect's Book'.

22

Charles Eames, 'Language of Vision: The Nuts and Bolts', *Bulletin of the American Academy of Arts and Sciences*, vol.28, no.1 (October 1974), pp.17–18.

23

Eero Saarinen and Associates, 'New York World's Fair for 1964, IBM Building: Report' (15 January 1962), p.2.

24

Photographs and ephemera relating to these exhibits can be found in the IBM Corporate Archive, World's Fair box 20, and Charles and Ray Eames Collection, Library of Congress, box 146.

25

IBM Fair (International Business Machines Corporation, New York 1964), p.21. The typography and design of the booklet are by Paul Rand; the text is adapted from the script for the Information Machine by Glen Fleck of the Eames Office. The emphasis is mine.

26

On Babbage, see the office of Charles and Ray Eames, *A Computer Perspective* (Cambridge, MA, 1973), a book edition of their exhibition for IBM of the same name. For a more conventional account, see Doron Swade, *The Difference Engine: Charles Babbage and the Quest to Build the First Computer* (New York 2001).

Expo '70 as Watershed: The Politics of American Art and Technology

Abbreviations used in these notes:

AAA: Archives of American Art, Smithsonian Institution, Washington, DC

GRI: Getty Research Institute of Arts and the Humanities, Los Angeles, CA

1

On the use of art as a political weapon during the Cold War, see: Max Kozloff, 'American Painting During the Cold War', originally published in *Artforum*, vol.11, no.9 (May 1973), pp.43–54; Eva Cockcroft, 'Abstract Expressionism, Weapon of the Cold War', originally published in *Artforum*, vol.12 (June 1974), pp.39–41; Jane de Hart Matthews, 'Art and Politics in Cold War America', originally published in *The American Historical Review*, vol.81 (February–December 1976), pp.762–87; and David and Cecile Shapiro, 'Abstract Expressionism: The Politics of Apolitical Painting', originally published in Jack Salzman (ed.), *Source: Prospectus*, vol.3 (1977), pp.175–214; all republished in Francis Frascina (ed.), *Pollock and After: The Critical Debate*, 2nd edn (London 2000), pp.130–96. See also Serge Guilbaut, *How New York Stole the Idea of Modern Art: Abstract Expressionism, Freedom, and the Cold War*, trans. Arthur Goldhammer (Chicago 1983); Frances Stonor Saunders, *The Cultural Cold War: The CIA and the World of Arts and Letters* (New York 1999).

2

The literature describing the transition from modernity to postmodernity is vast; for two insightful descriptions of this philosophical and historical shift during the 1960s, see Frederic Jameson, 'Periodizing the 60s', in Sohnya Sayres, Anders Stephanson, Stanley Aronowitz and Frederic Jameson (eds), *The 60s Without Apology* (Minneapolis 1984), esp. pp.194–201; and Rosalind Krauss, 'Sculpture in the Expanded Field', in Hal Foster (ed.), *The Anti-Aesthetic: Essays on Postmodern Culture* (Seattle 1983), pp.31–42.

3

In a meeting of 30 December 1957 with Secretary of Health, Education, and Welfare Marion Folsom, Eisenhower stressed that 'The most important point to get across to the American people ... is "that a football player is no more important than a person who does well in mathematics or a good well-balanced student."' (Robert Divine, *The Sputnik Challenge* [New York 1993], pp.90 and 223, note 34). On the NDEA see Divine 1993, pp.164–6.

4

See, for example, a 1961 report on the view of college students about scientists. David C. Beardslee and Donald D. O'Dowd, 'The College-Student Image of the Scientist', in Bernard Barber and Walter Hirsch (eds), *The Sociology of Science* (New York 1962), p.249.

36
Books by Khan-Magamedov include *Alexander Vesnin and Russian Constructivism* (New York 1986); *Pioneers of Soviet Architecture: The Search for New Solutions in the 1920s and 1930s* (New York 1987); *Alexander Rodchenko: The Complete Work* (Cambridge, MA, 1987) and *Vkhutemas: Moscou 1920-1930*, 2 vols (Paris 1990).

37
Bojko was the author of one of the first books on Soviet graphic design in English, *New Graphic Design in Revolutionary Russia* (London 1972).

38
Various essays in *Výtvarné umění*, vol.17 (1967).

39
Susan Reid, 'Design, Stalin and the Thaw', *Journal of Design History*, vol.10, no.2 (1997), p.112.

40
S. Frederick Starr, 'Writings from the 1960s on the Modern Movement in Russia', *Journal of the Society of Architectural Historians*, vol.30, no.2. (May 1971), p.171.

41
Igor Kazus, 'Cosmic architecture the Russian avant-garde', *Project Russia*, vol.15 (2000/01), pp.81-8.

42
Grigory Revzin, 'A prayer in recreation mode', *Project Russia*, vol.15 (2000/01), p.6.

43
Demartini (1969), cited in Ludmila Hájková and Rostislav Švácha, 'Where We Will Live Tomorrow', in *Acke Slovo Pohyb Prostor. Experimenty v Umění Šedesátých*, exh. cat., Galerie Hlavního Města Prahy (Prague 1999), p.397.

44
Camilla Gray, 'Revolutionary Poster', *Architectural Design*, vol.2 (1968), p.51.

45
Benjamin H.D. Buchloh, 'Cold War Constructivism', in Serge Guilbaut (ed.), *Reconstructing Modernism: Art in New York, Paris, and Montreal 1945-1969* (Cambridge, MA, 1990), p.91.

46
Editorial, 'Cuba: Che Si!', *Opus International* (October 1967), p.12.

47
R. Hart Phillips, 'Kidnappers Kind, Fangio Asserts', *The New York Times* (26 February 1958), p.3.

48
Richard Gott, *Cuba: A New History* (New Haven 2004), p.167.

49
See Richard R. Fagen, *The Transformation of Political Culture in Cuba* (Stanford, CA, 1969).

50
Fidel Castro, *Palabras a los Intelectuales* (Havana 1961), n.p.

51
Ernesto Guevara, cited in David Kunzle, 'Public Graphics in Cuba: A Very Cuban Form of Internationalist Art', *Latin American Perspectives*, vol.2, no.4 (1975), p.90.

52
See William Taubman, *Khrushchev: The Man and his Era* (London 2004), pp.578-619; Aleksandr Fursenko and Timothy Naftali, *Khrushchev's Cold War: The Inside Story of an American Adversary* (New York 2007).

53
Gott 2004, p.210. See also Jacques Levesque, *L'URSS et la Revolution Cubaine* (Montreal 1976).

54
Similar co-productions were entered into with the East Germans (*Preludio 11/Prelude 11*, directed by Kurt Maetzig, 1964) and with the Czechs (*Para quien baila La Habana/For Whom Havana Dances/Komu tancí Havana*, directed by Vladimír Čech, 1962). See Michael Chanan, *The Cuban Image* (Bloomington, IN, 1986), pp.130-31.

55
See Yevgeny Yevtushenko, *A Precocious Autobiography* (New York 1963).

56
Steven P. Hill, 'The Soviet Film Today', *Film Quarterly*, vol.20, no.4 (summer 1967), p.51.

57
Dina Iordanova, 'I Am Cuba – film review', *Russian Review*, vol.56, no.1 (January 1997), p.125.

58
Iskusstvo kino (March 1965), pp.24-37.

59
Richard Gott, 'From Russia with love', *The Guardian* (12 November 2005) - see www.guardian.co.uk.

60
French film-maker Chris Marker's early documentary, *Cuba Si*, displayed this trait. Filming in 1961, at a time when Cuba anticipated an American invasion, he arranged for a conga player to play whilst children danced, apparently spontaneously, on the streets, recalling: 'That was Havana in 1961: machine guns on the roofs and conga on the streets.' Marker, cited in Lupton, *Chris Marker: Memories of the Future* (London 2005), p.74.

61
See, for instance, Michael Richardson (ed.), *Refusal of the Shadow: Surrealism and the Caribbean* (London 1996).

62
Lowery Stokes Sims, *Wifredo Lam and the International Avant-Garde, 1923-1982* (Austin, TX, 2002).

63
John A. Loomis, *Revolution of Forms: Cuba's Forgotten Art Schools* (New York 1999).

64
David Kunzle, 'Public Graphics in Cuba: A Very Cuban Form of Internationalist Art', *Latin American Perspectives*, vol.2, no.4 (1975), pp.89-110.

65
Susan Sontag 'Posters: Advertisement, Art, Political Artifact, Commodity', in Douglas Stermer (ed.), *The Art of Revolution, Castro's Cuba 1959-1970* (London 1970), p.xvii.

66
See, for instance, Jean-Paul Sartre, *Sartre on Cuba* (New York 1961).

67
Benigno E. Aguirre, 'Social Control in Cuba', *Latin American Politics and Society*, vol.44, no.2 (summer 2002), pp.67-98.

68
Philip Brenner, 'Cuba and the Missile Crisis', *Journal of Latin American Studies*, vol.22, no.1 (February 1990), pp.115-42.

69
For an excellent study of the global impact of Cold War politics, see Odd Arne Westad, *The Global Cold War Third World Interventions and the Making of Our Times* (New York 2005).

70
David Kunzle, 'Uses of the Portrait: The Che Poster', *Art in America*, vol.63 (September-October, 1975), pp.66-73.

71
Sontag 1970, p.xxii.

72
Raoul Vaneigem, *The Revolution of Everyday Life* (London 1967), chap.18: 'Spurious Opposition'.

73
Hans Magnus Enzensberger, 'Constituents for a Theory of the Media', *New Left Review*, vol.1, no.64 (November-December 1970) p.18.

74
Ibid.

75
For a sophisticated defence of Godard's Maoism, see Colin MacCabe, *Godard: A Portrait of the Artist at Seventy* (New York 2003), pp.189-97.

76
Li Zhensheng, *Red-Color News Soldier* (London 2003).

77
Marco, cited in J. Aulich and M. Sylvestrová, *Political Posters in Central and Eastern Europe 1945-1995* (Manchester 2000), p.42.

78
Kundera, in ibid., p.41.

79
Claire Clouzot, review of *Loves of a Blonde*, *Film Quarterly*, vol.21, no.1 (autumn 1967), p.48.

80
Clouzot, review of *Daisies*, *Film Quarterly*, vol.21, no.3 (spring 1968), p.37.

81
'2000 words to workers, farmers, Scientists, Artists and Everyone', in Robin Alison Remington (ed.), *Winter in Prague* (Boston 1969), pp.196-202.

82
'Czechoslovak Censors Calls for an End to Censorship' (14 March 1968), in Remington 1969, p.54.

83
Louis Aragon and Raoul-Jean Moulin (eds), *Jiří Kolář* (Paris 1973), p.39.

84
A glossary of terms coined by Kolář to describe his various collage techniques appears in *Jiří Kolář Collages 1952-82*, exh. cat., Albemarle Gallery (London, June-July 1987), p.13.

85
K. Kaplan, *Report on the Murder of the General Secretary* (London 1990).

86
Alain Jaubert, *Making People Disappear: An Amazing Chronicle of Photographic Deception* (Washington, DC, 1989).

87
Arsén Pohribny, 'The Legacy of the Weeks of 1968', in *Jiří Kolář: Diary 1967*, exh. cat., Modern Art Oxford (Oxford 1984), p.17.

88
For a discussion of the events of Osaka and their repercussions, see Verena Wasmuth, 'Czech Glass in the Limelight: The Great Exhibitions Abroad', in Helmut Ricke (ed.), *Czech Glass: Design in an Age of Adversity, 1945-1980* (Düsseldorf 2005), pp.100-1.

89
'Sovereignty and the International Obligation of Socialist Countries' (26 September 1968), quoted in Remington 1969, p.413.

90
'Fidel Castro Speech on the Czechoslovak Situation' (23 August 1968), quoted in ibid., pp.334-6.

91

Svetlana Boym, 'From the Russian Soul to Post-Communist Nostalgia', *Representations*, no.49 (winter 1995), p.149.

92

'Kuznetzov recalls the Reaction of Russians to the Invasion of Czechoslovakia a Year Ago', *New York Times* (21 August 1969), p.14.

93

Natalia Gorbanevskaya, *Red Square at Noon* (New York 1972).

94

In 1968 Sakharov wrote: 'The universal human need for intellectual freedom has been understood in particular by the Czecho-Slovaks, and there can be no doubt that we should support their bold initiative, which is valuable for the future of socialism and all mankind. That support should be political and, in the early stages, include increased economic aid.' Quoted in William Henry Chamberlin, 'The Voice of Silent Russia', *Russian Review*, vol.28, no.2 (April 1969), p.157.

95

Robert Horvath, *The Legacy of Soviet Dissent: Dissidents, Democratisation and Radical Nationalism in Russia* (London 2005); Mark Boobbyer, *Conscience, Dissent and Reform in Soviet Russia* (London 2005). For a good overview of dissent in Central Eastern Europe during the Soviet period, see Barbara J. Falk, *The Dilemmas of Dissidence of East-Central Europe* (Budapest 2003).

96

See Jeremy Varon, *Bringing the War Home: The Weather Underground, The Red Army Faction, and the Revolutionary Violence of the 1960s and 1970s* (Berkeley, CA, 2004); Walter Laquer, *Guerrilla Warfare: A Historical and Critical Study* (New Brunswick/London 1998) pp.326–81.

Protest by Design: Giancarlo De Carlo and the 14th Milan Triennale

Translated by Emma-Louise Bassett.

1

Giancarlo De Carlo, in *L'Unità* (11 June 1968).

2

Arata Isozaki created an environment called *Electronic Labyrinth*, which focused on the macrotransformations of the contemporary landscape. See H.U.Obrist, 'Triennale de Milano '68: A case study and beyond', in *Iconoclash*, eds B.Latour and P.Weibel (Cambridge/London 2002).

3

The occupation lasted until the evening of 7 June, when those remaining were removed by the police. In spite of the damage sustained – the cost of repairing the exhibits and the damaged spaces came to approximately 244 million lire – the exhibition reopened from 23 June to 7 July.

4

Giancarlo De Carlo, letter to Arata Isozaki, 22 July 1968, Archivio De Carlo. Atti/038(1) Triennale di Milano. Archivio Progetti IUAV.

5

H. Hollein, *Austriennale l'Austria alla 14. Triennale di Milano 1968: il grande numero* (Vienna 1968).

6

S. Sadler, *Archigram. Architecture without Architects* (Cambridge/London 2005); Archigram, *MilanoGram. Report, Milan Triennale 1968* (Milan 1968).

7

Core members of Team 10, a breakaway group from the Congrès Internationaux d'Architecture Moderne (CIAM), included Alison and Peter Smithson, Aldo Van Eyck, Jaap Baakema, Georges Candilis, Shadrach Woods and Aldo Van Eyck. De Carlo became involved with CIAM at its final Conference in Otterlo, 1959, and then joined Team 10 in 1966. Several Team 10 members contributed installations to the 14th Triennale, including the Smithsons, who produced a somewhat eccentric exploration of 'urban ornament' and the way in which social events transformed the city ('Wedding in the City'). For a discussion of the 14th Triennale in relation to Team 10, see Mirko Zardini, 'Triennale Milano: "Il Grande Numero"', in Dirk van den Heuvel and Max Risselada, *Team 10 1953–81: In Search of A Utopia of the Present* (Rotterdam 2005), pp.158–9.

8

The 'Italian Exhibition of Decorative Arts' began its life in 1923 in Monza, but in 1929 was given state recognition and retitled 'The International Triennial Exhibition of Modern Decorative and Industrial Arts and Modern Architecture'. It was moved to Milan in 1933, to the Palazzo dell'Arte, designed by the Italian architect Giovanni Muzio.

9

The five members of the Executive Council were the architects Giancarlo De Carlo, Alberto Rosselli, Vittoriano Viganò and Marco Zanuso, the graphic designer Albe Steiner and the engineer Marcello Vittorini.

10

Immediately after the Second World War, the 'Greater Number' and the need for new housing design were developed as urban issues in Morocco and Algeria, mainly by ATABAT – Afrique, the African branch of Atelier des bâtisseurs, founded in 1947 by Le Corbusier, Vladimir Bodiansky, André Wogenscky and Marcel Py. In 1951 ATABAT – Afrique opened an office in Tangiers, run by two students of Le Corbusier who were members of the Team 10: George Candilis and Shadrach Woods. The latter was a close friend of De Carlo, who invited him to the 14th Triennale in Milan. See T. Avermaete, *Another Modern. The Post-War Architecture and Urbanism of Candilis-Josic-Woods* (Rotterdam 2005); J.L. Cohen, M. Eleb, *Casablanca: mythes et figures d'une aventure urbane* (Paris 1998).

11

De Carlo edited and directed a book series on urbanization, technology and communication for the Milan-based publisher Il Saggiatore, entitled *Struttura e Forma Urbana*. Among the authors he selected – and had translated for the first time into Italian – were: Patrick Geddes, with 'Cities in Evolution' ('Citta in evoluzione', 1970), Kevin Lynch with 'What Time is the place' and 'Site Planning' ('Il tempo dello spazio', 1977; 'Il senso del territorio', 1981), Nicholas Negroponte with 'The Architecture Machine' ('La macchina per l'architettura', 1977) and Colin Rowe and Fred Koetter with 'Collage City' (1981).

12

A. Pansera, 'Le Triennali del boom economico', in *Storia e cronaca della Triennale* (Milan 1978), pp.68–104 and related bibliography

13

Ibid.

14

The conference 'De Divina Proportione' was held on the occasion of the 9th Milan Triennale. Participants included international figures such as Rudolf Wittkower, James Ackermann, Max Bill, Ernesto Nathan Rogers and Le Corbusier. See 'Convegno Internazionale di Studi De Divina Proportione', *Atti del Convegno* (Milan 1952). The acts of the symposium are now available in A.C. Cimoli and F. Irace, *La Divina Proportione: Atti del convegno (Milano, 27–29 settembre 1951)* (Milan 2007).

15

Umberto Eco, *La Struttura Assente* (Milan 1968).

16

Dino Buzzati, 'Incubi e speranze della folla alla Triennale di Milano', in *Corriere della Sera* (28 May 1968).

17

XIV Triennale, Catalogo Generale (Milan 1968), p.35.

18

In these years strong similarities could be traced back between the way De Carlo conceived the exhibition display at the Triennale and his aim to rethink the academic study of architecture. Indeed, in 1968 he summarized his thoughts on university teaching criteria in his book *La Piramide Rovesciata* (Bari 1968), where he once more addressed the need for a process of discarding all traditional notions of discipline.

19

Press release distributed by the assembly on 3 June 1968 (Archivio Storico della Triennale di Milano).

20

From 'Documents of the occupation group', document read during the assembly of the Milan Triennale on 3 June 1968 (Archivio storico della Triennale di Milano).

21

Enzo Mari, *Interni* (September 1968), Special Number.

22

Similar protests beset the Venice Art Biennale in the same year. The protests of 1968 contributed to a crisis in the arts and provoked criticism of their institutional basis, which led the Biennale to abandon all prize categories in favour of a non-competitive thematic exhibition. See L. Alloway, *The Venice Biennale 1895–1968: From Salon to Goldfish Bowl* (Greenwich, CT, 1968); G. Dorfles, 'Dopo Venezia, dopo Kassel, che cosa?', in *Metro*, no. 17 (September–October 1968), pp.14–17; C. Lonzi, *Autoritratto* (Bari 1969); *Venezia e le Biennali: I percorsi del gusto*, ed. Comune di Venezia (Milan/Venice 1995).

23

For further information see the letters of Arnaldo Pomodoro, published in *Che Fare*. In particular A. Pomodoro, 'Short Letter from San Francisco', *Che Fare*, no.1 (29 May 1967), pp.58–60; *Che Fare*, no.4 (winter 1968-9).

24

See G. Agamben, 'Nel Mondo di Odradek', in *Stanze* (Turin 2006; 1st edn 1977), pp.39–70.

25

H. Rosenberg, *The De-Definition of Art* (Chicago/London 1972).

26

H. Rosenberg, *The Anxious Object: Art Today and its Audience* (Chicago/London 1964). This book, and in particular Rosenberg's analysis of art and audience in the media society, was quoted in the leaflets distributed by the protesting artists and students during the occupation of the Triennale.

The Personal Visions and Public Spaces of the Movement Group (Dvizhenie)

1
Many accounts of the dialogues that took place between Khrushchev and the artists invited to participate have been published, most recently by Vladimir Yankilevsky, 'Memoirs of the Manezh Exhibition, 1962', *Zimmerli Journal*, vol.1, pt 1 (2003), pp.67–77, and Susan Reid, 'In the Name of the People: the Manège Affair Revisited', *Kritika*, vol.6, no.4 (autumn 2005), pp.673–716.

2
Nussberg and Infante received much recognition in the 1960s in the Eastern Bloc through prominent art journals in Czechoslovakia and Poland; Nussberg's work was included in Documenta 6, and the Venice Biennale of 1977; Infante's work has been published in several recent catalogues, including that for a major retrospective of his work which was held in 2006 at the Museum of Contemporary Art in Moscow (see note 12).

3
This and all subsequent references to Infante's presentation of the group's history are from a book published by the artist entitled *Negativnye siuzhety* (Moscow 2006), see esp. pp.70–74.

4
Nussberg's redaction of this same history may be found in several of his publications, including most recently *Prisheltsy v lesu* (Moscow 2004). The primary document of Nussberg's history, a book he has been compiling for years, has not yet been published; at the present time the most complete source remains *Lew Nussberg und die Gruppe Bewegung 1962-1977*, exh. cat., Museum Bochum Kunstsammlung (1978). Nussberg refers to a 1965 publication of his draft manifesto in a Zagreb exhibition catalogue of kinetic art; an early variation also appeared in an article by the artist entitled 'Project for the Cinema', *Studio International* (August 1966), pp.64, 90–2. The full and final version of the manifesto was first published in the Czech art journal *Výtarné Umení*, nos 8–9 (1967), p.465.

5
Lev Nussberg, *Manifesto of Russian Kineticists* (1966), as translated in Igor Golomshtok and Alexander Glezer, *Soviet Art in Exile* (New York 1977), p.164.

6
Nussberg cites the impact in particular of the first Russian translation of Norbert Wiener's book, *Human Use of Human Beings: Cybernetics and Society* (Boston 1954), *Kibernetika i obshchestva* (Moscow 1958).

7
For images of influential works by these artists in the collection Costakis was allowed to take with him when he emigrated from the Soviet Union in 1977, see Angelica Zander Rudenstine, *Collecting Art of the Avant-Garde* (New York 1981).

8
In conversation with the author, 8 October 2007.

9
A few of Nussberg's large-scale projects bear more directly on this political context as he expressly designed and sought to realize installations marking historical commemoratives such as the Leningrad celebration of 50 years of Soviet power.

10
Infante has stated that he considers this to be his own individual project and does not list it with his Movement Group activities; he was sole author and creator of the diagrams and model (now destroyed).

11
As described by the artist in conversation with the author, 8 October 2007.

12
The most recent interview given by the artist and published at the time of the writing of this essay is with Evgeniia Kikodze and dates from 2002. *Francisco Infante, Nonna Goriunova: katalog artefaktov, retrospektivnoi vystavki v Moskovskom myzee sovremennogo iskusstva*, exh. cat., Museum of Contemporary Art (Moscow 2006), pp.15–19. Representative works from the spiral cycles are reproduced on pp.52–79.

13
These extracts are from the author's own translation of Infante's 1965 text 'Proekty rekonstruktsii zvezdnogo neba', reproduced in *Francisco Infante 2006*, p.81.

14
The project was installed in the Pavilion of People's Industrial Products (*Pavilion tovarov narodnogo upotrebleniia*).

15
Georg Kantor developed a 'sets theory' which led to significant revisions of the concept of infinity as a philosophical and mathematical problem. Infante refers to these theories as he explains his own course of discovery (independently of Kantor at first). *Francisco Infante 2006*, p.517.

16
This inscription, 'Annotation for the Spiral' (1965), appears on the reverse of a spiral image by Infante entitled *Requiem* (located at the Zimmerli Art Museum, New Brunswick, NJ, inv.CF2939). It is published in the original Russian with a parallel English translation in *Francisco Infante, Artefakty: Retrospektiva* (Moscow 2004), p.61.

Architecture or Revolution? – Vienna's 1968

The author would like to thank Hans Hollein, Günter Zamp Kelp, Timo Huber, and Martina Kandeler-Fritsch for valuable information given during interviews in summer 2007.

1
Hollein in Hans Hollein and Walter Pichler, *Architektur, Work in Progress*, exh. cat., Galerie St Stephan, Vienna, 1963, n.p.

2
The two artists met at a lecture given by Hans Hollein entitled 'Back to Architecture' at the Galerie St Stephan in 1962. The gallery is now better known as Galerie nächst St Stefan; the adjective, meaning 'next', was added some years later.

3
For a detailed discussion of the exhibition and the associations of technology and ritual, power and sensual beauty of the suggested designs, see Gabriele Koller, *Die Radikalisierung der Phantasie, Design aus Österreich* (Salzburg 1987), pp.200ff.

4
Banham promoted the view that the existing urban centres were poorly equipped to cope with contemporary urban living, mobility, technology, etc. Megastructures, characterized by buildings on a massive scale, were imposing structures to which partitions could be added or taken away, according to spatial demand. See Rayner Banham, *Megastructure. Urban Futures of the Recent Past* (London 1976). Similar approaches can be found with other architects of the period, e.g. Hollein's Austrian colleague Raimund Abraham and his project 'Megastructures' (1965), where the city is compacted into a transport system of enormous pipes containing dwellings and stretching out over the sea.

5
Similarly important and influential for the architectural avant-garde were the 'Clubseminar' inaugurated by Günther Feuerstein and the courses in rationalist methods and technologies by Konrad Wachsmann at the Salzburg Summer Academy.

6
A similarly influential show was Günther Feuerstein's exhibition 'Urban Fiction' in 1966-7, also at the Galerie St Stephan.

7
See Peter Cook, *Experimental Architecture* (New York 1970), p.71. Here Cook describes the 'decadence' as a 'feeling among young Austrians that their country represents a cultural remnant which is out of all proportions to its dynamic role'.

8
As mentioned in conversation by Timo Huber on 17 July 2007 in Vienna.

9
For architecture, three manifestos, all issued in 1958, were seminal in formulating a critique of post-war functionalism, initiating a new thinking in architecture: *Mould Manifesto against Rationalism in Architecture* (*Verschimmelungsmanifest gegen den Rationalismus in der Architektur*) by Fritz Stowasser (later Friedensreich Hundertwasser), *Architecture with Hands* (*Architektur mit den Händen*) by Arnulf Rainer and Markus Prachensky, and *Theses for an Incident Architecture* (*Thesen zur inzidenten Architektur*) by Günther Feuerstein.

10
Wiener Aktionismus (Viennese Actionism) showed strong links to ritual, liturgy and theatre in general, and in particular to medieval mystery plays and the baroque theatre.

11
See Friedrich Achleitner, 'Comments on Viennese Architectural History: Motifs and Motivations, Background and Influences, Therapeutic Nihilism', in *A New Wave of Austrian Architecture*, published by the Institute for Architecture and Urban Studies, Catalogue 13 (New York 1980), p.16.

12
Ibid., p.16.

13
Cook 1970, p.71.

14
The most important schools were the Technische Hochschule (Technical University) and the Akademie der Bildenden Künste (Academy of Applied Arts), in Vienna, and the Technische Universität (Technical University), in Graz.

15
See Frank Werner, *Covering + Exposing, the Architecture of Coop Himmelb(l)au* (Basel/Berlin/Boston 2000), p.8.

16
See Martina Kandeler-Fritsch and Thomas Kramer, *Get off my Cloud, Wolff D. Prix, Coop Himmelb(l)au, Texts 1968-2005* (Ostfildern-Ruit 2005), p.24.

17
For a detailed discussion of the term in the work of Haus-Rucker-Co, see Dieter Bogner, *Haus-Rucker-Co, Denkräume, Stadträume 1967-1992*

(Klagenfurt 1992), pp.274ff.

18
Haus-Rucker-Co, *Phy-Psy, Typscript*, HRC-Archive Düsseldorf, undated. See Bogner 1992, p.274 (author's translation).

19
See p.181 above, where headsets by Haus-Rucker-Co and a helmet by Walter Pichler are described.

20
Hollein presented a series of simulated spaces: a television set as extension of the university (1966), the 'non-physical' environments, an architecture pill (1967) and 'Svobodair', an environmental spray (1968).

21
In the project 'Imaginary Space' (1968), Friedrich St Florian designed transient spaces with light and laser beams.

22
See Coop Himmelblau, *Architecture is now. Projects, (Un)Buildings, Actions, Statements, Sketches, Commentaries. 1968–1983* (London 1984), p.188.

23
'Villa Rosa' was built on a 1:1 scale for an international congress on architecture at the Technische Hochschule in Vienna, and later displayed at the Museum für Angewandte Kunst in 1968.

24
Coop Himmelblau, 'Villa Rosa', loc. cit., p.188. See Werner 2000, p.28.

25
'Mobile Office' or 'In the suitcase transportable atelier' was constructed by Hans Hollein on the occasion of filming *Das österreichische Portrait* (*The Austrian Portrait*), screened by ORF (Österreichischer Rundfunk) on 7 December 1969.

26
See Kandeler-Fritsch et al. 2005, p.25.

27
See Marie-Ange Brayer, Frédéric Migayrou and Fumio Nanjo (eds), *Archilab's Urban Experi-ments: Radical Architecture, Art and the City* (London 2005), p.73.

28
The project emerged in the context of the exercise 'Design 2' at the Institut für Gebäudelehre und Entwerfen, Technische Hochschule, taught by Karl Schwanzer. Zamp Kelp was one of the tutors.

29
For a detailed description of the project, see 'The Great Vienna Auto-Expander', in Martina Kandeler-Fritsch (ed.), *Zünd-Up, Acme Hot Tar and Level, Dokumentation eines Architektur-experiments an der Wende der Sechziger Jahre* (Vienna/New York 2001), pp.66ff.

30
Author's interview with Timo Huber on 17 July 2007 in Vienna.

31
See Bogner 1992, p.279 (author's translation).

32
Ibid., p.57.

33
Ibid., p.285.

34
See Werner 2000, p.8. The foundation of the group itself gives an indication of the rebellious and uncompromising character of its members, as it was preceded by the interruption of their architectural studies (which they never finished).

35
See Coop Himmelblau 1984, p.166. The actions referred to are 'Restless Sphere' (Basel 1971) and 'City Soccer' (Vienna 1971).

36
Most of the subsequent, more politicized and aggressive work was realized in performances which various members of Zünd-Up co-presented under the group name '*Salz der Erde*' ('Salt of the Earth') between 1970 and 1972. Zünd-Up existed as a distinct group only until 1971.

37
Hans Hollein, 'Alles ist Architektur', in *Bau: Schrift für Architektur und Städtebau*, vol.20, no.1/2 (1968). For further discussions of the manifesto, see Liane Lefaivre, 'Everything is Architecture: Multiple Hans Hollein and the Art of Crossing Over', in *Harvard Design Magazine*, no.18 (spring/summer 2003), pp.65–8, and Craig Buckley, 'From Absolute to Everything: Taking Possession', in '*Alles ist Architektur*', *Grey Room*, no.28 (summer 2007), pp.108–22.

8 / LOOKING DOWN ON SPACESHIP EARTH: COLD WAR LANDSCAPES

1
Richard Buckminster Fuller, *Operating Manual for Spaceship Earth* (Carbondale 1969), p.47.

2
Ibid., p.52.

3
Michael Shamberg and Raindance Corporation, *Guerrilla Television* (New York 1971), p.3.

4
Anon., 'Earth Day and Space Day', *New York Times* (19 April 1970), p.174.

5
Martin Friedman, *Noguchi's Imaginary Landscapes* (Minneapolis 1978), p.45.

6
Charles Merewether, 'Irresistible Decay: Ruins Reclaimed', in Michael S. Roth, Claire Lyons and Charles Merewether (eds), *Irresistible Decay* (Los Angeles 1997), pp.1–13. See also Christopher Woodward, *In Ruins* (London 2002).

7
Arata Isozaki, 'Invisible City' (1966), in Joan Ockman and Edward Eigen (eds), *Architecture Culture 1943-1968* (New York 1993), p.403.

8
Georg Simmel, 'The Ruin', in Kurt H. Wolff (ed.), *Essays on Sociology, Philosophy and Aesthetics* (New York 1965), pp.259–66.

9
For the most apocalyptic vision of consumerism in the period, see Gordon Rattray Taylor, *Doomsday Book* (London 1970).

10
Barry Weisberg, *Ecocide in Indochina: The Ecology of War* (San Francisco 1970).

11
Frank Bardacke, 'Reclaim the Earth!', speech made in 1969 in Berkeley, CA, reproduced in Peter Stansill and David Zane Mairowitz (eds), *BAMN. Outlaw Manifestos and Ephemera 1965–70* (Harmondsworth 1971), p.182.

12
Theodore Roszak, *Sources: An Anthology of Contemporary Materials Useful for Preserving Personal Sanity while Braving the Great Technological Wilderness* (New York 1972), pp.xv–xvi. See also Theodore Roszak, *The Making of a Counter Culture: Reflections on the Technocratic Society and its Youthful Opposition* (New York 1970).

13
Douglas R. Weiner, *A Little Corner of Freedom. Russian Nature Protection from Stalin to Gorbachev* (Berkeley/London 1999), p.38.

14
Hans-Ulrich Obrist, 'Milano Triennale 68: A Case Study and Beyond / Arata Isozaki's Electronic Labyrinths', in Bruno Latour and Peter Weibel (eds), *Iconoclash: Beyond the Image Wars in Science, Religion and Art* (Cambridge, MA, 2002), pp.360–82.

15
Reyner Banham's *Megastructure: Urban Futures of the Recent Past* (London 1976) was the key publication in the production of a movement in retrospect.

16
There is a growing new literature on these various groups. See, for instance, Felicity D. Scott, *Architecture or Techno-Utopia. Politics after Modernism* (Cambridge, MA, 2007); Simon Sadler, *Archigram: Architecture Without Architecture* (Cambridge, MA, 2005); Martin Van Schaik and Otakar Máčel (eds), *Exit Utopia. Architectural Provocations 1956–76* (Munich 2004); Terence Riley (ed.), *The Changing of the Avant-Garde. Visionary Drawings from the Howard Gilman Collection* (New York 2002); Marie-Ange Brayer (ed.), *Architectures Experimentales 1950-2000* (Paris 2003); Larry Busbea, *Topologies: The Urban Utopia in France, 1960–1970* (Cambridge, MA, 2007).

17
See Kisho Kurokawa, *From Metabolism to Synthesis* (London 1992).

18
See, for instance, Neil Levine, 'The Significance of Facts: Mies's Collages Up Close and Personal', *Assemblage*, vol.37 (December 1998), pp.70–101.

19
Herron cited in Brandon Taylor, *Collage: The Making of Modern Art* (London 2004), p.192.

20
'At a 1963 London exhibition … a walking city was shown, with all buildings conceived as steel tanks moving mechanically and certainly crushing, as tanks do, nature and any person outside them. The example is appalling, not only because it represents an inhuman conception of the city of the future by a small group of people, but because it received wide publicity without, as far as I know, any corresponding protest.' Constantinos Doxiadis, 'Ecumeno-polis: Tomorrow's City' (1968), at www.doxiadis.org (accessed August 2007).

21
Udo Kultermann, *Kenzo Tange, 1946–1969* (Zurich 1970).

22
David E. Nye, *American Techno-logical Sublime* (Cambridge, MA, 1996).

23
Ibid., p.32.

24
Walter Pichler and Hans Hollein, 'Absolute Architecture' [1962], in Ulrich Conrads (ed.), *Programmes and Manifestoes in 20th-Century Architecture* (Cambridge, MA, 1971), p.182. See also Craig Buckley, 'From Absolute to Everything: Taking Possession in "Alles ist Architektur"', *Grey Room*, no.28 (summer 2007), pp.108–22.

25
Cherie Wendelken, 'Putting Metabolism Back in Place: The Making of Radically Decon-

textualized Architecture in Japan', in Sarah Williams Goldhagen and Réjean Legault (eds), *Anxious Modernisms. Experiments in Postwar Architectural Culture* (Cambridge, MA, 2001), p.281.

26
For a good overview of the international contacts of experimental architects in Czechoslovakia, see Ludmila Hájková and Rostislav Švácha, 'Where We Will Live Tomorrow', in *Acke Slovo Pohyb Prostor. Experimenty v Umění Šedesátých*, exh. cat. Galerie Hlavního Města Prahy (Prague 1999), pp.390-99.

27
Frei Otto's structural innovations were widely reported in Poland in the late 1950s. His books were also translated: Frei Otto, *Dachy Wiszące. Forma i Konstrucja* (Warsaw 1959). The professional magazines *Projekt* and *Architektura* featured experimental engineering structures by Otto and Robert Le Ricolais.

28
Hansen had worked in Pierre Jeanneret's studio in Paris in the late 1940s and was in the orbit of Le Corbusier's ideas. A clearline can be drawn between his notion of the Linear Continuous System and Le Corbusier's conception of the linear city developed before the Second World War. A comprehensive bibliography of reports of his work appears in Oskar Hansen, *Towards Open Form. Ku Formie Otwartej*, ed. Jola Gola (Warsaw 2005).

29
Priscilla Chapman, 'The Plug In City', *Sunday Times Magazine* (24 September 1964), p.31.

30
Peter Cook, 'The NER Group', *Architectural Design* (October 1968), p.481.

31
Anatole Kopp, *Town and Revolution* (New York 1970), p.237.

32
Peter Cook, *Experimental Architecture* (London 1970); Justus Dahinden, *Urban Structures for the Future* (New York/London,

1971); Ulrich Conrads and Hans G. Sperlich, *Fantastic Architecture* (London 1960).

33
Peter Blake, 'Cape Kennedy', *Architectural Forum* (January-February 1967), pp.50-59.

34
Arthur Rosenblatt, 'The New Visionaries', *The Metropolitan Museum of Art Bulletin*, vol.26, no.8 (April 1968), p.322.

35
Sarah Deyong, 'Planetary Habitat: the origins of a phantom movement', *The Journal of Architecture*, vol. 6 (summer 2001), pp.113-27.

36
Cook 1970, p.112.

37
Michel Ragon, *Les cités de l'avenir* (Paris 1966), p.119.

38
Friedman cited in Busbea 2007, p.70.

39
GEAM statement issued in 1960, cited in Busbea 2007, p.63.

40
Kultermann 1970, pp.112-52.

41
Sandr Kaji-O'Grady and Peter Raisbeck, 'Prototype cities in the sea', *The Journal of Architecture*, vol.10, no.4 (2005), pp.443-61.

42
Frei Otto, *Das hängende Dach*, dissertation, Technical University Berlin, 1953 (Berlin 1954), pp.116-17.

43
Frei Otto, *Zugbeanspruchte Konstruktionen*, vol. 1 (1962), p.36. See also Frei Otto (ed.), *Tensile Structures: Design, Structure, and Calculation of Buildings of Cables, Nets, and Membranes* (Cambridge, MA, 1967).

44
See Michael L. Bressler, 'Water Wars. Siberian Rivers, Central Asian Deserts, and the Structural Sources of a Policy Debate', in Stephen Kotkin and David Wolff (eds), *Rediscovering Russia in Asia:*

Siberia and the Russian Far East (Armonk, NY, 1995), pp.240-54.

45
Simon Ertz, 'Building Norilsk', in Paul R. Gregory and Valery V. Lazarev (eds), *The Economics of Forced Labor: The Soviet Gulag* (Stanford 2003), pp.127-49.

46
According to Radio Free Europe reports on Soviet media, an article by V. Shubkin published in *Kommunist* (March 1965) included a frank admission of the need to make the Soviet East a more inviting prospect for industrial workers by providing better housing, childcare and leisure facilities. The appeal to idealism made by Khrushchev to attract young workers to Siberia was viewed as a failure. See Radio Free Europe Research Institute report 'Kommunist Worries About Post-War Baby Boom' (23 March 1965), OSA archives 62-3-20, pp.2-3.

47
See anon., 'Arctic Cities', *Architectural Design*, vol.6 (1971), p.333.

48
Murray Feshbach, *Ecocide in the USSR: Health and Nature Under Siege* (New York 1993).

49
See Sarah Deyong, 'Memories of the Urban Future: the Rise and Fall of the Megastructure', in *The Changing of the Avant-Garde. Visionary Architectural Drawings from the Howard Gilman Collection* (New York 2002), pp.23-36, for an excellent overview.

50
Manfredo Tafuri, *Architecture and Utopia: Design and Capitalist Development* (Cambridge, MA, 1976) p.40.

51
Manfredi G. Nicoletti, 'The End of Utopia', *Perspecta*, vol.13 (1971), pp.268-79.

52
Alex Mlynarčik and Ľudovít Kupkovič and Viera Mecková, *VAL. Cesty a aspekty zajtrajšška* (Žilina 1995), pp.15-25.

53
Cf. Matthias Schirren, *Bruno Taut:*

Alpine Architecture – A Utopia (Munich 2004); Nancy Perloff and Brian Reed, *Situating El Lissitzky: Vitebsk, Berlin, Moscow* (Los Angeles 2003).

54
Nicoletti 1971, p.273.

55
Herbert Marcuse, *One Dimensional Man* (London 1964), p.154. See also Charles Jencks and Nathan Silver, *Adhocism: The Case for Improvisation* (London 1972); E.F. Schumacher, 'Buddhist Economics', *Resurgence* (January-February 1968), reproduced in *Small is Beautiful* (London 1973), pp.48-56; Victor J. Papanek, *Design for the Real World: Human Ecology and Social Change* (London 1972).

56
For period interpretations of the commune movement, see Ron Roberts, *The New Communes* (Englewood Cliffs, NJ, 1971); Rosabeth M. Kanter, *Commitment and Community: Communes and Utopias in Sociological Perspective* (Boston, MA, 1972).

57
Anon., 'The Sweep of the 60s', *Life* (22 December 1969), pp.27-8.

58
Nicoletti 1971, p.273.

59
See Tom Holert, 'Deserts of the Political', at www.medien-kunstnetz.de (accessed August 2007); Alessandra Ponte and Marisa Trubiano, 'The House of Light and Entropy: Inhabiting the American Desert', *Assemblage*, no.30 (August 1996), pp.12-31; Peter Reyner Banham, *Scenes in America Deserta* (Cambridge, MA, 1982).

60
See W.J.T. Mitchell, 'Holy Landscape: Israel, Palestine, and the American Wilderness', *Critical Inquiry*, vol.26, no.2 (winter 2000), pp.193-223.

61
P. Rabbit, cited in Turner, 'Where the Counterculture Met the New Economy', in *Technology and Culture*, vol.46, no.3 (July 2005), p.492.

62
Bill Voyd, 'Drop City', in Roszak 1972, p.279.

63
Cook 1970, p.26.

64
Rita Reif, 'It's taken Twenty Years, but the Dome as Home is Catching On', *New York Times* (17 November 1971), p.54.

65
This was an impression that its founders rejected: 'We were not models, hippies, or a commune ... Those trademarks are strictly the invention of establishment media.' Bernofsky, cited in Simon Sadler, 'Drop City Revisited', *Journal of Architectural Education*, vol.58, no.1 (2006), p.6.

66
Reichert, cited by Paul Hildebrandt, 'Zome-inspired Sculpture', available at www.lkl.ac.uk (accessed July 2007).

67
Peter L. Douthit, 'Drop City: A Report from the Energy Center', *Arts Magazine*, vol.41 (1967), p.50, cited in Felicity D. Scott, 'Acid Visions', *Grey Room*, no.23 (spring 2006), p.31.

68
Michael Shamberg and Raindance Corporation, *Guerrilla Television* (New York 1971), p.6.

69
'Whole Earth Catalog', *Architectural Design*, vol.4 (1970), p.169.

70
The best source on this is Fred Turner, *From Counterculture to Cyberculture: Stewart Brand, the Whole Earth Network, and the Rise of Digital Utopianism* (Chicago 2006).

71
See Murray Bochlin, *Post-Scarcity Anarchism* (Berkeley 1971).

72
Fred Turner, 'Where the Counterculture Met the New Economy: The WELL and the Origins of Virtual Community', *Technology and Culture*, vol.46, no.3 (July 2005), p.488.

73

The history of the counter-culture of the late 1960s and 1970s in the Eastern Bloc has yet to be written. Some authors have, however, provided valuable insights into the phenomenon. See, for instance, Mark Svede, 'All you Need is Lovebeads: Latvia's Hippies Undress for Success', in Susan E. Reid and David Crowley, *Style and Socialism: Modernity and Material Culture in Post-War Eastern Europe* (Oxford 2000), pp.189-208; Artemy Troitsky, *Back in the USSR: The True Story of Rock in Russia* (London/Boston 1988); Timothy W. Ryback, *Rock Around the Bloc* (Oxford 1990).

74

Roszak 1972, p.xvi.

75

E.F. Schumacher, *Small is Beautiful. Economics as if People Mattered* (New York 1973).

76

The United States Information Agency rejected the internationalist vision of 'World Game' (and in fact the ground-floor entrance to the Pavilion was dominated by a massive wall-mounted eagle fashioned in golden panels). Nevertheless, Fuller continued to develop his idea, organizing a prototype world game at the New York Studio School in 1969.

77

The Dymaxion map designed in the mid-1940s by Buckminster Fuller is a projection of a map of globe onto polyhedron that can be unfolded, and reproduces the distances and proportions between land masses with less distortion than the Mercator projection used conventionally for world maps. See Thomas W. Leslie, 'Energetic geometries: The Dymaxion Map and the skin/structure fusion of Buckminster Fuller's geodesics', *Architectural Research Quarterly*, vol.5 (2001), pp.161-70.

78

Fortune magazine had commissioned Fuller to edit a tenth-anniversary issue of the publication in 1940. Fuller was given the funds to collect enormous amounts of data on world resources. This material was kept up to date by Fuller in the years that followed. See Lloyd Steven Sieden, *Buckminster Fuller's Universe* (New York 2000), pp.374-5.

79

Richard Buckminster Fuller, *Critical Path* (New York 1981), p.221.

80

Sieden 2000, p.385.

81

Richard Buckminster Fuller in J. Krausse (ed.), *R. Buckminster Fuller, Your Private Sky: The Art of Design Science* (Baden 2003), p.473.

82

Richard Buckminster Fuller, '10 Solutions by Fuller for the Crucial World Problems', *New York Times* (29 June 1972), p.41.

83

There were a few attempts to span this divide in the early 1970s. For instance, Jacques Rougerie's developed the concept of 'Thalassopolis', a floating city in the Banda Sea in Indonesia, developed with a team of biologists and sociologists. It combined local building techniques with modern architecture's preoccupation with systems and networks. See J. and E. Rougerie, 'Thalassopolis', *Architecture d'Aujourd'hui*, vol.164 (October–November 1972), pp.80-84.

84

See Peter Lang and William Menking (eds), *Superstudio: Life Without Objects* (Turin 2003); Felicity D. Scott, 'Architecture Or Techno-Utopia', *Grey Room*, no.3 (spring 2001), pp.112-26; 'Superstudio: The Fundamental Acts/Five Stories by Superstudio (1972-73)', in Martin van Schaik and Otakar Matáčel (eds), *Exit Utopia: Architectural Provocations 1956-76* (New York/London 2004), pp.191-211.

85

Charles Jencks, *Modern Movements in Architecture* (Harmondsworth 1973), p.56.

86

A. Natalini, 'Inventory, Catalogue, Systems of Flux ... a Statement' (a lecture given at the Architectural Association in London in 1971), in Lang and Menking 2003, pp.164-7.

87

See Sarah Deyong, 'Memories of the Urban Future: The Rise and Fall of the Megastructure', in *The Changing of the Avant-Garde: Visionary Architectural Drawings from the Howard Gilman Collection* (New York 2002), p.31.

Select Bibliography

A

Abelshauser, Werner, *The Dynamics of German Industry: Germany's Path Toward the New Economy and the American Challenge* (Oxford 2005)

Abercrombie, Stanley, *George Nelson: The Design of Modern Design* (Cambridge, MA, 1995)

Abramov, Isaak P., and A. Ingemar Skoog, *Russian Spacesuits* (Chichester 2003)

Acke Slovo Pohyb Prostor. Experimenty v Umění Šedesátých, exh. cat., Galerie Hlavního Města Prahy (Prague 1999)

Agamben, G., *Stanze* (1977; rev. edn Turin 2006)

Agel, Jerome (ed.), *The Making of Kubrick's 2001* (New York 1970)

Albrecht, D., et al., *The Work of Charles and Ray Eames: A Legacy of Invention* (New York 1997)

Ali, Tariq, *Street Fighting Years: An Autobiography of the Sixties* (Glasgow 1987)

Alloway, L., *The Venice Biennale 1895–1968: From Salon to Goldfish Bowl* (Greenwich, CT, 1968)

Åman, Anders, *Architecture and Ideology in Eastern Europe during the Stalin Era: An Aspect of Cold War History* (Cambridge, MA, 1992)

Ambasz, Emilio (ed.), *Italy: The New Domestic Landscape, Achievements and Problems of Italian Design*, exh. cat., Museum of Modern Art (New York/Florence 1972)

Anderson, Jon Lee, *Che Guevara: A Revolutionary Life* (New York 1998)

Aragon, Louis, *Avez-vous lu Victor Hugo?* (Paris 1952)

Aragon, Louis, and Raoul-Jean Moulin (eds), *Jiří Kolář* (Paris 1973)

Arendt, Hannah, *The Human Condition* (Chicago 1958)

Aron, Raymond, *Le Grand Schisme* (Paris 1948)

Aron, Raymond, *Guerres en chaine* (Paris 1951)

Aron, Raymond, *L'opium des Intellectuels* (Paris 1955)

Atelier Populaire Présenté par Lui-même: 87 Affiches de Mai-Juin 1968 (Paris 1968)

Atkins, Guy, *Asger Jorn* (London 1964)

Attfield, Judy (ed.), *Utility Reassessed* (Manchester 1999)

Aulich, J., and M. Sylvestrová, *Political Posters in Central and Eastern Europe 1945–1995* (Manchester 2000)

Avermaete, T., *Another Modern: The Post-War Architecture and Urbanism of Candilis-Josic-Woods* (Rotterdam 2005)

B

Banham, Reyner, *The New Brutalism* (London 1966)

Banham, Reyner, *Megastructure: Urban Futures of the Recent Past* (London 1976)

Banham, Reyner, *Design by Choice*, ed. Penny Sparke (New York 1981)

Banham, Reyner, *Scenes in America Deserta* (Cambridge, MA, 1982)

Barbrook, Richard, *Imaginary Futures: From Thinking Machines to Global Villages* (London 2007)

Barghoorn, Frederick C., *The Soviet Cultural Offensive: The Role of Cultural Diplomacy in Soviet Foreign Policy* (Princeton 1960)

Barnstone, Deborah Ascher, *The Transparent State: Architecture and Politics in Postwar Germany* (London 2005)

Barthes, Roland, *The Eiffel Tower and Other Mythologies* (New York 1982)

Baudrillard, Jean, *Utopia Deferred: Writing for Utopie (1967–1978)*, trans. Stuart Kendall (New York 2005)

Beeren, Wim, et al., '1947–1957: Ten years of "Opbouw"', in *Het Nieuwe Bouwen in Rotterdam 1920–1960* (Delft 1982)

Bell, Daniel, *The End of Ideology: On the Exhaustion of Political Ideas in the Fifties* (Harvard 1962)

Benton, Charlotte (ed.), *Figuration/Abstraction: Strategies for Public Sculpture in Europe 1945–1968* (London 2004)

Benton, Tim (ed.), *Le Corbusier, Architect of the Century*, exh. cat., Hayward Gallery (London 1987)

Berend, Ivan T., *Central and Eastern Europe, 1944–1993: Detour from the Periphery to the Periphery* (Cambridge 1996)

Berger, John, *Renato Guttuso* (Dresden: 1957)

Berger, John, *Permanent Red: Essays in Seeing* (London 1960)

Berghahn, Volker, *America and the Intellectual Cold Wars in Europe: Shepard Stone between Philanthropy, Academy and Diplomacy* (Princeton 2001)

Berkeley, E.C., *Giant Brains, or Machines that Think* (New York 1949)

Bernatowicz, Piotr, *Picasso za Żelazną Kurtyną. Recepcja artysty i jego sztuki w krajach Europy Środkowo-wschodniej w latach 1945–1970* (Cracow 2006)

Bertsch, Georg, and Ernst Hedler, *SED: Schönes Einheit Design* (Cologne 1994)

Betts, Paul, *The Authority of Everyday Objects: A Cultural History of West German Industrial Design* (Berkeley, CA, 2004)

Betts Paul, 'The twilight of the idols. East German memory and material culture', *The Journal of Modern History*, vol.72 (2000), pp.731–6

Betts Paul and Greg Eghigian, *Pain and Prosperity: Reconsidering Twentieth Century German History* (Stanford, CA, 2003)

Bibrowski, Mieczysław, *Picasso w Polsce* (Cracow 1979)

Bill, Max (ed.), *Le Corbusier and P. Jeanneret: Oeuvre complète 1934–38* (Zurich 1939)

Binkiewicz, Donna M., *Federalizing the Muse: United States Art Policy and the National Endowment for the Arts, 1965–1980* (Chapel Hill/London 2004)

Birtwistle, Graham, and Peter Shield, 'Asger Jorn's Solutions for Architecture', *AA Files*, vol.52 (summer 2005), pp.34–54

Blake, Peter, *No Place Like Utopia* (New York 1993)

Blakesley, Rosalind P., and Susan E. Reid (eds), *Russian Art and the West: A Century of Dialogue in Painting, Architecture, and the Decorative Arts* (Deklab 2006)

Bochlin, Murray, *Post-Scarcity Anarchism* (Berkeley 1971)

Bogner, Dieter, *Haus-Rucker-Co, Denkräume, Stadträume 1967–1992* (Klagenfurt 1992)

Boobbyer, Mark, *Conscience, Dissent and Reform in Soviet Russia* (London 2005)

Booker, Christopher, *The Neophiliacs* (London 1969)

Boorstin, Daniel, *The Image* (New York 1961)

Boyer, Paul, *By the Bomb's Early Light: American Thought and Culture at the Dawn of the Atomic Age* (Raleigh, NC, 1994)

Brands, H.W., *The Devil We Knew: America and the Cold War* (Oxford 1993)

Branzi, Andrea, *The Hot House: Italian New Wave Design* (London 1984)

Brayer, Marie-Ange (ed.), *Architectures Experimentales 1950–2000* (Paris 2003)

Brayer, Marie-Ange, Frédéric Migayrou and Fumio Nanjo (eds),

Archilab's Urban Experiments: Radical Architecture, Art and the City (London 2005)

Brougher, Kerry, et al., *Visual Music, Synaesthesia in Art and Museum Since 1900* (London/New York 2005)

Brooks, Jeffrey, *Thank You, Comrade Stalin!: Soviet Public Culture from Revolution to Cold War* (Princeton 2000)

Brown, Andrew, *J.D. Bernal: The Sage of Science* (Oxford 2005)

Bruce, Gordon, *Eliot Noyes: A Pioneer of Design and Architecture in the Age of American Modernism* (London/New York 2006)

Brumfield, William Craft, and Blair A. Ruble (eds), *Russian Housing in the Modern Age: Design and Social History* (Cambridge 1993)

Bryson, Philip, *The Consumer under Socialist Planning: The East German Case* (New York 1984)

Buchli, Victor, *An Archaeology of Socialism* (Oxford 1999)

Buckminster Fuller, Richard, *Operating Manual for Spaceship Earth* (Carbondale 1969)

Buckminster Fuller, Richard, *Utopia or Oblivion: The Prospects for Humanity* (New York 1969; London 1970)

Buckminster Fuller, Richard, *Critical Path* (New York 1981)

Buck-Morss, Susan, *Dreamworld and Catastrophe: The Passing of Mass Utopia in East and West* (Cambridge, MA, 2000)

Bud, Robert, and Philip Gummett (eds), *Cold War, Hot Science: Applied Research in Britain's Defence Laboratories 1945-1990* (London 1999)

Burdick, Eugene and Henry Wheeler, *Fail-Safe* (New York 1962)

Burgess, Anthony, *A Clockwork Orange* (Harmondsworth 1972)

Burk, Kathleen, *The Troublemaker* (London 2000)

Burstow, Robert, 'The Limits of Modernist Art as a "Weapon of the Cold War": Reassessing the Unknown Patron of the Monument to the Unknown Political Prisoner', *Oxford Art Journal*, vol.20, no.1 (1997), pp.68–80

Busbea, Larry, *Topologies: The Urban Utopia in France, 1960–1970* (Cambridge, MA, 2007)

C

Calvesi, Maurizio, James Hyman, Sarah Whitfield and Massimo Onofin, *Guttuso*, exh. cat., Whitechapel Art Gallery (London 1996)

Carter, Erica, *How German is She? Postwar West German Reconstruction and the Consuming Woman* (Ann Arbor 1997)

Castillo, Greg, 'Domesticating the Cold War: Household Consumption as Propaganda in Marshall Plan Germany', *Journal of Contemporary History*, vol.40, no.2 (April 2005), pp.261–89

Caute, David, *The Fellow-Travellers: A Postscript to the Enlightenment* (London 1973)

Caute, David, *Sixty-Eight: The Year of the Barricades* (London 1988)

Caute, David, *The Dancer Defects: The Struggle for Cultural Supremacy during the Cold War* (Oxford 2005)

Chanan, Michael, *The Cuban Image* (Bloomington 1986)

Cimoli, A., and F. Irace, *La Divina Proportione: Atti del convegno (Milano, 27–29 settembre 1951)* (Milan 2007)

Cockcroft, Eva, 'Abstract Expressionism: Weapon of the Cold War', *Artforum*, vol.12 (June 1974), pp.38–41

Cocroft, Wayne D., and Roger J.C. Thomas, *Cold War: Building for Nuclear Confrontation 1946–89*, ed. P.S. Barnwell (London 2003)

Cohen, Jean-Louis, *Le Corbusier and the Mystique of the USSR* (Princeton 1992)

Cohen, Jean-Louis, and Hubert Damisch, *Scenes of the World to Come: European Architecture and the American Challenge, 1893–1960* (Paris/Montreal 1995)

Cohen, Jean-Louis, and M. Eleb, *Casablanca: mythes et figures d'une aventure urbane* (Paris 1998)

Colomina, Beatriz, *Domesticity at War* (Cambridge, MA, 2007)

Colomina, Beatriz, Annmarie Brennan and Jeannie Kim (eds), *Cold War Hothouses: Inventing Postwar Culture from Cockpit to Playboy* (New York 2004)

Colomina, Beatriz, 'Unbreathed Air 1956', *Grey Room*, no.15 (spring 2004), pp.28–59

Congrès Mondial des Intellectuelles pour la Paix, Wroclaw – Pologne, 25–28 août 1948, Compte-rendu présenté pour le Bureau du Secrétaire General (Warsaw 1949)

Conrads, Ulrich (ed.), *Programmes and Manifestoes in 20th-Century Architecture* (Cambridge, MA, 1971)

Conrads, Ulrich, and Hans G. Sperlich, *Fantastic Architecture* (London 1960)

Conway, F., and J. Siegelman, *Dark Hero of the Information Age: In Search of Norbert Wiener, the Father of Cybernetics* (New York 2005)

Cook, Peter, *Experimental Architecture* (New York 1970)

Coop Himmelblau, *Architecture is Now: Projects, (Un)Buildings, Actions, Statements, Sketches, Commentaries. 1968-1983* (London 1984)

Crew, David (ed.), *Consuming Germany in the Cold War* (Oxford/New York 2003)

Crowley, David, 'Building the World Anew: Design in Stalinist and Post-Stalinist Poland', *Journal of Design History*, vol.7, no.3 (1994), pp.187–204

Crowley, David, *Warsaw* (London 2003)

Crowley, David, 'Making the Post-War Home in Eastern Europe', in Mark Pittaway (ed.), *Globalization and Europe* (Milton Keynes 2003)

Crowley, David, and Susan E. Reid (eds), *Socialist Spaces: Sites of Everyday Life in the Eastern Bloc* (Oxford 2003)

Cullerne Bown, Matthew, and Brandon Taylor (eds), *Art of the Soviets: Painting, Sculpture and Architecture in a One-Party State, 1917-1992* (Manchester 1993)

Curtis, Barry, 'The Heart of the City', in Jonathan Hughes and Simon Sadler (eds), *Non-Plan: Essays on Freedom, Participation and Change in Modern Architecture and Urbanism* (Oxford 2000), pp.52–65

Curtis, William J.R., *Le Corbusier: Ideas and Forms* (London 1992)

Cushing, Lincoln, *Revolucion!: Cuban Poster Art* (San Francisco 2003)

D

Dahinden, Justus, *Urban Structures for the Future* (New York/London, 1971)

Daix, Pierre, *J'ai cru au matin* (Paris 1976)

Daix, Pierre, *Tout mon temps: mémoires* (Paris 2001)

Daniels, Robert Vincent, *The Rise and Fall of Communism in Russia* (New Haven 2007)

Day, Richard B. (ed.), *Cold War Capitalism: The View from Moscow, 1945-1975* (New York 1995)

De Carlo, Giancarlo, *La Piramide Rovesciata* (Bari 1968)

de Hooghe, Alexander, 'Siberia as Analogous Territory: Soviet Planning and the Development of Science Towns', *AA files*, vol.51 (winter 2005), pp.14–27

Deckker, Thomas (ed.), *The Modern City Revisited* (London 2000)

de Grazia, Victoria, *Irresistible Empire: America's Advance through Twentieth-Century Europe* (Cambridge, MA/London 2005)

Dent, Roger N., *Principles of Pneumatic Architecture* (London 1971)

Dessauce, Marc, *The Inflatable Moment: Pneumatics and Protest in '68* (Princeton 1999)

Devos, Rika, and Mil de Kooning, *L'Architecture Moderne à L'Expo 58 'Pour un Monde Plus Humain'* (Brussels 2006)

Divine, Robert, *The Sputnik Challenge* (New York 1993)

Documents: 7 CIAM Bergamo (Neneln 1979)

Doherty, Thomas, *Cold War, Cool Medium: Television, McCarthyism, and American Culture* (New York 2004)

Dolff-Bonekämper, Gabi, and Franziska Schmidt, *Das Hansaviertel. Internationale Nachkriegsmoderne in Berlin* (Berlin 1999)

Duggan, Christopher, and Christopher Wagstaff, *Italy in the Cold War: Politics, Culture and Society, 1948-58* (Oxford/Washington, DC, 1995)

Durant, Sam, et al., *Black Panther: The Revolutionary Art of Emory Douglas* (New York 2007)

Durth, Werner, Jörn Düvel and Niels Gutschow, *Ostkreuz: Personen, Pläne, Perspektiven: Architektur und Städtebau der DDR*, vol.1 (Frankfurt 1998)

E

Eames, Office of Charles and Ray, *A Computer Perspective: Background to the Computer Age* (Cambridge, MA, 1973)

Ebert, Hildtrud (ed.), *Drei Kapitel Weißensee (Dokumente zur Geschichte der Kunsthochschule Berlin-Weißensee, 1946-1957)* (Berlin 1996)

Edwards, Paul N., *The Closed World: Computers and the Politics of Discourse in Cold War America* (Cambridge, MA, 1996)

Egbert, Donald D., *Social Radicalism and the Arts – Western Europe: A Cultural History from the French Revolution to 1968* (London 1970)

Eidelberg, Martin (ed.), *Design 1935–65: What Modern Was, Selections from the Liliane and David M.Stewart Collection* (Montreal 1991)

Elderfield, John (ed.), *The Museum of Modern Art at Mid-Century: At Home and Abroad, Studies in Modern Art*, vol.4 (New York 1994)

Ernyey, Gyula, *Made in Hungary* (Budapest 1993)

Evans, Harriet, and Stephanie Donald, *Picturing Power in the People's Republic of China: Posters of the Cultural Revolution* (Lanham, MD, 1999)

EXAT 51 1951–1956, exh. cat., Centro Cultural de Cascais (Cascais 2001)

F

Falk, Barbara J., *The Dilemmas of Dissidence of East-Central Europe* (Budapest 2003)

Fehér, Ferenc, Ágnes Heller and György Márkus, *Dictatorship over Needs: An Analysis of Soviet Societies* (Oxford 1984)

Fejtö, François, *A History of the People's Democracies* (Harmondsworth 1974)

Fehrenbach, Heide, and Uta G. Poiger (eds.), *Transactions, Transgressions and Transformations: American Culture in Europe and Japan* (New York/Oxford 2000)

Ferkai, András, *Housing Estates* (Budapest 2005)

Feshbach, Murray, *Ecocide in the USSR: Health and Nature Under Siege* (New York 1993)

Fischer, David, *History of the International Atomic Agency: The First Forty Years* (Vienna 1997)

Fisher, Franklin M., et al., *I.B.M. and the U.S. Data Processing Industry: An Economic History* (New York 1983)

Folga-Januszewska, Dorota, *Picasso – Przemiany*, National Museum in Warsaw (Warsaw 2002)

Folgarait, Leonard, *Mural Painting and Social Revolution in Mexico, 1920-1940: Art of the New Order* (New York 1998)

Forty, Adrian, 'Cold War Concrete', in Mart Kalm and Ingrid Ruudi (eds), *Constructed Happiness: Domestic Environment in the Cold War Era* (Tallinn 2005), pp.28-45

Frampton, Kenneth, *Modern Architecture: A Critical History* (London 1980)

Francisco Infante, Artefakty: Retrospektiva (Moscow 2004)

Francisco Infante, Nonna Goriunova: katalog artefaktov, retrospektivnoi vystavki v Moskovskom myzee sovremennogo iskusstva, exh. cat., Museum of Contemporary Art (Moscow 2006)

Frascina, Francis, *Pollock and After: The Critical Debate* (New York 1985; 2nd edn London 2000)

Free (Abbie Hoffman), *Revolution for the Hell of It* (New York 1968)

Frei, Otto (ed.), *Tensile Structures: Design, Structure, and Calculation of Buildings of Cables, Nets, and Membranes* (Cambridge, MA, 1967)

Friebe, Wolfgang, *Buildings of The World Exhibitions* (Leipzig 1985)

Friedman, Martin, *Noguchi's Imaginary Landscapes* (Minneapolis 1978)

Frisch, Max, *Sketchbook: 1946-1949* [1950], trans. Geoffrey Skelton (New York/London 1977)

Fursenko, Aleksandr and Timothy Naftali, *Khrushchev's Cold War: The Inside Story of an American Adversary* (New York 2007)

C

Gaddis, John Lewis, *We Now Know: Rethinking Cold War History* (Oxford 1997)

Gaddis, John Lewis, *The Cold War: A New History* (Harmondsworth 2005)

Galbraith, John Kenneth, 'The Cold War and the Corporations', *Progressive*, vol.31, no.7 (1967), pp.14-18

Galison, Peter, 'War against the Center', *Grey Room*, no.4 (summer 2001), pp.6-33

Galjer, Jasner, *Design of the Fifties in Croatia: From Utopia to Reality* (Zagreb 2004)

Gerovitch, Slava, *From Newspeak to Cyberspeak: A History of Soviet Cybernetics* (Cambridge, MA, 2002)

Gervereau, Laurent, and Philippe Buton, (eds), *Le Couteau entre les dents* (Paris 1989)

Gilot, Françoise, and Carlton Lake, *Life with Picasso* (Harmondsworth 1966)

Gingrich, Arnold, *Business and the Arts: An Answer to Tomorrow* (New York 1969)

Global Village: The 1960s, exh. cat., Montreal Museum of Fine Arts (Montreal 2003)

Goban-Klas, Tomasz, *The Orchestration of the Media* (Boulder, CO, 1994)

Goldzamt, Edmund, *Architektura Zespołów Śródmiejskich I Problemy Dziedzictwa* (Warsaw 1956)

Golomshtok, Igor and Alexander Glezer, *Soviet Art in Exile* (New York 1977)

Gorbanevskaya, Natalia, *Red Square at Noon* (New York 1972)

Goscilo, Helena, and Beth Holmgren (eds), *Russia Women Culture* (Bloomington 1996)

Gosselin, Gérard and Jean-Pierre Jouffroy, *Picasso et la Presse: un peintre dans l'histoire* (Paris 2000)

Gott, Richard, *Cuba: A New History* (New Haven 2004)

Grabowska-Konwent, Anna (ed.), *Roman Cieślewicz 1930-1996* (Poznań 2006)

Gray, Chris Hables, *The Cyborg Handbook* (London 1995)

Greenhalgh, Paul (ed.), *Modernism in Design* (London 1990)

Groves, Leslie R., *Now it Can be Told: The Story of the Manhattan Project* (1962; rev. edn New York 1983)

Groys, Boris, *The Total Art of Stalinism* (Princeton 1993)

Guilbaut, Serge, *How New York Stole the Idea of Modern Art: Abstract Expressionism, Freedom, and the Cold War*, trans. Arthur Goldhammer (Chicago 1983)

Guilbaut, Serge (ed.), *Reconstructing Modernism: Art in New York, Paris, and Montreal 1945-1964* (Cambridge, MA/London 1990)

Gunther, Hans (ed.), *The Culture of the Stalin Period* (New York 1990)

H

Haddow, Robert H., *Pavilions of Plenty: Exhibiting American Culture Abroad in the 1950s* (Washington, DC, 1997)

Hammer, Martin and Lodder, Christina, *Constructing Modernity: The Art and Career of Naum Gabo* (London 2000)

Hanhimäki, Jussi M., and Odd Arne Westad (eds), *The Cold War: A History in Documents and Eyewitness Accounts* (Oxford 2004)

Hansen, Oskar, *Towards Open Form: Ku Formie Otwartej*, ed. Jola Gola (Warsaw 2005)

Hanson, Philip, *Advertising and Socialism: The Nature and Extent of Consumer Advertising in the Soviet Union, Poland, Hungary and Yugoslavia* (London/Basingstoke 1974)

Haraszti, Miklos, *The Velvet Prison: Artists Under State Socialism* (Harmondsworth 1989)

Harvey, Brian, *Russia in Space: The Failed Frontier?* (Chichester 2001)

Harvey, Sylvia, *May 68 and Film Culture* (London 1978)

Harwood, John, *The Redesign of Design: Multinational Corporations, Computers and Design Logic, 1945-1976* (New York/Ann Arbor 2006)

Harwood, John, 'The White Room: Eliot Noyes and the Logic of the Information Age Interior', *Grey Room*, no.12 (summer 2003), pp.5-31

Henket, Hubert-Jan and Hilde Heynen (eds), *Back from Utopia: The Challenge of the Modern Movement* (Rotterdam 2002)

Henriksen, Margot A., *Dr Strangelove's America: Society and Culture in the Atomic Age* (Berkeley 1997)

Heuvel, Dirk van den, and Max Risselada, *Team 10 1953-81: In Search of A Utopia of the Present* (Rotterdam 2005)

Hewlett, Richard, and Jack M. Holl, *Atoms for Peace and War 1953-1961: Eisenhower and the Atomic Energy Commission* (Berkeley 1989)

Highmore, Ben, 'Rough Poetry: Patio and Pavement Revisited', *Oxford Art Journal*, vol.29, no.2 (2006), pp.269-90

Highmore, Ben, 'Machinic Magic: IBM at the 1964-65 New York World's Fair', *New Formations*, vol.51 (winter 2003), pp.128-48

Hill, Katie (ed.), *The Political Body: Posters from the People's Republic of China* (London 2004)

Hirdina, Heinz, *Gestalten für die Serie: Design in der DDR, 1949-1985* (Dresden 1988)

Hixson, Walter L., *Parting the Curtain: Propaganda, Culture and the Cold War, 1945-1961* (London/Basingstoke 1997)

Hlaváčková, Konstantina, *Czech Fashion 1940-1970: Mirror of the Times* (Prague 2000)

Hobsbawm, Eric J., *Age of Extremes: The Short Twentieth Century, 1914-1991* (London 1994)

Hollein, Hans, *Austriennale l'Austria alla 14. Triennale di Milano 1968: il grande numero* (Vienna 1968)

Hollein, Hans, and Walter Pichler, *Architektur, Work in Progress*, exh. cat., Galerie St Stephan (Vienna 1963)

Honzík, Karel, *Architektura Všem* (Prague 1956)

Honzík, Karel, *Cestou k socialistické architektuře* (Prague 1960) (Russian trans. *Po puti k sotsialistcheskoi arkhitekture*, Moscow 1967)

Hopkins, M.F., and M.D. Kandiah (eds), *Cold War Britain, 1945-1962: New Perspectives* (Basingstoke 2003)

Horvath, Robert, *The Legacy of Soviet Dissent: Dissidents, Democratisation and Radical Nationalism in Russia* (London 2005)

Hughes, Jonathan and Simon Sadler (eds), *Non-plan: Essays on Freedom, Participation and Change in Modern Architecture and Urbanism* (London 1999)

Hutchings, Raymond, 'Soviet Design: The Neglected Partner of Soviet Science and Technology', *Slavic Review*, vol.37, no.4 (1978), pp.567-83

Hüttingered, Eduard (ed.), *Max Bill* (Zurich 1978)

Hyman, James, *The Battle for Realism* (New Haven/London 2001)

I

Ibelings, Hans (ed.), *Americanism: Dutch Architecture and the Transatlantic Model* (Rotterdam 1997)

Ikonnikov, Andreï, *L'architecture russe de la période soviétique* (Moscow 1990)

Il Modo Italiano: Italian Design and Avant-garde in the 20th Century, exh. cat., Montreal Museum of Fine Art (Montreal 2006)

Industrie und Handwerk schaffen neues Hausgerät in USA, exh. cat., Landesgewerbemuseum, Stuttgart (Berlin 1951)

Infante Arana, Francisco, *Negativnye siuzhety* (Moscow 2006)

International Sculpture Competition: The Unknown Political Prisoner (London 1953)

Isaacs, Reginald, Gropius: An Illustrated Biography of the Creator of the Bauhaus (Boston 1991)

Italienische Realisten, 1945 bis 1974, Neue Gesellschaft für Bildende Kunst und Kunstamt, Kreuzberg (Berlin 1974)

Italy At Work: Her Renaissance in Design Today, exh. cat. (Rome 1950)

J

James-Chakraborty, Kathleen, Bauhaus Culture: From Weimar to the Cold War (Minneapolis 2006)

Jankowski, Stanisław (ed.), MDM. Marszałkowska 1730-1954 (Warsaw 1955)

Jencks, Charles, Modern Movements in Architecture (Harmondsworth 1973)

Jiří Kolář: Diary 1967, exh. cat., Modern Art Oxford (Oxford 1984)

Jiří Kolář Collages 1952-82, exh. cat., Albemarle Gallery (London 1987)

Jiroutek, Jiří, Fenomenen Ještěd (Liberec 2005)

Johnson, Priscilla, and Leopold Labedz, Khrushchev and the Arts: The Politics of Soviet Culture 1962-1964 (Cambridge, MA, 1965)

Jones, Polly (ed.), The Dilemmas of Destalinisation: A Social and Cultural History of Reform in the Khrushchev Era (London 2006)

Joselit, David, 'Yippie Pop: Abbie Hoffman, Andy Warhol, and Sixties Media Politics', Grey Room, no.8 (summer 2002), pp.62-79

Joselit, David, Feedback: Television Against Democracy (Cambridge, MA, 2007)

Josephson, Paul R., New Atlantis Revisited: Akademgorodok, The Siberian City of Science (Princeton, NJ, 1997)

Josephson, Paul R., Red Atom: Russia's Nuclear Power Programme from Stalin to Today (Pittsburgh 2005)

Judt, Tony, Past Imperfect: French Intellectuals, 1944-1956 (Berkeley/Los Angeles/Oxford 1992)

Judt, Tony, Postwar: A History of Europe since 1945 (London 2005)

Junker, Detlef (ed.), The United States and Germany in the Period of the Cold War: A Handbook 1945-68 (London 2004)

K

Kahn, Herman, On Thermonuclear War (Princeton/London 1960)

Kalm, Mart, and Ruudi, Ingrid (eds), Constructed Happiness: Domestic Environment in the Cold War Era (Tallinn 2005)

Kandeler-Fritsch, Martina (ed.), Zünd-Up, Acme Hot Tar and Level, Dokumentation eines Architekturexperiments an der Wende der Sechziger Jahre (Vienna/New York 2001)

Kandeler-Fritsch, Martina, and Thomas Kramer, Get off my Cloud, Wolff D. Prix, Coop Himmelb(l)au, Texts 1968-2005 (Ostfildern-Ruit 2005)

Kanter, Rosabeth M., Commitment and Community: Communes and Utopias in Sociological Perspective (Boston, MA, 1972)

Kaplan, K., Report on the Murder of the General Secretary (London 1990)

Kaszynski, William, The American Highway: The History and Culture of Roads in the United States (Jefferson, NC, 2000)

Kaufmann, Edgar, Jr, What is Modern Design? (New York 1950)

Khrushchev, Nikita, The Dethronement of Stalin: The Full Text of the Khrushchev Speech (Manchester 1956)

Khrushchev, Nikita, O kontrol'nykh tsifrakh razvitiia narodnogo khoziaistva SSSR na 1959-1965 gody (Moscow 1959)

Kint, M., Expo '58 als belichaming van het humanistisch modernisme (Rotterdam 2001)

Kirk, Terry, The Architecture of Modern Italy, vol.2: Visions of Utopia 1900-Present (Princeton/New York 2005)

Kirkham, Pat, Charles and Ray Eames, Designers of the Twentieth Century (Cambridge, MA, 1995)

Klotz, Heinrich (ed.), Haus-Rucker-Co 1967 bis 1983 (Brunswick/Wiesbaden 1984)

Klüver, Billy, Julie Martin and Barbara Rose (eds), Pavilion by Experiments in Art and Technology (New York 1972)

Koch, Stephen, Double Lives: Spies and Writers in the Secret Soviet War of Ideas Against the West (New York/Ontario 1994)

Koller, Gabriele, Die Radikalisierung der Phantasie, Design aus Österreich (Salzburg 1987)

Kopp, Anatole, Town and Revolution (New York 1970)

Kopstein, Jeffrey, The Politics of Economic Decline in East Germany, 1945-1989 (Chapel Hill, NC, 1996)

Kornai, János, Economics of Shortage, 2 vols (Amsterdam 1980)

Koshar, Rudi, From Monuments to Traces: Artifacts of German Memory, 1870-1990 (Berkley, CA, 2000)

Koshalek, Richard (ed.), Blueprints for Modern Living. The History and Legacy of the Case Study Houses (Cambridge, MA, 1990)

Kotkin, Stephen, and Wolff, David (eds), Rediscovering Russia in Asia: Siberia and the Russian Far East (Armonk, NY, 1995)

Kowalska, Bożena, Polska Awangarda Malarska 1945-1980: Szanse i mity (Warsaw 1988)

Krausse, J. (ed.), R. Buckminster Fuller, Your Private Sky: The Art of Design Science (Baden 2003)

Kuisel, Richard F., Seducing the French: The Dilemma of Americanization (Berkeley, CA, 1993)

Kula, Marcin, Religiopodobny komunizm (Warsaw 2003)

Kultermann, Udo, Kenzo Tange - 1946-1969 (Zurich 1970)

Kunz, Diane B., Butter and Guns: America's Cold War Economic Diplomacy (New York 1997).

Kurlansky, Mark, 1968: The Year That Rocked the World (London 2003)

Kurokawa, Kisho, Metabolism in Architecture (London 1977)

Kurokawa, Kisho, From Metabolism to Synthesis (London 1992)

Kuznick, Peter J., and James Gilbert (eds), Rethinking Cold War Culture (Washington 2001)

L

Lackenbauer, P. Withney, Matthew J. Farish and Jennifer Arthur-Lackenbauer, The Distant Earl Warning (DEW) Line: A Bibliography and Documentary Resources List (Calgary 2005)

Ladd, Brian, The Ghosts of Berlin: Confronting German History in the Urban Landscape (Chicago/London 1997)

Lahusen, Thomas, and Evgeny Dobrenko (eds), Socialist Realism without Shores (Durham, NC, 1997)

Landsman, Mark, Dictatorship and Demand: The Politics of Consumerism in East Germany (Cambridge, MA, 2005)

Lane, Christel, The Rites or Rulers? Ritual in Industrial Society: The Soviet Case (Cambridge 1981)

Lang, Peter, and William Menking (eds), Superstudio: Life Without Objects (Turin 2003)

Lapp, Ralph, Must We Hide? (Boston 1949)

Lapp, Ralph, The Voyage of the Lucky Dragon (New York 1958)

Laquer, Walter, Guerrilla Warfare: A Historical and Critical Study (New Brunswick/London 1998)

Latour, Bruno, and Peter Weibel (eds), Iconoclash: Beyond the Image Wars in Science, Religion and Art (Cambridge, MA/London 2002)

Lecombre, Sylvain, and Helena Staub, Ossip Zadkine, l'oeuvre sculpté (Paris 1994)

Le Corbusier, The Modulor (London 1951)

Lefebvre, Henri, Critique of Everyday Life, trans. John Moore (London 1991)

Lefebvre, Henri, The Production of Space (Oxford 1991)

Les Années Pop 1956-68, exh cat., Centre Pompidou (Paris 2001)

Leslie, Stuart W., The Cold War and American Science: The Military-Industrial-Academic Complex at M.I.T. and Stanford (New York 1993)

Levesque, Jacques, L'URSS et la Revolution Cubaine (Montreal 1976)

Levin, Thomas, Ursula Frohne and Peter Weibel (eds), Rhetorics of Surveillance from Bentham to Big Brother (Cambridge, MA, 2002)

Lew Nussberg und die Gruppe Bewegung 1962-1977, exh. cat., Museum Bochum Kunstsammlung (Bochum 1978)

Lewallen, C.M. (ed.), Ant Farm 1968-1978 (Berkeley 2004)

Liebknecht, Karl, Die nationalen Aufgaben der deutschen Architektur (Berlin 1954)

Liivak, Ami (ed.), Tallinn-Moskva/Moskva-Tallinn, 1956-1985, exh. cat., Tallinn Art Hall (Tallinn 1996)

Loehlin, J.A., From Rugs to Riches: Housework, Consumption and Modernity in Germany (Oxford 1999)

Loewy, Raymond, Never Leave Well Enough Alone (1950; rev. edn Baltimore 2002)

Lonzi, C., Autoritratto (Bari 1969)

Loomis, John A., Revolution of Forms: Cuba's Forgotten

Art Schools (New York 1999)

Lumley, Robert, States of Emergency, Cultures of Revolt in Italy from 1968–78 (London 1990)

Lupton, Catherine, Chris Marker: Memories of the Future (London 2005)

M

Mabb, David, Menas Kasdienybei, exh. cat., Contemporary Art Centre, Vilnius (Vilnius 2006)

MacCabe, Colin, Godard: A Portrait of the Artist at Seventy (New York 2003)

MacFarquhar, Roderick and Michael Schoenhals, Mao's Last Revolution (Cambridge, MA, 2006)

Macharáčková, Marcela (ed.), Jiří Kroha (1893–1974) – architekt, malíř, designer, teoretik – v proměnách umění 20. Století (Brno 2007)

McLuhan, Marshall, The Gutenberg Galaxy (London 1962)

McLuhan, Marshall, Understanding Media (London 1967)

McLuhan, Marshall, The Medium Is the Message (Harmondsworth 1967)

McLuhan, Marshall, War and Peace in the Global Village (Corta Madera 2001)

McQuiston, Liz, Graphic Agitation: Social and Political Graphics Since the Sixties (London 1993)

Mamiya, Christin J., 'We the People: The Art of Robert Rauschenberg and the Construction of American National Identity', American Art, vol.7, no.3 (summer 1993), pp.40–64

Maniaque, Caroline, Les Cahiers de la recherche architecturale et urbaine (Paris 2002)

Marchand, Philip and Marshall McLuhan, The Medium and the Messenger (Toronto 1989)

Marcuse, Herbert, Eros and Civilisation (London 1969)

Marcuse, Herbert, One Dimensional Man (Boston 1964)

Marling, Karal Ann, As Seen on TV: The Visual Culture of Everyday Life in the 1950s (Cambridge, MA, 1994)

Martin, Reinhold, The Organizational Complex: Architecture, Media, and Corporate Space (Cambridge, MA, 2002)

Marx, Leo, The Machine in the Garden (New York 1964)

Mašinisti, exh. cat., Jaroslav Fragner Gallery (Prague 1996)

Mastanduno, Michael, Economic Containment: CoCom and the Politics of East–West Trade (Ithaca 1992)

Max Bill, exh. cat., Buffalo Fine Arts Academy and Albright-Knox Art Gallery (Buffalo, NY, 1974)

May, Elaine Tyler, Homeward Bound: American Families in the Cold War Era (New York 1988)

Meikle, Jeffrey L., American Plastic: A Cultural History (Chapel Hill, NC, 1995)

Merkel, Ina, Utopie und Bedürfnis: Die Geschichte der Konsumkultur in der DDR (Cologne 1999)

Merkel, Ina (ed.), Wunderwirtschaft. DDR-Konsumkultur in den 60er Jahren, exh. cat., Neue Gesellschaft für Bildende Kunst, Berlin (Cologne/Weimar/Vienna 1996)

Merkel, Jayne, Eero Saarinen (London 2005)

Mestre, Marie-Eve (ed.), Celebrating Air-Air, Monaco (Monaco 2000)

Michalski, Sergiusz, Public Monuments: Art in Political Bondage 1870–1997 (London 1998)

Michl, Jan, Institutional Framework Around Successful Art Forms in Communist Czechoslovakia (Budapest 1999)

Mieczkowski, Bogdan, Personal and Social Consumption in Eastern Europe (New York 1975)

Minck, Scott and Jiao Ping, Chinese Graphic Design in the Twentieth Century (London 1990)

Mlynarčik, Alex, Ľudovít Kupkovič and Viera Mecková, VAL. Cesty a aspekty zajtrajsška (Zilina 1995)

Moeller, Robert G. (ed.), West Germany Under Construction: Politics, Society and Culture in the Adenauer Era (Ann Arbor 1997)

Mokyr, Joel, Lever of Riches: Technological Creativity and Economic Progress (Oxford 1992)

Moore, R. Laurence, and Maurizio Vaudagna (eds), The American Century in Europe (Ithaca/London 2003)

Morris-Suzuki, Tessa, The Past Within Us: Media, Memory, History (New York 2005)

Moss, John, and Linda Morra (eds), At the Speed of Light There Is Only Illumination: A Reappraisal of Marshall McLuhan (Ottawa 2004)

Mumford, Eric, The CIAM Discourse on Urbanism, 1928–1960 (Boston 2000)

Mumford, Lewis, From the Ground Up (New York 1956)

Mumford, Lewis, The City in History (New York 1961)

N

Nelson, Deborah, Pursuing Privacy in Cold War America (New York 2002)

Nelson, Michael, War of the Black Heavens: The Battles of Western Broadcasting in the Cold War (Syracuse 1997)

Neuhart, John, Marilyn Neuhart and Ray Eames, Eames Design: The Work of the Office of Charles and Ray Eames (New York 1989)

Neumaier, Diane (ed.), Beyond Memory: Soviet Nonconformist Photography and Photorelated Works of Art (New Brunswick, NJ, 2004)

Noble, David F., America by Design: Science, Technology, and the Rise of Corporate Capitalism (New York 1977)

Nove, Alec, Stalinism and After (London 1975)

Nussberg, Lev, Prisheltsy v lesu (Moscow 2004)

Nuttall, Jeff, Bomb Culture (London 1968)

Nye, David E., American Technological Sublime (Cambridge, MA, 1996)

O

Ockman, Joan with Edward Eigen (eds), Architecture Culture 1943–1968 (New York 1993)

Oldenziel, Ruth and Karin Zachmann (eds), Kitchen Politics in the Cold War: Americanization, Technology, and European Users (Cambridge, MA, forthcoming)

O'Mahony, Michael, Sport in the USSR: Physical Culture–Visual Culture (London 2006)

Orvell, Miles, After the Machine: Visual Arts and the Erasing of Cultural Boundaries (Jackson 1995)

P

Packard, Vance, The Hidden Persuaders (New York 1957)

Packard, Vance, The Status Seekers (New York 1959)

Packard, Vance, The Waste Makers (New York 1960)

Padgett, Stephen, and William E. Paterson, A History of Social Democracy in Post War Europe (London/New York 1991)

Pan Picasso I Ja, exh. cat., Muzeum Narodowe (Warsaw 2003)

Pansera, A., 'Le Triennali del boom economico', in Storia e cronaca della Triennale (Milan 1978)

Paperny, V., Architecture in the Age of Stalin: Culture Two (Cambridge 2000)

Parks, J.D., Culture, Conflict and Co-Existence: American-Soviet Relations, 1917–1958 (Jefferson, NC, 1983)

Parmelin, Hélène, Le massacre des Innocents (Paris 1954)

Pawley, Martin, Buckminster Fuller (London 1990)

Pawłowski, A., Inicjacje: O sztuce, projektowaniei kształceniu projektowaniu (Warsaw 1989)

Pearce, Susan M. (ed.), Experiencing Material Culture in the Western World (London 1997)

Pelkonen, Eava-Liisa, and Esa Laaksonen (eds), Architecture + Art: New Visions, New Strategies (Helsinki 2007)

Pendergrast, Mark, For God, Country & Coca-Cola: The Definitive History of the World's Most Popular Soft Drink (London 2000)

Peter, Frank-Manuel, Das Berliner Hansaviertel und die Interbau 1957 (Erfurt 2007)

Picon, Antoine (ed.), L'art de l'ingénieur (Paris 1997)

Piotrowski, Piotr, Awangarda w cieniu Jałty Sztuka w Europie Środkowo-Wschodniej w latach 1945–1989 (Poznań 2004)

Pittaway, Mark (ed.), Globalization and Europe (Milton Keynes 2000)

Poiger, Uta G., Jazz, Rock and Rebels: Cold War Politics and American Culture in a Divided Germany (Berkeley/Los Angeles 2000)

Proccacci, Giuliano, et al., The Cominform. Minutes of the Three Conferences, 1947, 1948, 1949 (Milan 1994)

Pucci, Lara, Picturing the Worker, Guttuso, Visconti, De Santis and the Partito Communista Italiano, 1944–1953, Ph.D. dissertation, University of London, 2007

R

Ragon, Michel, Les Cités de l'avenir (Paris 1966)

Rainer, János M., and György Péteri (eds), Muddling Through in the Long 1960s: Ideas and Everyday Life in High Politics and the Lower Classes of Communist Hungary (Trondheim 2005)

Ramet, Sabina P., Rocking the State: Rock Music and Politics in Eastern Europe and Russia (Boulder, CO, 1994)

Rapaport, B.K., and K.L. Stayton, *Vital Forms: American Art and Design in the Atomic Age, 1940–1960* (New York 2001)

Rathgeb, Markus, *Otl Aicher* (London 2006)

Régnier, Philippe, *La propagande anticommuniste de Paix et Liberté, France, 1950–1956* (Brussels 1986)

Reichardt, Jasia (ed.), *Cybernetics, Art and Ideas* (London 1971)

Reid, Susan E., 'Destalinization and Taste, 1953–1963', *Journal of Design History*, vol.10, no.2 (1997), pp.177–202

Reid, Susan E., 'The Khrushchev Kitchen: Domesticating the Scientific-Technological Revolution' *Journal of Contemporary History*, vol.40 (2005), pp.289–316

Reid, Susan E., 'In the Name of the People: The Manege Affair Revisited', *Kritika*, vol.6, no.4 (autumn 2005), pp.673–716

Reid, Susan E., and David Crowley, *Style and Socialism: Modernity and Material Culture in Post-War Eastern Europe* (Oxford 2000)

Remington, Robin Alison (ed.), *Winter in Prague* (Boston 1969)

Richards, Simon, *Le Corbusier and the Concept of the Self* (New Haven 2003)

Richie, Alexandra, *Faust's Metropolis: A History of Berlin* (New York 1998)

Richmond, Yale, *Cultural Exchange and the Cold War: Raising the Iron Curtain* (Pennsylvania 2003)

Ricke, Helmut (ed.), *Czech Glass 1945–1980: Design in an Age of Adversity* (Stuttgart 2005)

Riesman, David, *Abundance for What? And Other Essays* (New York 1964)

Riley, Terence (ed.), *The Changing of the Avant-Garde: Visionary Drawings from the Howard Gilman Collection* (New York 2002)

Risselada, Max, and Dirk van den Heuvel (eds) *Team 10, 1953–1981: In Search of a Utopia of the Present* (Rotterdam 2005)

Robbins, D. (ed.), *The Independent Group: Postwar Britain and the Aesthetics of Plenty* (Cambridge, MA, 1990)

Robbins, D. (ed.), *Pierre Bourdieu* (London/Thousand Oaks, CA/New Delhi 2000)

Roberts, Geoffrey, *The Soviet Union in World Politics: Coexistence, Revolution and Cold War, 1945–1991* (London 1999)

Rome, Adam, '"Give Earth a Chance": The Environmental Movement and the Sixties', *Journal of American History*, vol.90, no.2 (September 2003), pp.525–54

Rose, Kenneth D., *One Nation, Underground: A History of the Fallout Shelter* (New York 2001)

Rosenberg, H., *The Anxious Object: Art Today and its Audience* (Chicago/London 1964)

Rosenberg, H., *The De-definition of Art* (Chicago/London 1972)

Ross, Kristin, *Fast Cars, Clean Bodies: Decolonization and the Reordering of French Culture* (Cambridge, MA, 1996)

Ross, Kristin, *May '68 and Its Afterlives* (Chicago 2002)

Roszak, Theodore, *The Making of a Counter Culture: Reflections on the Technocratic Society and its Youthful Opposition* (New York 1970)

Roszak, Theodore, *Sources: An Anthology of Contemporary Materials Useful for Preserving Personal Sanity while Braving the Great Technological Wilderness* (New York 1972)

Rouard-Snowman, Margo, *Roman Cieślewicz* (London 1993)

Rudenstine, Angelica Zander, *Collecting Art of the Avant-Garde* (New York 1981)

Ruff, Lajos, *The Brain-Washing Machine* (London 1959)

Rupnik, Jacques, *The Other Europe* (London 1988)

Rüthers, Monika, *Moskau bauen von Lenin bis Chruscev. Öffentliche Räume zwischen Utopie, Terror und Alltag* (Cologne, 2007)

Ryback, Timothy W., *Rock Around the Bloc: A History of Rock Music in Eastern Europe and the Soviet Union* (Oxford 1990)

S

Sadecký, Petr, *Octobriana and the Russian Revolution* (London 1971)

Sadler, Simon, *Archigram: Architecture Without Architecture* (Cambridge, MA, 2005)

Sartre, Jean-Paul, *Sartre on Cuba* (New York 1961)

Saunders, Frances Stonor, *Who Paid the Piper? The CIA and the Cultural Cold War* (London 1999)

Sauvage, Tristram (aka Arturo Schwartz), *Nuclear Art* (Gallery Schwartz, Milan), trans. John A. Stephens (Milan 1962)

Sayres, Sohnya, Anders Stephanson, Stanley Aronowitz and Frederic Jameson (eds), *The 60s Without Apology* (Minneapolis 1984)

Schaik, Martin van, and Otakar Mačel (eds), *Exit Utopia: Architectural Provocations 1956–76* (New York/London/Munich 2004)

Schapiro, Leonard, and Albert Boiter, *The U.S.S.R. and the Future: An Analysis of the New Program of the CPSU* (New York 1963)

Schulz, Stefanie and Carl-Georg Schulz, *Das Hansaviertel – Ikone der Moderne. 50 Jahre Interbau* (Berlin 2007)

Schumacher, E.F., *Small is Beautiful: Economics As if People Mattered* (New York 1973)

Schwartz, Richard Alan, *Cold War Culture: Media and the Arts, 1945–1990* (New York 2000)

Schwartz, Thomas Alan, *America's Germany: John J. McCloy and the Federal Republic of Germany* (Cambridge, MA, 1991)

Scott, Alison, and Christopher Geist (eds), *The Writing on the Cloud: American Culture Confronts the Atomic Bomb* (Lanham 1997)

Scott, Felicity D., *Architecture or Techno-Utopia. Politics after Modernism* (Cambridge, MA, 2007)

Scott-Smith, Giles, *The Politics of Apolitical Culture: The Congress for Cultural Freedom, the CIA and Post-War American Hegemony* (London 2002)

Scrivano, Paolo, 'Signs of Americanisation in Italian Domestic Life: Italy's Postwar Conversion to Consumerism', *Journal of Contemporary History*, vol.40 (2005), pp.317–40

Scrivano, Paolo, and Bonifazio, Patrizia, *Olivetti Builds: Modern Architecture in Ivrea* (Milan 2001)

Sedláková, Radomíra, *Sorela: Česká architektura padesátých let*, exh. cat., Národní Galerie (Prague 1994)

Shamberg, Michael, and Raindance Corporation, *Guerrilla Television* (New York 1971)

Shaw, Jeffrey, and Peter Weibel (eds), *Future Cinema: The Cinematic Imaginary after Film* (Cambridge, MA, 2003)

Shiomi, Haruhito, and Kazu Wada, *Fordism Transformed: The Development of Production Methods in the Automobile Industry* (Oxford 1995)

Sieden, Lloyd Steven, *Buckminster Fuller's Universe* (New York 2000)

Siegelbaum, L. (ed.), *Borders of Socialism: Private Spheres of Soviet Russia* (Houndmills 2006)

Siegfried, Detlef, and Axel Schildt (eds), *Between Marx and Coca-Cola: Youth Cultures in Changing European Societies 1960–1980* (Oxford/New York 2005)

Sims, Lowery Stokes, *Wilfredo Lam and the International Avant-Garde, 1923–1982* (Austin, TX, 2002)

Ślusarczyk, J., *Powstanie i działalność ruchu obrońców pokoju w latach 1948–1957* (Wrocław 1987)

Smith, P.D., *Doomsday Men: The Real Dr Strangelove and the Dream of the Superweapon* (London 2007)

Smith, Terry, *Making the Modern: Industry, Art, and Design in America* (Chicago 1993)

Sparke, Penny (ed.), *Design by Choice* (London 1981)

Spigel, Lynn, *Welcome to the Dreamhouse: Popular Media and Postwar Suburbs* (Durham, NC, 2001)

Spitz, René, *hfg ulm, The View Behind the Foreground: The Political History of the Ulm School of Design, 1953–1968* (Fellbach 2002)

Spufford, Francis, and Jenny Uglow (eds), *Cultural Babbage: Technology, Time and Invention* (London/Boston 1996)

Staniszewski, Mary Anne, *The Power of Display: A History of Exhibition Installations at the Museum of Modern Art* (Cambridge, MA, 1998)

Stanley Kubrick, exh. cat., Deutsches Film Museum and Deutsches Architektur Museum (Frankfurt 2004)

Stansill, Peter, and David Zane Mairowitz (eds), *BAMN. Outlaw Manifestos and Ephemera 1965–70* (Harmondsworth 1971)

Steinberg, Leo, *Other Criteria: Confrontations with Twentieth-Century Art* (London 1972)

Steiner, André, *Von Plan zu Plan: Eine Wirtschaftsgeschichte der DDR* (Munich 2004)

Stermer, Douglas (ed.), *The Art of Revolution, Castro's Cuba 1959–1970* (London 1970)

Stimson, Blake, *The Pivot of the World: Photography and Its Nation* (Cambridge, MA, 2006)

Stitziel, Judd, *Fashioning Socialism: Clothing, Politics and Consumer Culture in East Germany* (Oxford/New York 2005)

Stokes, Raymond G., *Constructing Socialism: Technology and Change in East Germany, 1945–1990* (Baltimore/London 2000)

Strasser, Susan, Charles McGovern and Matthias Judt (eds), *Getting and Spending: European and American Consumer Societies in the Twentieth Century* (New York/Cambridge 1998)

Summer of Love: Psychedelische Kunst der 60er Jahre, exh. cat., Schirn Kunsthalle (Frankfurt 2006)

Sutton, Antony C., *Western Technology and Soviet Economic Development, 1930 to 1945* (Stanford, CA, 1971)

Švácha, Rostislav, and Marie Platovská (eds), *Dějiny českého výtvarného umění V, 1939–1958* (Prague 2005)

Sviták, Ivan (ed.), *The Czechoslovak Experiment 1868–1969* (New York/London 1971)

Swann, Brenda, and Francis Aprahamian (eds), *J.D. Bernal: A Life in Science and Politics* (London/New York 1999)

Sylvestrová, Martá (ed.), *Česky plakát 60. let*, exh. cat., Moravské Galerie (Brno 1997)

Syrkus, Helena, *Społeczne cele urbanizacji. Człowiek i środowisko* (Warsaw 1984)

T

Tafuri, Manfredo, *Modern Architecture*, vol.2 (Milan 1976)

Tafuri, Manfredo, *Architecture and Utopia: Design and Capitalist Development* (Cambridge, MA, 1976)

Tarkhanov, Alexei, and Sergei Kavtaradze, *Stalinist Architecture* (London 1992)

Taubman, William, *Khrushchev: The Man and his Era* (London 2004)

Taylor, A.J.P., *A Personal History* (London 1983)

Taylor, Brandon, *Collage: The Making of Modern Art* (London 2004)

Taylor, Frederick, *The Berlin Wall: A World Divided, 1961–1989* (London 2007)

Taylor, Gordon Rattray, *Doomsday Book* (London 1970)

Taylor, Ronald, *Berlin and its Culture: A Historical Portrait* (New Haven/London 1997)

Thomas, Kenneth S., and Harold J. McMann, *US Spacesuits* (Chichester 2006)

Tichi, Cecilia, *Shifting Gears: Technology, Literature, and Culture in Modernist America* (Chapel Hill /London 1987)

Tompson, William J., *Khrushchev: A Political Life* (Basingstoke 1995)

Topolski, Feliks, *Fourteen Letters* (London 1984)

Treib, Marc, *Space Calculated in Seconds* (Princeton 1996)

Triolet, Elsa, *Le Monument* (Paris 1957)

Troitsky, Artemy, *Back in the USSR: The True Story of Rock in Russia* (London/Boston 1988)

Tuchman, Maurice (ed.), *Art and Technology: A Report on the Art and Technology Program of the Los Angeles County Museum of Art, 1967–1971*, exh. cat., Los Angeles County Museum of Art (Los Angeles 1971)

Turner, Fred, *From Counterculture to Cyberculture: Stewart Brand, the Whole Earth Network, and the Rise of Digital Utopianism* (Chicago 2006)

Tusa, Ann, and John Tusa, *The Berlin Airlift* (Boulder, CO, 1998)

Tyler, Parker, *Underground Film* (New York 1969)

Tyrannei Des Schönen: Architektur Der Stalin-Zeit, exh. cat., Österreichisches Museum für angewandte Kunst (Vienna 1994)

Tyszkiewicz, Jakub, *Sto wielkich dni Wrocławia: Wystawa Ziem Odzyskanych we Wrocławiu a propaganda polityczna ziem zachodnich i północnych w latach 1945–1948* (Wrocław 1997)

U

Utley, Gertje R., *Picasso: The Communist Years* (New Haven/London 2000)

V

Václav Cigler A Absolventi Oddelenia Sklo V Architektúre na Vysokéj škole výtvarných umění v Bratislavě 1965–1979, exh. cat., Galérie Porkorná, Prague and Slovenská Národná Galéria, Bratislava (Prague 2003)

Vaïsse, M., *Le pacifisme en Europe des années 1920 aux années 1950* (Brussels 1993)

Vanderbilt, Tom, *Survival City: Adventures Among the Ruins of Atomic America* (New York 2002)

Vaneigem, Raoul, *The Revolution of Everyday Life* (London 1967)

Varon, Jeremy, *Bringing the War Home: The Weather Underground, The Red Army Faction, and the Revolutionary Violence of the 1960s and 1970s* (Berkeley, CA, 2004)

Venezia e le Biennali: I percorsi del gusto, ed. Comune di Venezia (Milan/Venice 1995)

Verdery, Katherine, *What was Socialism and What Comes Next?* (Princeton 1996)

Virilio, Paul, *Cinema and War: The Logistics of Perception* (London 1989)

Virilio, Paul, *Bunker Archeology* (Princeton 1996)

Vismann, Cornelia, 'Tele-Tribunals: Anatomy of a Medium', in *Grey Room*, no.10 (winter 2003), pp.5–21

W

Walker, Martin, *The Cold War: A History* (New York 1993)

Wall, Irwin M., *The United States and the Making of Postwar France 1945–54* (Cambridge 1991)

Walsh, Victoria, *Nigel Henderson: Parallel of Life and Art* (London 2001)

Weiner, Douglas R., *A Little Corner of Freedom: Russian Nature Protection from Stalin to Gorbachev* (Berkeley/London 1999)

Weisberg, Barry, *Ecocide in Indochina: The Ecology of War* (San Francisco 1970)

Werner, Frank, *Covering + Exposing, the Architecture of Coop Himmelb(l)au* (Basel/Berlin/Boston 2000)

Westad, Odd Arne, *The Global Cold War Third World Interventions and the Making of Our Times* (Cambridge/New York 2005)

Westad, Odd Arne (ed.), *Reviewing the Cold War: Approaches, Interpretations, Theory* (London 2000)

Wharton, Annabel Jane, *Building the Cold War: Hilton International Hotels and Modern Architecture* (Chicago 2001)

White, Nicola, *Reconstructing Italian Fashion: America and the Development of the Italian Fashion Industry* (New York 2000)

Whitfield, Stephen J., *The Culture of the Cold War* (Baltimore 1991)

Wiener, Norbert, *Cybernetics: Or Control and Communication in the Animal and the Machine* (Cambridge, MA, 1948)

Wiener, Norbert, *The Human Use of Human Beings: Cybernetics and Society* (Boston 1950)

Wiesen, S. Jonathan, 'Miracles for Sale: Consumer Displays and Advertising in Postwar West Germany', in David Crew, *Consuming Germany in the Cold War* (Oxford/New York 2002), pp.151–78

Wigley, Mark, 'Network Fever', in *Grey Room*, no.4 (summer 2001), pp. 82–122

Wilk, Christopher (ed), *Modernism: Designing a New World 1914–1939* (London 2006)

Williams Goldhagen, Sarah, and Réjean Legault (eds), *Anxious Modernisms: Experimentation in Postwar Architectural Culture* (Cambridge, MA, 2001)

Wilson, Sarah, *Art and the Politics of the Left in France, c.1935–1955*, Ph.D. dissertation, University of London, 1992

Wilson, Sarah, et al., *Paris: Capital of the Arts, 1900–1968*, exh. cat., Royal Academy of Arts (London 2002)

Wolff, Kurt H. (ed.), *Essays on Sociology, Philosophy and Aesthetics* (New York 1965)

Wood, Ghislaine (ed.), *Surreal Things: Surrealism and Design*, exh. cat., Victoria and Albert Museum (London 2007)

Wright, Patrick, *Iron Curtain: From Stage to Cold War* (London 2006)

X

XIV Triennale, Catalogo Generale (Milan 1968) *50. Léta Užité Uměni a Design*, exh. cat., Uměleckoprůmyslové Muzeum (Prague 1988)

Y

Yevtushenko, Yevgeny, *A Precocious Autobiography* (New York 1963)

Yoshimi, S., '"Made in Japan": The cultural politics of "home electrification" in postwar Japan', *Media, Culture and Society*, vol.21 (1999), pp.149–71

Youngblood, Gene, *Expanded Cinema* (New York 1970)

Z

Zabierowski, S., and M. Krakowiak (eds), *Realizm Socjalistyczny w Polsce z perspektywy 50 lat* (Katowice 2001)

Zaslavsky, Victor, and E. Agarossi, *Togliatti e Stalin. Il Partito comunista italiano e la politica estera sovietica* (Bologna 1998)

Zatlin, Jonathan R., *The Currency of Socialism: Money and Political Culture in East Germany* (Cambridge 2007)

Zervos, Christian, *Pablo Picasso*, vol.10: *Oeuvres de 1939 et 1940* (Paris 1959)

Zhensheng, Li, *Red-Color News Soldier* (London 2003)

Exhibition Object List

Note: the Exhibition Object List was correct at the time of going to press.

Introduction

Sergei Korolev, Design Studio No 1, Sputnik, 1957
Metal
620 x 3800 mm
The K. E. Tsiolkovsky State Museum of the History of Cosmonautics, Kaluga
Plate 6.2

1 / Anxiety and Hope in the Aftermath of War

Divided World

Anonymous, American Sector sign, Berlin, 1945
Plywood, paint lacquer
100 x 1920 x 2780mm
Deutsches Historisches Museum, Berlin: 1990/1571.1

Max Bill, poster for 'USA Builds' (USA baut), 1945
Colour lithograph
1312 x 950mm
V&A: E.217-1982
Plate 2.10

Karel Šourek (designer), Tibor Honti (photographer), Hail to the Red Army Protectors of the New World, (Sláva Rudé Armádě – záštitě nového světa), Czechoslovakia, poster, 1945
Printed paper
810 x 1154mm
Private collection: P 631
Frontispiece

Tadeusz Trepkowski, Keep aware of enemies of the people (Bądź czujny wobec wroga narodu), poster, 1953
Offset
1000 x 700 mm
National Museum, Warsaw

Ossip Zadkine, model for monument La Ville Détruite (The Destroyed City)
Bronze
1280 x 560 x 580mm
Musée Zadkine, Paris: MZS 249
Plate 1.19

Constant (Constant A. Nieuwenhuys), Scorched Earth (Verschroeide Aarde), 1951
Oil on canvas
1200 x 750mm
Stedelijk Museum, Schiedam: S/68
Plate 4.11

Walerian Borowczyk, America Gifts (Amerykanskie dary), 1952
Lithograph on paper
470 x 360mm
National Museum, Warsaw: Gr.W.176

Walerian Borowczyk, The Free World (Wolny swiat), 1953
Lithograph on paper
358 x 262mm
National Museum, Warsaw: Gr.W.1060

The Bomb in the Brain

Isamu Noguchi, model for Memorial to the Dead of Hiroshima, 1952
Black Brazilian granite, stainless steel, wood
800 x 1500 x 495mm
The Isamu Noguchi Foundation and Garden Museum, New York: 400B-1/2

Enrico Baj, Two Atomic Figures (Due figure atomizzate), 1951
Oil and enamel on canvas
600 x 1200 x 20mm
Enrico Baj Collection
Plate 4.8

Enrico Baj, Manifesto Bum, 1952
Varnish and acrylic on canvas
1030 x 940mm
Private collection
Plate 4.6

Enrico Baj, Atomic Figure (Figura Atomica), 1952 (remade 1997)
Bone, chalk and wood
490 x 480 x 320mm
Enrico Baj Collection
Plate 4.7

Le Corbusier and Edouard Trouin, Basilique La Sainte-Baume, 1948
Heliotype
220 x 730mm
Fondation Le Corbusier, Paris: FLC 17760
Plate 4.19

Paul László, Longitudinal section, John A. Hertz Residence Fallout Shelter, Woodland Hills,
California. 1955
Ink and graphite on board
393.7 x 698.5mm
Architecture & Design Collection, University Art Museum, University of California, Santa Barbara
Plate 4.15

Frederick Kiesler, model of Endless House, 1950-60
Plaster
200 x 500 x 152mm
The Museum of Modern Art, New York: MC 25

Frederick Kiesler, Endless House, sections of storage areas and perspectives, 1951
Ink and ink wash on paper
375 x 451mm
The Museum of Modern Art, New York: SC29.1966

Frederick Kiesler, Endless House, section, 1951
Ink and ink wash on paper
(b: ink and cut-and-pasted paper on tracing paper)
378 x 454mm
The Museum of Modern Art, New York: SC38.1966.a-b
Plate 4.16

Swords to ploughshares

Charles and Ray Eames, leg splint, designed 1941-2. Manufactured by Plyformed Wood Company, Los Angeles 1942-3; Evans Products Company 1943-5
Moulded plywood
203 x 114 x 1067mm
V&A: W.49-1983
Plate 3.13

Charles and Ray Eames, Armchair, manufactured by Zenith Plastics for Herman Miller. 1950.
Grey moulded shell with rope-edge, seng swivel mechanism and dowel legs
686 x 810 x 635 mm
V&A: W.15-2007
Plate 1.14

Edgar Kaufmann, Prize designs for modern furniture from the International Competition for Low-Cost Furniture Design, exhibition catalogue, New York, 1950
Printed magazine
254 x 193mm
V&A/NAL: 47.K Box 1
Plate 3.15

Charles and Ray Eames, storage unit, designed 1949-50, manufactured by Herman Miller Furniture Co.
Zinc-plated steel, birch-faced plywood, plastic-coated plywood and lacquered fibreboard (masonite)
1489 x 1194 x 425mm
V&A: W.5:3-1991/ W.5:4-1991/ W.5:5-1991
Plate 3.18

Eero Saarinen, Womb Chair, designed 1946, manufactured by Knoll Associates, Inc., 1948
Upholstered latex foam on fibreglass-reinforced plastic shell and chrome-plated steel rod base
923 x 1026 x 910mm
Private collection
Plate 3.16

Gaston Van den Eynde, European Corporation for a Higher Standard of Living with the Marshall Plan, poster, printed by Mouton Cy, 1950
Colour offset lithograph
704 x 513mm
V&A: E.1900-1952
Plate 3.5

Corradino D'Ascanio, Vespa 125CC, motorscooter, manufactured by Piaggio & Co., 1951
Dark grey lacquered metal
940 x 840 x 1780mm
Die Neue Sammlung, Munich: 227
Plate 3.8

Gio Ponti, 'La Cornuta', coffee-making machine with horizontal boiler and four dispensers, manufactured by La Pavoni, 1947/8
Metal
520 x 920 x 620mm
Private collection
Plate 3.10

Marcello Nizzoli, Lexikon 80 typewriter, designed 1947, manufactured by British Olivetti Ltd., Glasgow
Pressed steel, chromed steel
and plastic
230 x 560 x 375mm
V&A: M.27-1993

Giovanni Pintori, Olivetti Lexikon, poster, designed for Olivetti S.p.A, Ivrea, 1953
Colour offset
693 x 484mm
V&A: Circ.634-1965
Plate 3.11

Fritz Fend, Messerschmitt Kabinenroller KR 200, designed 1955, manufactured by Fahrzeug-und Maschinenbau GmbH, Regensburg, 1959
Silver-coloured metal, silver
1270 x 1320 x 2850mm
Die Neue Sammlung, Munich: 10/99
Plate 3.9

Design and Defence Research

Richard Buckminster Fuller, model of Geodesic Dome, 1952
Elastic cord and metal
514 x 991mm
The Museum of Modern Art, New York: MC 27, Gift of the Architect

Geodesics Inc. (engineers) and Jack Masey (Co-ordinating designer, United States Information Agency), copy of drawing no. D2 for a 100-ft dome for the US Pavilion, International Trade Fair, Kabul, 1956, concept design by Richard Buckminster Fuller
Print on paper
880 x 920mm
Private collection (Jack Masey, New York)

Konrad Wachsmann, design for large aeroplane hangars, structure based on a standard construction element, 1953
Ink on transparency
630 x 2245mm
Deutsches Architekturmuseum, Frankfurt am Main: 272-001-006

Konrad Wachsmann, design for aeroplane hangars, perspective, 1950-53
Ink on transparency
185 x 435mm
Deutsches Architekturmuseum, Frankfurt am Main: 272-001-001

Konrad Wachsmann, design
for aeroplane hangars, bird's-
eye perspective, 1950–53
Ink on transparency
185 x 430mm
Deutsches Architekturmuseum,
Frankfurt am Main: 272-001-002

Konrad Wachsmann, designs
for aeroplane hangars, perspective,
1950–53
Ink on transparency
185 x 449mm
Deutsches Architekturmuseum,
Frankfurt am Main: 272-001-003

IBM Corporation, Military
Products Division, excerpts
from film *On Guard! The Story
of SAGE*, 1956
IBM Archive, New York

An Iron Curtain Descends
Dmitrii Chechulin (architect)
and I. Tigranov (structural
engineer), administrative building
in Zariad'e, the eighth high-rise
tower-block planned for Moscow
(unbuilt), 1947–9
Watercolour and ink on paper
2165 x 1370mm
Schusev State Museum of
Architecture (MUAR), Moscow:
Kpof 4678/4
Plate 2.1

Yevgenii Vuchetich, *We'll
Hammer Our Swords into
Ploughshares! (Perekuem mechi
na orala!)*, 1957
Bronze; granite base
2800 x 400 x 800mm
State Tretyakov Gallery: SKS-482

City Visions
Hermann Henselmann,
*Stalinallee, East-Berlin,
Perspective Straussberger
Platz*, 1952
Pen on transparency
1488.6 x 1200mm
Berlinische Galerie,
Landesmuseum für Moderne
Kunst, Fotografie und Architektur,
Berlin: BG-AS-81.1.2

Hermann Henselmann, *Façade
of building on Marchlewskistrasse,
East Berlin*, c.1952
Charcoal on transparency
550 x 1415mm
Berlinische Galerie,
Landesmuseum für Moderne
Kunst, Fotografie und Architektur,
Berlin: BG-AS-81.2.1
Plate 2.9

Anonymous, *Socialism is
Winning (Der Sozialismus
siegt)*, poster, 1950s
Printed paper
621 x 876mm
Stiftung Haus der Bundesrepublik
Deutschland Bonn: 1990/2/229

Anonymous, poster showing
Stalinallee, a project of the
National Development
Programme, Berlin, 1952
('Nationales Aufbauprogramm
Berlin 1952'), printed by Greif
Graphischer Grossbetrieb,
East Berlin, 1952
Printed paper
832 x 1185mm
Stiftung Haus der Bundesrepublik
Deutschland Bonn: 1995/11/0485

Johannes H. van den Broek and
Jacob B. Bakema, *Apartment
block Bartningallee 7*, 1956, built
for Interbau housing exhibition,
West Berlin, 1957
Ink on paper
Nederlands Architectuur Instituut,
Rotterdam, Van den Broek and
Bakema archive: 1135 t 1
Plate 2.17

Le Corbusier and Wogenscky
workshop after a drawing by
Tobito, site plan and side elevation,
East and South of the Unité
d'Habitation, Charlottenburg,
West Berlin, 1: 500, 17.03.1956
India ink on gelatin print, print
from tracing paper
930 x 1430mm
Fondation Le Corbusier, Paris:
FLC 23681

Le Corbusier, model of the Unité
d'Habitation, Charlottenburg,
West Berlin, 1957–8, model
made c.1980
Wood
153 x 260 x 565mm
Berlinische Galerie,
Landesmuseum für Moderne
Kunst, Fotografie und Architektur,
Berlin

Socialist Realism in the
Eastern Bloc
Zdzisław Głowacki and
Aleksander Kromer (design),
tapestry on the themes of the
reconstruction of Warsaw,
American dockers destroying
armaments and the war in Korea,
woven by students in Maria
Kańska-Piotrowska's atelier
at the State High School of Fine
Art in Łódź, Poland 1950–52
Wool

1650 x 3030mm
The Central Museum of Textiles,
Łódź: CMW 10102/w/1139
Plate 1.7

Viktor Ivanov, *Long live Moscow!
(Da zdrazwute Moskva)*, poster,
1947
Printed paper
750 x 560mm
Private collection: P 2752

Viktor Koretsky, *It is not possible
to break the will of the Korean
people (Koreiskii narod ne slomit')*,
poster, 1953
Printed paper
855 x 550mm
Private collection: P 1957

Mikhail Posokhin and Ashot
Mndoiants (architects), V.
Lagutenko (engineer), A.
Bartashevich (main constructor)
and S. Shkol'nikov (main
engineer), model of a 6- and
10-storey panel-construction
residential house in district
surrounding Peschanaia square,
Moscow, 1953 (model early
1970s)
Plastic, wood and metal net
435 x 205 x 810mm
Schusev State Museum of
Architecture (MUAR), Moscow:
R II 271

An Alternative Path: Exat 51 in
Yugoslavia
Ivan Picelj (Exat 51), *Composition
54*, 1954
Tempera on paper
640 x 640mm
Museum of Contemporary Art,
Zagreb

Exat 51 (Vjenceslav Richter,
Zvonimir Radic, Ivan Picelj
and Aleksandar Srnec), *Spatial
depiction of the Exhibition
Brotherhood and Unity Motorway*,
Art Pavilion Zagreb, 1950
Architectural drawing, collage
Museum of Contemporary Art,
Zagreb: 1326/1

Exat 51 (Vjenceslav Richter,
Zvonimir Radic, Ivan Picelj and
Aleksandar Srnec), *Spatial
depiction of the Exhibition
Brotherhood and Unity Motorway*,
Art Pavilion Zagreb, 1950
Architectural drawing, collage
Museum of Contemporary
Art, Zagreb: 1326/2
Plate 1.10

Vjenceslav Richter (Exat 51),
armchair, 1952
Wood and metal
Applied Arts Museum, Zagreb
Plate 1.11

Vjenceslav Richter, Model of
Yugoslavian pavilion, Expo '58,
Brussels, 1958, model made by
Department of Architecture and
Urbanism, Faculty of Engineering,
University of Ghent (date
unknown)
Wood, metal and plastic
500 x 1350 x 1012mm
Department of Architecture and
Urbanism, Faculty of Engineering,
University of Ghent

2 / The Conscription of the Arts

Morality of Objects: the Origins
of the HfG Ulm
Otl Aicher, *Man and technology
(Mensch und Technik)*, lecture
poster for the Volkshochschule,
1947–50
Lithograph on paper
830 x 405mm
Ulmer Museum/HfG-Archiv Ulm
Plate 3.21

Otl Aicher, *Wiederaufbau
(Reconstruction)*, lecture poster
for the Volkshochschule, 1947–50
Lithograph on paper
820 x 400mm
Ulmer Museum/HfG-Archiv Ulm
Plate 3.21

Otl Aicher, *Wie wohnen? (How
to live?)*, lecture poster for the
Volkshochschule, 1947–50
Lithograph on paper
820 x 400mm
Ulmer Museum/HfG-Archiv Ulm
Plate 3.21

Max Bill, irradiation lamp,
manufactured by Novelectric
AG, Zurich, 1951
Metal (aluminium, stainless steel),
light grey or silver lacquered,
black plastic
585 x 385mm
V&A: New acquisition

Max Bill and Hans Gugelot,
Ulmer Hocker (Ulm stool), 1954,
manufactured for the Hochschule
für Gestaltung, Ulm, Germany
Unlacquered spruce and beech
450 x 400 x 290mm
Die Neue Sammlung, Munich:
384/95

Max Bill and Ernst Moeckl,
kitchen clock with timer,

manufactured by Gebrüder
Junghans AG, Schramberg,
Germany, 1956–7
Metal, glass, ceramic and plastic
260 x 190 x 65mm
V&A: M.224-2007
Plate 3.20

Dieter Rams and Hans Gugelot,
Phonosuper, SK55 (a later version
of the 1956 SK4 model),
manufactured by Braun AG,
Taunus, West Germany, 1963
Metal, wood and acrylic plastic
240 x 580 x 290mm
V&A: W.51-1978
Plate 3.22

Peter Staudacher, *Object Assembly
(Objektverband)*, student design,
tutor: Tomas Maldonado, 1962/3
Wood (13 parts)
150 x 180 x 90mm
Ulmer Museum/HfG-Archiv Ulm

Peter Hofmeister, *Topological
sculptural experiment
(Topologische Plastik)*, student
design, 1968
Material unknown
400 x 460 x 550mm
Ulmer Museum/HfG-Archiv Ulm

Art and Peace
Le Corbusier, *The Hands (Les
Mains)*, tapestry, 1951
Tapestry (wool)
2190 x 2730mm
Fondation Le Corbusier, Paris:
FLC 7
Plate 4.25

Le Corbusier, *Poème de l'angle
droit*, folio, published by Editions
Verve, Paris, 1955
Lithograph
421 x 317mm
V&A/NAL: RC.CC.2
Plate 2.12

Andrzej Wróblewski, *Surrealistic
Execution (Rozstrzelanie
surrealistyczne)*, 1949
Oil on canvas
1290 x 1980mm
National Museum, Warsaw:
MPW 1125

Pablo Picasso, *Dove*, 1949
Lithograph on paper
547 x 697mm
Tate, London: P 11366

Pablo Picasso, scarf for the Festival
Mondial de la Jeunesse
et des Etudiants pour la Paix,
Berlin, 5–19 August 1951
Printed cotton

810 x 745mm
National Museum, Warsaw:
Wrz.t.3010
Plate 1.28

Pablo Picasso, *Paix Stockholm*,
Paris, 1958 (22-Jul-58), poster,
printed by Schuster, Paris
Colour lithograph, ink on paper
777 x 497mm
V&A: E.1843-2004, Gift of the
American Friends of the V&A;
Gift to the American Friends by
Leslie, Judith and Gabri Schreyer
and Alice Schreyer Batko

Anonymous, *Jo-Jo-la Colombe*
(*Jo-Jo the Dove*), anti-communist
propaganda poster issued by
Imprimerie Spéciale de Paix
et Liberté, France, 1952
Ink on paper, colour lithograph
779 x 561mm
V&A, E.629-2004, Gift of the
American Friends of the V&A;
Gift to the American Friends by
Leslie, Judith and Gabri Schreyer
and Alice Schreyer Batko
Plate 1.24

Constant (Constant A.
Nieuwenhuys) and Jan Elburg,
The Dove's View (*Het uitzicht
van de duif*), edition no.100/125,
1952; poem by Elburg, woodcuts
by Constant
Woodcut and letterpress on paper
340 x 540mm
Stedelijk Museum, Schiedam:
G/94/1-10 and G/1352/1-10,
donated by Mr and Mrs Verweij,
1959
Plate 4.12

Vojtěch Němeček, *Build the
nation - you shall strengthen
peace* (*Buduj vlast posílíš mir*),
poster, 1951
Printed paper
555 x 738mm
Private collection: P 325

Alexander Zhitomirsky, *In
the name of peace they travelled
halfway around the world*,
1950
Photomontage
345 x 275mm
Private Collection: PH 15

Feliks Topolski, *Confessions
of a Congress Delegate: being an
account of the adventures of an
artist-delegate to the International
Congress of Intellectuals for Peace,
held in Wroclaw (Poland) in
August 1948*, Gallery editions,
London, 1949

Booklet
279 x 445mm
V&A/NAL: Box I G 28 G
Plates 1.30 and 1.31

Paul Hogarth, *Nowa Huta*, 1953
Black crayon on yellow paper
396 x 517mm
V&A: E. 550-1986

Pablo Picasso, *Scene with
Minotaur* (*Scena z minotaurem*),
1947
Ceramic
40 x 380 x 315mm
National Museum, Warsaw:
SZC 1318

Pablo Picasso, *Bull's Head*
(*Glowa Byka*), 1947
Ceramic
40 x 380 x 315mm
National Museum, Warsaw:
SZC 1312

Pablo Picasso, *Face of Faun*
(*Twarz Fauna*), 1947
Ceramic
40 x 380 x 315mm
National Museum, Warsaw:
SZC 1329

Pablo Picasso, *Dove* (*Gołąb*),
1947
Ceramic
40 x 380 x 315mm
National Museum, Warsaw:
SZC 1325

Pablo Picasso, *Owl* (*Sowa*),
1947
Ceramic
40 x 380 x 315mm
National Museum, Warsaw:
SZC 1316

Pablo Picasso, *Still Life with
Scissors* (*Martwa Natura z
Nożycami*), 1947
Ceramic
40 x 380 x 315mm
National Museum, Warsaw:
SZC 1313

**The Competition for a Monument
to the Unknown Political Prisoner**
Reg Butler, final maquette for
the *Monument to the Unknown
Political Prisoner*, 1955-6
Forged and painted steel,
bronze and plaster
854 x 2238 x 879mm
Tate, London: T02332
Plate 1.9

Reg Butler, photomontages
of maquette for the *Monument
to the Unknown Political Prisoner*

on the proposed site, Humboldt
Hain, Wedding, West Berlin, 1957
Print
Estate of Reg Butler, Berkhamsted
Plate 1.8

Naum Gabo, maquette for the
*Monument to the Unknown
Political Prisoner*, 1952
Plastic and wire mesh
381 x 89 x 95mm
Tate, London: T02187
Plate 1.20

Bernhard Heiliger, maquette
for the *Monument to the
Unknown Political Prisoner*, 1953
Bronze and other metal
901 x 594 x 901mm
Tate, London: T03897

Eduardo Paolozzi, maquette for
the *Monument to the Unknown
Political Prisoner*, 1952
Plaster
356 x 432 x 612mm
Pallant House Gallery, Chichester:
CH CPH 1303

Le Corbusier and Iannis Xenakis
(architects) and Edgard Varèse
(composer), excerpts from film
Poème Électronique, 1958, made
for the Philips Pavilion, Brussels
Expo '58
Philips Archive
Plate 6.27

3 / The Competition to be Modern

Kitchen Debate
Vice President Richard Nixon with
USSR First Secretary Nikita
Khrushchev during the 'Kitchen
Debate' at the American National
Exhibition, Moscow, 1959
Photograph (reproduction)
Associated Press Photos
Plate 5.27

Richard Hamilton, $*he*, 1958-61
Oil, cellulose paint and collage
on wood
1219 x 813mm
Tate, London: T01190
Plate 1.2

Reproductions of photographs
taken at the American National
Exhibition, Moscow, 1959
Photographs
Private Collection (Jack Masey,
New York)
Plate 5.28

Charles and Ray Eames, excerpts
from film *Glimpses of the USA*,
1959, made for the United States

Information Agency, American
National Exhibition, Moscow,
1959,
Eames Office LLC
Plate 6.26

**Thaw Modern: Design in the
Soviet Bloc**
South-west district of Moscow,
the first wave of construction
of panel housing quarters near
the Kaluga motorway, panoramic
view, 1960s
Paper, pencil, ink and watercolour
1050 x 2510mm
Schusev State Museum of
Architecture (MUAR), Moscow:
R1a 11917

SAKB 2 (Special Architectural-
construction Studio), housing
complex for 1,500 people for
the New Cheremushki quarter,
Moscow, 1961
Ink and gouache on paper
990 x 1588mm
Schusev State Museum of
Architecture (MUAR), Moscow:
R1a 6557
Plate 5.20

School-studio Ivan Zholtovskii,
fragment of a building site
of a new housing quarter,
perspective drawing, 1950s
Paper, ink, watercolour
and gouache
885 x 1980mm
Schusev State Museum of
Architecture (MUAR), Moscow:
R1a 11970/4

Early competition drawing of
the Pioneer Palace on Lenin Hills,
Moscow, designed by Vladimir
Kubasov, Felix Novikov, B. Palui,
Igor Pokrovskii, M. Khazhakian
and I. Ionov (engineer), 1958,
built 1959-62
Pencil, ink, gouache and
watercolour on paper
585 x 3820mm
Schusev State Museum of
Architecture (MUAR) Moscow:
RIa6560/2
Plate 5.8

Construction of residential quarter,
1953-5, built on Kousinena Street,
Moscow, in 1957-9 to a design
by Mikhail Posokhin and
Ashot Mndoiants (architects),
V. Lagutenko (engineer), A.
Bartashevich (chief constructor)
and S. Shkol'nikov (chief engineer)
Pencil, watercolour and ink
on paper
620 x 1772mm

Schusev State Museum of
Architecture (MUAR), Moscow:
R1a 9944
Plate 5.6

Herbert Rappaport (director)
and Dmitri Shostakovich
(composer), excerpts from film
Cheremushki (*Cherrytown*), 1962
Lenfilm, St Petersburg

Walter Ende, P70 coupé,
manufactured by VEB
Automobilwerk AWZ, Zwickau,
East Germany, 1954
Duroplast (plastic) body
1480 x 1580 x 3800mm
Die Neue Sammlung, Munich:
259/96
Plate 5.14

Viktor Koretsky, *From oil we
take for the needs of our country a
river of gasoline, oil and petroleum
and in addition thousands of items
for the home and for domestic
comfort!* (*Iz nefti my berem dlia
nuzhd strany svoei potok
benzina,masel i mazuta,
a k nim v pridachu tysiachu
veshchei dlia doma i domashnego
uiuta!*), poster, 1960
Printed paper
1025 x 570mm
Private collection: P 2279
Plate 5.30

Albert Krause, set of dishes,
manufactured by VEB Presswerk
Auma resp. VEB Plasta-Werke
Sonneberg, East Germany, 1959
Meladur (plastic)
1 a,b: h. 29mm, w. 235mm,
d. 139mm (ivory, turquoise, 1a,b)
2 a-f: h. 29mm, w. 208mm,
d. 101mm (sand, grey, pink,
blue, yellow, turquoise)
3 a-b, c-f, g-h: h. 29mm, 102 x
102mm (ivory, yellow, turquoise)
Die Neue Sammlung, Munich: 489/
2006, 1a, b, 2a-f, 3a-h
Plate 5.11

Hans Merz, camping set,
manufactured by VEB Presswerk
Tambach, Tambach-Dietharz,
East Germany, 1958
Meladur (plastic)
Pot: 133 x 200 x 138mm; jug:
53 x 105 x 85mm; sugar bowl
64 x 109mm; cup: 55 x 112 x
86mm; saucer: 14 x 123mm
Die Neue Sammlung, Munich:
493/2006, 1-3, 4a, b, 5a, b

Hedwig Bollhagen, coffee set,
model 558, manufactured by
HB-Werkstätten für Keramik,

Marwitz bei Velten, East
Germany, 1961
Ceramic, with black glaze
Pot: 210 x 180 x 79mm;
jug: 85 x 80 x 51mm; sugar
bowl: 60 x 87mm
Die Neue Sammlung, Munich:
683/2006, 1-3
Plate 5.12

Walter Womacka, *Mosaikfries
'Unser Leben' vom Haus des
Lehrers am Alexanderplatz
in Berlin* (*Mosaic Frieze 'Our
Life' from the Teachers' House
at Alexanderplatz Berlin*),
poster printed by DEWAG
Handelswerbung Berlin,1964
Printed paper
610 x 856mm
Stiftung Haus der Bundesrepublik
Deutschland Bonn:
H 1998/09/0046
Plate 2.20 (photograph of frieze)

Władysław Garlicki, decorative
textile (no title), 1956
Printed cotton
4000 x 100mm
National Museum, Warsaw:
WRZ.t.1019
Plate 5.15

Lubomir Tomaszewski, Ina coffee
service, manufactured by Ćmielów
Porcelain Tableware Industries,
Ceramics and Glass Workshop
of the Industrial Design Institute,
Warsaw (prototype), 1964
Porcelain decorated with
monochrome slip
Coffee pot: h. 120mm, diam.
232mm; cup: h. 63mm, diam.
40mm; saucer diam. 115mm;
creamer h.90mm, diam. 55mm
National Museum, Warsaw:
Wzr.c. 491/1,2,8,9 MNW
Plate 5.16

Eugen Jindra, table with music
system and lamp, part of the
Music Room displayed at Milan
Triennale, 1962
Wood, metal and upholstery
Lower part: 300 x 1500 x 600mm;
radio: 240 x 450 x 405mm;
loudspeaker: 410 x 460 x 460mm;
lamp: 480 x 1000 x 700mm
Museum of Decorative Arts,
Prague: 57114a-d
Plate 5.17

Roman Modzelewski, armchair,
1959-60 (patented 1961)
Fibreglass
V&A: New acquisition
Plate 1.15

Stanislav Libenský & Jaroslava
Brychtová, *Head I*, made by
Železnobrodské sklo (ZBS)
Glassworks, 1957/8
Mould-melted and etched
transparent brown glass
H. 355mm
Museum of Decorative Arts,
Prague: 54876

Stanislav Libenský and Jaroslava
Brychtová, *Zoomorphic Stones*,
8 glass objects in 3 parts,
manufactured by Železnobrodské
sklo Glassworks, 1957-8
Glass stones set in panels
(embedded in original concrete
within iron frame)
a: 520 x 1220mm; b: 520 x 1160
mm; c: 520 x 970 mm
Steinberg Foundation, Vaduz:
SF 264-1 (a), SF 264-2 (b),
SF 264-3 (c)
Plate 4.17

René Roubíček, *Blue Glass Form*,
made by Borské sklo Glassworks,
Hantich workshop. 1959
Blue glass, hand-blown and
hot-worked
460 x 280 mm
V&A: C.21-1998
Plate 5.22

Stanislav Libenský and Jaroslava
Brychtová, *Sphere in Cube*,
manufactured by Železnobrodské
sklo (ZBS) Glassworks, 1970
Mould-melted and cut
colourless glass
220 x 222 x 222mm
Steinberg Foundation,
Vaduz: SF 266

Václav Cigler, glass object with
concave surfaces, manufactured
by Borské sklo Glassworks,
Kamenicky Senov workshop,
1968-70
Optical cut glass
60 x 400 x 400mm
Museum of Decorative Arts,
Prague: 73420
Plate 1.16

Pavel Hlavá, *Cosmos*, orange glass
sphere, manufactured by Ceský
krišt'ál Glassworks, Chlum u
Trebone, 1971
Blown, hot-shaped transparent
red glass on cut stand, glued
Diam. 400mm
Museum of Decorative Arts,
Prague: 75374

4 / Crisis and Fear

Technocracy

Marco Zanuso and Richard Sapper,
Black 201 television set, 1966-74
(manufactured 1969),
manufactured by Brionvega
S.p.A., Italy
Acrylic plastic
254 x 292 x 305mm (cover:
300 x 400 x 300mm)
V&A: CIRC 5:3-1974

Dieter Rams, T 1000 radio world
receiver, manufactured by Braun
AG, Taunus, West Germany, 1963
Coloured aluminium
140 x 360 x 250mm
V&A: W.12-2007
Plate 3.23

Sony Corporation, 8 301 W,
portable television, manufactured
by Sony Corporation, Tokyo, 1959
Metal, grey lacquered, partially
chromed
210 x 210 x 280mm
Die Neue Sammlung, Munich:
22/90
Plate 3.6

Dieter Rams, RT 20, table radio
('Tischsuper'), manufactured by
Braun AG, Taunus, West Germany,
1961
Beech and white plastic
510 x 180 x 260mm
V&A: W.13-2007

Eliot Noyes and Associates,
Selectric 1, golfball typewriter,
manufactured by IBM, USA, 1961
Steel and plastic
190 x 470 x 375mm
V&A: M.225:1-2007
Plate 6.32

Television, Panasonic model TR
005, manufactured by Matsushita
Electric Industrial Co. Ltd., Japan,
c.1970
Plastic
250 x 290mm
Die Neue Sammlung, Munich:
329/92

Nuclear Fears

F.H.K. Henrion, *Stop Nuclear
Suicide*, poster issued by
the CND, 1963
Offset lithograph
708 x 504mm
V&A: E.3910-1983
Plate 4.29

Alexander Zhitomirsky,
General Dynamics, 1961
Photomontage

405 x 314mm
Private collection: PH 13

Mieczyslaw Berman, *Ten tons
of Trotyl* (*Dziesiec ton trotylu*),
1965
Collage, photomontage on paper
420 x 300mm
National Museum, Warsaw:
Rys.W.3070

Kenneth Adam, design for the
War Room, final concept, 1962
(extended 1999), for *Dr
Strangelove Or: How I Learned
To Stop Worrying and Love
The Bomb*, directed by Stanley
Kubrick, 1964
Felt-tip pen on card
320 x 810mm
Sir Kenneth Adam, London:
SK-1499
Plate 4.30

Kenneth Adam, the Bomb Release
Sequence, 1962, story board for
*Dr Strangelove Or: How I Learned
To Stop Worrying and Love The
Bomb*, directed by Stanley
Kubrick, 1964
Ink and wash on paper
530 x 720mm
Sir Kenneth Adam, London:
SK-1505
Plate 4.2

Crisis

Robert Rauschenberg, *Kite*, 1963
Oil and colour serigraphied on
canvas
2130 x 1530mm
Museum of Modern and
Contemporary Art, Rovereto/
Trento, Courtesy Ileana Sonnabend
Plate 1.6

Gerhard Richter, *Phantom
Interceptors* (*Phantom
Abfangjäger*), 1964
Oil on canvas
1400 x 1900mm
Sammlung Fröhlich, Leinfelden/
Echterdingen

Hans Hollein, 'Aircraft Carrier
City in Landscape' project, exterior
perspective, 1964
Cut-and-pasted printed paper
on gelatin silver photographs
mounted on board
337 x 1086mm
The Museum of Modern Art,
New York: 434.1967, Philip
Johnson Fund
Plate 7.34

Wolf Vostell, *Betonierung
(Potsdamer Platz)* (*Concreting

(*Potsdamer Platz*)), 1972
Pencil, watercolour and plaster
on board
1050 x 750 x 130mm
Mauermuseum – Museum
Haus am Checkpoint Charlie,
Berlin
Plate 1.5

Richard Buckminster Fuller,
dome for covering part of New
York City, photomontage, 1962
Photograph (reproduction)
The Estate of R. Buckminster
Fuller, Santa Barbara
Pages 8/9

Espionage

Kenneth Adam, design for Dr No's
underwater apartment, set design
for the James Bond film *Dr No*,
directed by Terence Young, 1962
Ink on paper
Dimensions unknown
EON Productions Ltd., London:
KA001

Kenneth Adam, design for rumpus
room, set design for the James
Bond film *Goldfinger*, directed
by Guy Hamilton, 1964
Ink on paper
405 x 800mm
EON Productions Ltd., London:
KA013

Kenneth Adam, design for the
brainwashing chamber in the
film *The Ipcress File*, directed
by Sidney J. Furie, 1965
Ink on paper
266 x 507mm
Sir Kenneth Adam, London
Plate 6.28

Secret camera, used to document
the 17 June 1953 uprising
in Berlin, 1953
Miniature camera disguised
in book
240 x 350mm
Stiftung Haus der Bundesrepublik
Deutschland Bonn

Male wristwatch with microphone
for 'Minifon P 55', manufactured
by Protona
GmbH, Hamburg, 1957
Metal, glass, leather and plastics
13 x 243 x 42mm
Stiftung Haus der Bundesrepublik
Deutschland Bonn: 2005/03/0314

Espionage camera type 'Kiew 303'
in cigarette packet 'Gerzegowina
Flor Jawa Cigaretui',
manufactured by Arsenal Kiew,
1960s-1980s

Metal, cardboard and paper
90 x 60 x 25mm
Stiftung Haus der Bundesrepublik
Deutschland Bonn:
H 2001/07/0200

KGB secret camera in a briefcase,
c.1968
Metal, plastic, glass, textile
and leather
410 x 670 x 370mm
Stiftung Haus der Bundesrepublik
Deutschland Bonn: 1992/06/474

Table lighter with masked
eavesdropping technology, 1970s
Metal and plastic
59 x 85 x 32mm
Stiftung Haus der Bundesrepublik
Deutschland Bonn: 2005/03/0315

5 / Space Odysseys

Andrei Tarkovsky (director),
excerpts from film *Solaris*, 1972
Mosfilm Cinema Concern, Moscow

House of the Future

Peter and Alison Smithson,
preliminary drawing for House of
the Future, designed for the Ideal
Home Exhibition 1956, 1955-6
Pencil on tracing paper
970 x 750mm
V&A: E.663-1978

Peter and Alison Smithson,
Pogo chair, 1956
Metal and perspex
889 x 457 x 445mm
V&A: Circ. 81-1975

Peter and Alison Smithson,
photograph of interior, House of
the Future, designed for the Ideal
Home Exhibition, living room
with hexagonal table, 1956
Gelatin-silver print
V&A: E.663B-1978
Plate 4.22

Joe Colombo, Mini-Kitchen,
manufactured by Boffi, 1963
Wood, plastic, steel and
electrical components
1020 x 650 x 1020mm
Private collection

Cosmic Visions

Eduardo Paolozzi, *Will man
outgrow the earth?*, c.1952-3, from
the series entitled *Bunk*, 1947-53
Collage
400 x 250mm
V&A: Circ.715-1971
Plate 4.28

Francisco Infante-Arana, *Space –
Movement – Infinity (Project
for a Kinetic Object)*, 1963
Tempera and ink on paper
mounted on fibreboard
703 x 910mm
Jane Voorhees Zimmerli Art
Museum, The Norton and Nancy
Dodge Collection of Nonconformist
Art from the Soviet Union, New
Brunswick, NJ: 05336/1995.0758
Plate 7.31

Lucio Fontana, *Spatial Concept,
The End of God (Concetto spaziale,
La fine di Dio)*, 1963
Oil, scratches, holes, and glitters
on canvas
1780 x 1230mm
Deposito Fondazione Lucio
Fontana, Milano, Museum of
Modern and Contemporary Art,
Rovereto/Trento
Plate 4.10

Jiří Kolář, *Mysterious Sea
(Tajemnicze Morze)*, 1965
Collage
1275 x 985 x 65mm
Muzeum Sztuki, Łódź: MS/SN/
RYS/240

Magdalena Abakanowicz,
Composition (Kompozycja),
tapestry, 1967
Tapestry (wool)
Centralne Muzeum
Włókiennictwa (Museum of
Textiles), Łódź: CMW 4295/w/382

Francisco Infante-Arana, *Star Rain*
from the series *Project
of the Reconstruction of the
Firmament*, 1965
Airbrush and gouache on paper
506 x 330mm
Jane Voorhees Zimmerli Art
Museum, The Norton and Nancy
Dodge Collection of Nonconformist
Art from the Soviet Union, New
Brunswick, NJ: 03771/1991.0863
Plate 7.30

Francisco Infante-Arana,
Nostalgia from the series *Project
of the Reconstruction of the
Firmament*, 1965
Tempera on paper
505 x 330mm
Jane Voorhees Zimmerli Art
Museum, The Norton and Nancy
Dodge Collection of Nonconformist
Art from the Soviet Union, New
Brunswick, NJ: 03772/L03772

Francisco Infante-Arana, *Star* from
the series *Project of the
Reconstruction of the Firmament*,

1965
Tempera on paper
500 x 319mm
Jane Voorhees Zimmerli Art
Museum, The Norton and Nancy
Dodge Collection of Nonconformist
Art from the Soviet Union,
New Brunswick, NJ: o3770

Nicolas Schöffer, *Chronos 8*, 1967
Animated sculpture with mirrors
which spin, connected to motors
3080 x 1250 x 1300mm
Musée nationale d'art moderne,
Paris: AM 1979-351

2001: Space Age Design

Model 1:3 of Vostok space
capsule, USSR, c.1960
Metal and plastic
H. 2200mm, diam. 800mm
The K.E. Tsiolkovsky State
Museum of the History of
Cosmonautics, Kaluga

Vadim Volikov, *Glory to Soviet
Science! Glory to Soviet Man –
the First Cosmonaut! (Sovetskoi
nauke slava!Slava Sovetskomu
cheloveku – pervomu kosmonavtu!)*,
poster, 1961
Printed paper
1080 x 660mm
Private collection: P1871

Joe Tilson, *Transparency 1: Yuri
Gagarin 12 April 1961*, 1968
Screenprint and mixed media on
plastic
1219 x 1219 x 51mm
Tate, London: P02330

Eero Aarnio, Globe Chair, designed
1962-5, manufactured by Asko
Finnternational, Helsinki, 1966
Red fibreglass, upholstery and
metal base
977 x 1190 x 660mm
V&A: Circ.12:1-3-1969

Gaetano Pesce, UP 3 chair, 1969,
manufactured by C&B Italia
S.p.A, Novedrate, Italy, 1970
Polyurethane foam, nylon jersey
cover
700 x 1040 x 1040mm
V&A: Circ.211.1970

Pierre Paulin, Chair 582,
manufactured by Artifort,
Maastricht, 1965
Tensioned rubber sheet over
tubular metal frame, with jersey-
covered latex foam upholstery,
lacquered wood base
695 x 1000 x 755mm
V&A: Circ.303-1970

Olivier Mourgue, chaise longue
of Djinn series, designed 1963,
manufactured by Airborne
International, 1964
Tubular steel structure filled
with polyether foam and
jersey (Ponant) cover
610 x 1700 x 650mm
V&A: Circ.201-1969
Plate 6.8

Olivier Mourgue, chair of Djinn
series, designed 1963,
manufactured by Airborne
International, 1964
Tubular steel structure with
polyester wadding and jersey
(Ponant) cover
670 x 740 x 660mm
V&A: Circ. 202-1969

Pascal Haüsermann, model
of *Théâtre mobile*, 1968
Solder metal, plastic
250 x 560 x 440mm
Collection FRAC Centre, Orléans:
997 01 53

Peter Ghyczy, Garden Egg Chair,
1968, designed for Elastogran
GmbH, Lemförde, West-Germany,
1971, manufactured by VEB
Synthesewerk Schwarzheide,
East-Germany, 1972-74/5
Lacquered, moulded polyurethane
with synthetic textile upholstery
over polyurethane foam padding
1000 x 740 x 860mm
V&A: W.8-2007
Plate 1.12

Cesare Leonardi and Franca Stagi,
Dondolo rocking chair,
manufactured by Elco, 1967
White moulded fibre-glass in one
long curved piece
H. 750mm
V&A: Circ.329.1970

Videosphere television set, 1970,
manufactured by JVC, Japan,
1971-4
ABS plastic, acrylic, glass, metal
Diam. 270mm
V&A: W.661-2001

Walter Pichler, Galaxy 1 chair,
manufactured by Möbelwerk
Svoboda GmbH & Co KG, St.
Pölten, Austria, 1966
Frame of aluminium sheet, 3mm,
laser cut, fine grinded and silver
anodized, all connections though
hollow aluminium rivets, seat
plate hung on rubber o-Rings
420 x 910 x 850mm
Private collection
Plate 1.1

Mario Bellini, TCV 250 Video
Display Terminal, manufactured
by Ing. C. Olivetti & C.S.p.A.,
Ivrea, Italy, 1966
Sheet steel and vacuum-cast
ABS plastic
937 x 916 x 559mm
The Museum of Modern Art,
New York: 434.1983, Gift of the
manufacturer

Yonel Lébovici, Satellite table
lamp, edition made by Yonel
Lébovici, Paris, 1965
Chrome-plated metal and
acrylic glass (PMMA)
410 x 400mm
Die Neue Sammlung, Munich:
205/95
Plate 6.3

Anonymous, poster for film
Solaris, directed by Andrei
Tarkovsky, 1972
Print on paper
1148 x 812mm
V&A: New acquisition

Designing for Space

Raymond Loewy, design for
a stateroom with individual
work and sleep mode, undertaken
for NASA, 1968
Postercolour, pen and ink
and chalk on brown card
379 x 592mm
V&A: E.3203-1980
Plate 6.11

Raymond Loewy and William
Snaith Inc., design for eating
and drinking aid, habitability
study for Saturn 5 Space Station,
undertaken for NASA, 1968
Colour wash and felt tip pen
on card
406 x 343mm
V&A: E.3202-1980

Raymond Loewy and William
Snaith Inc., study for a space
taxi (extravehicular activity),
undertaken for NASA (series
reproduction 1978), c.1970
Print
334 x 501mm
V&A: E.647-1981

Raymond Loewy and William
Snaith Inc., habitability study
(extravehicular activity) for NASA
Saturn 5 Space Station (series
reproduction 1978), c.1970
Print
532 x 711mm
V&A: E.650-1981

Space Age Bodies

X-1B flight suit, worn by
Neil Armstrong, USA military,
late 1950s
Various materials
Private collection

Berkut full-pressure space suit,
USSR, 1960s
Various materials
Private collection

Orlan research prototype EVA
(extra-vehicular activity) space
suit, USSR, 1970s
Manufactured by Zvezda
Various materials
Private collection

Frank Hess, protective suit,
student work in Industrial Design
department at HfG, Ulm, tutor:
Tomas Maldonado, 1965
PVC-coated nylon fabric
330 x 1890 x 680mm
Ulmer Museum/HfG-Archiv Ulm

Gijs Bakker, Emmy van Leersum
and Tiny Leeuwenkamp, *Clothing
Suggestions*, 1970
Artificial material, white tricot
1800 x 1000 x 1000mm
Gemeente Museum, Den Haag:
K 12-1995

Gijs Bakker, Emmy Van Leersum
and Tiny Leeuwenkamp, *Clothing
Suggestions*, 1970
Black artificial material and 14
rings
1800 x 1000 x 1000mm
Gemeente Museum, Den Haag:
K 20-1995

Eva Fiavola, evening dress,
manufactured by UBOK, 1967
Bobbin lacework, silver metal
thread and black cotton thread
910 x 450mm
Museum of Decorative Arts,
Prague: 76934

Václav Cigler, neckpiece, 1965
Chrome-plated metal
540 x 100mm
Museum of Decorative Arts,
Prague: 97.049

Pierre Cardin, Cosmos menswear,
1967
Woollen jersey, vinyl, plastic
and leather
Tunic 790 x 450mm; trousers
1080 x 350mm
V&A: T.703-1974

Pierre Cardin, Cosmos
womenswear, 1967
Woollen jersey, vinyl, plastic
and leather
Dress 850 x 420mm
V&A: T.75D-1974
Paco Rabanne, Disc Dress, 1967
Plastic pailletes joined with
metal wire
700 x 410mm
V&A: T.165-1983

Stephen Willats, Variable
Sheets dress, 1965
PVC and metal zippers
815 x 500mm
V&A: T.19-1991

Techno-Utopia

Karel Hubáček (chief architect
of state office, Stavoprojekt 7),
model of Ještěd
telecommunications tower,
Liberec, 1968–73
Materials unknown
1350mm; base: 1605 x 1000mm
Vitkovice, Ostrava
Plate 6.16

Otakar Binar, drawings of the
interior of Ještěd
telecommunications tower
and hotel, Liberec, 1968–73
Ink on paper
Each drawing 205 x 205mm
Private collection
Plate 6.17 (photograph of interior)

Model of Berlin Teletower, upper
section, project realization of
tower by Fritz Dieter and Günter
Franke after a design by Hermann
Henselmann; model constructed
by the model-maker Lehne, 1991
Wood and plaster, grey paint
1550 x 800mm
Museum für Kommunikation,
Frankfurt am Main
Plate 6.18 (photograph of building)

Gera Wernitz, costume designs
for telecommunications tower
staff in East Berlin. 1968
Pen, watercolour and sample
swatches
358 x 478mm
Stiftung Stadtmuseum, Berlin:
No. 204
Plate 6.19

Gera Wernitz, costume designs
for telecommunications tower
staff in East Berlin. 1968
Pen and watercolour
358 x 478 mm
Stiftung Stadtmuseum, Berlin:
No. 202

Nikolai Nikitin (designer), Leonid
Batalov and D. Burdin (architects),

Ostankino, Teletower, Moscow,
model constructed by A-Models,
London, 2008
MDF, plywood veneer and plastic
6000mm
V&A
Plate 6.15

Photographs of Post Office Tower,
now BT Tower, Eric Bedford
(chief architect), Ministry of Public
Building and Works,
built 1961-4, opened 1965
BT Archive, London
Plate 6.14

Archigram (designed by Peter
Cook, model by Dennis Crompton),
model for the Montreal 67 Tower,
1967
Acrylic, plastic, cork, plywood
and metal
1170 x 850 x 850mm
Deutsches Architekturmuseum,
Frankfurt am Main: 009-008-014

Archigram (Peter Cook), Montreal
67 Tower, elevation, 1963
Ink on transparency
1260 x 750mm
Deutsches Architekturmuseum,
Frankfurt am Main: 009-008-002

Archigram (Peter Cook), Montreal
67 Tower, section A–A with
descriptions of functions, 1963
Ink on transparency
1235 x 740mm
Deutsches Architekturmuseum,
Frankfurt am Main: 009-008-003
Plate 6.20

Frei Otto, *Roofed Futurist
City*, 1963
Pencil on cardboard
300 x 400mm
Deutsches Architekturmuseum,
Frankfurt am Main: 187-002-033
Plate 8.6

Frei Otto, *Futurist City*, 1963
Pencil on board
300 x 400mm
Deutsches Architekturmuseum,
Frankfurt am Main: 187-002-030

Arata Isozaki, *Cluster in
the Air*, model, 1962
Wood, cork and metal on
laminated chipboard
270 x 1200 x 905mm
Deutsches Architekturmuseum,
Frankfurt am Main: 121-001-001
Plate 8.10

Arata Isozaki, *Re-ruined
Hiroshima*, project Hiroshima,
perspective, 1968

Ink and gouache with cut-
and-pasted gelatin silver print
on gelatin silver print
419 x 1004mm
The Museum of Modern Art,
New York: 1205.2000, Gift of the
Howard Gilman Foundation
Plate 8.5

Kisho Kurokawa, *Nagakin-
Capsule-Highrise*, isometric
drawing of the interior
of a capsule, 1972
Transparent reproduction
on film
840 x 590mm
Deutsches Architekturmuseum,
Frankfurt am Main: 144-002-003
Plate 6.10

Peter Cook (Archigram), section
of *Plug-in City*: Maximum Pressure
Area, 1964
Ink and gouache on
photomechanical print
730 x 1336mm
The Museum of Modern Art,
New York: 1185.2000, Gift
of The Howard Gilman Foundation
Plate 8.8

Ettore Sottsass, *The Future of
Architecture; Buckminster Fuller,
Stranded* (*Die Zukunft der
Architektur, Buckminster Fuller,
gestrandet*) from his series *Planet
as Festival* (7/17), 1973
Zinc lithography, coloured pencil
on paper
685 x 518mm
Deutsches Architekturmuseum,
Frankfurt am Main: 227-001-001
Plate 8.12

Nikolai Tsitsin (scientific
consultant), I. Petrov (architect)
and S. Yaroslavtseva with the
assistance of A. Vinogradova,
Klimatron, Botanical Gardens,
Moscow (section), 1964-5
Ink and watercolour on paper
678 x 1234mm
Schusev State Museum of
Architecture (MUAR), Moscow:
P1a 10275/11

6 / Revolution

Cuba

Anonymous, poster issued by
Comision de Orientacion
Revolucionaria, XVII Anniversario
Viva el 26 de Julio, 1971
Screenprint on card
970 x 494
V&A: E.783-2003

Niko, *The Tenth Anniversary of the
Victory at the Bay of Pigs*, poster
commissioned by the Instituto
Cubano del Arte e Industrias
Cinematográfico, Cuba, 1971
Screenprint
765 x 510mm
V&A: E.760-2003
Plate 7.14

Anonymous, *We Will Win*
(*Venceremos*), student poster
from Mexico, c.1970
Print
700 x 475mm
V&A: E. 685-2004, Gift of the
American Friends of the V&A; Gift
to the American Friends by Leslie,
Judith and Gabri Schreyer and
Alice Schreyer Batko
Plate 7.4

Anonymous, poster published by
OSPAAAL for Solidarity with the
African American People, Cuba,
18 August 1968
Offset lithograph
540 x 357mm
V&A: E.798-2004, Gift of the
American Friends of the V&A;
Gift to the American Friends by
Leslie, Judith and Gabri Schreyer
and Alice Schreyer Batko

Mikhail Kalatozov (director),
excerpts from *Soy Cuba*
(*I am Cuba*), 1965
Film
Mosfilm Cinema Concern, Moscow
Plate 7.13

Evgenii Svidetelev, reproductions
of set drawings for film *Soy
Cuba* (*I am Cuba*), 1965
Photographs
Cinema Museum, Moscow

Protest

Erró (Gudmundur Gudmundsson),
American Interior No. 7, 1968
Oil on canvas
970 x 1150mm
Sammlung Ludwig, Ludwig Forum
für Internationale Kunst, Aachen
Plate 7.15

Li Zhensheng, reproduction
of photograph showing public
humiliation of local officials during
the Cultural Revolution, Harbin,
China, c.1967
Photograph
Contact Press Images
Plate 7.17

Anonymous, *Down with US
Imperialism, Down with Soviet
Revisionism*, poster produced

during the Cultural Revolution
in China, 1967
Printed paper
750 x 522mm
V&A: New acquisition
Plate 7.16

Anonymous, *Cultural Revolution –
2*, 1967
Printed paper
733 x 518mm
V&A: New acquisition

Boris Mikhailov, 6 photographs
from the *Red Series*, 1960s/1970s
Type-C prints on paper
205 x 305mm (each photograph)
Jane Voorhees Zimmerli Art
Museum, The Norton and Nancy
Dodge Collection of Nonconformist
Art from the Soviet Union, New
Brunswick, NJ: 12982, 12983,
12985, 15449, 15450, 15452
Plate 7.9

Anonymous, *Nixon – La Peste
dehors!* (*Oust the Menace!*), French
Anti-Vietnam War poster, 1969
Colour offset lithograph
884 x 695mm
V&A: E.137-2004, Gift of the
American Friends of the V&A; Gift
to the American Friends by Leslie,
Judith and Gabri Schreyer and
Alice Schreyer Batko

Atelier Populaire, *SS*, 1968
Lithograph
552 x 433mm
V&A: E.225-1985

Atelier Populaire, *To vote
is to die a little* (*Voter c'est
mourir un peu*), 1968
Lithograph
680 x 540mm
V&A: E.668-2004, Gift of the
American Friends of the V&A;
Gift to the American Friends by
Leslie, Judith and Gabri Schreyer
and Alice Schreyer Batko

Atelier Populaire, *The Police
Speak to You Every Evening
at 8pm* (*La Police vous Parle
tous les soirs a 20h*), 1968
Lithograph
618 x 457mm
V&A: E.671-2004, Gift of the
American Friends of the V&A; Gift
to the American Friends by Leslie,
Judith and Gabri Schreyer and
Alice Schreyer Batko
Plate 7.6

Roman Cieślewicz, cover
illustration for *Opus
International* magazine, no.4,

1968
Magazine 210 x 125mm
V&A: New acquisition
Plate 7.7

Josef Koudelka, *Prague 1968*,
1968
Gelatin silver print
227 x 360mm
V&A: Ph1442-1980
Plate 7.22

Jiří Kolář, *Diary 1968: But Deliver
Us From Evil*, sheet no.22, 1968
Collage
446 x 325mm
Neues Museum - Staatliches
Museum für Kunst und Design,
Nuremberg: 549

Jiří Kolář *Diary 1968: Vienna:
A Tower grows and grows, far
out over the water*, sheet no. 24,
1968
Collage
446 x 331mm
Neues Museum - Staatliches
Museum für Kunst und Design,
Nuremberg: 549

Jiří Kolář, *Diary 1968: Entrée*,
sheet no.26, 1968
Collage
447 x 329mm
Neues Museum - Staatliches
Museum für Kunst und Design,
Nuremberg: 549
Plate 7.19

Jiří Kolář, *Diary 1968: Mladý
Svet* (*Young World*), sheet
no.34d, 1968
Collage
446 x 328mm
Neues Museum - Staatliches
Museum für Kunst und Design,
Nuremberg: 549
Plate 7.20

Jiří Kolář, *Diary 1968: Literární
Listy*, sheet no. 35c, 1968
Collage
446 x 328mm
Neues Museum - Staatliches
Museum für Kunst und Design,
Nuremberg: 549

Jiří Kolář, *Diary 1968: After
the Finish*, sheet no.43, 1968
Collage
448 x 328mm
Neues Museum - Staatliches
Museum für Kunst und Design,
Nuremberg: 549

Milan 1968
Reproduction of photograph of
installation by Giancarlo de Carlo,

Marco Bellocchio and Bruno
Caruso, 'The Protest of the Young
People' at the 14th Milan
Triennale, 1968
Photograph
Triennale Archive Milan
Plate 7.26

Reproduction of photograph
of the Student occupation
of the 14th Milan Triennale, May 1968
Photograph
Triennale Archive Milan
Plate 7.25

7 / The Last Utopians

Haus-Rucker-Co (Laurids Ortner,
Günter Zamp Kelp, Klaus Pinter
and Manfred Ortner), *Oasis No 7*,
1972, reconstructed for the
exhibition; original concept by
Haus-Rucker-Co, reconstruction
advised by Günter Zamp Kelp,
exhibition architects Universal
Design Studio, London, 2008
Inflatable structure
Diam. 8000mm
V&A
Plate 7.38

The Inflatable Moment
Arthur Quarmby, inflatable
plastic pouffe, 1965
Clear plastic
180 x 830mm
V&A: Circ.744-1968

Jonathan De Pas, Donato
d'Urbino, Paolo Lomazzi and
Carla Scolari, Blow Chair, 1967,
manufactured by Zanotta
S.p.A, 1968-9
PVC film seam-welded by
radio-frequency
830 x 1035 x 975mm
V&A: Circ.100:1-1970
Plate 1.13

Antoine Stinco (Utopie), hall
for a travelling exhibition for
everyday objects project, 1967-9
Ink and watercolour on paper
690 x 1690mm
Collection FRAC Centre,
Orléans: 996 01 86

Peter Cook (Archigram), *Instant
City in a Field Long Elevation*
1/200, 1969
Silk screen on paper
565 x 2200mm
Collection FRAC Centre,
Orléans: 998 01 69

Coop Himmelblau, *Villa Rosa*,
M 1:20, 1968
Black ink on tracing paper,

Letraset
542 x 865mm
Collection FRAC Centre,
Orléans : CE 999 17 02
Plate 7.36

Coop Himmelblau, model
of *Villa Rosa*, 1967
Wood, plastic, metal and paint
400 x 680 x 680mm
Collection FRAC Centre, Orléans:
999 01 01

Haus-Rucker-Co (Günter Zamp
Kelp), *Leisuretime Explosion*,
1968
Collage
480 x 680mm
Collection FRAC Centre, Orléans:
002 14 02

Coop Himmelblau, *Cloud* (*Wolke*),
1970
Photo, pencil and coloured
pencil on paper
397 x 602mm
Deutsches Architekturmuseum,
Frankfurt am Main: 050-001-001

Haus-Rucker-Co (Günter Zamp
Kelp), *Pneumatic Skin Protecting
a Farm House*, 1970
Print on paper
530 x 640mm
Archive Günter Zamp Kelp, Berlin

Haus-Rucker-Co (Klaus Pinter),
Cover, Klima 1, Museum
Haus Lange, 1971
Mixed media
300 x 700mm
Archive Klaus Pinter, Paris
Plate 1.18

Graham Stevens, excerpts
from *Atmosfields*, 1971
Film
British Film Institute

Soft Machines – The Cybernetic Body
Haus-Rucker-Co (Laurids Ortner,
Günter Zamp Kelp and Klaus
Pinter), 'Environment
Transformers', helmet with visor
and mobile central disc, 1968
Plastics, colour adhesives and
metal
170 x 260 x 280mm
Musée nationale d'art moderne,
Paris: AM 2000-2-150
Plate 6.23

Haus-Rucker-Co (Laurids Ortner,
Günter Zamp Kelp and Klaus
Pinter), 'Environment
Transformers', helmet with visor
and supple membrane, 1968
Plastics and metal

240 x 300 x 350mm
Musée nationale d'art moderne,
Paris: AM 2000-2-151
Plate 6.23

Haus-Rucker-Co (Laurids Ortner,
Günter Zamp Kelp and Klaus
Pinter), *Mindexpander 2*, 1968
Inflatable PVC and polyester,
aluminium
2100 x 1400 x 1600mm
Archive Günter Zamp Kelp,
Berlin

Haus-Rucker-Co (Laurids Ortner,
Günter Zamp Kelp and Klaus
Pinter), *Electric Skin 1*, 1968
Plastic
1500 x 1250 x 200mm
Archive Günter Zamp Kelp,
Berlin

Walter Pichler, TV helmet,
'Portable Living Room' ('Das
tragbare Wohnzimmer'), 1967
Polyester, varnished white,
integrated TV monitor with
TV cable
590 x 1200 x 430mm
Generali Foundation, Vienna:
GF0001972.00.0-1998
Plate 6.22

Walter Pichler, *Standard Suit*
(*Standardanzug*), 1968
Pencil and colour pen on paper,
laminated on aluminium (foldable)
2000 x 1000mm
Generali Foundation, Vienna:
GF0002124.00.0-2000

Walter Pichler, *Kleiner Raum*
(*Prototyp 4*), 1967 (reconstruction
of base 1998)
Helmet: polyester, white lacquer,
integrated microphone, front
perforated; base: aluminium,
natural rubber, PVC-foil; b/w
photograph: silver gelatin on
canvas, integrated speaker,
aluminium hanging
Helmet: 480 x 400 x 400mm; base:
200 x 1000 x 1000mm;
photograph: 2020 x 1020mm
Generali Foundation, Vienna:
GF0001971.00.0-1998

Krzysztof Wodiczko, 'Personal
Instrument', 1969
Metal
453 x 505 x 604mm
Muzeum Sztuki, Łódź: MS/SN/
R/251/1-6
Plate 6.24

Krzysztof Wodiczko, Leporello
for 'Personal Instrument', 1969
Print

1520 x 300mm
Muzeum Sztuki, Łódź
Plate 6.24

Critical Utopias
Lev Nussberg and Natalia
Prokuratova, *Altar for the Temple
of the Spirit (Sketch for the
Creation of an Altar at the Institute
of Kinetics)*, 1969–70
Tempera and photo collage
on paper
618 x 864mm
Jane Voorhees Zimmerli Art
Museum, The Norton and Nancy
Dodge Collection of Nonconformist
Art from the Soviet Union, New
Brunswick, NJ: 25274/2003.0154
Plate 7.27

Movement Group, design for a
*Kinetic City: Labyrinth for Children
in Tuapse, Caucasus*, 1968 (The
Movement Group portfolio),
Nuremburg, 1972–4
Screenprint
647 x 650mm
Jane Voorhees Zimmerli Art
Museum, The Norton and Nancy
Dodge Collection of Nonconformist
Art from the Soviet Union, New
Brunswick, NJ:
07108.09/1995.0886.009

Movement Group, design for an
installation *Ten Years of the
Development of Kinetic Art in
Russia* (The Movement Group
Portfolio), Nuremburg, 1972–4
Screenprint
650 x 650mm
Jane Voorhees Zimmerli Art
Museum, The Norton and Nancy
Dodge Collection of Nonconformist
Art from the Soviet Union, New
Brunswick, NJ:
07108.12/1995.0886.012

Igor Korbut, *Starfish* (Master
Plan for Moscow), 1969
Ink and tempera on board
540 x 486mm
Private collection

Francisco Infante-Arana, *Scheme
for the kinetic illumination of the
old architectural buildings in the
Moscow Kremlin (the Spasskaya,
Nikol'skaya towers, the Kremlin
wall, the cathedral of Basil-the
Blessed) and the mausoleum
on the Red Square*, 1968
Tempera and Indian ink on
cardboard
50 x 1500mm
Francisco Infante-Arana, Moscow
Plate 7.29

NER Group, Architectural Scheme
for Triennale '68 in Milan, 1968
Typographic paint on tracing paper
780 x 1450mm
V&A: New acquisition
Plate 8.9

Viera Mecková, Alex Mlynarčik
and Ľudovít Kupovič (VAL),
Heliopolis, design for an Olympic
village, 1966–7
Plaster, with plastic, painted
architectural sculpture
1000 x 1000 x 750mm
VAL, Žilina
Plate 8.13

Ron Herron (Archigram),
*Walking City, Walking Cities
in the Desert*, 1973
Spraying technique, paper
on board
880 x 1820mm
Deutsches Architekturmuseum,
Frankfurt am Main: 009-004-001
Plate 8.7

Ron Herron (Archigram), *Instant
City, Tuned Suburb* (part 1), 1968
Airbrushed ink and paper collage
on board
610 x 890mm
Deutsches Architekturmuseum,
Frankfurt am Main: 009-011-001

Ron Herron (Archigram), *Instant
City, Tuned Suburb* (part 2), 1968
Airbrushed ink and paper collage
on board
610 x 880mm
Deutsches Architekturmuseum,
Frankfurt am Main: 009-011-002

Archigram, *Air-Hab*, model, 1966
Wood, metal, rubber, textile,
artificial lawn, plastics and
black and white photograph
260 x 390 x 255mm
Deutsches Architekturmuseum,
Frankfurt am Main: 009-027-001

Raimund Abraham, *Air-Ocean-
City*, 1966
Photo and paper collage on
cardboard
237 x 142mm
Deutsches Architekturmuseum,
Frankfurt am Main: 140-015-001
Plate 6.1

Hans Hollein, *Rolls Royce Grill on
Castle Schrattenberg (Rolls Royce
Grill auf Schloss Schrattenberg)*,
transformation, 1966
Black-and-white photomontage
104 x 215mm
Generali Foundation, Vienna:
GF0002446.00.0-2004

Zünd-Up (Bertram Mayer, Michael
Pühringer, Hermann Simböck
and Timo Huber), *The Great
Vienna Auto-Expander, Standort
Karlsplatz, Vienna*, 1969
Photomontage
763 x 711mm
V&A: E.469-2008
Plate 7.37

Superstudio (Adolfo Natalini),
*Continuous Monument, New
York (Il Monumento Continuo,
New York)* (75/100), 1969
Colour lithograph on paper
704 x 997mm
Deutsches Architekturmuseum,
Frankfurt am Main: 178-003-001
Plate 8.20

Superstudio (Adolfo Natalini),
*Vita Educazione Cerimonia Amore
Morte, Vita (Supersuperficie)*
(75/100), 1971
Colour lithograph on paper
700 x 1000mm
Deutsches Architekturmuseum,
Frankfurt am Main: 178-004-001

Superstudio, *Interplanetary
Architecture*, 1971
Photomontage
Private collection

Superstudio, excerpts from
*Supersurface: An alternative
model for life on the earth
(Vita)*, 1972
Film
GianPiero Frassinelli/Archivio
Superstudio

Anonymous, *Save Our Planet,
Save Our Cities*, poster produced
by Olivetti, 1971
Print on paper
690 x 745mm
V&A: E.137-1972
Plate 8.1

Reproduction of photograph
Earthrise taken by Apollo 8
mission crew, 24
December 1968
Photograph
NASA
Plate 8.2

Picture Credits

6.9 2001: A Space Odyssey © Turner Entertainment Co. Warner Bros. Entertainment Company. All Rights Reserved

6.11 Raymond Loewy™/® by CMG Worldwide, Inc./www.Raymond Loewy.com/Victoria and Albert Museum, London

6.12 Zvezda Archive, Moscow

6.13 Photo: Dennis Crompton © Archigram Archives 2008

6.14 By courtesy of BT Archives

6.16 Photograph:Jiří Jiroutek/ Jiří Jiroutek, Liberec

6.17 Photograph: P. Štecha/ Jiří Jiroutek, Liberec

6.18 Institut für Regionalentwicklung und Strukturplanung, Wissenschaftliche Sammlungen, Erkner

6.19 Reproduction: Oliver Ziebe, Berlin/Stiftung Stadtmuseum Berlin

6.20, 7.24 © Archigram Archives 2008

6.21, 8.2 NASA

6.22 © Generali Foundation Collection, Vienna. Photo: Werner Kaligofsky

6.23 Archive Günter Zamp Kelp, Berlin

6.24 Muzeum Sztuki, Łódź

6.25 Estate of John and James Whitney, USA, Copyright © 2008

6.27 Philips Company Archives

6.29 University of California and Berkeley Art Museum and Pacific Film Archive

6.30 Photo: Gui Bonsiepe

6.31 © SODRAC, Montreal and DACS, London 2008/Coll. François Dallegret, Montréal

6.32, 6.33 Courtesy of IBM Corporate Archives, New York

6.38 Library of Congress

6.40, 6.41, 6.42 Photo Shunk-Kender, courtesy Experiments

in Art and Technology. All Rights Reserved

6.43 Photography by Mark Gulezian/Smithsonian Institution, Washington, DC

7.5 © Henri Cartier-Bresson/ Magnum Photos

7.7 © ADAGP, Paris and DACS, London 2008/Victoria and Albert Museum, London

7.8 Photograph by M. Churakov, 1967. Schusev State Museum of Architecture (MUAR), Moscow

7.9 © DACS 2008/Jane Voorhees Zimmerli Art Museum, Rutgers, The State University of New Jersey, The Norton and Nancy Dodge Collection of Nonconformist Art from the Soviet Union. Photo by Jack Abraham. 12982, 12983, 12985, 15449, 15450, 15452

7.10 Prometheus Institute

7.11, 7.29 Francisco Infante-Arana, Moscow

7.13 © Mosfilm Cinema Concern, 1964

7.15 Ludwig Collection. Photographer © Anne Gold Aachen

7.17 © Li Zhensheng/Contact/ nbpictures

7.18, 7.22 © Josef Koudelka/ Magnum Photos

7.19, 7.20 Neues Museum – State Museum for Art and Design in Nuremberg

7.21 Jaroslava Brychtová and Stanislav Libenský (artists), Arnošt Kořínek (photo)

7.23 Photograph by Franz Hubmann, 1968. Hans Hollein, Vienna

7.25, 7.26 Courtesy Photo Archive © Foundation La Triennale di Milano

7.27, 7.30, 7.31, 7.32, 7.33 Jane Voorhees Zimmerli Art Museum, The Norton and Nancy Dodge Collection of Nonconformist Art from the Soviet Union

7.28 Jane Voorhees Zimmerli Art Museum, Gift of Dieter and Jutta Steiner

7.35 © COOP HIMMELB(L)AU

7.36 Courtesy Collection FRAC Centre, Orléans, France/ Photographer: François Lauginie

7.38, 7.39 Archive Günter Zamp Kelp, Berlin

8.3 © The Isamu Noguchi Foundation and Garden Museum/ ARS, New York and DACS, London 2008/Photo: Soichi Sunami

8.8 DIGITAL IMAGE © 2008, The Museum of Modern Art/Scala, Florence © Archigram Archives 2008

8.11 Photo: Fritz Dressler © Atelier Frei Otto Warmbronn

8.13 Alex Mlynarčik, Ľudovít Kupovič and Viera Mecková

8.15 © Eve Arnold/Magnum Photos

8.21 © Superstudio/Gian Piero Frassinelli, © Photo CNAC/MNAM Dist. RMN

8.22 Photo by Time Life Pictures/ NASA/Time Life Pictures/Getty Images

All other illustrations, unless otherwise stated above, are © V&A Images.

Index

Figures in *italics* refer to captions